GRANVILLE SHARP'S

CASES ON SLAVERY

The purpose of this book is twofold: first, it is to publish previously unpublished legal materials principally in three important cases in the eighteenth century on the issue of slavery in England, and specifically the status of black people who were slaves in the American colonies or the West Indies and who were taken to England by their masters. The unpublished materials are mostly verbatim transcripts made by shorthand writers commissioned by Granville Sharp, one of the first Englishmen to take up the cause of the abolition of the slave trade and slavery itself. Other related unpublished material is also made available for the first time, including an opinion of an attorney general and some minor cases from the library of York Minster.

The second purpose, in the Introduction, is to give a social and legal background to the cases and an analysis of the position in England of black servants/slaves brought to England and the legal effects of the cases, taking into account the new information provided by the transcripts. There was a conflict in legal authorities as to whether black servants remained slaves, or became free on arrival in England. Lord Mansfield, the chief justice of the Court of King's Bench, was a central figure in all the cases and clearly struggled to come to terms with slavery. The material provides a basis for tracing the evolution of his thought on the subject. On the one hand, the huge profits from slave production in the West Indies flooded into England, slave owners had penetrated the leading institutions in England and the pro-slavery lobby was influential. On the other hand, English law had over time established rights and liberties which in the eighteenth century were seen by many as national characteristics. That tradition was bolstered by the ideas of the Enlightenment. By about the 1760s it had become clear that there was no property in the person, and by the 1770s that such servants could not be sent abroad without their consent, but whether they owed an obligation of perpetual service remained unresolved.

Granville Sharp's

Cases on Slavery

Andrew Lyall

PhD (Lond.) LLD (Lond.) FLS

Barrister of Gray's Inn

OXFORD AND PORTLAND, OREGON
2017

Hart Publishing

An imprint of Bloomsbury Publishing Plc

Hart Publishing Ltd	Bloomsbury Publishing Plc
Kemp House	50 Bedford Square
Chawley Park	London
Cumnor Hill	WC1B 3DP
Oxford OX2 9PH	UK
UK	

www.hartpub.co.uk

www.bloomsbury.com

Published in North America (US and Canada) by
Hart Publishing
c/o International Specialized Book Services
920 NE 58th Avenue, Suite 300
Portland, OR 97213-3786
USA

www.isbs.com

HART PUBLISHING, the Hart/Stag logo, BLOOMSBURY and the

Diana logo are trademarks of Bloomsbury Publishing Plc

First published 2017

© Andrew Lyall

Andrew Lyall has asserted his right under the Copyright, Designs and Patents
Act 1988 to be identified as Author of this work.

All rights reserved. No part of this publication may be reproduced or
transmitted in any form or by any means, electronic or mechanical, including
photocopying, recording, or any information storage or retrieval system,
without prior permission in writing from the publishers.

While every care has been taken to ensure the accuracy of this work, no
responsibility for loss or damage occasioned to any person acting or refraining
from action as a result of any statement in it can be accepted by the authors,
editors or publishers.

.

British Library Cataloguing-in-Publication Data

A catalogue record for this book is available from the British Library.

ISBN: HBK: 978-1-50991-121-9
ePDF: 978-1-50991-123-3
ePub: 978-1-50991-122-6

A catalogue record for this book is available from the Library of Congress.

Typeset in LaTeX 2_ε Palatino by Andrew Lyall
Printed and bound in Great Britain by
CPI Group (UK) Ltd, Croydon, CR0 4YY

for Victor and Kevin

CONTENTS

Preface xi
Abbreviations xiii
Cases Cited xv
Unreported Cases xvii
Table of Statutes xix

INTRODUCTION 1

Granville Sharp (1735–1813) 1
The Manuscripts 2
    Jonathan Strong 2
    The King (Lewis) v Stapylton 3
    Somerset v Stuart 4
    Gregson v Gilbert (The Zong) 5
Black Servants Brought to England 7
    Factual Background 7
    State of the Law 22
        The Case Law 22
        Blackstone 38
        The Royal Navy 41
    The Cases 42
        Jonathan Strong 42
        The King (Lewis) v Stapylton (1771) 46
        Somerset v Stewart 48
            Versions of the Judgment 50
            The Order 56
            Scope of the Judgment 56
            Attempts to Evade *Somerset* 61
            Habeas Corpus and Foreigners 65
            Slave Law in the Colonies 66
            Villeinage in England 69
        Gregson v Gilbert (The Zong) 70
            The "Absolute Necessity" 75
            Marine Insurance and Slave Trade Acts 78
            Navigation and the Longitude Problem 81
            Did it Really Happen? 83

TRANSCRIPTIONS 89

Jonathan Strong 91

King (Lewis) v Stapylton 101
Proceedings in the King's Bench 101
Motions for Judgment 136
Granville Sharp's Argument 139
Granville Sharp's Remarks on the Case 145

Somerset v Stuart 153
First Hearing in the King's Bench 153
Third Day, "Second Hearing" in the King's Bench 199
Lord Mansfield's Judgment 221
   1. The Scots Magazine/Estwick version 221
   2. Granville Sharp MS of the Judgment 224
   3. Letter to the *General Evening Post* 226
   4. Lincoln's Inn, Hill MS version 228
   5. Lincoln's Inn, Ashhurst Paper Book 230
   6. Lofft's Report 232
Sharp's Memoranda on Somerset v Stuart 235

Gregson v Gilbert 239
The Declaration in the King's Bench 239
Proceedings on a Motion for a New Trial 243
Letter from Granville Sharp to Admiralty 291
An Account of the Murder of Slaves on the *Zong* 297
Letter from Granville Sharp to Duke of Portland 307
Bill in the Court of Exchequer 311
James Kelsall's Answer 335
Gregson's Answer 353
Extract from Martin Dockray MS 361

Minor Cases 375
De Grey Opinion 375
Cay v Crichton 376
Hylas v Newton 377
Sharp's Remarks on Hylas v Newton 379

Legislation 385
Habeas Corpus Act 1679 385
Act of the Scottish Parliament, 1701 c 6 386
Slave Trade Act, 1788 388

> Slave Trade Act, 1793 389
> Slave Trade Act, 1798 390
> Slave Trade Act, 1799 392

Letters 395
> Letter from Blackstone to Sharp 395
> Letter from Dr Fothergill to Sharp 397

Blackstone's Commentaries 399

Bibliography   401
Index of People, Places & Things   409
Index of Subjects   419

Preface

In the last few years academic research has been transformed by the development of the internet. About two years ago I had an interest in Granville Sharp, the Englishman who took up the cause of the abolition of slavery, and so I typed his name into Google. Among the entries was a link to the New York History Society (NYHS) website and its archives. There is a collection of some of Granville Sharp's manuscripts, including the unreported first hearing in *Somerset v Stewart* and an account of the proceedings, also unreported, in the case of *The King (Thomas Lewis) v Stapylton*. Greatly to its credit, the NYHS had digitised the manuscripts and so I did not even have to make a trip to New York.

I had also heard that Professor Martin Dockray of the City University, London, who died tragically early, at the time of his death had been collecting materials for a book on the infamous case concerning the slave ship *Zong (Gregson v Gilbert)*. He had made a transcript of the proceedings in the King's Bench on a motion for a new trial from a manuscript volume of Granville Sharp that is now in the possession of the National Maritime Museum (NMM) at Greenwich. A more detail account of these manuscript sources are to be found below in the Introduction, in the section headed "Manuscripts". Professor Dockray's papers have now been deposited with the Squire Law Library in the University of Cambridge in accordance with Mrs Dockray's wishes.

Professor James Oldham, as the acknowledged expert on Lord Mansfield, encouraged me to produce this volume and has been an inspiration. Professor Hamilton Bryson at an early stage made valuable suggestions as to sources. Dr Ruth Paley, the Honorary Editor of the British Records Association, and Dr Kevin Barker of the University of Suffolk have both been of great help and we have had many conversations that illuminated issues and suggested other lines of inquiry and sources. They have also made useful comments that improved the text. I am also grateful to Dr Nicholas Rodger of All Souls College, Oxford for his comments on the *Zong* case.

Editorial Conventions

In transcribing the manuscripts the aim has been to reproduce the text as faithfully to the original as possible. Where the original omits a full stop at the end of a sentence it has generally been supplied within square brackets ([.]) to show that it has been inserted by the editor. Sometimes a sentence in the original ends, with or without a full stop, and a new sentence begins, but the first letter of the first word of the new sentence is not capitalised. The lower case has been retained in such cases, again to be faithful to the original, but also because there might be some doubt as to whether the writer in fact intended to end a sentence and start a new one at that point. Other punctuation, where necessary to make the sense clear, has been inserted in the same way. Original spellings have been retained, except occasionally "ye" and "yt" have been rendered as "the" and "that" since they are, in effect, abbreviations. Abbreviations in the original have been expanded to aid readability and there is a list of the abbreviations commonly used in the table at the beginning of this volume. The spelling of names in the manuscripts sometimes varies. For example, the Lincoln's Inn, Ashhurst Paper Book version of Mansfield's judgment in *Somerset v Stewart* is headed "Ex Parte Summerset". In the first hearing on the return to the writ of habeas corpus it is spelled "Summersett", the name by which he was in fact baptised, and in Lofft's report it is spelled "Somerset", which is the more usual modern form. In transcriptions the original spelling has been retained, but the modern form is used in the text of the Introduction.

Andrew Lyall
Hampton Hill
September 2016

Abbreviations

Editor's abbreviations

G#	("G Sharp" in musical notation) Granville Sharp (His own abbreviation of his name. Used in these transcripts to indicate a footnote added by Sharp. In transcripts, footnotes added by the editor are preceded by "Ed.")
AV	The Bible, Authorized Version
B	Baron
BSBE	Black slave/servant brought to England
CB	Chief Baron
CJ	Chief Justice
CP	Common Pleas
JCP	Justice of the Common Pleas
KB	King's Bench
LCB	Lord Chief Baron
LCJ	Lord Chief Justice
MS/MSS	manuscript/manuscripts
ODNB	Oxford Dictionary of National Biography
OUP	Oxford University Press
Seld Soc	Selden Society
St Realm	Statutes of the Realm
TNA	The National Archives, Kew

Abbreviations in manuscripts expanded in transcript

'd (as in convey'd, happen'd, etc.) = ed

afsd = aforesaid

Cap:^{n}, Captn = Captain

Chf = Chief

Dec:^{r} = December

Dft(s) = Defendant(s)

Lords:^{p} = Lordship

Nov:^{r} = November

Plf(s) = Plaintiff(s)

sd = said

Sept^r = September

Serjt = Serjeant

Sol:^{r} Gen:^{l} = Solicitor General

tho' = though

ye = the

yt = that

Cases Cited

A v Secretary of State for the Home Department [2005] 2 AC 68 65

Beckford v Beckford (1783) 4 Bro 38, 2 ER 26 268

Boumediene v Bush 553 US 723, 128 S Ct 2229 66

Butts v Penny (1676) 2 Lev 201, 83 ER 518,
(1676) 3 Keb 785, 84 ER 1011 .... 23, 49, 179, 179, 180

Chamberline (or Chamberlain) v Harvey (1696) 1 Ld Raym 146, 91 ER 994;
(1701) 5 Mod 182, 87 ER 598 .... 24, 49, 180, 202, 208,

Colt & Glover v Bishop of Coventry & Lichfield
(1612) Hob 140 at 159, 80 ER 290 261

Coventry v Woodhall (1615) Hob 134, 80 ER 284 .... 63, 219

Fleyer v Crouch (1568) 3 Dyer 283b, 73 ER 636 169

Grace, The Slave, (1827) 2 Hagg 94, 166 ER 179 64

Gregson v Gilbert (1783) 3 Doug 232, 99 ER 629 .... 5, 243

Khawaja v Secretary of State for the Home Department [1984] AC 74 ... 65

Knight v Wedderburn (1772) St Tr 2–7n 59

Lockyer and Others v Offley (1786) 1 Term Rep 252, 99 ER 1079 21

Pearne v Lisle (1749) Ambler 75, 27 ER 47 30

Pigg v Caley (1617) Noy 27, 74 ER 997 .... 49, 169

R. v The Inhabitants of Thames Ditton (1785) 4 Doug KB 300,
99 ER 891 34

Shanley v Harvey (1762) 2 Eden 126, 28 ER 844 .... 32, 65, 202

Smith v Brown and Cooper (1705) 2 Salk 666, 91 ER 566 .... 24, 182

Smith v Gould (1706) 2 Ld Raym 1274, 92 ER 338;
(1705) 2 Salk. 666, 91 ER 567 181

Somerset v Stewart (1772) Lofft 1, 98 ER 499 .... 4, 22, 28, 32, 153,

Tatham v Hodgson (1796) 6 T.R. 656 79

Thorne v Watkins (1750) 2 Ves. Sen. 35, 28 ER 24 216

Vernon v Vernon (1837) 2 My & Cr 145, 40 ER 596 268

Year Books
YB Mich 19 Hen 6 p 65 fol 32b, Seipp 1440.083 .... 50, 217

Unreported Cases

Barton v Cooper, Court of Exchequer 369

Cartwright, Case of, 11 Eliz 1 (1569) Rushworth, "Historical Collections", Vol 2: 1629–38 (1721), pp 461–481 .... 22, 170, 192, 198

De Pinna v Henriques (1732) unreported, Guildhall. 31

Galway v Caddee, (c 1739) unreported, Thompson B, Guildhall. 31

Hylas v Newton Dec 1768, case stated, Wilmot CJCP 7, 186, 377

Lockyer v Offley, Lincoln's Inn, Buller Paper Books, bundle 428–79 21

Wager v Webb Easter, 21 Geo II 184

Table of Statutes

1377	1 Ric II, c 6 (villeinage)	165
1547	1 Edw VI, c 3 (vagabonds adjudged slaves)	166
1535	27 Hen VIII, c 4 (Admiralty)	292
1536	28 Hen VIII, c 15 (Admiralty)	292
1549	3 & 4 Edw VI, c 16 (1 Edw. VI c 3, rep.)	166
1562	5 Eliz I, c 4 (wages)	35
1603	1 Jac I, c 6 (labourers, wages)	36
1646	Court of Wards, Abolition, February 24, 1645–1646	225
1656	Court of Wards and Liveries, Abolition, November 27, 1656	225
1660	12 Car II c 24 (Tenures Abolition Act, 1660)	50, 213, 222, 226
1679	31 Car II c 2, (Habeas Corpus Amendment)	57, 380, 385
1701	Criminal Procedure Act 1701 (Scottish, unlawful detention)	61
1713	13 Anne, c 14 (Longitude)	81
1731	5 Geo II, c 7 (Recovery of Debts, North America)	186
1756	29 Geo II, c 4 (Recruiting, impressment)	150
1756	29 Geo II, c 35 (Recruiting, North America)	202
1788	28 Geo III, c 54 (Slave Trade, Marine Insurance)	79, 388
1789	29 Geo III, c 54 (Slave Trade, Marine Insurance)	388
1790	30 Geo III, c 33 (Slave Trade, Marine Insurance)	388
1791	31 Geo III, c 54 (Slave Trade, Marine Insurance)	388
1792	32 Geo III, c 52 (Slave Trade, Marine Insurance)	388
1793	33 Geo III, c 73 (Slave Trade, Marine Insurance)	389
1794	34 Geo III, c 80 (Slave Trade, Marine Insurance)	390
1795	35 Geo III, c 90 (Slave Trade, Marine Insurance)	390
1797	37 Geo III, c 104 (Slave Trade, Marine Insurance)	390
1816	56 Geo III, c 100 (Habeas Corpus Amendment)	58
1819	59 Geo III, c 120 (Registration of slaves)	64
1833	3 & 4 Will 4 c 73 (Slavery Abolition)	27

1898	Criminal Evidence Act 1898	149
2005	Prevention of Terrorism Act 2005	65

Statutes of Virginia

1662	14 Car II., Act 12	67
1667	19 Car II, Act 3	69
1670	21 Car II, Act 1	178
1682	34 Car II, Act 1	172
1705	4 Anne, Act 22	172

INTRODUCTION

Granville Sharp (1735–1813)

The collection of manuscripts (MSS) presented here were in most cases commissioned by Granville Sharp who pursued a number of legal cases as part of his anti-slavery work. Sharp was the first English person to devote his life to the fight against slavery and the slave trade.

He was a civil servant at the Ordnance office. When the American Revolution broke out, Sharp sympathised with the colonists and was opposed to the use of force against them. He resigned his post which also had the effect of freeing him to pursue the campaign against slavery. He has been called "the force behind Wilberforce".[1] He was a devout Anglican, on the evangelical wing of the church. He was a younger son in a large family and had to leave Grammar school before completing his studies. After getting the worse of a discussion on religious doctrine he taught himself Greek and Hebrew. He later published numerous works on religious doctrine and on Greek grammar and Hebrew. He was also an accomplished musician.[2]

It was chance encounter one morning in 1765 with a young black man, Jonathan Strong, which set Sharp off on his campaign to challenge slavery in the courts and which culminated in the *Somerset* case. He wrote an account of this incident which started him on his life's work and it is to be found today in the Gloucestershire Archives.[3] An account of the incident and the legal proceedings which followed is given below in the section entitled "The Cases".[4]

Sharp's activism led to the formation of the Society for the Abolition of the Slave Trade in 1797. He initially resisted being associated with the Society on the ground that it should have been devoted to the abolition of slavery itself, but was persuaded to join it. He lived to see the abolition of the slave trade in 1807, but not of the abolition of slavery itself throughout the British Empire in 1834.

---

[1] [http://what-when-how.com/ social-sciences/sharp-granville-social-science/], accessed 7 May 2016; [http://www.encyclopedia.com/topic/Granville_Sharp.aspx], accessed 7 May 2016.

[2] Prince Hoare, *Memoirs of Granville Sharp, Esq., Composed from his own Manuscripts and Other Authentic Documents in the Possession of his Family and of the African Institution*, London, 2 vols 1820, 2nd edn, 1828; E C P Lascelles, *Granville Sharp and the Freedom of Slaves in England*, Oxford, 1928; G M Ditchfield, 'Sharp, Granville (1735–1813)', ODNB, 2004; online edn, September 2012 [http://www.oxforddnb.com/view/article/25208], accessed 23 April 2016.

[3] D 3549/13/3/28; D 3549 13/3/38; D 3549 13/4/2 book G. Below, page 91.

[4] Page 42.

Sharp never married and died childless in 1813. His papers passed to the family of his niece Mary, who in 1800 had married Thomas Lloyd Baker of Uley in Gloucestershire. In 1977, Sharp's papers were deposited, along with other papers of the Sharp family, at the Gloucestershire Archives.

Sharp was one of the founders of the colony of Sierra Leone as a refuge for freed slaves. The Americans later followed this example in the founding of Liberia.

Sharp used the witty abbreviation of his own name "G#" ("G Sharp" in musical notation) which has been used in this book to indicate those footnotes which Sharp inserted into the MSS.

The Manuscripts

There are at least four repositories of Granville Sharp's MSS. The largest one is in the Gloucestershire Archives.[5]

The New York Historical Society (NYHS) acquired a number of his MSS and has digitised them and made them available on its website.

The third source is the volume devoted to the case of *Gregson* v *Gilbert* (the slave ship *Zong*) in the National Maritime Museum, Greenwich, London.

The fourth source is a small deposit of MSS in York Minster Library of minor cases.

The MSS transcribed in this volume were produced by Granville Sharp who employed shorthand writers to take verbatim notes of proceedings in court. One such writer is identified. The transcript of *The King (Lewis)* v *Stapylton* was the work of William Isaac Blanchard, who practised in Westminster Hall from 1767 until his death in 1796.[6]

Given the importance at least of the *Somerset* and *Zong* cases and the academic discussion of their significance, it is remarkable that these MSS have not been published to date.

Jonathan Strong

The MS is an account written by Granville Sharp himself, some years after the events, of the incident which was to set the course of his life.

---

[5] Clarence Row, Alvin Street, Gloucester, GL1 3DW, [www.gloucestershire.gov.uk/archives].

[6] Page Life, 'Blanchard, William Isaac (bap 1741?, d 1796)', ODNB, 2004 [http://www.oxforddnb.com/view/article/2605], accessed 1 February 2012. According to Page Life, his offices were at 4 Dean Street, Fetter Lane, and 10 Clifford's Inn, although according to the note at the end of the transcript, his office was at 69 Fetter Lane in February 1771. It was estimated that Blanchard could take down about 150 words a minute.

Introduction

The manuscript is in the Gloucestershire Archives and the catalogue entry is entitled "A draft written by Granville Sharp and a fair [contemporary] copy [in another hand]". The original has many crossings-out and amendments. The transcript presented here is from a typed transcript prepared by the staff of the Gloucestershire Archives from the fair copy, with the addition of some footnotes.

The King (Lewis) v Stapylton

To date this case is unreported, although Thomas Clarkson wrote a brief account of it in his book on the history and abolition of the slave trade.[7] The source of the MSS presented here is the New York Historical Society (NYHS) Granville Sharp Collection.

The main MS is a verbatim account of proceedings in the King's Bench in 1771, with the examination and cross-examination of witnesses, including Lewis himself and the captain of the ship on which Lewis had been incarcerated, interspersed with comments and interventions by Lord Mansfield. Verbatim records of trials in the eighteenth century are very rare.

A further MS consists of an argument prepared by Sharp "in haste at a Coffeehouse near the [Westminster] Hall just before the Trial came on". Sharp was not a trained lawyer although he studied law from books. He relies on general principles and maxims, citing Coke and St Germain's *Doctor and Student*, etc, but his argument appears naïve. The MS shows his indignation that human beings could be regarded as property. He castigates Mansfield's reluctance and equivocation. Sharp never developed any appreciation for the barrister's taxi-rank principle, at least in cases involving slavery. At one point, where Dunning is insisting that there is no such thing as property in slaves in England (MS p 63), Sharp adds an amusing and rather charming footnote:[8]

> NB. When Mr Dunning spoke these Words, he held in his hand G. Sharp's Book on *the illegality of Tolerating Slavery in England* (printed in 1769) having one Finger in the Book to hold open a particular part: and yet after so solemn a Declaration he appeared on the opposite side of the Question against James Somerset, the very next year. This is an

---

[7] Thomas Clarkson, *History of the Rise, Progress and Accomplishment of the Abolition of the African Slave Trade*, 2 vols, London, 1808, vol 1, chapter III.

[8] Below, page 129.

abominable and insufferable practice of Lawyers to undertake causes diametrically opposite to their own declared opinions of Law and Common Justice!!!

Somerset v Stuart

The MS is in the NYHS Granville Sharp Collection and is a digitised copy available online.

The report is undated but is of the earlier first hearing rather than that reported by Lofft.[9] Shyllon from newspaper reports gives the date of first hearing as 7 February 1772.[10] Lofft himself says his report was of the "second hearing", on 14 May 1772 and consists of the arguments of Hargrave, which Hargrave later published himself, and then Alleyne and Wallace. Shyllon, on the other hand, mentions a brief hearing on Saturday, 9 May 1772.[11] Mansfield (counsel for Somerset) "went very spiritedly into the natural rights and privileges of mankind" but counsel on the same side "not being well enough to attend" further hearing was postponed to 14 May. Lofft's report should therefore really be counted as the third hearing. The case was then adjourned to seven days later, ie 21 May 1772 and Lofft reports (on the fourth day) the arguments of Dunning and Serjeant Davy on that day. Mansfield's judgment of 22 June 1772 appears from Lofft to be the only event in the case on that day. Since it was a habeas corpus proceeding, more correctly the case should be known as *R v Knowles, ex parte Somerset*, Knowles being the commander of the ship to whom the writ was addressed, but it is generally referred to as *Somerset v Stewart*. The Sharp MS spells the alleged slave owner's name as Stuart. To summarise, the hearings in *Somerset* are as follows:

First Day, Friday, 7 February 1772.
    Arguments of Serjeants Davy and Glynn.
    Source: Sharp MS NYHS, from shorthand. Below.

Second Day, Saturday 9 May 1772.
    Mansfield (counsel).
    Source: Shyllon, *Black Slaves*, pp 94–95, from newspaper reports.

---

[9] *Somerset v Stewart* (1772) Lofft 1, 98 ER 499. Lofft's report is reproduced in (1772) 20 St Tr 1 with added notes.

[10] Shyllon, *Black Slaves*, p 90. Clarkson, *History of the Rise, Progress and Accomplishment of the Abolition of the African Slave Trade*, i.55 gives the date as "January 1772", but that may have been from memory.

[11] Shyllon, *Black Slaves*, p 94; *The Gazetter and New Daily Adviser*, Wednesday, 13 May 1772.

Third Day (Lofft, "Second hearing") Thursday, 14 May 1772.
Francis Hargrave (first appearance in court since call to bar); Alleyne.
Source: (1772) Lofft 1, 98 ER 499; Howell (1772) 20 St Tr 1 at 70. Shyllon, *Black Slaves*, pp 95–103.

Fourth Day, Thursday, 21 May 1772.
Mr Dunning (for Stewart), Serjeant Davy (for Somerset).
Source: Shyllon, *Black Slaves*, pp 103–108, from newspaper reports.

Fifth Day, Monday, 22 June 1772.
Judgment. Lord Mansfield. Source: various, five versions reproduced below. The NYHS MSS contains a separate MS of a version of Mansfield's judgment.

The second and fourth day arguments have not been reproduced in this volume as an account of the newspaper reports are available in Professor Shyllon's book. Lofft mentions Serjeant Glynn's argument at the start of his report: "Upon the second argument [third in fact], (Serjeant Glynn was in the first and, I think, Mr. Mansfield) the pleading on behalf of the negro was opened by Mr. Hargrave." He seems to have forgotten that it was Davy and not Mansfield (who had changed his name from Manfield)[12] in the "first argument" and Lofft describes his own report as a "summary note".

Gregson v Gilbert (The Zong)

Sharp was first told about the the *Zong* case by Olaudah Equiano.[13] The MSS concerning proceedings in the King's Bench on a motion for a new trial and the bill in the proposed action in the Court of Exchequer are contained in a vellum-bound volume which also contains other MSS concerning the same case.

The report in Douglas[14] is an abbreviated version of the arguments and the judgment on the motion for a new trial and differs in a number of respects from the National Maritime Museum MS reproduced in this volume, which was commissioned by Granville Sharp, and taken down in shorthand.

---

[12] Sir James Mansfield, formerly Manfield, bap 1734, d 1821, appointed Solicitor General on 1 September 1780. Michael T. Davis, 'Mansfield, Sir James (bap 1734, d 1821)', ODNB, 2004; online edn, January 2008 [http://www.oxforddnb.com/view/article/17995], accessed 16 July 2016.

[13] Below, page 9.

[14] *Gregson v Gilbert* (1783) 3 Doug 232, 99 ER 629.

The late Professor Martin Dockray, who was possibly the first legal historian to examine the volume, produced a transcript of the arguments in the King's Bench on the motion for a new trial. His widow, Mrs Alison Dockray, handed his papers to Professor Andrew Lewis of University College London (UCL). He then retired from UCL and handed over Professor Dockray's papers to the present author with Mrs Dockray's approval. The papers have now been deposited with the Squire Law Library at the University of Cambridge in accordance with Mrs Dockray's wishes, so that other scholars may have access to them.

Among those papers are some draft chapters of a book devoted to the *Zong* case, which Professor Dockray was working on when he died. The extract in this volume at the end of the other *Zong* transcripts is a draft chapter from the MS, on the "Captives and Captors" on the *Zong*, with a discussion of the Africans, the crew members and in particular the captain, Luke Collingwood, and Robert Stubbs, an extremely dubious former slave ship captain and employee of the African Company who was in command of the ship when the notorious incident took place. It is clear from the transcript that Professor Dockray was a very tenacious and accomplished researcher and had unearthed a great deal of information, in many cases from sources that might not have occurred to others. He discovered that Wentworth in his *A Complete System of Pleading*, published in ten volumes between 1797 and 1799, had used pleadings in actual cases. As an example of a declaration in the King's Bench he had used the pleading in *Gregson* v *Gilbert*, so that is also transcribed in this volume.

Professor Lewis gave a copy of the *Zong* King's Bench transcript to Professor James Oldham who checked the MS against the original and made some changes. I expressed an interest in the transcript, which was the inspiration for this volume, and Professor Oldham has generously made it available to me. I examined the MS book in the National Maritime Museum at Greenwich (NMM) and digitally photographed the whole volume. I checked the transcript against the original and found that some corrections needed to be made. I have also added footnotes to explain certain references in the text.

I then transcribed the MS of the bill in the Exchequer. The answers to the bill are to be found in the National Archives (TNA) at Kew and those have been transcribed and are also included in this volume.

Black Servants Brought to England

In this section we shall consider in particular a special category of servants: black slaves/servants brought to England from colonies where they were held as slaves under laws applicable there. The abbreviation "BSBE" is used here to refer to that category. The section below, on "The State of the Law" discusses whether their legal status differed from that of English servants.

Factual Background

There were several thousand black people in England at the end of the eighteenth century. Estimates of the black population vary from between 3,000 to 15,000.[15] Granville Sharp in his comment on the case of *Hylas* v *Newton*,[16] quoted Sir Fletcher Norton as saying there "is now in Town upwards of 20,000 Negroes" and commented that "I could have told him that there would soon be 20,000 more".

There had been black people in England since at least the Roman period. A unit of Moorish auxilliaries, the *Numerus Maurorum Aurelianorum* was stationed on Hadrian's Wall at Aballava, a fort on the wall at what is now Burgh-by-Sands.[17] The unit[18] was raised in Roman provinces in North Africa and in adjacent lands such as Mauretania south of modern day Morocco. The information comes from an inscription dating from the 3rd century.[19]

There had been a small black population in England since at least

---

[15] Ruth Anna Fisher, "Granville Sharp and Lord Mansfield" (1943) 28 *The Journal of Negro History*, No 4 (Oct, 1943), pp 381–389.

[16] See page 382.

[17] Locally pronounced "Bruff-by-Sands".

[18] A *numerus* was an auxilliary military unit of Roman allies who were not integrated into the regular Roman army.

[19] The name "Aurelianorum" refers to the unit being named in honour of the Emperor Marcus Aurelius (161–80 AD). The unit was raised during the reign of the Emperor Septimius Severus (193–211 AD) who was himself a native of Libya and an inscription recording their presence dates from the 3rd century AD: Richard Benjamin, "Whose Wall: Roman Wall, Barrier or Bond?" *British Archaeology Magazine*, Issue 77 York, Council for British Archaeology, 2004; Anthony R Birley, *The African Emperor: Septimius Severus*, London, Batsford, 1988; James L Forde-Johnston, *Hadrian's Wall*, London, Michael Joseph, 1978; Alistair Moffat, *The Wall*, London, Birlinn Limited Press, 2008; [http://www.blackpast.org/gah/africans-hadrians-wall], accessed 30 August 2016; David Dabydeen, John Gilmore, and Cecily Jones, eds *The Oxford Companion to Black British History* Oxford, 2007; David Olusoga, *Black and British: A Forgotten History*, London, 2016; the book accompanies the BBC 2 series of the same name, broadcast in November 2016.

Tudor times[20] and their descendants were still present in the eighteenth century. By the eighteenth century there was a population of free black people in England, particularly in London.

Kathleen Chater[21] has made an extensive study of the black population in England and Wales in the period 1660 to 1807 and presents a wealth of material drawn from many sources. As a whole it presents, as Chater sees it, a counterpoint to some studies based on the American experience. The American experience was of separate and segregated communities in which there was little contact between black and white populations and a fairly widespread wish, on both sides, to preserve a separate identity. Chater argues that England in the eighteenth century presented a very different picture. Most black people were domestic servants who necessarily lived in the same household as white families. The group most discriminated group against in the period were Catholics, given the Penal Laws, and not black people. There were no laws that applied specifically to black people. There was no ban on marriage between black and white people or on sexual relations and there were numerous examples of black men marrying white women. She examines baptism, birth and death records, wills, etc. In baptism records they are never referred to as slaves, with the exception of one woman. Black people, mostly men, occupied many different jobs, usually in the poorer strata but not always. Among the occupations of black people she found actress, beggar, cabinet maker, churchwarden, coal trader (Cesar Picton) parish constable, drummer, gardener, groom, market gardener, member of the militia, minister of religion (Brian Mackey, parish priest of Coates in Gloucestershire), prostitute, sailor and seaman, servant (the most numerous), soldier, teacher of sword fighting, victualler and barrister (Robert Laing, of Lincoln's Inn).[22] Nathaniel Wells, son of a West Indian slave owner, became deputy lieutenant of Monmouthshire.[23] Black children, the offspring of adult black servants, were often baptised at the same time as the master's children. The eighteenth century concept was that servants were part of the family of the male head of the household. Dr Johnson defined "family" in this way in his dictionary.[24]

---

[20] Onyeka [Nubia], *Blackamoores: Africans in Tudor England, their Presence, Status and Origins*. Narrative Eye, 2013; Thomas F Earle, Kate J P Lowe, eds, *Black Africans in Renaissance Europe* Cambridge, Cambridge UP, 2005.

[21] Kathleen Chater, *Untold Histories: Black People in England and Wales during the period of the British Slave Trade c 1660–1807* Manchester, 2009.

[22] Chater, *Untold Histories*, p 238.

[23] ibid, pp 237–38.

[24] Johnson's *Dictionary*: Family "1. Those who live in the same house; household."

Most black people tried to get on with their lives as best they could and in doing so interacted with white people in similar roles. Chater argues that assimilation was the English model, not segregation. Black people came together on occasion and she gives examples, but she concludes that most black people were not active in the anti-slavery movement and that the role of activist groups within the black community has been exaggerated.

Nevertheless, there was undoubtedly a small group of Africans who had an influence in the abolitionist movement and in wider society far in excess of their numbers and who collaborated with white English abolitionists including Granville Sharp and Thomas Clarkson. They were able to describe in fluent English and from first hand knowledge the horrors of the slave trade and of slavery.

The *Sons of Africa* was a group of free Africans living in London who campaigned to end slavery. The leading members were as follows.

Olaudah Equiano (c 1745–31 March 1797),[25] who was baptised as "Gustavus Vassa" but often preferred to use his African name, wrote a remarkable account of his life which became a best-seller.[26] He became a leading abolitionist in England and a collaborator with Granville Sharp and Thomas Clarkson.

Ignatius Sancho (c 1729–1780),[27] was the first black Briton known to have voted in a British election[28] and to have his obituary published in the press. He ran a well-known grocer's shop in Westminster and had a reputation as a man of letters and culture. Frances Crewe, one of Sancho's younger correspondents, edited and published the two-volume *Letters of the Late Ignatius Sancho, an African* which was sold by subscription. His fame grew when one of his letters appeared in the posthumously published *Letters* (1775) of Laurence Sterne, with whom he had initiated a correspondence on 21 July 1766, in which he

---

The secondary meaning he gives is the primary one today: "2. Those that descend from one common progenitor; a race; a tribe; a generation."

[25] James Walvin, 'Equiano, Olaudah (c 1745–1797)', ODNB, 2004; online edn, October 2006 [http://www.oxforddnb.com/view/article/57028], accessed 29 December 2015.

[26] Olaudah Equiano, *The Interesting Narrative of the Life of Olaudah Equiano, or Gustavus Vassa, the African*, 2nd edn, London, printed and sold for the Author, by T Wilkins, etc, [1789].

[27] Vincent Carretta, 'Sancho, (Charles) Ignatius (1729?–1780)', ODNB, 2004 [http://www.oxforddnb.com/view/article/24609], accessed 29 December 2015.

[28] Ibid.

appealed to Sterne to support the campaign against slavery.[29]

Chater has pointed out that virtually all that is known of the Sons of Africa as a group is that they signed five letters to newspapers under that name and there is no evidence that they had regular meetings.[30] She points out that Equiano never mentioned meeting Ignatius Sancho in his autobiography, as one would expect if he had done so.[31] Nevertheless, the individuals who signed the letters made significant contributions in their own right.

Ottobah Cugoano,[32] or Quobna Ottobouh Cugoano as he preferred to sign himself,[33] who was born on the coast of present-day Ghana, in the Fante village of Agimaque (present-day Ajumako), was captured by other Africans, sold to a European slave trader and taken to Grenada, and then brought to England in 1772 where he obtained his freedom. In 1786 he joined William Green, another Afro-Briton, in successfully appealing to Granville Sharp to save a black person, Harry Demane, from being forced into West Indian slavery. He published *Thoughts and Sentiments on the Evil and Wicked Traffic of the Slavery and Commerce of the Human Species* (1787), and a shorter version of it, *Thoughts and Sentiments on the Evil of Slavery…* in 1791.[34] He gave a harrowing account of his capture and voyage on a slave ship and time as slave in Grenada. He argued that enslaved people had not only the right but also a moral duty to rebel against their enslavement and called for the total abolition of slavery. By the 1780s he was employed as a domestic servant by the artists Richard and Maria Cosway who lived at 81 Schomberg House in Pall Mall and whose patron was the Prince Regent. The artist Gainsborough lived next door at number 80. An etching of 1784 by Cosway is entitled *The artist and his wife in a garden, with a black servant*.[35] It is assumed that the servant is Cugoano. There are other identifiable likenesses of him in the work of

---

[29] Carretta, ODNB.

[30] Chater, *Untold Histories*, pp 161, 172 n 5.

[31] Ibid, p 39.

[32] Martin Hoyles, *Cugoano Against Slavery*, Hertford, 2015; Vincent Carretta, 'Cugoano, Ottobah (b. 1757?)', ODNB, 2004 [http://www.oxforddnb.com/view/article/59531], accessed 29 December 2015.

[33] Below, note 34.

[34] The British Library has a copy of the 1791 edition in which the author's name is printed at the end as "Quobna Ottobouh Cugoano". Ray A Kea, *A Cultural and Social History of Ghana from the Seventeenth to the Nineteenth Century*, Lewiston, NY, 2012 notes that the modern version of "Quobna" would be "Kwabena", meaning "born on Tuesday", and "Ottobouh" meant "second-born", so he must have had a brother or sister.

[35] Hoyles, *Cugoano Against Slavery*, pp 104, 106.

Cosway.³⁶ In his role of servant, Cugoano met many prominent people who came to see Cosway and put this acquaintance to good effect in the fight against slavery. He wrote letters to George III, the Prince of Wales, Edmund Burke, Sir William Dolben, and Sharp.³⁷

Ukawsaw Gronniosaw, baptised as James Albert, (c 1705–1775) was a freed slave and autobiographer. The title page of his autobiography explained that it was committed to paper by "the elegant pen of a young lady of the town of Leominster". It was entitled *A Narrative of the Most remarkable Particulars in the Life of James Albert Ukawsaw Gronniosaw, an African Prince, As related by himself*. It was the first book published by a black person in England and the first account in England of slavery by a former slave. It was published in Bath, Somerset, in December 1772, and gave a vivid account of Gronniosaw's life, from his capture in Africa, followed by a life of poverty in Colchester and Kidderminster, later becoming a weaver in Norwich. He was born in Nigeria of a noble family but at the age of fifteen he was taken by a Gold Coast ivory merchant. He was bought by an American in Barbados and later resold to a Calvinist minister in New York. When the minister died, Gronniosaw chose to stay with his widow, and subsequently their orphans, until he was left without support. Gronniosaw then enlisted as a cook with a privateer, and later as a soldier in the British army. He served in Martinique and Cuba, before obtaining his discharge and crossing to England.

Evidence that black people came together for social reasons or to celebrate in England at that time is scarce, but it does exist. When a young undergraduate, Noel Turner, called on Dr Johnson: "The Doctor was absent, and when Francis Barber, his black servant, opened the door to tell me so, a group of his African countrymen were sitting round the fire in the gloomy anti-room..."³⁸ It was probably unusual for a servant to be allowed to entertain his friends in this way and Johnson was known to be indulgent of Francis.

Other examples exist of black people meeting socially. John Baker in his diary,³⁹ covering the years 1751–1778, mentions that his servant, Jack Beef, attended a "Ball of Blacks" and in 1764 the *London*

---

³⁶ Carretta, 'Cugoano, Ottobah', ODNB.
³⁷ Ibid.
³⁸ *New Monthly Magazine*, vol X (July – December 1818), 386. Michael Bundock, *The Fortunes of Francis Barber: The True Story of the Jamaican Slave Who Became Samuel Johnson's Heir*, New Haven, London, 2015, pp 99, 238 n 4.
³⁹ John Baker, *The Diary of John Baker*, ed P Yorke, London, Hutchinson, 1931. Chater, *Untold Histories*, p 162.

Chronicle reported a dance to which white people were not admitted.[40] The servants who attended probably wished to be free to talk among themselves without fear of any remarks critical of their masters or mistresses being reported. There were black people present at every hearing of the *Somerset* case and many were present when Mansfield delivered his judgment.[41] A few days later nearly 200 black people gathered at an unnamed public house in Westminster to celebrate "the triumph which their brother Somerset had obtained over Stewart his master. Lord Mansfield's health was echoed round the room, and the evening concluded with a ball. The tickets to this Black assembly were 5s.".[42] Chater goes perhaps too far in questioning the existence of a black community.

There were also black people in England who were not, and never had been, enslaved. Some had left West Africa in some form of employment or had been sent to England by their parents for education.[43]

Apart from the individuals mentioned above, there were other black people in England who, though not active in the fight against slavery, made significant contributions to British life and no doubt contributed to changes in attitude towards people of African descent in England. Mtubani mentions some interesting examples.[44] Francis Williams[45] from Jamaica went to Cambridge University in the 1720s, read law and was called to the bar.[46] He was sponsored by the Duke of Montagu[47] who also sponsored the education of Ignatius Sancho. Williams returned to Jamaica and became a writer.[48] Another protégé of Montagu

---

[40] 17 February 1764; quoted in Shyllon, *Black People*, p 80; Chater, ibid.

[41] *The London Chronicle*, 22 June 1772; *The Middlesex Journal*, 23 June 1772; Shyllon, *Black Slaves*, p 110; Chater, *Untold Histories*, p 162.

[42] *The London Packet*, 26–29 June 1772.

[43] Chapter 4, 'Princes, Students and Scholars', in Folarin Shyllon, *Black People in Britain 1555–1833*, Oxford, 1977,

[44] Victor C D Mtubani, "The Black Voice in Eighteenth-Century Britain: African Writers against Slavery and the Slave Trade" *Phylon* (1960–), Vol 45, No 2 (2nd Qtr, 1984), pp 85–97.

[45] John Gilmore, 'Williams, Francis (c.1690–1762)', ODNB, 2004; online edn, Jan 2015 [http://www.oxforddnb.com/view/article/57050], accessed 22 September 2016.

[46] Mtubani writes: "Dr. James Beattie, Professor of Moral Philosophy and Logic in the University of Aberdeen, was to praise his intellect and use his example to refute Hume's charge that Africans were inferior to Europeans." Ibid p 86.

[47] John Montagu, 2nd Duke of Montagu, KG GMB PC (1690–5 July 1749). Montagu's house in Bloomsbury was on the site of what is now the British Museum and housed the original collection provided by Sir Hans Sloane, the founder of the Museum.

[48] Williams seems to have had considerable property in Jamaica and so may not

was Ayuba Suleiman Diallo (1701–1773), aka Job ben Solomon.[49] He was born in Bundu, Senegal, the son of a prominent Fulbe political and Islamic leader.[50] He was enslaved on a plantation in Maryland. When it was discovered that he knew Arabic (as well as several African languages), he was rescued from slavery and brought to England in 1733 after James Oglethorpe, the army officer and founder of the colony of Georgia, received a letter from him and purchased his freedom. He became a celebrity and was asked to translate Sir Hans Sloanes' Arabic manuscripts.[51] Mtubani notes that "as the ultimate mark of recognition, he was elected to the Gentlemen's Society of Spalding, an exclusive society of scholars."[52] Diallo later returned to Gambia.

George Augustus Bridgetower[53] was a virtuoso violinist who was hailed as an "extraordinary genius" and as one of the "musical wonders of the Age."[54] He had been born in Poland, the son of a West Indian (possibly Barbadian) servant of the Hungarian Prince Esterházy. His mother was from Germany, and was probably a domestic servant in the household of Sophie von Thurn und Taxis. He performed with Beethoven and in concerts in England and the Prince of Wales employed him in his private orchestra in Brighton.

A further sub-category were young black children, mostly boys, brought to England as retainers and as a kind of fashionable accessory or luxury item. They were often dressed in silk livery and turbans and would act as pages, opening the front door to visitors. Samuel Pepys mentions them in his diary:[55] "Here we saw a little Turk and a negroe, which are intended for pages to the two young ladies." Horace

---

have needed sponsorship: Gilmore, above.

[49] David Killingray, 'Diallo, Ayuba Suleiman [Job Ben Solomon] (c.1701–1773)', ODNB, September 2015 [http://www.oxforddnb.com/view/article/100405], accessed 22 September 2016.

[50] He had himself sold some slaves to a European dealer, but on the return journey was captured by a hostile tribe and was sold by them to the same European trader he had just dealt with. His furious protests fell on deaf ears.

[51] Walvin, *Black and White: the Negro and English society, 1555–1945*. London, 1973, p 83; Mtubani, p 86.

[52] Mtubani, p 86.

[53] George Augustus Polgreen Bridgetower (11 October 1778–29 February 1860). W B Squire, 'Bridgetower, George Augustus Polgreen (1780–1860)', rev David J Golby, ODNB, 2004; online edn, May 2010 [http://www.oxforddnb.com/view/article/3398], accessed 22 September 2016.

[54] Barker, Anthony J, *The African Link: British Attitudes to the Negro in the Era of the Atlantic Slave Trade, 1550–1807*, London, 1978, p 26; Mtubani, p 86.

[55] *Diary of Samuel Pepys*, 30 May 1662.

Walpole[56] wrote in a letter of 1788: "I was in Kingston with the sisters of Lord Milford; they have a favourite black, who has been with them a great many years and is remarkably sensible." "Sensible" in the eighteenth century meant having "sensibility", ie responsive to emotional or aesthetic influences. He was referring to Cesar Picton who was brought in 1761 from Senegal by Captain Parr, an officer of the British army who had been serving there.[57] There is no evidence that Captain Parr "bought" Cesar in a slave market. Cesar may have been left behind after his parents were taken in a slave raid and Captain Parr took pity on him. In a meeting with Sir John Philipps, Captain Parr "gave" Cesar to the Philipps family, or perhaps more accurately, entrusted him to their care. Cesar was educated by the family, and when Lady Phillips died in 1788 she left Cesar £100 in her will. In his early thirties he set himself up as a coal merchant in Kingston upon Thames and became a wealthy man, allegedly the wealthiest black person in England at the time. He bought a substantial house in Thames Ditton as well as his place of business at 52, High Street, Kingston. Both were named "Picton House" after him. In recent years commemorative plaques have been put up on both properties.

Thomas Lewis, who features in *The King (Thomas Lewis) v Stapylton* the transcript of which is in this volume, is sometimes referred to as a "slave"[58] but by his own account he took a job on a ship to see the world and learn English. He admitted to being the servant of Stapylton but not his slave and Stapylton failed to prove that Lewis was his slave. Nor was there evidence in the case that Lewis had been the slave of anyone else.

English domestic servants at this time were by no means "free", as they were bound to remain with their masters, ie employers, during the term of their service which was determined by contract. Indeed, if they left their employer without permission they could be sent to prison and often were, a sitiation which continued until well into the

---

[56] Actually Horatio Walpole, but known as Horace. He was son of Robert Walpole, the first Prime Minister. Paul Langford, 'Walpole, Horatio, fourth earl of Orford (1717–1797)', ODNB, 2004; online edn, May 2011 [http://www.oxforddnb.com/view/article/28596], accessed 3 November 2015.

[57] Howard Benge, *Cesar Picton, A Black Merchant In 18th Century Kingston*, 1 December 2006, [http://www.culture24.org.uk/history-and-heritage/art41941], accessed 16 March 2015.

[58] Folarin Olawale Shyllon, *Black Slaves in Britain*, London, OUP for the Institute of Race Relations, 1974, at p 43; James Oldham, "New Light on Mansfield and Slavery" (1988) 27 *Journal of British Studies* 45–68, at p 48.

nineteenth century.[59] Similarly, apprentices were bound to their masters for the term of their apprenticeship. The service of white English servants would have its origin in contract. In Sir Henry Maine's terms, contract gave rise to a status in their case. The status of BSBEs, whatever it was, had not begun by contract and so that was sometimes an issue in the legal cases. It is not possible to say how many black people in England were free and how many were domestic servants, but probably the majority were domestic servants. The question "was slavery legal in England?" therefore resolves itself into a more specific question: "did BSBEs suffer from any disability in addition to those of domestic servants in England generally?" This question will be discussed in a later section.

It is certainly the case from the point of view of social fact that many masters of black servants treated them as if they were their property, but it was not universally the case. There were many advertisements for the return of black servants who had run away, with promise of reward. In the *The London Gazette* of 18 March 1685 a reward was advertised for bringing back John White, a black boy of about fifteen years of age who had run away from a Colonel Kirk's house. He had a silver collar round his neck on which was engraved the colonel's coat of arms and cipher, supposedly indicating that the colonel claimed he was his "property". Anyone who returned him to the colonel would be "well rewarded".[60] *The Daily Journal* of 28 September 1728 contained an advertisement for a runaway black boy, who had the legend "My Lady Broomfield's black, in Lincoln's Inn Fields" engraved on a collar round his neck.[61] In the *London Advertiser* for 1756 Matthew Dyer, a goldsmith of Duck Lane, Westminster, advertised that he made "silver padlocks for Blacks and Dogs; collars, &c.".[62] The portrait of the Jacobite James Drummond, 2nd titular Duke of Perth, 1673–1720, in the National Gallery of Scotland shows the duke with a young black boy wearing a collar which appears to be secured with a padlock.[63]

---

[59] Douglas Hay, "England, 1562–1875: The Law and Its Uses", in Douglas Hay and Paul Craven, eds, *Masters, Servants, and Magistrates in Britain and the Empire, 1562–1955*, Chapel Hill and London, 2004.

[60] [https://www.thegazette.co.uk/London/issue/2122/page/2]; Folarin O Shyllon, *Black Slaves*, p 9; *The London Gazette* was then, as it is now, under the title of *The Gazette*, the official organ of the British government, though at that time it accepted advertisements from private persons.

[61] Shyllon, *Black Slaves*, p 9.

[62] Ibid, p 9.

[63] Ibid, p 117; National Gallery of Scotland.

The Proceedings of the Old Bailey, 1674–1913[64] for 13 January 1716 features a silver collar worn by a black servant. A Mr William Jordan had sent his boy, Richard, "a negro", on an errand. Richard met Anne Smith of the parish of St. Martin in the Fields and complained to her that he had been a long time on his errand and was afraid to go home. It is unclear if Richard previously knew her or not. She told him "his collar would betray him" and advised him to let her take it off. She took him to a fruit cellar, where she and her associate, Jane Evans,"broke the collar with their teeth." Anne and Jane then ran off with it. Richard returned home and told his master what had happened. Mr Jordan "took up the prisoner" and took her to a magistrate, where she confessed that Jane had removed the collar and that she, Anne, had sold it. The jury found her guilty of assault and robbery. She and her friend were sentenced to be branded on the hand, which by this time meant that it was done with a cold iron, so it was the equivalent of a slap on the wrist.[65] The fact that the collar could be removed with the teeth suggests it was made of very thin silver.

There are newspaper reports of the sale of black people in Liverpool and elsewhere. On 28 September 1769 the *Bath Chronicle and Weekly Gazette,* announced: "To be Sold, a likely Negro Boy, about fourteen Years of Age, who understands English, is very tractable, and of a good Country. For particulars, enquire of Mr Thomas Cadell, Bookseller, in Wine Street, Bristol." However, it seems that the idea that Black Boys Hill in Bristol was so-called because small black boys were sold there, is a myth. It was named after a public house in the 17th century called "The Black Boy" which was a popular nick-name of King Charles II, who was dark skinned. Several public houses are today called "The Black Boy" for the same reason.

Black boys were not always sold separately from other "goods". The *Manchester Mercury* of 1 February 1763 announced: "Yesterday Mr Rice the Broker's Coach, Horses &c were sold by Auction as under, viz. one Pair of Coach Geldings, 67 l. one pair ditto, 61 l. one Saddle Horse, 26 l. one ditto, 8 l. 8 s. a Coach and Harness for four Horses, 107 l. 1 s. a Post Chariot, 42 l. a *Negro Boy*, 32 l." The boy was valued at about the price of one of a pair of coach horses. As Shyllon has pointed out,[66] advertisements for the return of servants became more common after the Yorke-Talbot opinion of 1729 which asserted that black people held as slaves in the colonies remained slaves in England.

---

[64] Old Bailey Proceedings Online, reference number t17160113-18.
[65] [https://www.oldbaileyonline.org/static/Punishment].
[66] *Black Slaves,* p 27.

This suggests that the number of black servants absenting themselves from their masters increased after the opinion and no doubt as a result of it.

When Benjamin Franklin returned to London[67] from America in 1757 he brought with him his son and secretary, William, together with Franklin's personal slave, Peter, and William's slave, whom they called "King".[68] Peter settled into life in London, but King soon ran off and was later found to be in the care of a lady in Suffolk who was paying for his education and personally teaching him the violin and French horn.[69] The Franklins were content to leave him there. In his early life in America Franklin had been an indentured servant and had run away before his term was up, so that may explain his attitude.

Franklin in the later part of his life was in principle opposed to slavery and indeed in London on 1 May 1760 he had met with Dr Johnson and others who had formed a committee to promote the education of "Negro children".[70] Johnson had a personal interest in this subject as his servant, Francis Barber, had been born a slave in Jamaica on the Bathurst plantation. Francis when young was also known by the name of Quashey.[71] This is known to be a Jamaican variant of Kwashi which comes from the Fante culture of what is today Ghana.[72]

He was brought to England in 1750 by Colonel Richard Bathurst, father to Johnson's friend, Dr Richard Bathurst. Colonel Bathurst had not made a success of running the plantation and by 1749 his finances were in a precarious position.[73] He was forced to sell the Bathurst estate and return to England. Francis was then about seven or eight years old.[74] At first the colonel and Francis stayed with Richard Bath-

---

[67] The house he lived in, at 36 Craven Street London WC2N 5NF, is now a museum, the Benjamin Franklin House. Franklin lived there for nearly sixteen years, between 1757 and 1775.

[68] George Goodwin, *Benjamin Franklin in London: the British Life of America's Founding Father*, London, 2016, p 69.

[69] Ibid, p 79.

[70] Ibid, pp 78–79.

[71] Ibid, pp 11–12.

[72] It is a day-name, meaning "born on Sunday". Variations of it, such as Kwasi, occur in other Akan cultures. I am grateful to Victor Akonta MA for this information.

[73] Bundock, *The Fortunes of Francis Barber*, p 26.

[74] Barber said this to Boswell, but there is uncertainty about Barber's age: ibid, p 10. If he was seven or eight years old in 1750 he would have been born in 1742 or 1743, but in the 1799 Poor Law examination he said he was "about 52 years old", which would mean he was born in 1747. However, that would mean he was only three years old when he came to England which seems much too young. Ibid.

urst. Colonel Bathurst had him baptised and named Francis Barber,[75] and sent him to a school in Barton in Teesdale, North Riding of Yorkshire, where he remained for two years. It was known as a "cheap school", but all that Bathurst could afford.

Dr Richard Bathurst was an opponent of slavery and when Francis returned from school in Yorkshire it was Richard Bathurst who suggested to Johnson that he take Francis into his household, which he did in 1752.[76] Francis would then have been nine or ten years of age. Johnson's wife had recently died and he was suffering from grief, so having to look after the young boy must have been a comfort to him. In the course of time Francis became both Johnson's manservant and his companion and became the principal beneficiary under his will.[77] Johnson never considered Frank (as he called him) to be a slave and would not have been willing to have a slave as a servant.[78] He sent Francis to school, first to a writing master and then to Bishop's Stortford Grammar School where he learned Greek and Latin.[79] Johnson's objection to slavery was of a particularly passionate kind. On one occasion "when in company with some very grave men at Oxford, his toast was, 'Here's to the next insurrection of the negroes in the West Indies.'"[80] Boswell went on: "His violent prejudice against our West Indian and American settlers appeared whenever there was an opportunity. Towards the conclusion of his *Taxation no Tyranny*, he says, 'how is it that we hear the loudest yelps for liberty among the drivers of negroes?'"

The toast was probably a response to Tacky's Rebellion in Jamaica in 1760.[81] Slave owners were in constant fear of slave revolts which occurred with some frequency in the eighteenth century, and particularly after the successful revolt led by Tousaint L'Ouverture which established the state of Haiti in 1804. The slave owners formed local militias and gave themselves the rank of "colonel", etc.

In 1754 Colonel Bathurst made his will in which he left Francis "his freedom and twelve pounds in money".[82] Colonel Bathurst died

---

[75] Ibid, p 33.

[76] Ibid, pp 39, 45.

[77] Ibid, pp 174–75. In his first will Johnson had bequeathed Barber £500 and £70 for life, but in his last will he made Barber his residuary legatee.

[78] Ibid, p 64.

[79] Ibid, pp 118–28.

[80] Ibid, p 112; *Boswell's Life of Johnson*, III, pp 200–201.

[81] Hoyles, *Cugoano Against Slavery*, p 58.

[82] Bundock, *The Fortunes of Francis Barber*, pp 28, 69; Will of Richard Bathurst, 24 April 1754, TNA PROB/11/824/149; William R Jones, 'Barber, Francis (c 1745–

the following year. Whatever the effect of the will, and its legal effect was necessarily unclear given the uncertain state of the law, Francis believed it had made him free. As Bundock has pointed out, Francis Barber told James Boswell some thirty years later that he considered himself a slave up to that point.[83] He had, after all, been brought up in a slave society and the Colonel's household. It is possible that he was Colonel Bathurst's son, although that is speculation. Nevertheless, from the Colonel's death Francis considered himself to be free and said so to Boswell.

In 1755 he was twelve or thirteen years old, and had money in his pocket. Johnson's household was a somewhat disturbing place for Francis. The nominal housekeeper, Anna Williams, was old and blind and bad-tempered. Francis left Johnson's house and worked for a time in Cheapside with an apothecary.[84] An advertisement in the *Daily Advertiser* for 14 and 15 February 1757,[85] inserted by Johnson, was in very different terms to some of those quoted above:

> Whereas Francis Barber, a black boy, has been some months absent from his master, and has been said to have lived lately in Wapping, or near it: This is to give him notice, that if he will come to his master, or apply to any of his master's friends, he will be kindly received.

The advertisement was addressed to Francis, there was no threat and no offer of reward, simply a plea for him to return. Johnson clearly did not treat Francis as his "property" but as a young member of his household and was concerned for his welfare. Francis did return, but later joined the Navy for about two years and only returned to Johnson after Johnson requested his release.[86] He then remained with Johnson for the rest of Johnson's life. On 28 January 1773 he married a white woman, Elizabeth Ball.[87] She was then seventeen or eighteen and

1801)', ODNB, 2004 [http://www.oxforddnb.com/view/article/59398], accessed 1 April 2016.

[83] Ibid, p 64.

[84] Bundock, ibid, pp 69–77.

[85] Ibid, p 71; The advertisement was found by Betty Rizzo, "The Elopement of Francis 'Barber'" *English Language Notes* (September 1985), pp 35–38.

[86] Bundock, *The Fortunes of Francis Barber*, pp 93–95. Johnson raised the matter with Tobias Smollett, the novelist, who had been a naval surgeon and had travelled to Jamaica where he had lived for some years before returning to England and married a wealthy Jamaican heiress. Smollett in turn wrote to John Wilkes who contacted the Admiralty.

[87] Ibid, p 144.

Francis was about thirty-one. They had several children. His first son, born in 1774, was named Samuel, no doubt after Johnson. Sadly, he died at the age of fourteen months.[88] In 1781 they had a daughter, Elizabeth Ann, and when another son was born in 1783, they named him Samuel also.[89] Samuel became a Primitive Methodist preacher and in 1811 married Frances Sherwin, who was also active in the movement. They had six children, three of whom had children of their own. After Johnson's death, the Francis's family moved to Lichfield and their descendants still live in Staffordshire.[90] On 28 July 2016 a plaque in honour of Francis was unveiled at Dr Johnson's House, 17 Gough Square, London. It was unveiled by Cedric Barber, the great-great-great-great-grandson of Francis. The plaque is one in a series made to commemorate the contribution of black people to British history and made in conjunction with David Olusoga's BBC 2 series, *Black and British: A Forgotten History*, broadcast in November 2016. Cedric Barber is interviewed in the first programme. A book of the same name accompanies the series.

Another case in point is that of Dido Elizabeth Belle,[91] whom Lord Mansfield took into his household. She was the natural daughter of Mansfield's nephew, Captain Sir John Lindsay, by a black woman, Maria Bell. Maria had been on board a Spanish vessel when it was captured as a prize by Lindsay. Even if she had been a slave of the Spanish, the Royal Navy regarded anyone who came aboard as thereby free.[92] It is therefore doubtful if Maria was a slave at the time she gave birth to Dido. Dido was baptised in London in 1766[93] and remained in Mansfield's household at Kenwood House for the next thirty years. Mansfield apparently provided for her education, since she was literate. A letter in Lincoln's Inn library, discovered by Professor James Oldham, dated 19 May 1786, is from Mansfield to puisne judge Buller, about a case at a time when Mansfield was too ill to write. He added at the end of the letter: "This is wrote by Dido. I hope you will be able

---

[88] Ibid, p 150.
[89] Ibid, p 160.
[90] Ibid, p 212.
[91] G Adams, "Dido Elizabeth Belle: a Black Girl at Kenwood" (1984) 12 *Camden Historical Review* 10.
[92] Below, page 42.
[93] Dido was baptised at St George's, Bloomsbury on 20 November 1766. The entry in the register states: "Dido Elizabeth D[aughte]r of Bell & Maria his wife aged 54." Thus, it did not show the real father's name and presumably the named father, "Bell", was fictitious. Presumably also "aged 54" refers to "Bell" and was also fictitious. There is no date of birth. Ancestry.co.uk, photograph of original entry.

to read it."[94] Oldham noted that the letter is perfectly legible.

In his will, Mansfield declared Dido to be free and left her well provided for.[95] Shyllon[96] has interpreted the declaration as evidence that Mansfield had previously considered her a slave, but this seems to be a misunderstanding. Mansfield had great affection for her and his other grandnieces, Lady Elizabeth Murray and Lady Anne Murray[97] who also lived at Kenwood. It is more likely that he was concerned to protect her from other people who might otherwise have regarded her as a slave.

In England, unlike in Virginia or the West Indies, black runaways might find employment elsewhere. However, absconding by black servants and the attempts to recapture them, although a social fact, rarely gave rise to legal proceedings. Slavery, was, as Sharp put it, "tolerated", but that is a different thing from saying that the law recognised slavery in England. Indeed, there are several thousand people held in captivity in England at the present day, as domestic servants or trafficked for prostitution. A recent analysis for the Home Office suggested there could be between 10,000 and 13,000 modern-day slaves.[98] But that does not mean it is legal. Today it is a crime and police are engaged in the search to identify the traffickers and prosecute them. In the eighteenth century there was no police force and there was no crime that might apply to the situation of a domestic servant who was not free under the law then in force to leave his or her employment if he or she wished. Some have characterised the eighteenth century situation as "near-slavery"[99] but that was not a recognised legal category, and could with some accuracy be applied metaphorically to the law of master and servant, of apprentices and of the press gang at the time. The fact that there were legal status relations in England restricting freedom of labour but falling short of chattel slavery complicates

---

[94] *Lockyer* v *Offley*, Buller Paper Books, bundle 428-79. Oldham, "New Light", p 67. The case is reported as *Lockyer and Others* v *Offley* (1786) 1 Term Rep 252, 99 ER 1079.

[95] Mansfield's will states: "I confirm to Dido Elizabeth Belle her freedom." Dido was left £500 and £100 for life. Will of William Murray, Lord Mansfield CJKB, TNA PROB/11/1230/147; James Oldham, *Mansfield Manuscripts & the Growth of English Law in the Eighteenth Century*, Chapel Hill, NC, 2004, ii.1240, n 74.

[96] *Black Slaves*, p 169.

[97] Oldham, *Mansfield Manuscripts*, ii.1239; Adams, "Dido Elizabeth Belle".

[98] BBC News online report, "Slavery levels in the UK 'higher than thought'", 29 November 2014. [http://www.bbc.co.uk/news/uk-30255084], accessed, 18 December 2015.

[99] George van Cleve, "'Somerset's Case' and Its Antecedents in Imperial Perspective" (2006) 24:3 *Law and History Review* 601–645.

the discussion. The relation of master and servant and apprentices arose out of contract, as far as English servants or apprentices were concerned. The relation between BSBEs and their masters when they arrived in England was clearly not based on contract. But if they were under an obligation to serve their masters for an indefinite period or for life, what was the basis for that obligation?

State of the Law

By the eighteenth century the state of English law regarding those who were slaves in the American or West Indian colonies and were brought to England by their masters (BSBEs) was far from coherent. It would be inaccurate to describe them unequivocally as "slaves".[100]

The Case Law

What has not generally been recognised is that there were two distinct lines of authority, or set of precedents before *Somerset* and they were diametrically opposed to one another. One line asserted that as soon as slave set foot on English soil, he or she became free. The other line of authority, stemming from the Yorke-Talbot opinion of 1729, asserted that the status of those who were slaves in the colonies did not change on their arrival in England. As to the latter line of authority, there was also the assertion that baptism, even after arrival in England, did not change that status either. One should also bear in mind, as Wiecek has pointed out[101] that few of the decisions cited here as reported were in print until the end of the eighteenth or the early nineteenth century. They might have circulated in manuscript, but the extent to which they influenced legal opinion is questionable.[102] On the other hand, the Yorke-Talbot opinion was widely circulated at the time by slave owners and their supporters.

The notion that as soon as a slave set foot in England he or she became free was first asserted at the time of Queen Elizabeth I. Rushworth[103] states that "In the Eleventh of Elizabeth [1568–69], one Cartwright brought a Slave from Russia, and would scourge him, for which he was questioned; and it was resolved, That England was too pure an

---

[100] Paul D Halliday, *Habeas Corpus: From England to Empire*, Cambridge, Mass; London, 2010, pp 174–175. Shyllon, *Black Slaves in Britain*, p 43; Baker, John H, (John Hamilton) *An Introduction to English Legal History*. 4th edn, London, 2002, pp 475–477.

[101] William M Wiecek, "Somerset: Lord Mansfield and the Legitimacy of Slavery in the Anglo-American World." (1974) 42 *University of Chicago Law Review* 94–95;

[102] Oldham, "New Light", p 49.

[103] 2 *Historical Collections* 468.

Air for Slaves to breath in". The origin of Rushworth's report was the proceedings against John Lilburne in 1637 in the Star Chamber for printing and publishing a libel. For refusing to answer he was imprisoned for contempt, whipped, pilloried and fined. His imprisonment continued until 1640 when he was released by the Long Parliament and the House of Commons impeached the judges of the Star Chamber for their proceedings against Lilburne. In speaking of the impeachment, the managers of the Commons cited the case of *Cartwright* and the Russian slave.[104] The notion that when a slave set foot in England he became free did not in fact originate in England, but had been invoked earlier by the Dutch[105] and was said to be the practice in other Christian nations.

The first reported case that put forward the view that black people could be the subject of property was *Butts v Penny*[106] in 1676, in which a master was permitted to bring the common law action of trover against a defendant who, it was alleged, was interfering with the master's right of possession over his slaves. Trover was an action to recover the value of goods or chattels, although not the thing itself. Levinz report states that the action was for "trover for 100 negroes". The special verdict found that "the negroes were infidels, and the subjects of an infidel prince , and are usually bought and sold in America as merchandise, by the custom of merchants", and that "the plaintiff bought these, and was in possession of them until the defendant took them". The King's Bench held that "negroes being usually bought and sold among merchants, as merchandise, and also being infidels, there might be a property in them sufficient to maintain trover" as a preliminary point but the hearing was then postponed to the next term as the Attorney General wished to be heard on the matter. No further action was taken. Another report[107] merely states the general opinion of the court that "they are by usage *tanquam bona*[108] and go to administrator untill they become Christians; and thereby they are infranchised". Keble's report however states, bizarrely, that the verdict was for "10 negroes and a half"(!), not 100, and that they were "usually bought and sold in India". The reference to an administrator may suggest an analogy was made to the property of a deceased slave owner in Eng-

---

[104] Catterall, *Judicial Cases*, i.16.
[105] Simon van Groenewegen van der Made, *Tractatus de Legibus Abrogatis in Hollandia*, p 5.
[106] (1676) 2 Lev 201, 83 ER 518.
[107] (1676) 3 Keb 785, 84 ER 1011.
[108] Ed. Meaning (treated) as goods.

land, but the references to America and India suggest that the slaves concerned were not in England. The case is also authority for the view that slaves became free by baptism.

In *Chamberline v Harvey*[109] in 1697 the legal seesaw swung the other way. Chief Justice Holt[110] specifically rejected the holding in *Butts v Penny*, holding that "Trover will not lie for a negro." The point was a narrow one on pleading. It was not enough for A to allege against B that B was in possession of A's "negro" because there was no assumption in the common law that black people were property, or necessarily servants. A should have alleged that B was in possession of A's servant. "Any man may maintain trespass for another, if he declares with a *per quod servitium amisit*" [ie for loss of services]. The case is also reported as *Chamberlain v Harvey*[111] where the court stated that:

> An action of trespass will not lie, because a negro cannot be demanded as a chattel, neither can his price be recovered in damages in an action of trespass, as in case of a chattel; for he is no other than a slavish servant, and the master can maintain no other action of trespass for taking his servant, but only such which concludes *per quod servitium amisit*,[112] in which the master shall recover for the loss of his service, and not for the value, or for any damages done to the servant.

In *Smith v Brown and Cooper*[113] in 1701 Chief Justice Holt restated the doctrine in *Cartwright*, that as soon as a slave set foot in England he became free. In 1705 the plaintiff brought an action for *indebitatus assumpsit* for £20 for "a negro" sold by the plaintiff to the defendant in Cheap, one of the wards in the City of London[114] and the verdict was given for the plaintiff. On a motion in arrest of judgment, Holt CJ held that "as soon as a negro comes into England, he becomes free: one may be a villein in England, but not a slave". Powell J commented that "the law took no notice of a negro", meaning that the common law

---

[109] (1701) 5 Mod 182, 87 ER 598. Court of King's Bench, 01 January 1701.

[110] Paul D Halliday, 'Holt, Sir John (1642–1710)', ODNB, 2004; online edn, October 2009 [http://www.oxforddnb.com/view/article/1361], accessed 13 August 2016.

[111] (1701) Carthew 396, 90 ER 830. King's Bench 1697; (1696) 1 Ld Raym 146, 91 ER 994.

[112] Ed. Meaning "the service is lost".

[113] (1705) 2 Salk 666, 91 ER 566. King's Bench 1701.

[114] "*viz. in parochia Beatæ Mariæ de Arcubus in warda de Cheape*", "in the parish of the Blessed Virgin Mary of the Arches in the ward of Cheap".

did not take account of race or colour.[115] Holt said that the plaintiff should have averred in the declaration that the sale was in Virginia, and "by the laws of that country, negroes are saleable". He directed the plaintiff to amend the pleading so that it stated "that the defendant was indebted to the plaintiff for a negro sold here at London, but that the said negro at the time of sale was in Virginia, and that negroes, by the laws and statutes of Virginia, are saleable as chattels." In other words, one could enter into a valid contract in London for the sale of a slave in Virginia, but could not validly contract for the sale of a black person if the black person at the time of the puported sale was in England.[116]

The next legal development came in 1729 when Sir Philip Yorke,[117] Attorney General, and Charles Talbot,[118] Solicitor General, gave an opinion on the legality of slavery. The practice of Christian nations seems to have been unknown to Yorke and Talbot who asserted that the legal position of slaves in the colonies was not affected by their coming to England, nor was it affected by baptism. Mansfield in *Somerset v Stewart* commented on the opinion as follows:[119]

> Lord Mansfield observes, The case alluded to was upon a petition in Lincoln's Inn Hall,[120] after dinner; probably, therefore, might not, as he believes the contrary is not unusual at that hour, be taken with much accuracy. The principal matter was then, on the earnest solicitation of many

[115] Harry Potter, *Law, Liberty and the Constitution: A Brief History of the Common Law*, Woodbridge, 2015, p 176.

[116] In *Cook v Kelly* the plaintiff sued for non-payment for a slave: cited in James Oldham, "New Light on Mansfield and Slavery" (1988) 27 *Journal of British Studies* pp 45–68, at p 64, and n 70, Mansfield, May 23, 1782, Middlesex, 495 nb 60. In Mansfield's notes the amount is stated originally to have been in dollars, suggesting the slave was not sold in England, or the slave was not in England.

[117] Peter D G Thomas, 'Yorke, Philip, first earl of Hardwicke (1690–1764)', ODNB, 2004; online edn, October 2007 [http://www.oxforddnb.com/view/article/30245], accessed 21 October 2015.

[118] Charles Talbot, first Baron Talbot of Hensol (bap 1685, d 1737). M Macnair, 'Talbot, Charles, first Baron Talbot of Hensol (bap. 1685, d. 1737)', ODNB, 2004; online edn, May 2008 [http://www.oxforddnb.com/view/article/26923], accessed 4 August 2016.

[119] (1772) 20 St Tr 1 at 70 (the second hearing, taken from Lofft's note in his reports), below, page 208.

[120] That would be the Old Hall in Lincoln's Inn. The Court of Chancery sat there rather than Westminster Hall out of term time: [http://www.lincolnsinn.org.uk/index.php/history-of-the-inn/ historic-buildings-ca/the-old-hall], accessed 29 October 2016. The Court of Chancery was always open to hear petitions from people seeking redress.

> merchants, to know, whether a slave was freed by being made a Christian? And it was resolved, not. It is remarkable, though the English took infinite pains before to prevent their slaves being made Christians, that they might not be freed...

Mansfield was clearly under the impression that the opinion had been given at the solicitation of owners of slave plantations, and this remained the accepted view until recently. Mansfield was writing some forty years after the opinion was given and the circumstances surrounding it seem to have been forgotten.

There certainly were social contacts between slave owners and leading lawyers during the period, as many slave owners had houses in England and some preferred to live there, such as the Codringtons.[121] One such contact, although much later than 1729, is worth mentioning. John Baker owned slave plantations in the Leeward islands, was also a member of the Middle Temple and was Solicitor General of the Leeward islands. He recorded in his diary[122] that on 2 August 1757 he went to Lincoln's Inn Hall (i.e. the Old Hall) and there met Sir Charles Pratt, the Attorney General, Charles Yorke, the second son of Lord Chancellor Hardwicke and Robert Henley, the Lord Keeper, who succeeded Hardwicke as lord chancellor that year. Unfortunately Baker did not record their conversation. Henley, as lord chancellor, was to take the view, as discussed later,[123] that slaves became free as soon as they arrived in England.

However, Glasson, in an important article,[124] has established beyond doubt that the opinion of Yorke and Talbot was sought by Bishop Berkeley[125] and his ecclesiastical associates who were seeking to establish what was known as the Bermuda scheme. This was partly to establish a missionary school but also had the aim of converting the slave population in the West Indies to Christianity. The chief obstacle to this was the attitude of the slave owners, who were convinced that baptism would make the slaves free. This was essentially a legal

---

[121] Madge Dresser and Andrew Hann (eds), *Slavery and the British Country House*, English Heritage, 2013, chapter 10, Natalie Zacek, "West Indian echoes: Dodington House, the Codrington family and the Caribbean heritage".

[122] John Baker, *The Diary of John Baker*, p 98.

[123] Below, page 32.

[124] Travis Glasson, "'Baptism doth not bestow Freedom': Missionary Anglicanism, Slavery, and the Yorke-Talbot Opinion, 1701–30" (2010) 67:2 *The William and Mary Quarterly* 279–318.

[125] M A Stewart, 'Berkeley, George (1685–1753)', ODNB, 2004; online edn, May 2005 [http://www.oxforddnb.com/view/article/2211], accessed 19 May 2016.

issue and Berkeley and his associates sought the opinion in order to reassure the owner of plantations that the status of their slaves would not be changed by baptism. Berkeley had written on the duty to obey established authority and was even opposed to passive resistance. It connected to the notion that suffering in this world was of less consequence than the saving of souls. Quite why such a duty should apply to people kidnapped and held as slaves, is something of a mystery, and he seemed less concerned with saving the souls of slave owners which would seem to be in far greater danger, but such was his view. Berkeley and his coterie argued that slave owners would find Christian slaves quiescent and easier to manage and would not need to resort to brutality and violence. The group was not the least interested in ending slavery itself and indeed their plan, stripped of its metaphysical aspects, would have disarmed the slaves not physically, but mentally, making them reject any form of resistance to their oppressive conditions.

The Church of England became involved in slavery as early as 1710 as a result of the "charitable bequest" under the will of Christopher Codrington by which the church's missionary wing, the Society for the Propagation of the Gospel in Foreign Parts, became owners of the Codrington Plantations in Barbados, which were slave plantations producing cane sugar. Granville Sharp specifically mentioned the Codrington family in a letter to the Archbishop of Canterbury.[126] The Codrington Library in All Souls College, Oxford still bears their name. On 8 February 2006 the General Synod of the Church of England voted to apologise to the descendants of victims of the slave trade.[127] The Rev Simon Bessant introduced the debate. He noted that the slaves on the plantations had the word "society" branded on their bodies with a red-hot iron. He added that when the emancipation of slaves took place in 1833,[128] compensation was paid, not to the slaves, but to their owners. The Bishop of Exeter and three colleagues were paid nearly £13,000 in compensation for 665 slaves. The descendants of the slaves have not yet been compensated for the vast wealth extracted from their ancestors.

The Catholic church was also involved with slavery from an early period.[129] On 13 August 1985 in Yaounde, Cameroon Pope John Paul

---

[126] Gloucestershire Archives D3549 13/1/C3. The Codrington family lived at Dodington Manor in Gloucestershire.
[127] BBC News online, Wednesday, 8 February 2006.
[128] Slavery Abolition Act 1833, 3 & 4 Will 4, c 73.
[129] In 1452 Pope Nicholas V issued the papal bull *Dum Diversas* to King Alfonso V

II apologised to black Africa for the involvement of white Christians in the slave trade.[130]

Despite the Yorke-Talbot opinion, black people in England continued to seek baptism throughout the eighteenth century. This may have been for a number of reasons, religious conviction no doubt being one,[131] but it seems that the idea persisted that it would confirm their freedom.[132] Bundock mentions the instance, reported in *Lloyd's Evening Post* in November 1760, of a runaway girl who had gone to a church in Westminster to be baptised. Her mistress heard of the plan, burst into the church while the minister was reading the service, and dragged the poor girl out, regardless of the girl's cries and tears, announcing to the congregation that "she was her slave, and would use her as she pleased".[133] Perhaps the idea that baptism freed a BSBE persisted also among slave owners.

Mansfield's comment also seems to disparage the value of the opinion, suggesting perhaps by the addition of the phrase "after dinner", that the port had been round a few times. The Yorke-Talbot opinion was promoted by the slave owners who sought to portray it as definitive of the legal status of BSBEs, which it was far from being, just as the abolitionists promoted Mansfield's judgment in *Somerset* as declaring that there was no such thing as slavery in England, which it did not.

---

of Portugal which authorised him "to invade, search out, capture and subjugate the Saracens and pagans and any other unbelievers and enemies of Christ...to reduce their persons into perpetual slavery". In 1454 Pope Nicholas explicitly confirmed the rights granted to King Alfonso V in *Dum Diversas* in *Romanus Pontifex* by which he granted to Alfonso "...the rights of conquest and permissions previously granted not only to the territories already acquired but also those that might be acquired in the future". On 13 March 1456, Pope Callixtus III issued the papal bull *Inter Cætera* (not to be confused with *Inter Cætera* of 1493) which reaffirmed the earlier bulls recognising Portugal's rights to territories along the West African coast, and the enslavement of "infidels" and non-Christians captured there. The bulls were renewed by Pope Sixtus IV in 1481. Finally, in 1514, Pope Leo repeated verbatim all these documents and confirmed them. Other popes sought to regulate the slave trade and slavery: John Francis Maxwell, *Slavery and the Catholic Church: The history of Catholic teaching concerning the moral legitimacy of the institution of slavery*, Chichester, the Anti-Slavery Society for the Protection of Human Rights, 1975.

[130] *New York Times*, 14 August 1985.

[131] One effect presumably would be that they could testify in court, as Thomas Lewis did.

[132] Bundock, *The Fortunes of Francis Barber*, p 34.

[133] Ibid, pp 34, 228 n 18; Seymour Drescher, "Manumissions in a Society without Slave Law: Eighteenth Century England" (1989) 10 *Slavery and Abolition* 85–101, at p 95.

Several leading lawyers regarded Mansfield's judgment as freeing the "slaves" in England, namely Edmund Burke,[134] Dr Hay of the Prerogative Court,[135] Lord Campbell,[136] who held the offices of lord chief justice and then lord chancellor,[137] Lord Stowell,[138] of the Admiralty court, and John Philpot Curran.[139] Black people held as slaves in America evidently shared this view. At the end of September 1773 a slave owner named John Austin Finnie placed an advertisement in the *Virginia Gazette* seeking the return of two of his slaves and expressed the view that they might try to reach "Britain, where they imagine they will be free (a Notion now too prevalent among the Negroes…".[140] A similar advertisement was put in a local newspaper in Georgia the following year by a slave owner called Gabriel Jones, who feared his slave would "attempt to get aboard some vessel for Great Britain, from the knowledge he has of the late Determination of Somerset's Case".[141]

Both views were used as propaganda in a political cause. Unfortunately both views have survived into modern times, no longer as propaganda, since the political battle was won long ago, but as orthodox views of the legal history. They have been conflated into the composite notion that there was slavery in England, but that Lord Mansfield abolished it. Neither part of that notion is true.

Recently, the view that *Somerset* was the decisive blow against slav-

---

[134] "…even a negro slave, who had been sold in the colonies and under an act of parliament, became as free as every other man who breathed the same air as him." *A Letter to the Sheriffs of Bristol*, 1777, quoted in Carretta, introduction to Cugoano, *Thoughts and Sentiments on the Evil of Slavery*, xi–xii, Harmondsworth, Penguin, 1999 and Bundock, *The Fortunes of Francis Barber*, p 140. Burke himself had a black servant, possibly brought from St Vincent, where his brother Richard had an interest in a plantation: ibid, p 101.

[135] Below, page 376.

[136] Gareth H Jones, Vivienne Jones, 'Campbell, John, first Baron Campbell of St Andrews (1779–1861)', ODNB, 2004; online edn, January 2008 [http://www.oxforddnb.com/view/article/4521], accessed 22 May 2016.

[137] "Lord Mansfield first established the grand doctrine that the air of England is too pure to be breathed by a slave." *Lives of the Chief Justices of England*, 1874, iv.291–93; Shyllon, *Black Slaves*, p 166. Shyllon describes Campbell's comment as a "fabrication" which is clearly accurate.

[138] Below, page 64.

[139] *Speeches*, Thomas Davis ed, Dublin, 1845, p 182. James Kelly, 'Curran, John Philpot (1750–1817)', ODNB, 2004 [http://www.oxforddnb.com/view/article/6950], accessed 22 May 2016.

[140] Olusoga, *Black and British*, p 145–146; Vincent Carretta, *Phillis Wheatley: Biography of a Genius in Bondage*, Georgia, 2011, p 130.

[141] Olusoga, *Black and British*, p 146; Alan Gilbert, *Black Patriots and Loyalists: Fighting for Emancipation in the War of Independence*, Chicago, London, 2012, p 9.

ery has been revised by many scholars.[142] On the other hand, the orthodox view of the Yorke-Talbot opinion has not been subjected to the same degree of academic criticism. It is equally in need of revision. It was neither a judgment given in court nor by judges. No reasons were given for the conclusions. The latter point is not surprising, because opinions given by lawyers often did not give the reasoning that led to the conclusions, merely the conclusions. But being in that form did not add to its authority, which rested only on the reputation of those who gave it. It was not based on credible legal foundations. A BSBE brought to England from the colonies, where slavery was legal by statute, could only remain a slave in England if colonial statutes somehow had force in England, which was untenable, or if the BSBE had acknowledged himself or herself in court proceedings to be a "villein in gross", a category with which he would be unlikely to be familiar, which had long since since become obsolete and whose members, if they existed, must have originated, or whose ancestors must have originated, in an English manor. The opinion seems imbued with the prejudiced view that slavery was somehow a characteristic of an enslaved person and passed with him or her as with any other personal characteristic, such as the colour of the skin. But there is no slave without a slave owner, just as there is no wife without a husband. What was asserted was a legal relationship, which, if it were to be valid, had to be based on some legal doctrine or provision in force in England.

Whatever the circumstances in which the Yorke-Talbot opinion was given, it seems also to have been Philip Yorke's own view of the law, since after he became lord chancellor with the title of Lord Hardwicke,[143] he sought to reinforce it in his judgment in *Pearne* v *Lisle*.[144] Indeed, he cited his own earlier opinion as Attorney General in support of his view.

The case did not, however, concern the status of BSBEs in England and therefore as obiter dicta, his statements on the point would not even bind lower courts. The plaintiff claimed he was entitled to "fourteen Negroes at Antigua", that his agent had let them to the defendant for hire, that the defendant refused to pay for two years' service and refused to deliver them to the plaintiff's agent. He claimed that the defendant had declared that he intended to leave England and go to

---

[142] William M Wiecek, "Somerset: Lord Mansfield and the Legitimacy of Slavery in the Anglo-American World" (1974) 42 *University of Chicago Law Review* 86–146. Shyllon, *Black Slaves*; Oldham, "New Light".

[143] Above, page 25 and n 117.

[144] (1749) Amb 75, 27 ER 47.

Antigua. The plaintiff sought a writ of *ne exeat regno* to prevent the defendant leaving the country. The court refused, holding that it would not grant *ne exeat regno* on a mere demand for money and that the defendant was in any case amenable to legal process in Antigua. Lord Hardwicke nevertheless went on to criticise Holt CJ's decisions. He attacked them for not being based on precedent, which ignored the *Cartwright* case. Lack of precedent was a fault that more appropriately applied to his own earlier opinion as Attorney General.

The seasaw had swung back again in favour of liberty in two minor cases cited by Granville Sharp, in his monograph, *A Representation of the Injustice and Dangerous Tendency of Tolerating Slavery*.[145] In *Galway v Caddee* tried before Baron Thompson in the Guildhall "abt 30 years ago", ie, 1739, a verdict was given in favour of a "negro", who was declared "free on his first setting foot on English ground". In *De Pinna v Henriques* decided in Guildhall in 1732 a black woman was claimed as slave. The defendant Henriques had given her protection. The verdict was given for the defendant.

A manuscript in the NYHS Granville Sharp collection is an opinion of Attorney General De Grey, (who became Lord Chief Justice of the Common Pleas). He was of the opposite opinion to Yorke-Talbot. It seems that one Storer, who claimed a woman as his slave, had instructed Swetman to "carry her away", possibly back to a colony, which would have separated her from her husband.

> Mr Storer might have an Interest by Contract in the Service of this Female Slave. But no property in her person by the Law of this Country. And therefore no authority to direct Swetman to carry her away. The Husband had a right by Marriage according to the Laws of this Country to that Relation, and Mr Storer having no property in her Person could have none by the Marriage.

De Grey interestingly makes a distinction between the right of property, which he says Storer did not have, and a right to her services, which he might have had, but only, in de Grey's view, if based on contract. The husband had a right to her company stemming from the marriage, and whatever rights Storer might have had did not override that. William De Grey became Attorney General in 1766 and lord chief justice of the Common Pleas in 1770, so the opinion must have been given between those dates.[146]

---

[145] At pp 5–6.
[146] Gordon Goodwin, 'Grey, William de, first Baron Walsingham (1719–1781)', rev M

In 1762 another lord chancellor also took the opposite view to Lord Hardwicke. In *Shanley v Harvey*[147] the plaintiff Shanley twelve years earlier had brought over the defendant, Harvey, as he was then known, as his slave, who was then only eight or nine years old, and given him to his niece, Margaret Hamilton, who had him baptised and changed his name to Joseph Harvey. In July 1752, about an hour before her death, she directed Harvey to take out a purse, which was in her dressing-case drawer, and delivered it to him, saying, "Here, take this, there is £700 or £800 in bank notes, and some more in money, but I cannot directly tell what, but it is all for you, to make you happy: make haste, put it in your pocket, tell nobody, and pay the butcher's bill." He then knelt down and thanked her. She said, "God bless you, make a good use of it." If Joseph Harvey were a free man, those facts would have amounted to a *donatio mortis causa*[148] and a valid gift. The bill in Chancery was brought by Shanley, ostensibly as administrator of Margaret Hamilton's estate, claiming against Joseph Harvey for an account of part of her personal estate under those circumstances. This was evidently a claim for the money and on the basis that Joseph Harvey was a slave and incapable of taking such a gift. It might also have been a claim to Joseph Harvey himself, as being property and part of Miss Hamilton's estate, but that would be a matter for the court to decide on an account. Lord Chancellor Henley[149] dismissed the bill, following Holt CJ's judgments and indeed going further, holding that: "As soon as a man sets foot on English ground he is free: a negro may maintain an action against his master for ill usage, and may have a Habeas Corpus if restrained of his liberty." His holding, that black people alleged to be slaves had the benefit of habeas corpus, is significant in that it was made some ten years before Lord Mansfield's judgment in *Somerset v Stewart*.

So far, one may conclude that there was something of a consensus emerging by the 1760s at least that there was no property in the person of a BSBE, so that he or she could not legally be sold in England and

---

J Mercer, ODNB, 2004 [http://www.oxforddnb.com/view/article/11571], accessed 23 March 2015.

[147] (1762) 2 Eden 126, 28 ER 844, Court of Chancery, 15 March 1762.

[148] Meaning gift in contemplation of death. A principle of Roman law which had found its way into the common law.

[149] Peter D G Thomas, 'Henley, Robert, first earl of Northington (c 1708–1772)', ODNB, 2004 [http://www.oxforddnb.com/view/ article/12931], accessed 21 October 2015. He was made lord keeper 30 June 1757, the last person to receive that title. He was made a peer on 27 March 1760, as Baron Henley. On 16 January 1761 he became lord chancellor, and on 19 May 1764, he was created Earl of Northington.

had other rights such as to habeas corpus and the protection that the common law accorded to any person. Physical abuse could give rise to an action for assault and battery. There is at least one instance of a conviction for murder for killing a black person.[150] On 20 December 1770 the *Bath Chronicle and Weekly Gazette* reported that: "This Day the Admiralty Sessions ended at the Old Bailey, before Sir Thomas Salusbury, when Capt. Ferguson, for the murder of a negro boy, about 13 years of age, was capitally convicted, and received sentence to be executed on Thursday next." The High Court of Admiralty had criminal jurisdiction over offences committed on the high seas.[151]

It may be objected that this view of the law paints an overly rosy picture, especially when set against what often happened in practice. Masters might simply resort to force and send people to drag back their servants by force. A distinction was made earlier between "slavery in fact" and slavery in law, but to some extent the two cannot be entirely separated. Jonathan Strong was arrested by a sheriff, who would have needed a warrant from a magistrate to do so. Nevertheless, once his case was heard by the magistrate, Strong was released. In the Scottish case of *Knight*,[152] under a different legal system, it was the sheriff, who was a judge with far greater powers than an English sheriff, who released him. More research needs to be done to get a clearer picture, if possible, of the involvement of English sheriffs and magistrates in these proceedings.

Lord Mansfield had not taken a clear position on the issue as to the personal liberty of BSBEs before *Somerset*. Indeed one of the surprising comments that he makes in the *Thomas Lewis* case that:[153]

> "I have granted several Writs of Habeas Corpus upon Affidavits of Masters for [36] their Negroes, two or 3 I believe upon affidavits of Masters deducing sale and property of their Negroe[.] upon being prest I have granted Habeas Corpuss to deliver them to their Masters; but whether they have this kind of property in England never has been solemnly determined[.]"

That is to say, when black servants had been impressed into the Navy, Mansfield had granted habeas corpus not to set the impressed men

---
[150] See below, Dr Fothergill's letter to Sharp, page 397: "A Master who stabbed his Black Servant, or any other Black would probably swing for it..."
[151] As to admiralty jurisdiction, see page 292. See also "The Royal Navy", below, page 41.
[152] Below, page 59.
[153] Below, page 117.

free, but at their masters' behest to return them to their masters. Granville Sharp was scathing in his comments on this remark of Mansfield's, as a misuse of a writ intended to protect liberty and also since it deprived the King of the service of these servants for the benefit of a private person. This was despite the fact that Mansfield also noted that no definitive ruling had been made on their status. Mansfield's comment is also interesting, in that habeas corpus would not be an appropriate remedy for the return of mere property. Perhaps such masters had already conceded that in England their servants were not property. Or perhaps they had been advised that they would not have succeeded in an action of trover or detinue. There are, indeed, examples of habeas corpus being granted to return apprentices who had been impressed.[154]

There were other specific issues which were unresolved or only partly resolved: could BSBEs sue their masters for wages, and were they obliged to work for the master for the rest of their lives? The wages question was the subject of an obiter dictum by Lord Mansfield in the case of *R. v The Inhabitants of Thames Ditton*.[155] It concerned Charlotte Howe, a black woman. The report says, that "the pauper was bought in America by Captain Howe as a negro slave, and by him brought to England in 1781". Captain Howe went to live in the parish of Thames Ditton, taking Charlotte with him, and she lived with him there in his service, until 7 June 1783, when he died.[156] Charlotte was baptised on 17 December 1783 in the parish of St Nicholas in Thames Ditton.[157] She continued to live with his widow and executrix, Mrs Howe, who soon afterwards moved to the parish of St Luke's, Chelsea. Charlotte lived with her in Chelsea for five or six months, but then left and returned to Thames Ditton where she applied for poor relief, ie, to be supported by the parish.[158] The overseers of Thames Ditton denied her poor relief because she had not resided in Thames Ditton for forty days. They decided that Charlotte's poor relief should be paid for and

---

[154] Paul D Halliday, *Habeas Corpus: From England to Empire*, London, 2010, p 175 n 161.

[155] (1785) 4 Doug KB 300, 99 ER 891. Court of King's Bench, 27 April 1785.

[156] "Will of Tyringham Howe, late Commander of His Majesty's Ship Thames of Thames Ditton, ...", TNA PROB 11/1106/110.

[157] See: [http://www.exploringsurreyspast.org.uk/themes/subjects/black_history/surrey/charlotte-howe], accessed 26 April 2016. I am grateful to Dr Ruth Paley for reference to this source.

[158] It appears that Mrs Elizabeth Howe died in 1786: "Will of Elizabeth Howe, Widow of Saint Luke Chelsea, Middlesex." TNA PROB 11/1142/103, probate, 10 May 1786.

provided by Chelsea and she was duly 'removed' to that parish. As was common practice, the parish of St Luke's appealed the decision and the matter was taken to the Court of King's Bench. The poor law statutes were aimed at providing for those who had been in work but had then lost their jobs and so they required proof of a "hiring", ie a contract. Charlotte could not prove a hiring and so Lord Mansfield held that she did not qualify for poor relief in Thames Ditton. The same would apply in Chelsea.

Counsel for St Luke's argued that the general scope of the Acts was that no settlement[159] should be gained by a service of an indefinite duration, which would be to impose too heavy a burden on the parish, adding that "the Court has never decided that a negro brought to England is there under an obligation to serve". Lord Mansfield interjected to remark that "The determinations go no further than that the master cannot by force compel him to go out of the kingdom", again insisting on the most narrow interpretation of his own judgment in *Somerset*. Later he added that, "in the case relating to villeins, it was held that the lord could not by force take them out of the country" and then that "The case of Somerset is the only one on this subject. Where slaves have been brought here, and have commenced actions for their wages, I have always nonsuited the plaintiff." The inability to sue for wages seems to have been a real disability of BSBEs. They could not prove a contract nor claim quantum meruit[160] for the reasonable value of their work, since quantum meruit was based on an implied contract. However, it is interesting to note that some BSBEs were suing in the King's Bench. They must have had supporters able to bear the costs. It is possible, of course, that some had been paid weekly sums, or had been promised wages.

The case shows the extreme vulnerability of BSBEs, especially women whose prospects of advancement in some calling were even more limited than for men. Some BSBEs, like Equiano and Cesar Picton, became well-connected, educated and financially independent, but they were exceptions.

Apart from the King's Bench, there was a procedure whereby menial servants could apply to two justices of the peace who could order payment under a statute of Elizabeth I[161] which had been modified

---

[159] A settlement in the context of the poor law meant "the right, depending on various circumstances, to be maintained by a particular locality, whether parish or union". Brown, *A New Law Dictionary* (1874), "Settlement, Poor Law".
[160] "what one has earned".
[161] (1562–3) 5 Eliz I, c 4, 4 St Realm 414. James Barry Bird, *Laws respecting Masters and*

under James I.[162] So it may be that some BSBEs obtained an order that way. But the picture is complicated, as Chater has pointed out, by the fact that English servants were often not paid wages either. They were supplied with food, lodging and clothes, but not necessarily money wages.[163] Non-payment of wages was therefore not a definite mark of slavery in England. On the other hand, payment of wages was inconsistent with the status of a slave. Lord Mansfield seems to imply this in his comment in *Somerset* on the third day that "the service performed by the slaves without wages, is a clear indication they did not think themselves free by coming hither".[164] Mansfield's assumption, that BSBEs were somehow free to choose, is another example of Mansfield's refusal to recognise the reality of a slave's powerless position. Even in *Somerset* he seems still to have been conflicted.

As noted in his diary, Dr Johnson paid Francis Barber wages of 7s a week in 1765 and other entries show the same in 1782.[165] On top of that Francis would have got board and lodging and clothes and probably vails,[166] ie tips expected to be given by guests to servants.

Nothing further is known of the fate of Charlotte Howe and the court was not called upon to decide other issues. The law seems clear that BSBEs were not property. If so, then it is not clear why counsel said that "The pauper was to be considered the servant of Captain Howe during his life, and the life of his widow after his death". If, when in England, she was not the property of Captain Howe, then she would not have been "inherited" by Howe's widow. Perhaps he had given Charlotte to his wife before they arrived in England under the law applicable in the American colony. It is interesting that Charlotte was baptised shortly after Captain Howe's death. If Charlotte survived her mistress then it would seem that there would then have been nothing to prevent her seeking employment for wages, if she was by then able to work. But since the court did not have to decide these points it is difficult to predict how it would have done, in view of its inconsistency on other points.

In 1786 the Committee for the Relief of the Black Poor was instituted to relieve the problem of the many black paupers living not only

Servants; articled clerks, apprentices, journeymen and manufacturers. Comprising as well the laws respecting... London, [1795], pp 47–50.

[162] (1603–4) 1 Jac I, c 6, 4 St Realm 1022.
[163] Chater, *Untold Histories*, pp 85–88.
[164] Below, page 219.
[165] Bundock, *The Fortunes of Francis Barber*, p 63.
[166] OED. From Old French *vail*, from *valoir* (to be worth), from Latin *valeō* (I am worth).

in London but also in other ports and towns in England. Some had found their way to England working on board ships trading with the West Indies. Thousands of black loyalists who had been held as slaves in America joined the British forces in the American War of Independence (1775–83)[167] and were promised their freedom if they did so. They were brought to England at the end of the war, but no provision was made for them and many became destitute. This was to give rise to the movement to establish Sierra Leone as a homeland for them in Africa, a movement in which Sharp was deeply involved.

There were other marked differences between the position of BSBEs in England and slaves in the colonies. They arose mainly not out of law, but from the absence of law. There was never a suggestion in England that their status, whatever it was, was inherited.[168] Black people born in England of BSBEs, or with a BSBE parent, were subjects and free. There was no law that said otherwise. There was never any prohibition in England of sexual relations between black and white people, or against their marriage.[169] There were in fact a number of instances of marriages, usually between black men and white women, in eighteenth century England.[170] There was no law on manumission. Drescher[171] maintained that there four methods in practice: indentures as a servant; a letter of reference from an employer; assumed prior manumission by self-assertion; and sacral manumission. Chater considers that the first two, which would also have applied to white people, stretched slavery beyond the point at which it had any meaning.[172] Drescher noted that there was no law in England that dealt specifically with slavery. It can nevertheless be argued that there might, however, be something in the nature of manumission in a limited sense. So long as there was a notion applied to BSBEs that they "possibly"[173] owed a duty of perpetual service to their original master, then an indication that their master renounced such a possible right, or acted in a manner inconsistent with it, such as paying wages, would presumably have freed the BSBE of any such "possible" obligation. The relation in any

---

[167] Simon Schama, et al, *Rough Crossings: Britain, the Slaves and the American Revolution*, London, 2005.
[168] Chater, *Untold Histories*, p 89.
[169] Walvin, *Black and White*, p 52.
[170] Ibid. Francis Barber married a white lady, Elizabeth Ball, in Lichfield in 1773: Bundock, *The Fortunes of Francis Barber*, p 144; Equiano married a Cambridgeshire lady: Walvin, *Black and White*, p 52.
[171] Drescher, "Manumissions", pp 85–101; Chater, *Untold Histories*, pp 83, 97 n 22.
[172] Chater, ibid, p 83.
[173] Blackstone, *Commentaries*, below, pages 41, 399.

case was between individual BSBEs and individual masters. If a master did not treat a BSBE as a slave, as for example, in the case of Dr Johnson and the young Francis Barber, then the relation did not have any effects on third parties. If a BSBE left his or her original master and went to live with a third party, there was no obligation by statute or otherwise on the third party to send the BSBE back if the master did not pursue the issue. An apprentice who had agreed to serve for a given number of years committed an offence if he absconded during the period, but a BSBE had not so agreed and therefore committed no criminal offence if he or she ran away. In the colonies a slave who ran away could be charged with stealing the clothes he wore, or even more bizarrely, himself,[174] whereas a BSBE was not, or was not held to be, property, and his clothes could be construed as a gift, as with other servants, so none of that applied.

Blackstone

In 1758 William Blackstone was appointed Vinerian professor of English law at the University of Oxford, the first professor of English law to be appointed in England. In 1765 he published the first volume of his *Commentaries on the Laws of England* which was to extend over four volumes and prove to be highly influential in the common law world. Blackstone presented English common law as the result of a long period of development in which the more primitive aspects of law had evolved through the spirit of liberty, which he saw as the particular genius of the English, to approach in his own time the perfection of reason and liberty of the subject. In his own closing words to the *Commentaries*, Blackstone asserted that the common law was "the best birthright, the noblest inheritance of mankind".[175] Blackstone's view has been the subject of critical analysis in an article by Duncan Kennedy.[176] Far from being a coherent body of rational law which protected liberty, Kennedy demonstrates that the common law in the age of Blackstone was a mixture of status relations and growing areas protecting freedom, especially the freedom of contract. In status relations legal obligations were imposed on individuals without their consent,

---

[174] Frederick Douglass on several occasions in addressing audiences said: "I appear this evening as a thief and a robber. I stole this head, these limbs, this body from my master, and ran off with them." [http://www.civilwar.org/education/history/biographies/frederick-douglass.html], accessed 1 December 2016.

[175] *Commentaries*, vol 4, p 436; Potter, *Law, Liberty and the Constitution*, p 177.

[176] "The Structure of Blackstone's Commentaries" (1978–1979) 28 *Buffalo Law Review* 205.

or if created originally with consent, then imposed pre-determined onerous obligations on one party which they could not negotiate or alter. The surviving status relations included the law of married women, master and servant, apprenticeship, impressed sailors and aspects of property law.

In view of this paean to liberty, it was of interest to many, both abolitionists and slave owners alike, to note what Blackstone had to say about slavery in England. In the first edition of the *Commentaries* he appeared at first sight to support Holt and Henley's view, stating:[177]

> And this spirit of liberty is so deeply implanted in our constitution, and rooted even in our very soil, that a slave or a negro, the moment he lands in England, falls under the protection of the laws, and so far becomes a freeman.

and further on page 412, that: "And now it is laid down, that a slave or negro, the instant he lands in England, becomes a freeman; that is, the law will protect him in the enjoyment of his person, his liberty, and his property". Blackstone was to qualify this view in his second and later editions and some have assumed that he was persuaded by someone that English law had not taken such an unequivocal stand and that he should correct that impression in the second edition onwards. The obvious candidate for that role was Mansfield, since Mansfield had been instrumental in the creation of the chair at Oxford on Blackstone's behalf.[178] However, in a letter first published by Professor Prest[179] from Blackstone to Sharp, in response to Sharp's having sent Blackstone a copy of the unpublished manuscript of his book against slavery,[180] Blackstone expressed some surprise that commentators, including Sharp apparently, had got the impression that he endorsed Holt's view, that a slave as soon as he landed on English soil became free in all respects. The passages from his *Commentaries* with their later amendments are set out below on page 399. In fact, in the first edition of the *Commentaries*, Blackstone's statements on pages 123

---

[177] Book 1, p 123.

[178] Potter, *Law, Liberty and the Constitution*, p 177.

[179] W R Prest, *The Letters of Sir William Blackstone, 1744–1780*, London, Selden Society, 2006, Letter 124 pp 138–139; reproduced in part in Shyllon, *Black Slaves*, p 66. Prest states that "the present whereabouts" of the original letter in the Gloucestershire Archives, D 3549 13/1/B25 were unknown. The letter reproduced in this volume is from a copy in the Granville Sharp Collection in the NYHS, as is that in Prest. Below, page 395.

[180] Granville Sharp, *A Representation of the Injustice and Dangerous Tendency of Tolerating Slavery...*, London, 1769.

and 412 quoted above are an unequivocal endorsement of the position of Holt CJ and Henley LC. But later, on page 412, he did indeed suggest a somewhat vague qualification:

> Yet, with regard to any right which the master may have acquired, by contract or the like, to the perpetual service of John or Thomas, this will remain exactly in the same state as before: for this is no more than the same state of subjection for life, which every apprentice submits to for the space of seven years, or sometimes for a longer term.

What is meant "by contract or the like"? What is "like" a contract if it is not a contract? If the master had acquired the right by a colonial statute, and without any consideration, that is in no way "like" a contract. Blackstone went on to say (on page 413) that baptism would make no alteration in the position and that it would "not dissolve a civil contract, either express or implied, between master and servant" and goes on to say that "the slave is entitled to the same liberty in England before, as after, baptism". He seems here to veer towards the Yorke-Talbot opinion, while asserting that any duty of perpetual service could only arise out of contract, which is not what the Yorke-Talbot opinion asserted, adding "express or implied", and also that the slave was entitled to "liberty" in England. There seems little ambiguity here, unless "or the like" was intended to leave some area of doubt. It is hardly surprising, then, that Sharp among others got the impression from the first edition that Blackstone supported the notion that slaves became free in England. In his letter, however, Blackstone says that he did not intend to express a view on whether BSBEs were under an obligation of perpetual service once they arrived in England:

> I have never peremptorily said, that "The master hath acquired any right to the perpetual Service of John Thomas", or that the Heathen Negroe did owe such Service to his American master. I only say that "if he did, that obligation is not dissolved by his coming to England and turning Christian." It did not become me to pronounce decisively, on a matter *Adhuc subjudice*;[181]

In the second edition Blackstone retreated from the notion of freedom. On page 412 the phrase "by contract or the like" is deleted and so too is the word "liberty", so that legal protection applies only to the servant's person and property, while the "civil contract" becomes "civil

[181] Ed. While still under judicial consideration.

Introduction

obligation" and "liberty" is replaced by "protection", so that perpetual service might not be based on contract at all and might arise without the consent of the servant. Yet in that case the obligation could arise only from slavery. Furthermore, on page 123 in the second edition, after the words "and so far becomes a freeman", he adds "though the master's right to his service may probably still continue". In the 4th edition, 1770, Blackstone seems to have thought this was going too far and he changed the word "probably" to "possibly".[182] A further amendment was made in the 5th edition, published in 1773. In Book 2, page 402 of the first edition Blackstone referred to:

> negro-servants, who are purchased, when captives, of the nations with whom they are at war, and continue therefore in some degree the property of their masters who buy them: though, accurately speaking, that property consists rather in the perpetual service, than in the body or person, of the captive.

In the 5th edition the phrase "(if it indeed continues)" was added after "perpetual service".[183] Blackstone introduced a new doubt as to perpetual service, perhaps as a result of the *Somerset* case. Blackstone reached the position by the 5th edition that a BSBE in England had protection of his person and property, but the question as to whether he or she was under an obligation of indefinite personal service was still left unresolved.

The Royal Navy

Finally, whatever the state of civilian law, the Lords of the Admiralty were quite clear. In 1751 a naval officer, James Jones, bought a black man, William Castillo, in Boston.[184] He brought him to England the following year and Castillo was baptised in Plymouth. Castillo considered this made him free and he left Jones and went to London. He was spotted there in 1758 and was sent in chains to Portsmouth under threat of being sent into slavery in Barbados. Castillo petitioned the prime minister, William Pitt, saying that he was held on board HMS

---

[182] *The Oxford Edition of Blackstone*, Wilfrid Prest, gen ed, 4 vols, vol 1, below page 399. Shyllon, *Black Slaves*, pp 59–61; Wilfrid Prest, *William Blackstone: Law and Letters in the Eighteenth Century*, Oxford, 2008, pp 250–251.
[183] Below, page 400.
[184] Bundock, *The Fortunes of Francis Barber*, p 83.

Neptune "with a collar on my neck in day and in irons att night." An inquiry was carried out by Admiral Holburne, the Portsmouth harbourmaster, who reported back to the Admiralty. The Lords of the Admiralty responded:[185]

> Acquaint Admiral Holburne that the laws of this country admit of no badges of slavery, therefore the Lords hope and expect whenever he discovers any attempt of this kind he should prevent it.

Black seamen ate the same food as their white counterparts, wore the same clothes, shared the same quarters, received the same pay and other benefits and undertook the same duties.[186]

The cases which are the subject of the transcripts published in this book are outlined below.

The Cases

Jonathan Strong

One day in 1765 Sharp visited his brother William Sharp who was a surgeon in Mincing Lane, and found Jonathan Strong,[187] a young black man about sixteen or seventeen years of age, waiting outside to be treated. He had been badly beaten about the head with a pistol by his master, David Lisle, who had then thrown him out into the street. Strong had suffered brain damage, had lost some of the use of one arm and was partially blind. William Sharp sent him to St Bartholomew's Hospital where he remained for about two months. When he was discharged he had nowhere to go and contacted Granville Sharp again. Sharp found him a position with a Mr Brown, a surgeon and apothecary in Fenchurch Street, as an errand boy. He stayed with Mr Brown for about two years. He was paid wages and given a livery and in Sharp's words "grew to be a good looking, stout, young man".

Lisle had read law at the Inner Temple and was admitted to the bar in 1747 but also had a slave plantation in Barbados. He was not successful and even sustained losses. He also had a foul temper, probably exacerbated by his personal failures. He had returned to London and

---

[185] Bundock, *The Fortunes of Francis Barber*, p 83; Vincent Carretta, *Equiano, the African: biography of a self-made man*, Athens, GA, c 2005, pp 86–88; Rodger, *The Wooden World*, p 161.

[186] Carretta, *Equiano the African*, pp 74–75.

[187] Kathleen Chater, 'Strong, Jonathan (c 1747–1773)', ODNB, September 2012 [http://www.oxforddnb.com/view/article/100415], accessed 23 April 2016.

brought Jonathan Strong with him. Many black people believed that baptism made them free and it is possible that Strong had been baptised and this may have been the reason behind cause of Lisle's vicious assault.[188]

About two years after Jonathan had begun working for Mr Brown, Lisle saw him in the street and had him arrested and imprisoned as a runaway. On 12 September 1767 Sharp received a letter from from the prison known as Poultry Counter.[189] It was from Jonathan Strong, and signed by him, imploring Sharp to protect him. Lisle was planning to send him to Barbados to be sold as a slave. Sharp did not remember Strong's name, but went the following day, a Sunday, to the prison and demanded to see Jonathan. When he saw him he remembered him at once and asked him what he had done to be imprisoned. Jonathan said he had done nothing, that Lisle had seen him in the street behind a hackney coach "attending his mistress", possibly Mrs Brown, and had followed him to Fenchurch Street. Lisle had purported to sell Jonathan to a Jamaican slave owner and had him committed to the prison until a ship was available. Sharp told the keeper of the prison not to deliver Jonathan to anyone until the matter should be examined by a magistrate. Sharp, with his brother James, then went to see the Lord Mayor, Sir Robert Kite, and asked that all people who "pretended to have a claim on the person" of Jonathan should be summoned before the Lord Mayor. When the appointed day came, Lisle did not appear, but William Macbean, a notary public appeared as attorney for a Jamaican slave owner, called James Kerr, and David Laird, captain of the ship *Thames* which was bound for Jamaica. Both claimed that Jonathan was the property of Kerr by virtue of a bill of sale, which they produced and which was signed by Lisle. Jonathan had never heard of either of them. Macbean and Sharp then engaged in a long argument, during which Jonathan nearly fainted with fear. The Lord Mayor then told Jonathan he was free to go wherever he pleased. The captain of the West Indiaman then grabbed hold of Jonathan by the arm and said he was the property of Kerr. At that, the Coroner of London, Thomas Beach, came up behind Sharp and whispered in his ear, "Charge him". Sharp then told Laird that he would demand that a constable should charge Laird with assault if he should try to take

---

[188] No record of Strong's baptism has been found by the author at this time.

[189] More properly, Poultry Compter. It was a small compter, or prison, run by a Sheriff of the City of London from medieval times until 1815. It took its name from a section of Cheapside called Poultry, so-called because poultry was sold in the street market.

Jonathan. Laird let go of Jonathan and "all the parties retired from the presence of the Lord Mayor, and Jonathan departed also, in the sight of all, in full liberty, nobody daring afterwards to touch him". The Lord Mayor had refused to recognise the validity of a bill of sale for a slave in London.

But that was not the end of the matter. Some time later James and Granville were served with copies of writs to answer to James Kerr in a plea of trespass and demanding £200 damages. They employed an attorney of the Lord Mayor's office and he showed them a copy of the Yorke-Talbot opinion. The attorney told them that in view of that opinion their case could not be defended, but Sharp refused to accept that the law of England was "so injurious to natural rights" and began his study of the law "tho' he had never before opened a law book in his life". He wrote his comments, attacking the many errors in the writs and discussing arguments against slavery. Among the authorities he collected which were opposed to the Yorke-Talbot opinion was the passage from the first edition of Blackstone's *Commentaries*[190] citing the opinion of Chief Justice Holt in Salkeld's Reports that as soon as a slave set foot in England he became free.[191] However, he later became aware of the third edition of the *Commentaries* in which Blackstone had changed his opinion "induced (as it is said) by the sentiments of Chief Justice of the King's Bench (Lord Mansfield) to withdraw that opinion". That issue has been discussed above. Nevertheless, Sharp made the interesting move of instructing his attorney to retain Blackstone as one of his counsel, since Blackstone was also practising as a barrister at that time. He also retained Sir James Eyre, then Recorder of London. Blackstone was given a copy of Sharp's comments. Blackstone advised that they should arrange a consultation with the Solicitor General, John Dunning, later to become Lord Ashburton. This was arranged at the chambers of the Solicitor. Sharp attended with his attorney and with the Recorder and Blackstone. There was some discussion before the Solicitor General came in. Blackstone said that the courts might take the view that there was an implied contract of apprenticeship, in the case of BSBEs, which he had hinted at in the second and third editions of his *Commentaries*.

There was a further objection to the implied apprenticeship suggestion because in London a proclamation of the Lord Mayor of 14 September 1731 had ordered that "for the future no *Negroes* or other

---
[190] Above, page 39.
[191] Above, page 24.

Blacks to be suffered to be bound Apprentices at any of the Companies of this City to any Freeman thereof".[192] This arose out of the John Satie affair. Satie was a BSBE who had become apprenticed to a joiner in London in 1718. In September 1731 Satie became entitled to become a Freeman of the City of London. Neither "aliens" nor their children could be apprenticed. Satie had been a slave in Barbados and had been brought to England at the age of about two by a merchant called Gerrard who was his master and possibly his father. Barbados was part of the king's dominions and on the face of it anyone born in the king's dominions was a subject of the king and not an alien. The aldermen debated whether Satie was a British subject. They decided that he should be given his freedom, but that in future no black person should be permitted to become Freemen. The order of the Lord Mayor is notable both in that it impliedly conceded that a black person born into slavery in the West Indies was a British subject, but also in that it was a rare if not unique example of a measure which applied to black people specifically on the basis of race.

Sharp immediately responded to Blackstone's point and objected that any contract, implied or otherwise, had to be based on free consent of the parties concerned. The Solicitor General then came in and expressed a similar view to that of Blackstone. Sharp remained silent "being no speaker" but decided to develop his comments into a more considered version. He had about twenty copies made in manuscript and lent them out among his friends and "the professors of the law". This probably included Blackstone and the Solicitor General. In any case, it had, he said, "the desired effect" of intimidating the plaintiff's lawyers. The case dragged on for two years until they were non-suited and ordered to pay costs. At one point Lisle had challenged Sharp to a duel. Sharp refused, saying Lisle should have satisfaction before the courts. It was this incident that also impelled Sharp to oppose the practice of duelling and he wrote against it.[193] Sharp then felt able to publish his answer to the Yorke-Talbot opinion which he did in 1769 as *A Representation of the Injustice and Dangerous Tendency of Tolerating Slavery, or of Admitting the least Claim of Private Property in the Persons of Men in England*.[194] It was the first publication in England to present

---

[192] Bundock, *The Fortunes of Francis Barber*, p 77.
[193] Granville Sharp, *A Tract on Duelling: wherein the Opinions of the most celebrated Writers on Crown Law are examined and corrected...*, Printed for B White and Son, Fleet Street; and C Dilly in the Poultry, 1773; Second edition with additions. London, 1790. Gloucestershire Archives, D3549/13/6/9.
[194] London, Printed for B White, 1769.

the legal and moral case against slavery. He also began to correspond and collaborate with the French-born American abolitionist Anthony Benezet and, from 1773, the Philadelphia abolitionist Benjamin Rush. Benezet and other Quakers had founded the the Society for the Relief of Free Negroes Unlawfully Held in Bondage on 14 April 1775, in Philadelphia, Pennsylvania. It was the first abolitionist society in America, and predated the English society. Sharp took up other cases of BSBEs in England, such as Thomas Lewis.

Sadly, Jonathan was to die only a few years after his release, on 17 April 1773, probably as a result of his injuries, at the age of 26.[195]

The King (Lewis) v Stapylton (1771)

Thomas Lewis was a young African, born on the coast of what is now Ghana. His original African name does not seem to have survived. Professor Oldham has reproduced Lord Mansfield's trial notes of Lewis's evidence.[196] According to that note, Lewis's uncle suggested to him he should go to sea with the captain of a Danish ship. According to Lewis's account in the NYHS manuscript, reproduced in this volume, he was brought up by his uncle after his father died, but then became a servant of the "general and governor of the place". It is not clear if this man was a local tribal leader or perhaps an appointee of the African Society. This man spoke English and it was he who suggested to Lewis that he might like join a Danish ship to travel abroad and learn English, a suggestion with which Lewis readily agreed. Lewis's account does not suggest that he left West Africa as a slave. The Danish ship was evidently not a slave ship but a trading vessel. Lewis did not say he was put in chains. He was a ship's boy or servant. He later worked for Stapylton on his ship and in a variety of jobs in Havana, New York and Pensacola, Florida. It was certainly an eventful voyage. On one occasion he was shipwrecked and later Stapylton's ship was taken by a Spanish privateer (or letter of marque).[197] Mansfield laid emphasis on this in his trial notes and it is clear he considered that the capture of Stapylton by the Spanish destroyed any title or claim Stapylton might otherwise have had to own Lewis as a slave.[198] Stapylton, as a captive, would himself have

[195] Chater, 'Strong, Jonathan', ODNB.
[196] Oldham, "New Light on Mansfield and Slavery" (1988) 27:1 *Journal of British Studies* 50.
[197] A letter of marque was a certificate from a state recruiting a private ship to be a man of war in the navy of the state. The phrase also came to be used to denote the ship itself. Such ships were also known as privateers.
[198] Oldham, "New Light", p 52; Oldham, *Mansfield Manuscripts*, ii.1226, 1243.

been in a position indistinguishable from a slave of the Spanish. Lewis spent some days with the Spanish, separated from Stapylton. Later, they were both released. Lewis later went with Stapylton to Chelsea in London and worked in a tavern there. Stapylton formed a plan to kidnap Lewis and have him sent to Jamaica to be sold as a slave. Lewis was set upon one night by two watermen employed by Stapylton, John Maloney and Aaron Armstrong, who bound and gagged him and took him down to a boat or snow at a wharf on the Thames at Chelsea. Lewis cried out and his cries were heard by Mrs Banks, the mother of Sir Joseph Banks, the naturalist, who lived nearby. She alerted Sharp who obtained a writ of habeas corpus. In the meantime, Lewis had been transferred to a West Indiaman, at Gravesend.[199]

The habeas corpus led to Lewis being released by the captain of the ship, Philip Sawyer, after the intervention of the mayor of Gravesend. Lewis, with the aid of Sharp, then brought a private prosecution against Stapylton and the other men who had assaulted and tried to kidnap him, which is the subject of the main MS. Stapylton's defence was that Lewis was his property and he was entitled to act as he did. Habeas corpus had no application to "goods".

The proceedings are remarkable in that Lewis gave evidence himself. He said he was a servant but was not, and never had been, a slave. Lord Mansfield expressed doubts about whether Lewis should give evidence of his own freedom, then said he would presume a person free until proved otherwise, so it was for Stapylton to prove Lewis was his property. Mansfield's comments make it clear that he was determined not to allow argument as to whether slavery was legal in general and to confine the issue to whether Lewis was specifically the property of Stapylton and that he would leave that issue to the jury. In his trial notes[200] Mansfield said that he considered the capture of Stapylton's ship by the Spanish privateer significant, ie that it would have negated any question of Lewis being Stapylton's slave at that point. The jury found that Lewis was not Stapylton's slave, with cries of "no property!" "no property!" Mansfield then instructed them that they must find Stapylton and the others guilty, which they duly did.

In the manuscript of the motions for judgment, in which Stapylton and the others did not appear, Mansfield said he had doubts about whether Lewis should have been allowed to give evidence, apparently contradicting his earlier opinion in the case that a person should

---

[199] Oldham, *Mansfield Manuscripts*, ii.1242. There is some apparent confusion in the G# MS over the name of the captain: see page 115.
[200] Oldham, *Mansfield Manuscripts*, ii.1243.

be presumed free until proven otherwise. There is no indication that judgment or sentence was given against Stapylton and the other defendants. Sharp expresses his indignation that the finding of guilty was not followed by judgment and sentencing, in violation of principles of the rule of law. In his trial notes[201] Mansfield says that Stapylton was "blind and old" which would seem to explain why no further action was taken. At any rate, Lewis was free.

The case is further evidence of Mansfield's reluctance to face the issue of the legality of slavery in England, which is also evident from his judgment in *Somerset*.

Somerset v Stewart

According to Stewart's case for the detention of Somerset, it was stated that James Somerset had been held by Charles Stewart (or Stuart) in Virginia where slavery was legal under local legislation. He had been brought to England by Stewart, had escaped and was recaptured on 26 November 1771. Somerset had been baptised "James Summersett [*sic*] an adult Negro aged about 30 years [of] Baldwins Gardens" on 12 February 1771 at St Andrew's, Holborn.[202] He had been detained on board ship to be transported to Jamaica where he was to be sold as the slave and property of Stewart. The writ of habeas corpus had been obtained from Lord Mansfield by Somerset's godparents who had witnessed Somerset's capture and had signed affidavits: Elizabeth Cade, a widow, Thomas Walkin, and John Marlow.[203]

As Shyllon has pointed out, Somerset was taken not from Virginia, but from Boston, Massachusetts, to London. This appears from the private papers of Charles Stewart, made available to Emory Washburn, a member of the Massachusetts Historical Society, in 1864.[204] According to the papers, Stewart was the cashier and paymaster of customs in North America and had lived for some years in Boston. It may be, therefore, that Somerset's status in America was governed not by the law of Virginia, but by that of Massachusetts. However, slavery had been established in Massachusetts since at least the seventeenth century and although there was growing opinion, including judicial opin-

[201] Oldham, *Mansfield Manuscripts*, ii.1243; Oldham, "New Light", p 50.
[202] Ancestry.co.uk, photograph of original entry.
[203] Gerzina, *Black England*, p 116; David Olusoga, *Black and British: A Forgotten History*, London, 2016, p 128.
[204] Shyllon, *Black Slaves*, pp 78–79; Emory Washburn, "Somerset's Case, and the Extinction of Villeinage and Slavery in England" *Massachusetts Historical Society, Proceedings for 1863–1864*, pp 307–26.

ion,[205] against the legality of slavery or a life-long obligation of service, that developed in the years after Somerset was brought to England.

However humiliating life was as a domestic servant in England, life as a slave on a sugar plantation in the West Indies was far worse. James Somerset must have been appalled at the prospect. It was famously described by the Rev John Newton, the slave ship captain who became an Anglican clergyman and also famously composed the hymn *Amazing Grace*, when he recounted a conversation he had in 1751:[206]

> One thing I cannot omit, which was told to me by the Gentleman to whom my ship was consigned, at Antigua, in the year 1751, and who was, himself, a Planter. He said, that calculations had been made, with all possible exactness, to determine which was the preferable, that is, the more saving method of managing Slaves:– "Whether, to appoint them moderate work, plenty of provision, and such treatment, as might enable them to protract their lives to old age? Or, by rigorously straining their strength to the utmost, with little relaxation, hard fare, and hard usage, to wear them out before they became useless, and unable to do service; and then, to buy new ones, to fill up their places?" He farther said, that these skillful calculators had determined in favour of the latter mode, as much the cheaper; and that he could mention several estates, in the island of Antigua, on which, it was seldom known, that a Slave had lived above nine years.

Serjeant Davy in this MS asserted that his main argument was addressed to the proposition that "no man at this day can be a slave in England" and went into the issue of the law of Virginia and villeinage in England in some detail and into case law such as *Pigg* v *Caley* (1617) Noy 27, 74 E.R. 997, *Butts* v *Penny* (1676) 2 Lev. 201, 83 E.R. 518, *Chamberline* v *Harvey* and other cases. At one point Mansfield interjected to say that the last case he found where someone was found to be a

---

[205] In *Quock Walker* v *Jennison* (Worcester County Court of Common Pleas) in 1781 Chief Justice William Cushing instructed a jury that "the idea of slavery is inconsistent with our own conduct and Constitution; and there can be no such thing as perpetual servitude of a rational creature, unless his liberty is forfeited by some criminal conduct or given up by personal consent or contract...". This was popularly believed to have abolished slavery in Massachusetts, but that was ten years after Somerset was brought to England.

[206] *Thoughts upon the African Slave Trade*, pp 38–39.

villein by confession was in the "19th of Henry the 6th". This seems to be a reference to a case in the Year-Books in 1440.[207]

Davy maintained that there were only two grounds for maintaining that people could be slaves in England, namely (1) that their status under the laws of Virginia and the West Indian colonies somehow continued in England when they were brought here, or (2) that they were villeins in gross, if such still existed. The first required the notion that the laws of the colonies, where slavery was legalised by statute, somehow applied in England, which was untenable. On villeinage, he maintained that it arose from manors in England, that villeins regardant, ie tied to a manor, had been abolished at the Restoration by the Tenures Abolition Act 1660 and, at most, only villeins in gross existed in theory, but had become obsolete in practice. Black servants brought to England had no connection with manors in England. He dismisses the notion that one could be a villein by confession on record, as there was no evidence of such in the present case and judges in the past had invented or recognised numerous means by which a claim to villeinage was barred or defeated. Also, if slavery was legal in England, it would apply equally to white and black, since the common law made no distinction of race. He finally deployed, somewhat teasingly, what could be called a racist argument against recognising slavery in England. If plantation owners could bring their slaves to England, what was to stop them deciding to establish slave plantations in England? He painted a fanciful picture of the arrival of large numbers of black people in England who, in the course of time, would become free and intermarry with the white population, producing a mixed-race population and causing much "heart ache"! As anyone familiar with the behaviour of slave owners would know, they had already made their own notable contribution to the "mixing" of the population.

Versions of the Judgment

Lord Mansfield appears to have delivered his judgment extempore, but it seems odd, given the importance that a ruling on the issue raised in the case, that there is no version written or approved by Mansfield himself. It was left to shorthand writers or lawyers and others sitting in court to produce versions of it for publication. Wiecek[208]

---

[207] YB Mich 19 Hen 6 p 65 fol 32b, Seipp 1440.083. Below, page 217.
[208] William M Wiecek, "Somerset: Lord Mansfield and the Legitimacy of Slavery in the Anglo-American World" (1974) 42 *University of Chicago Law Review* 86–146.

lists four versions.[209] Professor James Oldham in an important article has brought to light two previously-unnoticed versions of Mansfield's judgment in the manuscript collections of Lincoln's Inn, London.[210] Scholars owe him a considerable debt for this notable contribution to the debate. One[211] is in the manuscript collection of Serjeant Hill[212] and the other is in the paper books of Ashhurst J in the Dampier Manuscripts[213]

Professor Oldham compared the various versions to assess which was likely to be the most accurate. He divided Mansfield's judgment into "six critical elements" leading up to the conclusion that Somerset was free and compared them in the different versions. On the Ashhurst version, he noted that despite the fact that Ashhurst was a judge and therefore the authenticity on that ground must be accepted, Ashhurst did not write shorthand and that some phrases are missing in his version which are present in other versions. He concludes that the Ashhurst version cannot be taken to include all the words spoken by Mansfield. He also rejects Lofft's version as it does not con-

[209] 1. Lofft 1, 18-19 (1772). 2. An account in the (London) *Gentleman's Magazine* 293-94 (June 1772) 24. 3. An account in 34 *Scots Magazine* 297 (June 1772) 225. 4. An unsigned handwritten document in the Granville Sharp transcripts, New York Historical Society, captioned "Trinity Term 1772 On Monday 22 June 1772 In Banco Regis.", reprinted in Prince Hoare, *Memoirs of Granville Sharp, Esq.* 89–91 (1820).

[210] Oldham, "New Light on Mansfield and Slavery" (1988) 27 *Journal of British Studies*, No 1, 45-68; see also Oldham, *Eighteenth-Century Judges' Notes: How They Explain, Correct and Enhance the Reports* (1987) 31 *American Journal of Legal History* 9; Oldham *Mansfield Manuscripts*, ii.1229.

[211] Hill MS 10 ff. 312–314; J H (Sir John Hamilton) Baker, *English Legal Manuscripts: vol II. Catalogues of the Manuscript Year Books, Readings, and Law Reports in Lincoln's Inn, the Bodleian Library and Gray's Inn.* Zug, Switzerland and London, c 1975–1978, ii.81.

[212] George Hill (1716–1808), King's Serjeant-at-Law, admitted to the Middle Temple in 1733; called to the Bar by that society in 1741; admitted *ad eundem gradum* to Lincoln's Inn in 1765, created serjeant-at-law November 1772. M Macnair, 'Hill, George (c 1716–1808)', ODNB, 2004, [http://www.oxforddnb.com/view/article/13273], accessed 1 April 2016. Baker, *English Legal Manuscripts*, ii.81. Baker notes that he was considered one of the most learned lawyers of his day, but "quite ignorant of the world, and so incapable of applying his learning that he acquired the nick-name of *Serjeant Labyrinth*" citing Polson, Archer, *Law and Lawyers: or, Sketches and Illustrations of Legal History and Biography.* London, 1840, i.78.

[213] APB 10.b. The Dampier manuscripts are described in Edmund Heward, "Dampier Manuscripts at Lincoln's Inn" (1988) 9 *Journal of Legal History* 357. There is an index to the Dampier MSS consisting of a box of paper slips noting the case name, date and the reference to the MS numbers of each cases prepared by Lincoln's Inn. The *Somerset* case is listed in the paper card file as "Summerset, Ex p." and as "unreported". The present author is currently engaged in transcribing the paper slips into a version which will be available at the Inn and possibly published on the Inn's web site or elsewhere in due course.

tain the "fuller and consistent expressions" contained in the other four versions. He notes that that the version that are closest are the *Scots Magazine* and Hill versions. Nevertheless he discounts language that appeared in the *Scots Magazine* version that appeared nowhere else, unless reprinted in newspapers. It should be noted here that a critical phrase appearing in the Sharp NYHS version was missing from the *Scots Magazine* version, but inserted by Sharp in the version published in his pamphlet and also reproduced by Hoare and by Shyllon, namely: "Tracing the subject to natural principles the claim of Slavery never can be supported." We shall refer to this as the "Sharp insertion" and return to it later. Oldham concludes that the *Scots Magazine* (without the Sharp insertion) and Hill versions are most similar and of the two prefers the Hill MS. Shyllon favoured the *Scots Magazine* version and reproduces it in his book [214] including the "Sharp insertion". Oldham refers to the work of the distinguished American cultural historian, David Brion Davis,[215] who also preferred the *Scots Magazine* version.

The present volume reproduces six versions as follows:

1. The Scots Magazine/Estwick version.
This was published in 34 *Scots Magazine* 297 (June 1772). It was reprinted by Granville Sharp, *The Just Limitation of Slavery, in the Laws of God, Compared with the Unbounded Claims of the African Traders and British American Slaveholders...* (1776), Appendix 8, p 65, from the second edition of a tract published in 1773 by Samuel Estwick, the government agent for Barbados and MP for Westbury. The "Sharp insertion" is in italics within brackets and noted as an addition by Sharp, who says they were taken from "the notes of a very ingenious and able counsellor, who was present when the judgement was given". This is also the version reproduced by Hoare in *Memoirs of Granville Sharp*, pp 89–91 and Shyllon notes that it was this version which was printed in a number of newspapers within a day or two of its being delivered.[216]

2. Granville Sharp MS of the Judgment
This MS, in the NYHS Granville Sharp Collection, differs slightly from the Scots Magazine/Estwick version. It was printed, with minor vari-

[214] Shyllon, *Black Slaves*, pp 108–110.
[215] *The Problem of Slavery in the Age of Revolution, 1770–1823*, Ithaca, NY, 1975, chapter 10.
[216] Shyllon, *Black Slaves in Britain*, p 110, note 1: *The London Evening Post* (24 June), *The Public Advertiser* (24 June), *Felix Farley's Bristol Journal* (27 June 1772).

ations in punctuation, in Prince Hoare, *Memoirs of Granville Sharp, Esq.* 89–91 (1820).

3. Letter, *General Evening Post*, London, 1772
This version was contained in an anonymous letter to the newspaper. Again, it differs in minor respect from the Scots Magazine/Estwick version.

4. Lincoln's Inn, Hill MS version
This is a transcript of the Hill MS 10 ff. 312–314 in Lincoln's Inn.

5. Lofft's Report in (1772) Lofft 1, 98 ER 499; (1772) 20 St Tr 1.

6. Lincoln's Inn, Ashhurst paper book. This is a transcript of the Dampier MS, APB 10b in Lincoln's Inn.

Professor Oldham's detailed comparison means that it is only necessary here to add some points to the existing debate. Some comentators have focussed on the use of the words "positive law" in the different versions. "Positive law" could be used in opposition to natural law, or it could mean statute law as opposed to case law.[217]

Davis favoured the *Scots Magazine* version and concludes that the passage:

> The state of slavery is of such a nature, that it is incapable of being now introduced by courts of justice upon mere reasoning, or any principles natural or political; it must take its rise from positive law; the origin of it can in no country or age be traced back to any other source. Immemorial usage preserves the memory of positive law long after all traces of the occasion, reason, authority, and time of its introduction, are lost, and in a case so odious as the condition of slaves must be taken strictly.

implied that "positive law" was used in the sense of case law and that Mansfield meant that the case law must be "taken strictly" and that did

---

[217] Mansfield used it in this sense in the later case of *R v The Inhabitants of Thames Ditton*, p 56, 99 ER 891 at 892: "Lord Mansfield.- We will not trouble Mr. Palmer. The poor law is a subsisting positive law, enforced by statutes which began to be made about the time of Queen Elizabeth, when villeinage was not abolished...For the pauper to bring herself under a positive law she must answer the description it requires."

not rule out some aspects of slavery. If so, then it seem to the present writer that the earlier words "inacapable of being *now* introduced" imply that slavery had not been recognised by case law up to that point, and could not "now" be introduced by "courts of justice". Moreover, to say that slavery could not be introduced on "upon mere reasoning" etc implies that it could not be introduced by case law, which was based on reasoning and argument, as opposed to statute law based on enacted words. In other words it, could only be introduced by statute law, and, clearly, there was none. This view is reinforced by a statement in Hoare quoted by Oldham[218] and made by Mansfield extra-judicially after the hearing of 7 February 1772: "If the merchants think the question of great consequence to trade and commerce, and the public should think so too, they had better think of an application to those that will make a law. We must find the law: we cannot make it." Again, the case law, as has been discussed, consisted of two conflicting lines of authority, the one against slavery being considerably the stronger, as we have argued. A strict view would require a strong line of authority in favour of slavery and there was none.

The statement that "A foreigner cannot be imprisoned here on the authority of any law existing in his own country" (the "foreigner" being James Somerset) seems a clear rejection by Mansfield of any suggestion that the laws of Virginia could somehow have force in England. The point contradicted the Yorke-Talbot assertion that the status of a person who was a slave in a foreign country did not change if he came to England, at least insofar as it was based on the laws of Virginia. The only other basis suggested was the law of villeinage in gross, which had been argued in some detail in the first hearing. Perhaps this is what Mansfield meant by his reference to "immemorial usage". Mansfield does not then go into the issue of whether the situation of a BSBE could be assimilated to villeinage in gross, but, apart from the difficulties already discussed and inherent in that context, he says that it must be treated "strictly" which would seem to rule it out. If on the other hand, as some have argued, he is referring to positive law in the sense of custom, which, in the context of relatively recent commercial custom, he had recognised, then again the passage seems to rule that out also. One of the requirements of the recognition of custom at common law was that it should have been practised from "time immemorial", which specifically meant since the coronation of King

---

[218] Oldham, *New Light*, p 59; Hoare, *Memoirs of Granville Sharp*, p 88.

Richard I, ie since 1189[219] and should be reasonable. Chattel slavery, in the sense of the practice of treating black people as slaves in England, the wearing of collars etc, can hardly be traced back further than the seventeenth century. Slavery might have been introduced in the colonies at first by recognising an existing practice on the basis of custom there, but that would be open to the same objection of introducing colonial law into England. Colonies had not existed since "time immemorial" and so it is difficult to see how slavery could have been introduced legally other than by local statute.

Another aspect of the *Scots Magazine*/Estwick version which would definitely rule out any recognition of slavery in England, are the words "Tracing the subject to natural principles the claim of Slavery never can be supported", which we refer to as the "Sharp insertion". The same words appear in the Sharp MS version and it seem likely therefore that Sharp took those words from the MS and added them to the *Scots Magazine*/Estwick version. Sharp's footnote says that they were taken from "the notes of a very ingenious and able counsellor, who was present when the judgement was given". That also suggests that the ingenious counsellor was the author of the Sharp MS version in the NYHS collection. But are the words reliable? The only reliable way of obtaining a verbatim transcript of an extempore judgment at the time was to take it down in shorthand. Sharp did indeed employ professional shorthand writers. However, he describes the author of the "Sharp insertion" as a lawyer, albeit an ingenious one, but does not say he was a shorthand writer. Nevertheless, it was the *Scots Magazine* version which Sharp chose to publish himself, including the insertion. None of the versions of the judgment can definitely be said to be the work of a shorthand writer and that makes it difficult to identify any one as definitive. If the Sharp MS in the NYHS collection was a shorthand note commissioned by Sharp, presumably he would have reproduced that and the fact that he did not seems to indicate that he did not have full confidence in it, but chose to include the "Sharp insertion" as a special note since it was not in the *Scots Magazine* version. It strengthened the case for asserting that Mansfield had ruled out slavery, but its insertion by Sharp with the special note shows that Sharp was meticulously honest in not claiming it as definitive. Nevertheless, using the criterion that two, or more, versions independently taken down which contain the same or very similar words or phrases are most likely to be accurate, the "Sharp insertion" should be discounted, since it was only

---

[219] Jacob, *Law Dictionary*, "Custom".

in the Sharp NYHS MS and then copied into the *Scots Magazine* version by Sharp. The present writer agrees with Oldham that the *Scots Magazine* (without the Sharp insertion) and Hill versions are most similar and are to be preferred, Oldham leaning in favour of the Hill version. As between the *Scots Magazine* and Hill versions, the present author sees little to choose between them.

The Order

The final words of Lord Mansfield's judgment are usually quoted, from Loffts report, as "and therefore the black must be discharged". In fact, none of the other versions refer to James Somerset as "the black", but use a more respectful term. Four of them refer to him as "the man". The *Scots Magazine* version, the letter to the *General Evening Post*, the Granville Sharp MS and the Lincoln's Inn, Ashhurst Paper Book, all have: "...therefore the man must be discharged". Finally, the Lincoln's Inn, Hill MS, refers to him by name: "therefore we are all of Opinion that James Somerset must be discharged". Since the preponderance of the versions use the words "the man", it seems more likely that those were the words spoken by Lord Mansfield.

Scope of the Judgment

If Somerset was free to go, then clearly he had no continuing obligation of service to Stuart, or not one that Stuart tried, or was able, to enforce. However, recent scholarship has tended to revise the notion that Mansfield in *Somerset* intended set all slaves in England free. Indeed, Mansfield himself denied that the decision went so far. In *R v The Inhabitants of Thames Ditton*[220] he intervened in the course of submission by counsel to say:[221] "The determination [in *Somerset*] go no farther than that the master cannot by force compel him [The BSBE] to go out of the kingdom." That is of course correct as to the issue directly before the court. But is difficult to accept that Mansfield by his other remarks was unaware of the implications. As Bundock has commented:[222]

> In spite of the narrowness of the judgment, however, he must have been well aware of the implications: if slavery could be established only by positive law, and there

---

[220] (1785) 4 Doug KB 300, 99 ER 891.
[221] Ibid, p 892; Shyllon, *Black Slaves*, p 169.
[222] Bundock, *The Fortunes of Francis Barber*, p 139.

Introduction

was no such positive law in England, then how could slavery continue? Moreover, how could slave-owners prevent their slaves from running away when they had lost their most potent threat, that of sending a slave back into colonial slavery?

When Thomas Hutchinson, governor of Massachusetts, dined with Lord Mansfield at Mansfield's home, Kenwood House, in 1779, Mansfield repeated his insistence on the "narrow rule" of his judgment. Hutchinson found it difficult to accept that, although he kept his doubts to himself:[223]

> I took occasion to remark that all the Americans who had brought Blacks had, as far as I knew, relinquished their property in them, and rather agreed to give them wages, or suffered them to go free. His Ld.ship remarked that there had been no determination that they were free, the judgment (meaning the case of Somerset) went no further than to determine the Master had no right to compel the slave to go into a foreign country, &c. I wished to have entered into a free colloquium, and to have discovered, if I am capable of it, the nice distinctions he must have had in his mind, and which would not make it equally reasonable to restrain the Master from exercising any power whatever, as the power of sending the servant abroad; but I imagined such an altercation would rather be disliked and forbore.

The Habeas Corpus Amendment Act 1679[224] had introduced some reforms to the writ. The Act applied to any "inhabitant or resiant" (ie, resident) of England, without limiting that description in any way, but only to detention "for criminal or supposed criminal matter".[225] Nevertheless it is worth considering it briefly to put Mansfield's decision in context. Under section 11 of that Act:[226]

> ...noe Subject of this Realme that now is or hereafter shall be an Inhabitant or Resiant [sic] of this Kingdome of England Dominion of Wales or Towne of Berwicke upon Twee-

---

[223] Thomas Hutchinson, *The Diary and Letters of His Excellency Thomas Hutchinson Esq.*, Boston, 1884–86, 2:274–77; quoted in Shyllon, pp 14–15 and by Oldham, "New Light", p 67.
[224] 31 Car II c 2, St Realm v.935.
[225] Ibid; Baker, *Introduction*, p 474; Halliday, *Habeas Corpus*, p 175.
[226] Ibid, p 937.

de shall or may be sent Prisoner into Scotland Ireland Jersey Gaurnsey Tangeir or into any Parts Garrisons Islands or Places beyond the Seas which are or at any time hereafter shall be within or without the Dominions of His Majestie His Heires or Successors and that every such Imprisonment is hereby enacted and adjudged to be illegall...

The proviso in section 12 exempted from the benefit of section 11 any person who should enter into a contract in writing by which they agreed to be so transported.

Section 11 had in fact been inserted because of the case of John Lilburne. In 1651 he had been held in contempt of parliament.[227] In 1654 he had been sent to the island of Jersey by the Council of State under Cromwell, in order to be beyond the reach of habeas corpus. Harry Potter (the barrister) has aptly described Jersey as "Cromwell's Guantanamo Bay". Lilburne was confined in Mont Orgueil castle in winter with no glass in the windows of his cell, and he died there.[228] The practice had been continued after the Restoration, but the "Lilburne clause" was passed to prevent such abuses in future.

Since James Somerset had not been accused of a criminal offence, Mansfield does not refer specifically to the section, although Hargrave made a passing reference to the Act, referring to Stuart as "taking an ill advantage of some inaccurate expressions in the Habeas Corpus Act" and to an "inadvertently worded" clause; in his submission.[229] He trusted that "that one statute, will not be allowed to over-rule the law of England".[230] Wallace, on the other hand, for Stuart, argued that "'Tis necessary the masters should bring them over; for they cannot trust the whites, either with the stores or the navigating the vessel. Therefore, the benefit taken on the Habeas Corpus Act ought to be allowed."[231] Mansfield clearly did not accept that because the 1679 Act did not apply that it followed that he should uphold the detention in the case of a writ at common law.[232] There had been a concern at the time that the 1679 Act had in some way undermined the writ at com-

---

[227] Potter, *Law, Liberty and the Constitution*, pp 154–161.
[228] Ibid, pp 154–155.
[229] Below, page 205; Halliday, *Habeas Corpus*, p 175.
[230] Below, page 205.
[231] Below, page 208.
[232] In 1816 a further statute extended the scope of the 1679 Act: Habeas Corpus Amendment Act 1816, 56 Geo. III, c 100. Baker, *Introduction*, p 474; Halliday, *Habeas Corpus*, p 246.

mon law but Lord Hardwicke had dismissed these suggestions.[233] The words in Mansfield's judgment (depending on what version you prefer) are: "No master ever was allowed here to take a slave by force to be sold abroad because he had deserted from his service, or for any other reason whatever" (*Scots Magazine*) or "No master was ever Allowed here to send his servant abroad because he absented himself from his service or for any other Cause" (Hill MS version). Sale implied that Somerset was Stuart's property, and it would seem to follow that Mansfield also refused to accept this.

Another point should be noted. Blackstone had replaced the word "liberty" in his *Commentaries* apparently because he thought it was inconsistent with a possible obligation of perpetual service. But the writ of habeas corpus is a remedy specifically and historically to protect liberty, not merely to protect the person, for which assault and battery etc, were already available. If habeas corpus was applicable to set at liberty an alleged slave, how could there still be an obligation of perpetual servitude without pay? If a slave owner had detained his BSBE in his house in England and asserted his right to perpetual service without a contract, would habeas corpus not also set the BSBE free? It would need a "nice distinction", in Hutchinson's phrase, to refuse it. But this issue did not come directly before the courts.

Shortly after the *Somerset* case, a Scottish court, by contrast to the ambiguity of *Somerset*, was to declare that slavery was contrary to the law of Scotland. It was in the case of *Knight v Wedderburn*.[234]

On 20 April 1765 the slave ship *Phoenix* arrived in Montego Bay in Jamaica. The captain was John Knight and the ship had left for the Caribbean on 5 March 1765, with a cargo of slaves acquired on the Guinea Coast at Anomabu and Cape Coast Castle.[235] One of the captured Africans on board was a boy aged about thirteen, who was to become known as Joseph Knight. John Knight sold the young African as a slave to John Wedderburn. Wedderburn was a Jacobite whose father, an impoverished baronet, had been executed for involvement in the Rebellion of 1745–46. Wedderburn had himself participated in the Rebellion and had fled to Jamaica with some of his brothers to wait for times to change so that he could safely return to Scotland. Knight became his personal servant. Wedderburn prospered in Jamaica, and

---

[233] Halliday, *Habeas Corpus*, p 246 and n 123.

[234] (1772) St Tr 2–7 n; Court of Session, unextracted processes, National Archives of Scotland (reference CS235/K/2/2); John W. Cairns, "After Somerset: The Scottish Experience" (2012) 33:3 *The Journal of Legal History* 291–312.

[235] Cairns, "After Somerset", p 291.

in 1768 he eventually returned to Scotland, taking Knight with him. The next year Wedderburn married Margaret Ogilvy, daughter of the Jacobite Earl of Airlie, in whose regiment he had fought at Culloden. He also acquired the house and estate of Ballindean in Perthshire, close to Dundee.

Joseph Knight later married a local girl who was employed by Wedderburn as a servant. When Wedderburn learned of their relationship, he sacked her. By the time that *Somerset* was decided, Joseph Knight was twenty or twenty-one. Like many at the time, he understood it to have declared slaves to be free. He also assumed that it applied throughout Great Britain, although of course it had no force in Scotland. He demanded wages from Wedderburn, in order to provide for his wife and himself. Wedderburn refused. Knight then left, but Wedderburn had him apprehended on a warrant from justices of the peace. The justices found "the petitioner entitled to Knight's services, and that he must continue as before". Knight then applied to the Sheriff of Perth, who found that "the state of slavery is not recognised by the laws of this kingdom, and is inconsistent with the principles thereof: That the regulations in Jamaica, concerning slaves, do not extend to this kingdom." He further held "that perpetual service, without wages, is slavery...".[236] In 1777 Wedderburn appealed to the Court of Session in Edinburgh, Scotland's highest civil court, arguing that Knight still owed service, in the same manner as an indentured servant or an apprenticed artisan, although in this case presumably they meant it to be perpetual. The case was heard by a full panel of judges, including Lord Kames. The case for Knight was helped in preparation by James Boswell and Samuel Johnson and there are many references to it in Boswell's *Life of Johnson*.[237] Lord Kames stated that: "we sit here to enforce right not to enforce wrong" and the court emphatically rejected Wedderburn's appeal. It ruled that:

> the dominion assumed over this Negro, under the law of Jamaica, being unjust, could not be supported in this country to any extent: That, therefore, the defender had no right to the Negros service for any space of time, nor to send him out of the country against his consent: That the Negro was likewise protected under the act 1701, c 6.[238] from being

---

[236] (1772) St Tr 2–7n. National Archives of Scotland, "Feature: Slavery, freedom or perpetual servitude? – the Joseph Knight case." [http://www.nas.gov.uk/about/071022.asp], accessed 23 December 2015.

[237] Shyllon, *Black Slaves*, pp 177–178.

[238] *Act for preventing wrongous Imprisonments and against undue delays in Tryals*, 1701

sent out of the country against his consent.[239]

Joseph Knight was free.

Attempts to Evade *Somerset*

Granville Sharp wrote to his brother James Sharp[240] describing how some slave owners attempted to circumvent the *Somerset* judgment. In *Keane v Boycott*[241] a black boy called Toney, who was about sixteen or seventeen years old, was a slave of the plaintiff on the island of St Vincent. The plaintiff was planning a trip to England. He induced Toney to execute an indenture whereby Toney bound himself to serve the plaintiff for five years as his servant. The plaintiff covenanted to provide him with food, lodging, clothing and medical assistance if he fell sick. The plaintiff arrived in England and went to live in Cheltenham.

The defendant was a captain in the army on a recruiting party. He noticed Toney on the street dressed in livery. He asked him whether he was an indentured servant, to which Toney replied that he was and that he was bound to the plaintiff for five years. After this the boy went to the defendant's lodgings where the defendant gave him two shillings and told him to go to Gloucester to the regiment where the boy duly went. On learning of this, the plaintiff obtained a warrant from a magistrate by virtue of which the boy was apprehended and brought back to the plaintiff's service. The defendant then sent two sergeants to take the boy back to the regiment, which they did, but it did not appear that the boy went unwillingly. The plaintiff brought an action on the case against the defendant for enticing his servant away from his service. The jury found for the defendant. On a motion for a new trial, the Court of Common Pleas held that the contract might have produced a manumission, since Toney was a slave under the laws of the island of St Vincent, and that since it was for his benefit, it was at most voidable only by Toney himself.[242] Chief Justice Eyre[243] said that

---

c.6, Criminal Procedure Act 1701, Short title given by Statute Law Revision (Scotland) Act 1964 (c 80), Sch 2.

[239] Court of Session, unextracted processes, National Archives of Scotland (reference CS235/K/2/2).

[240] Hoare, *Memoirs of Granville Sharp, Esq.*, p 159.

[241] (1795) 2 H Blackstone 512, 176 ER 676.

[242] Contracts with minors are void, where they are to the prejudice of the minor, and, if for their benefit, are binding unless repudiated by the minor during his minority or within a reasonable time after attaining his majority.

[243] Eyre was created serjeant-at-law, knighted, and made a baron of the exchequer on 6 November 1772, becoming chief baron on 26 January 1787. He became chief

whether it was void or voidable, the defendant had no concern with the relation between the plaintiff and his servant and, "to speak of his conduct in the mildest terms", had interfered with it officiously in his zeal for the recruiting service. Further, possibly in order to anticipate events by which Toney or others in his position might simply present themselves voluntarily at a recruiting office or a drumhead, Eyre CJ suggested that is a such a case a recruiting officer should refuse to accept an indentured servant. The court held that there should be a new trial.

It should also be recalled that Eyre, when a barrister, had advised Sharp and his brother, when sued in connection with the Jonathan Strong incident, that their case was hopeless in view of the Yorke-Talbot opinion.[244] In the Common Pleas he had also opposed some of Mansfield's innovations.[245] It would not seem that a supposed apprenticeship entered into with a slave was likely to be an effective device. Since Eyre considered it at most to be voidable at the BSBE's instance, why did he not hold that Toney had avoided it by joining the colours?

Another example of the device is furnished by the case of John Hamlet in 1799.[246] He had been held as a slave on St Christopher. When his master took him to England he had been induced to sign articles of apprenticeship during the voyage. He had "absented himself" from his master, partly because he had been threatened with being sent back to slavery in the West Indies. He alleged that his master had a ship bound for St Christopher and intended to put him on it. He applied for habeas corpus but it was refused by Lord Kenyon's[247] King's Bench, apparently on the basis he was an apprentice, and he was returned to the West Indies.[248] If Hamlet was treated as an apprentice, then Lord Kenyon seems to have ignored the case in Hobart's

---

justice of common pleas on 11 February 1793. Douglas Hay, 'Eyre, Sir James (bap 1734, d 1799)', ODNB, 2004; online edn, January 2008 [http://www.oxforddnb.com/view/article/9032], accessed 5 April 2016.

[244] Shyllon, *Black Slaves*, pp 22–23, 31, 159.

[245] Douglas Hay, 'Eyre, Sir James (bap 1734, d 1799)', ODNB, 2004; online edn, Jan 2008.

[246] Ruth Paley, "After *Somerset*: Mansfield, Slavery and the Law in England, 1772–1830", in *Law, Crime and English Society, 1660-1830*, ed Norma Landau Cambridge, 2002, 165–184, p 178.

[247] Douglas Hay, 'Kenyon, Lloyd, first Baron Kenyon (1732–1802)', ODNB, 2004; online edn, October 2009 [http://www.oxforddnb.com/view/article/15431], accessed 13 August 2016.

[248] Ibid, p 179; PRO KB1/30, affidavits 26 April 1799.

reports cited by Lord Mansfield during the third day (Lofft's "second hearing") in *Somerset*, namely *Coventry v Woodhall*[249] in which it had been held that a master had no right to send an apprentice out of the kingdom against his will.

Commenting on *Keane v Boycott*, Sharp poured scorn on the idea that a slave could enter into a valid contract with his master, and the decision of the court was open to a number of objections. First, the contract should have been held void *ab initio*, since Toney, as a slave in St Vincent where the contract was allegedly formed, lacked capacity to contract. It is also difficult to see how it was for Toney's benefit, since it seems, despite the court's remarks, that the contract would not have constituted a manumission in St Vincent, whose law had required sums of money to be paid to the colonial government before any manumission.[250]

Shyllon describes the case of *Keane v Boycott* as revealing a "gaping hole" in the *Somerset* ruling.[251] However, one can hardly blame Mansfield for the error of Eyre CJ or indeed Lord Kenyon.[252] Some judges who were unsympathetic to the *Somerset* decision were evidently prepared to accept at face value a cynical device. In the case of Hamlet, the case seems to have been decided *per incuriam*. One can say that the writ was wrongly refused in the Hamlet case, although that would have been little comfort to John Hamlet.

On the question of apprenticeship, it is of interest to note that when Granville Sharp took up the case of Jonathan Strong, the issue of an "implied apprenticeship" was raised when he and his brother were sued in trespass by Kerr. Sharp engaged "Dr Blackstone", then practising as a barrister, who suggested a consultation with Dunning, the Solicitor General. Before Dunning arrived, Blackstone told Sharp that "it would be uphill Work in the Court of KB"[253] because "the Case of

---

[249] (1615) Hob 134, 80 ER 284. See below, page 219.

[250] (1795) 2 Blackstone (H) 511 at 516 note. *Statutes of St Vincent*, published in 1788, page 46, the 24th section of the Act entitled "An Act for making slaves real estate, and the better government of slaves and negroes": "That no person or persons whatsoever shall hereafter manumit or set free any slave or slaves, except he, she, or they, or the representatives of such person or persons, previous to such manumission, pay into the public treasury of this island one hundred pounds current money..."

[251] Shyllon, *Black Slaves*, p 160.

[252] Kenyon had replaced Mansfield as chief justice in 1788, an appointment which had been delayed because Mansfield was reluctant to give way to Kenyon. Kenyon had said, in criticism of Mansfield, that "I do not think that the Courts ought to change the law so as to adapt it to the fashions of the times: Douglas Hay, 'Kenyon, Lloyd, first Baron Kenyon (1732–1802)', ODNB, 2004.

[253] Below, page 95.

the Boy may be considered in the Nature of an Apprenticeship, that it was a contract implyed, the Service having been Due to the Master in the West Indies it was imply'd to be due also here".[254] Sharp immediately pointed out that "a Contract could not be implyed without implying at the same time the free Consent of both Parties to the making of the Contract, which free Consent was impossible in the Case of A Slave". This was impressive, given that Sharp had only just begun to study law. Then Dunning joined them and put forward the same theory. Sharp said no more at this point, "being no speaker", but decided to study the issue further and put down his objections to it in writing. The theory of "implied apprenticeship" was not in fact taken up by the courts, but from this evidence it seems to have been canvassed among the Bar in 1765.

One other case in 1827 was thought by some to restrict the ratio of *Somerset*. In *The Slave, Grace*,[255] Grace had been held as a domestic slave in Antigua. She had accompanied her mistress, Mrs Allen, to England in 1822, remained there a year and then returned with her to Antigua. After Grace had remained there for about two years in 1825 she was seized by an official of the customs at Antigua "as forfeited to the King, on suggestion of having been illegally imported in 1823". It was alleged that her owner, Mr Allen, had "imported" her into Antigua in breach of a statute[256] which required registration of colonial slaves, consequent on the abolition of the Slave Trade in 1807. The Vice-Admiralty Court of Antigua restored her to her owner. An appeal was taken by the Crown to the High Court of Admiralty. The issue raised by the Crown was "whether, under the circumstances, slavery was so divested by landing in England that it would not revive on a return to the place of birth and servitude?" Lord Stowell,[257] who was conservative-minded but also regarded as a leading civilian lawyer of his day,[258] held that Mansfield's decision to discharge Somerset had established "that the owners of slaves had no authority or control over them in England, nor any power of sending them back to the colonies",[259] but he did not consider that the statute in question

---

[254] Below, page 95.

[255] (1827) 2 Hagg 94, 166 ER 179, High Court of Admiralty.

[256] 59 Geo III, c 120 (1819), s 12.

[257] R A Melikan, 'Scott, William, Baron Stowell (1745–1836)', ODNB, 2004; online edn, January 2008 [http://www.oxforddnb.com/view/article/24935], accessed 13 April 2016].

[258] He was called to the bar in 1780, and in the previous year had received his doctorate in civil law and was admitted to the Faculty of Advocates at Doctors' Commons.

[259] 2 Hagg at 106, 166 ER at 183.

was ever intended to apply to domestic servants accompanying their masters or mistresses to England or back again. He held that on her return to Antigua, Grace's status as a slave revived. The case was governed by the law of Antigua which he saw as unaffected by the *Somerset* case in England. Stowell was personally opposed to slavery,[260] but regarded the issue of one of the conflict of laws. Stowell clearly believed, nevertheless, that her status had changed when she arrived in England and that she was free when in England.

Habeas Corpus and Foreigners

An important point of law which was accepted in *Somerset* and which has led to its being cited as an authority in recent times is the proposition that the scope of habeas corpus is not limited to citizens, but is available to anyone within the jurisdiction. That point as to habeas corpus is the modern legacy of *Somerset*. It was cited by Lord Scarman in *Khawaja* v *Secretary of State for the Home Department*[261] in the context of illegal immigration and by Lord Bingham in *A* v *Secretary of State for the Home Department*[262] in the context of detention under anti-terrorism laws.[263]

In fact, as has been seen, the point can be traced back to Lord Chancellor Henley, who stated it explicitly, in *Shanley* v *Harvey*[264] and to Chief Justice Holt in *Smith* v *Brown and Cooper*[265] in 1701. It was also

---

[260] Melikan, above, n 257. He was a friend of Dr Johnson and one of the executors of his will: Bundock, *The Fortunes of Francis Barber*, p 63.

[261] [1984] AC 74, House of Lords, at pp 111G–112A: "There is no distinction between British nationals and others. He who is subject to English law is entitled to its protection. This principle has been in the law at least since Lord Mansfield freed 'the black' in Sommersett's Case (1772) 20 St Tr 1." In fact, only Lofft reports Mansfield as referring to "the black". In other versions he is referred to as "the man": above, page 56.

[262] [2005] 2 AC 68, at p 77: "The distinction in legal status between alien and citizen, while permissible in terms of immigration control, is impermissible in the context of national security in respect of powers of detention: see *R* v *Secretary of State for the Home Department, Ex p Khawaja* [1984] AC 74; Sommersett's Case (1772) 20 State Tr 1..."; Tom Bingham, *The Rule of Law*, London, 2010, Kindle edition, loc. 2528; Potter, *Law, Liberty and the Constitution*, p 274.

[263] The Prevention of Terrorism Act 2005, is aimed at individuals suspected of being terrorists but who cannot be prosecuted for various reasons. It provides for a system of "control orders", falling short of detention, under which individuals, may be subject to restrictions on association, on movement, to curfews, and which may restrict access to the internet or the use of mobile phones. The powers are designed to disrupt and prevent terrorist activity.

[264] (1762) 2 Eden 126, 28 ER 844. Above, page 32.

[265] Above, page 24.

accepted without argument in the *Lewis* case. *Somerset* has also been cited in the U.S. Supreme Court in *Boumediene v Bush*.[266]

Slave Law in the Colonies

Serjeant Davy in the first hearing of the *Somerset* case points out the wide disparity between the law of England and the laws of Virginia.[267]

In Virginia there was an extensive statutory code which applied specifically to black people and put them under the most severe restrictions and penalties, based purely on colour. There were also extensive provisions dealing with the punishment of slaves. In England there was no such body of laws. Race or ethnicity was not a concept known to the common law. One might point out that there is one qualification on that, but it had become obsolete by the eighteenth century. Up to the fourteenth century there was a collective punishment imposed on hundreds called *murdrum* when someone had been killed and the killing was in secret or the killer was undetected. The punishment was a fine and had been introduced either at the Norman Conquest or perhaps at the earlier conquest by the Danish King Canute. It was not payable if the murdered person could be shown to have been English by a group of his or her kin. By the mid-thirteenth century the proof seems to have become simply proof that the victim was unfree. In other words, it punished the English only when the murdered person was Norman, or perhaps Danish.[268] Apart from that, however, the common law was indifferent to race or ethnicity. In Virginia, by contrast, there was a plethora of laws applying specifically to people of colour. Under a 1682 statute all black people and others, except "Turks and Moors in Amity with Her Majesty", that could not make due proof of being free in England or in any other Christian Country "shall be accounted as Slaves and as such be bought and sold notwithstanding their being converted to Christianity".[269] Under an act of 1705 "All Negro, mulatto and Indian slaves... within this dominion... shall be held to be real estate...". It mattered not what status a black person had in his country of origin: he was a slave in

---

[266] 553 US 723, 128 S Ct 2229, at 2248B. Note that Justice Kennedy, delivering the opinion of the court, states the point more narrowly than either Lord Scarman or Lord Bingham: "We know that at common law a petitioner's status as an alien was not a categorical bar to habeas corpus relief. See, eg, Sommersett's Case, 20 How St Tr 1, 80–82 (1772)..."; Potter, *Law, Liberty and the Constitution*, p 274.

[267] Below, page 172.

[268] I am grateful to Professor Paul Brand for this information.

[269] Below, page 173.

Virginia, unless he was a Christian before he arrived there. Davy refers to the famous instance of Abdul-Rahman Ibrahim Ibn Sori (aka Abdul-Rahman) who was a prince from West Africa who had been captured while leading a military expedition and then sold as a slave. He spent forty years in slavery in Mississippi before being freed in 1828 by order of President John Quincy Adams and Secretary of State Henry Clay after the Sultan of Morocco requested his release. Davy also refers to the short novel *Oroonoko: or, the Royal Slave* by Aphra Behn (1640?–1689), one of the earliest women writers in English, which had been published in 1688. It was a work of fiction, but anticipated the actual case of Abdul-Rahman by many decades.[270] There was also the case of William Ansah Sessarakoo, son of the ruling family at Annamaboe (Anomabu) who was sold as a slave in Barbados in 1744, but eventually freed. He visited England in 1749.[271]

At common law, the status of a child born of a "mixed marriage" between a male villein and a free woman depended on the status of the father, but in the sense that if a free woman went to live with a villein on his unfree tenement and the children were born there, the children were villeins.[272] If a free man had children by a villein woman (naif), then if the children were born in the unfree tenement, according to Bracton, they would be villeins.[273] Since there was no such thing as villeinage in the American colonies, but there was slavery as to black people, there arose a doubt as to the rule in such a case. The Virginia House of Burgesses changed this in 1662 so that the status of children depended on the status of their mother.[274] Other states soon followed. This had been the rule in Roman law.[275]

---

[270] Below, page 173. Abdul-Rahman's case was the subject of a book: Terry Alford, *Prince Among Slaves*, New York, London, c 1977, and a PBS Home Video DVD with the same title.

[271] [William Ansah Sessarakoo], *The Royal African: or, Memoirs of the young Prince of Annamaboe, etc*, London, W Reeve, etc, 2nd edn, c 1750.

[272] P & M i.423.

[273] Ibid.

[274] 14 Car II Act XII, December 1662:

> Whereas some doubts have arisen whether children got by any Englishman upon a Negro woman should be slave or free, be it therefore enacted and declared by this present Grand Assembly, that all children born in this country shall be held bond or free only according to the condition of the mother...

William Waller Hening, *Statutes at Large; Being a Collection of all the Laws of Virginia*, Richmond, Va, 1809–23, vol 2, pp 170, 260, 266, 270, [http://vagenweb.org/hening/vol02-09.htm], accessed 17 March 2015.

[275] W W Buckland, *The Roman Law of Slavery*, Cambridge, 1st edn, 1908, reprint 1970,

There was a very practical reason for the change of the rule in the American colonies. It was not uncommon for male slave owners to rape their female slaves and thus have children by them. One has to use the ugly word "rape" because in the relationship of master and slave there was no such thing as consent on the part of the slave. Clearly, the legislators of the American slave states had no wish to allow the development of a free, biracial population. Yet this in itself is not enough to explain the change of the rule. Indeed, given that slave owners generally regarded their slaves as less than human, and subjected them to the most cruel indignities, it requires some explanation as to why they would be attracted sexually to their female slaves. By changing the rule the slave owners ensured that the children of such liaisons would be slaves. As such, they would be the property of the owner of their mother. By having sex with his slaves, the slave owner would increase his own property, an advantage which was probably not absent from the minds of the slave owners. It seems not unlikely that the motive of increasing their wealth made the objects of their lust seem more attractive in their eyes. In any case, the slave owners rarely regarded the offspring as their own children or treated them as such, although there are individual instances of this. Their treatment of their offspring no doubt depended on individual character. The Jefferson-Hemings controversy is a case in point. The concensus of modern historians is that Thomas Jefferson, the principal author of the Declaration of Independence (1776), and the third President of the United States, was the father of the children of his slave, Sally Hemings.[276] He did not acknowledge them in his lifetime, but the Hemings children were the only slaves he manumitted in his will, apart from three elderly men who had spent their lives working at Monticello. There are, on the other hand, examples of slave owners selling their own children, as Frederick Douglass noted.[277]

pp 397–398:

> The child born of a female slave was a slave, whatever be the status of the father, and conversely, if the mother was free the child was free, whatever the status of the father. This, says Gaius, is the rule of the *ius gentium*...It may be added that the slave issue belongs to the owner of the mother at the time of birth, not at the time of of conception.

---

[276] Annette Gordon-Reed, *Thomas Jefferson and Sally Hemings: An American Controversy*. Charlottesville, Virginia, 2000; it was argued by some that the father was one or other of Jefferson's nephews, but DNA analysis has ruled that out: 89:3 *National Genealogical Society Quarterly*, September 2001, pp 207, 214–218.

[277] "...slaveholders have ordained, and by law established, that the children of

A Virginia law of September 1667 specifically provided that baptism would not emancipate a slave.[278]

Villeinage in England

Serjeant Davy addresses the issue of whether a BSBE could be considered a villein in gross, the suggestion made in the Yorke-Talbot opinion. There were two methods: by prescription and by confession on the record. Davy rules out the first on the ground that "it was necessary to prove a Man a Villein to shew that he had been in his Stock and had been a Villein beyond all Memory".[279] Clearly, that was impossible in the case of a BSBE.

As to confession on the record, he argues that no free man could be supposed willingly to confess himself to be unfree. This was a more subtle argument than perhaps first appeared. Confession on the record required an act on the part of the BSBE. But what of his status immediately after he landed in England and before any such hypothetical act? English courts would presume a person free unless proved otherwise – if there was an "otherwise" – as Mansfield himself had held in the *Lewis* case.[280] So a BSBE arriving in England would initially have been presumed free before the question of any hypothetical confession

---

slave women shall in all cases follow the condition of their mothers; and this is done too obviously to administer to their own lusts, and make a gratification of their wicked desires profitable as well as pleasurable;... The master is frequently compelled to sell these slaves, out of deference to the feelings of his white wife. Cruel as this deed may strike anyone to be, for a man to sell his own children to human flesh-mongers, it is often the dictate of humanity for him to do so. Unless he does this, he must not only whip them himself, but must stand by and see one white son tie up his brother, of but few shades darker complexion than himself, and ply the gory lash to his naked back..." Frederick Douglass, *Narrative of the Life of Frederick Douglass*, Boston, Anti-Slavery Office, 1845, chapter 1.

[278] 19 Car II, Act 3.

> Whereas some doubts have risen whether children that are slaves by birth, and by the charity and piety of their owners made partakers of the blessed sacrament of baptism, should by virtue of their baptism be made free, it is enacted and declared by this Grand Assembly, and the authority thereof, that the conferring of baptism does not alter the condition of the person as to his bondage or freedom; that diverse masters, freed from this doubt may more carefully endeavor the propagation of Christianity by permitting children, though slaves, or chose of greater growth if capable, to be admitted to that sacrament.

[279] Below, page 161.
[280] Below, page 107.

arose. Courts would be unlikely to hold that a free man had made himself unfree by a confession. The whole concept had fallen into decline so that "not only that Courts of Law never would suffer a Man in any other Form to become a Villein but upon the Contrary a Thousand Devices and thousand Modes of Manumitted them by Implication were devised by the Lawyers from time to time".[281]

Furthermore, admitting to being a servant, or even a slave in the colonies, was a different thing from confessing to being a villein in England. A villein was not the same as a slave. Vinogradoff,[282] writing of villeinage in the fourteenth and fifteenth centuries, explains that "villein regardant" and "villein in gross" were not two separate categories of villein in terms of status, but were forms of pleading by which a lord might claim title to a villein. He might claim title to the villein by prescription, that is, he might rely on his title to a manor with which the alleged villein and his ancestors had been associated time out of mind. Or he might rely on a deed or recorded confession by which the villein admitted that he belonged to the lord, that is, the lord could claim him as a villein in gross. The same villein might therefore be claimed as "regardant to a manor" in one case, but as "in gross" in another. This was the case at the time of Littleton. The implication was that villeinage was concerned with "peasants tilling the earth and dependent on manorial organisation".[283] The notion that there were two separate kinds of villein was the product of a misunderstanding and of a later time. All this was far from the situation of an imported domestic servant, who was not engaged in tilling the soil, and the owner of slave plantations in the colonies who was unlikely to be a lord of an English manor.

Gregson v Gilbert (The Zong)

The *Zong* was a slave ship which had been a Dutch ship, named the *Zorge* or *Zorg*, which had been captured as a prize by a privateer. The original Dutch name, which, by a great irony, given the subsequent events, meant "care", had been renamed, probably by mistake or ignorance, as the *Zong*, which was meaningless. The name nevertheless has acquired an evil connotation through the events which apparently occurred on board on its voyage as a slave ship from Africa to Jamaica.

[281] Serjeant Davy at page 162.
[282] Sir Paul Vinogradoff, *Villainage in England*, Oxford, 1st edn, 1892, reprint 1968, at pp 48–56.
[283] Ibid, p 57.

Introduction

This infamous case concerned the murder in 1781 of 132 Africans who were thrown overboard in chains from the slave ship *Zong*, by the captain and other members of the crew, ostensibly because, as a result of a navigation error, on the voyage from the West Coast of Africa, they had sailed past Jamaica, believing it to be the island of Hispaniola, and had run short of fresh water and food.

The case was not, however, a trial for murder. The owners of the ship, the William Gregson syndicate of Liverpool, claimed the loss on the insurance policy as arising from the "perils of the seas" and that it fell within the principle of general average, which permitted ships in difficulties to cast cargo over the side in order to save the ship. Counsel in the case, Mr Pigot noted[284] that it was not the first instance (nor would it be the last[285]) of enslaved Africans being thrown overboard from a slave ship, but it was the first case in which the owners had attempted to claim the loss under an insurance policy. The fact that the Gregson syndicate had no concern for the bad publicity itself shows the confidence that the slave interest had at the time. The declaration in the King's Bench, reproduced here, claimed the delay arose from storms and adverse currents and the ship becoming foul and leaky and that the captain, after consultation with the crew, had decided the only option was to throw a portion of the slaves overboard in order to save themselves and the remainder of the slaves. The jury found in favour of the owners.

The underwriters brought the motion for a new trial, because the evidence in the King's Bench varied from the facts alleged in the declaration. The captain of the *Zong* was Luke Collingwood, who had been ill since the beginning of the voyage. James Kelsall was the chief mate and formally second in command. The solicitor general read out an affdavit sworn by Kelsall,[286] but it is not reproduced in the MS and it has not been traced at the present time. He was subpoenaed, but not found.[287] The oral evidence at the trial was given by Robert Stubbs. He had been a passenger on the *Zong* but was in charge of the ship at the relevant time. Stubbs had been a captain of slave ships before and latterly had been the Governor of Anomabu, a slave port on the coast of what is today Ghana.[288] Collingwood, apparently feeling unable to

---

[284] MS p 19, below, page 254.
[285] James Walvin, *The Zong: A Massacre, The Law and The End of Slavery*, New Haven and London, 2011, pp 200–203.
[286] Below, page 274.
[287] Below, page 251.
[288] Below, page 244, presumably under the African Company.

carry on the day to day command of the ship, had appointed Stubbs to be in charge of the ship. Kelsall, not surprisingly, objected to this and as a result of this disagreement, Collingwood suspended Kelsall as chief mate. Collingwood then became delirious, according to Kelsall. Kelsall declined to take over, as he was still suspended. So Stubbs continued in command.

Stubbs' evidence was that the delay was caused by the captain mistaking Jamaica for Hispaniola, in other words an error of navigation. Mansfield with Willes and Buller JJ, held that this vitiated the proceedings at trial. First, the plaintiffs had not proved the facts alleged in the declaration, but different facts. Secondly, it was suggested in passing by Buller J, that an error in navigation did not come within the scope of "perils of the sea" in the insurance policy.[289] The suggestion was that navigation was the responsibility of the captain and if he made an error, the owners could not seek to throw responsibility for that onto the underwriters. The application in the King's Bench for a new trial was successful.

At the original trial, the log of the *Zong* was not produced, nor any other papers relating to the voyage, which, if they existed, would have been in the possession of the owners. The underwriters had been at a great disadvantage at the trial in King's Bench as there was no discovery of documents in a common law court. They had no opportunity to challenge effectively the assertions of the owners by examining the log or any other documents regarding the voyage. The underwriters therefore brought an action on the equity side of the Court of Exchequer, where discovery of documents was available, demanding that the owners produce the log book and any other documents. Their bill also set out a series of detailed questions, or interrogatories, to which they wanted answers. The final manuscript in the NMM volume is the draft bill, with a *quo minus* clause,[290] on the equity side of Exchequer by the insurers. It is addressed to the nominal head of the Court of Exchequer, the treasurer, who was in fact William Pitt, the prime minister, but that was a mere formality.

The underwriters also claimed an injunction to prevent further proceedings at law until the documents were produced. From the bill one can conclude that the underwriters suspected the claim was fraudu-

---

[289] Below, Buller J at page 290: "I will suppose the Law clear for the Underwriters are not liable for a mistake made by the Captain[.] you don't understand me giving any opinion upon this particular Case but for the purpose of the Argument I mention it[.]"

[290] Below, page 312.

lent, that there was no absolute necessity to throw the Africans overboard, that it had rained in the days before the incident and the rainwater had been collected, and that the ship might have reached other islands to obtain supplies. If the ship had arrived in Jamaica with a cargo of intended slaves many of whom were sick or dying it would have resulted in a financial disaster for the owners and it was suspected that the action of the captain and crew was an attempt to cast the loss on the insurers.

The first mate, James Kelsall, in his answer, alleged essentially the same facts as Stubbs had given in evidence in the King's Bench, ie that the delay and the throwing overboard of slaves was a result of a navigation error. He also maintained that the *Zong* had run short of drinking water and this had given rise to the "absolute necessity" of throwing the Africans into the sea. He further maintained that it was not sickly Africans who had been thrown overboard, but healthy ones, apparently to counter the suggestion that the crew had thrown overboard the less valuable, or valueless, slaves in order to cut the losses of the voyage.

Probably neither Stubbs nor Kelsall knew much about the law of insurance or the law relating to pleadings and so did not appreciate the implications of this for the owners' claim. The ship owners appear to have abandoned their claim as there is no record of a new trial, probably because they were unable to produce any documents and also because, even if they had established that the loss had occurred through a navigation error, that would not have been held to be a loss by "perils of the sea" and would not have resulted in the underwriters being liable, as Lord Mansfield and Buller J had remarked on the motion for a new trial.

The other manuscripts concern Sharp's attempts to have the captain and crew tried for murder: a letter to the Admiralty, with his own summary of the case, and to the Prime Minister, the Duke of Portland. He warned the Prime Minister that there were signs that God had already punished the English for their involvement in the slave trade and slavery. He cited as examples the loss of the American colonies and unusually violent thunderstorms of late in the West Indies, and asserted his belief that worse would follow!

There was to be no trial for murder. In such a criminal trial there would have been no defence of necessity. It is worth noting that even in the insurance case itself there was no suggestion either at the bar or from the bench, that necessity would excuse an act of murder.[291] In a famous case in the nineteenth century the issue was directly in point. In *R v Dudley and Stephens*[292] the yacht *Mignonette* had foundered in heavy seas when about 1,500 miles from land and the crew, Edmund Brooks, Tom Dudley, Edwin Stephens and Richard Parker, who was then 17 years old, had taken to an open boat. After many days at sea and after great suffering from hunger, thirst and exposure and with no rescue in sight, Dudley and Stephens, after praying for forgiveness, killed Parker, who had drunk sea water and was near to death, and ate his heart and liver in order to save themselves. Brooks took no part in the killing but ate part of the body. Four days later they were rescued. After their return to England Dudley and Stephens were prosecuted for murder. They were convicted. Necessity, even if it had been proved, was no defence. They were initially sentenced to death, as the law then required, although there were already indications before sentence that they would not be executed. Their sentence was later commuted to a few months in prison. In 1837 Edgar Allen Poe had published the "Narrative of Arthur Gordon Pym", in a magazine. It was a fictional tale of starving castaways who killed one of their number and ate him. By an extraordinary coincidence Poe named the unfortunate victim "Richard Parker".[293]

In his extensively-researched book on the case[294] Simpson also recounts the affair of the *William Brown* and the American case of *US v Holmes*[295] in 1842. On a passage from Liverpool to Philadelphia the ship struck an iceberg and started to sink. Before it did so, the passengers and crew took lifeboats. They drifted apart. One boat started to leak and despite efforts to bale it out, it was clear it would soon sink also. The crew then threw overboard some of the passengers in order to save themselves and the rest. The remaining passengers and crew were spotted by a ship, the *Crescent*, and picked up. The survivors were taken to Le Havre but eventually made it back to Philadelphia. Holmes, a member of the crew who had thrown some passengers overboard on the instructions of the mate, was the only member of the crew then in the city. A grand jury declined to indict him for murder and he was indicted for manslaughter. David Paul Brown, the best criminal

---

[291] *Kenny's Outlines of Criminal Law*, 18th edn by J W C Turner, Cambridge, 1962, p 67.
[292] (1884) 14 QBD 273.
[293] A W B Simpson, *Cannibalism and the Common Law*, Chicago, 1984, p 144.
[294] Ibid.
[295] US Circuit Court, 1842.

lawyer in Philadelphia at the time, represented Holmes. He argued that in situations of necessity, conventional law ceased to operate and gave way instead to "natural law", ie, "the law of self preservation". Holmes was convicted and sentenced to six months in jail and given a $20 fine. He received a Presidential pardon for the fine but he served the full sentence. He then returned to the sea, as had the rest of the crew, none of whom was ever charged over the affair. One press comment was that "The frightful necessity of sacrificing part of the passengers for the safety of the rest is fully proved". Simpson notes that a letter, signed only by "Homo", appeared in *The Times* of London on 18 May 1842 in which the author said he was not persuaded that "any circumstance whatever can possibly justify so gross an outrage". He congratulated his countrymen that no such thing "has ever been heard of, amd I trust never will, on board an English ship". Simpson points out that "his chauvinism was hardly justified" since it was from an English ship, the *Zong* of Liverpool, that Captain Collingwood had had 132 Africans thrown alive into the sea.

The "Absolute Necessity"

As Walvin[296] has pointed out, it is impossible to be confident about what happened on board the *Zong*. We only have the accounts of Stubbs and Kelsall for what happened. Neither can be considered as reliable witnesses. Stubbs was a scoundrel and Kelsall, along with the owners, had a motive to misrepresent or lie about the facts. If the *Zong* had arrived in Jamaica with a "cargo" of enslaved Africans many of whom were either starving or dying of thirst, they would be worth little or nothing to slave dealers and the voyage would have been a financial disaster, whereas under the insurance policy, each slave was insured for £30. As to other witnesses, the captain, Luke Collingwood, had died of disease in Jamaica, the crew had dispersed to other ships and the surviving enslaved Africans were, to put it mildly, unavailable. Kelsall in his written answer in the Exchequer was evasive as to who was responsible for the navigation error. In theory, Collingwood was responsible as captain, but he was already ill. It would have been convenient for both Stubbs, Kelsall and the ship's owners to blame the late captain to divert any blame from themselves. Kelsall himself had been suspended and Stubbs was effectively acting first mate, but Kelsall did not ascribe the blame to Stubbs. Nor, interestingly, did he blame Collingwood. He maintained that Collingwood

[296] Walvin, *The Zong*, p 96.

was deceived by currents but that "many regular bred Seamen Captains in the African Trade from Liverpool"[297] had made similar mistakes in those waters. It may be that Kelsall had in mind that if he wanted another command, blaming his late captain would not ingratiate himself with prospective future employers.

Sharp, in his account of the massacre, made it clear that he had spoken to Stubbs[298] and also to another "person on board" whom he did not identify.[299] He said that Stubbs was staying at No 75 King Street, Westminster.[300]

Before considering Sharp's account, a précis of Kelsall's version will be given.

James Kelsall in his answer[301] in the Exchequer case said that on 14 November 1781 differences arose between himself and the captain, Luke Collingwood, as a result of Collingwood having appointed Stubbs to take charge of ship. Collingwood then suspended Kelsall as chief mate and he remained suspended until 29 November, the day the ship was found to be to the leeward of Jamaica.

On 20 or 21 November Kelsall said that the the second and third mates who were in charge of the water and provisions found that a large quantity of water had leaked from the lower tier of water casks. This caused a general survey to be made of what water remained. They found that there were nearly twenty butts of water which was thought sufficient to last the voyage to Jamaica.

On 27 November they made land, which the captain thought was Hispaniola but was in fact Jamaica, at a distance of nine leagues, or 27 nautical miles.

On 29 November the slaves had had their full allowance of water and it was not until the evening a little after sunset that the captain discovered the error or navigation. Kelsall acquitted the captain of any blame for this, and attributed it to currents. The captain then set a course for Jamaica. In view of the "small stock of water" then on board, the captain then called all the hands together "to consult what was best to be done" when it was "the general opinion that it was impracticable" for the ship to reach any British island. Kelsall also asserted that he did not hear the captain or any person on board the ship at the consultation say that by putting the slaves on short allowance

---

[297] Below, page 86.
[298] Below, page 299.
[299] Below, page 300.
[300] Below, page 294.
[301] Below, page 335.

of water they would be weak or emaciated when they came to market and sell for little or nothing or that the voyage would be ruined or any such words. Nor did he hear the captain say that they should throw into the sea such of the slaves as were weak, sickly and of little value or words to that effect, although he believed he heard some one of the crew say, after the slaves were thrown overboard, that the throwing overboard such slaves would be no loss to the owners of the ship if she was insured or some such words. Kelsall said he was shocked by the proposal to throw slaves overboard and accompanied the captain into the cabin and urged him instead to put the slaves and crew on short measure for a day or two and that they might possibly in the meantime come across some ship or "that Providence might afford them some Showers of Rain" which might supply them with water. The captain rejected this idea as impractical. About 8 o'clock on the night of 29 November Collingwood ordered fifty or sixty of the Africans to be taken out of the women's and boys' rooms indiscriminately and fifty-four of them were thrown alive singly through the cabin windows of the ship into the sea.

Sharp in his account[302] argued that there was no genuine necessity and that sick and dying slaves were thrown overboard, and that the incident was an attempted insurance fraud.

He asserted that on 29 November, or the preceding day, they discovered that the stock of fresh water was reduced to 200 gallons "as Mr Stubbs has informed me" and "yet the same day, or in the Evening of it, before any soul had been put to short allowance (V.2 p.5.6.18 & 52)[303] & before there was any present or real want of water..." the captain proposed to throw Africans overboard. The conclusion that there was not at that time "any present or real want of water" is taken from the bill of the underwriters, who alleged that this came from Kelsall.[304] Kelsall in his answer merely said that when in the captain's cabin he had suggested putting the Africans and crew on short allowance.[305] Sharp quoted the bill in the Exchequer filed by the underwriters when he alleged that, contrary to Kelsall's sworn answer, on the evening of 29 November the captain "called together a few of his officers & told them that if the slaves died a natural death it would be the loss of the owners of the ship but if they were thrown alive into the Sea it would

---

[302] Below, page 298.
[303] Below, page 318.
[304] Ibid.
[305] Below, page 341.

be the loss of the underwriters".[306] He also asserted, again taking the allegation from the bill in the Exchequer, that "in order to palliate his said inhuman proposal the said Luke Collingwood pretended that it would not be so cruel to throw the poor sick wretches (meaning such slaves) into the sea as to suffer them to linger out a few days under the disorder with which they were afflicted or expressed himself to the like effect".[307] There is nothing about a meeting of "a few of his officers" in Kelsall's answer. Where the allegations in the bill came from, again it is not possible to say. They must have come from one of the officers, or from Stubbs or members of the crew to whom the conversation was relayed and who were interviewed by the underwriters, unless they were entirely invented.

As to the question of rainfall, Sharp asserted that on 1 December 1781 before the stock of water was consumed "there fell a plentiful rain, which by the confession of one of their own advocates 'continued a day or two' (V.2 p.50)[308] & enabled them to collect 6 casks of Water which was full Allowance for 11 days (V.2 p.24)[309] or for 23 days, at half Allowance, whereas the ship actually arrived at Jamaica in 24 days afterwards vizt. on the 22nd December 1781 (V.1 p.2)".[310] Sharp quoted "a person on board", whom he did not further identify, as telling him that they seem to have had an opportunity of sending the ship's boat for water on 9 December when they "made the West end of Jamaica distant 2 or 3 leagues only,... as I am informed by a person who was on board",[311] so that the 6 casks of rainwater "caught on the 1st and 2d December (only 7 days before this opportunity of obtaining water from Jamaica) was not only a providential supply but providentially demonstrated the iniquity of pretending a necessity".

Marine Insurance and Slave Trade Acts

The marine insurance aspect of the *Zong* affair have been dealt with in depth in two recent articles by Oldham[312] and by Lobban.[313] This is

[306] Below, page 299, and see the statement in the bill, page 318.
[307] Below, page 318.
[308] This is stated on page 79 of the transcript by Mr Chambre, below, page 285.
[309] Page 35 of the MS, below, page 263.
[310] Below, page 300 and see Kelsall's answer, page 348.
[311] Below, page 300.
[312] James Oldham, "Insurance Litigation Involving the Zong and Other British Slave Ships, 1780–1807" (2007) 28:3 *The J Leg Hist* 299–318.
[313] Michael Lobban, "Slavery, Insurance and the Law" (2007) 28:3 *The Journal of Legal History* 319–328.

not an area of expertise of the present author and readers who wish to pursue this aspect are referred to those articles. What follows is a brief précis of some of the main points and some supplementary remarks.

Sir William Dolben (1727–1814)[314] was a baronet and Tory member of parliament who took up the cause of abolishing the slave trade. Given the strong opposition to such a measure, in the short term he attempted to regulate it and to improve conditions on board slave ships making the voyage from Africa to the West Indies on the middle passage. Despite opposition from the merchants of Bristol and Liverpool and with with Pitt's support, he successfully promoted a bill in the Commons in 1788 designed to limit the number of slaves allowed on a vessel in proportion to its tonnage, initially, for a trial period of a year.[315] Dolben developed a close alliance in parliament with William Wilberforce on the slave trade. He also got annual bills through parliament to extend Dolben's Act of 1788, which gave him the chance to speak against the iniquities of the trade. Section 12 of Dolben's Act was the first measure to regulate the insurance of slaves. It provided that no marine insurance could be made except against "perils of the sea" and other losses such as capture by the king's enemies and fire, etc. It did not explicitly ban loss by throwing slaves overboard, but both Lord Mansfield and Buller J had implied, without deciding the point, that a navigation error might not qualify as a "peril of the sea".[316]

Section 8 of the 1790 Act repeated the words of section 12 of the 1788 Act as did section 10 of the 1794 Act, but section 8 of the 1790 Act added the words: "no Loss or Damage shall be hereafter recoverable on account of the Mortality of Slaves by natural Death or ill Treatment, *or against Loss by throwing overboard of Slaves, on any account whatsoever,*" [emphasis supplied]. The phrase was repeated in the Slave Trade Act 1794, section 10. These words were in response to the *Zong* case.

Another case of mass murder of Africans occurred in 1796 and it was fought on section 8 of the 1790 Act and section 10 of the 1794 Act. That was *Tatham v Hodgson*.[317] A Liverpool merchant sued on the

---

[314] Nigel Aston, 'Dolben, Sir William, third baronet (1727–1814)', ODNB, 2004 [http://www.oxforddnb.com/view/article/7780], accessed 29 December 2015; Shyllon, *Black Slaves*, pp 205–207.

[315] Sir William Dolben's Act 1788 (Slave Trade Act, 1788), 28 Geo 3 c 54.

[316] Below, pages 289-290. Both Mansfield and Buller make the procedural or evidential objection that the declaration based the claim on "perils of the sea", namely winds and contrary currents, whereas the evidence at trial alleged a different cause, namely the navigation error, which seems to imply that a navigation error might not fall within the phrase "perils of the sea".

[317] (1796) 6 TR 656; Shyllon, *Black Slaves*, p 207; Oldham, "Insurance Litigation", pp

policy of insurance to recover the loss of 128 Africans who had died on the middle passage. The slave ship had sailed from the the coast of Africa with 168 slaves on board bound for the West Indies. The voyage was delayed by storms and did not have sufficient or proper food on board. In fact the voyage lasted an incredible six months and eight days, as against an ordinary crossing which was from six to nine weeks. The Africans had been fed with Indian corn which was unsuitable for them. Many of them died and the cargo of slaves was reduced from 168 to 40. It seems the rudder had also been damaged shortly after the ship set sail. After the corn ran out, the slaves starved to death.

At the trial in Liverpool the judge held the plaintiff was barred by section 8 of the 1790 Act and section 10 of the 1794 Act, but he reserved the point to the Court of King's Bench. Lord Kenyon who had succeeded Lord Mansfield as chief justice in 1788, together with Grose and Lawrence JJ, heard the application on the single point as to whether the loss could be attributed to the perils of the sea. Serjeant Cockell, for the ship-owner, argued that the loss arose from the extraordinary length of the voyage, and not from any negligence in the supply of food and that no precautions could have prevented the slaves from being starved to death. According to a newspaper report[318] Lord Kenyon intervened at this point and "asked whether the Captain of the ship was starved to death? He was answered in the negative." It was clear from the statutory provisions that the ship-owners could not recover if the slaves died a "natural death". Lord Kenyon held that to hold that if the captain took a number of slaves which was disproportionate to the quantity of provisions on board and then caused the slaves to starve to death, to allow the ship-owners to recover on the policy would contradict the intention of the Act and violate principles of humanity. Lord Kenyon clearly had misgivings about holding that the deaths could be described in any sense as "natural", but continued: "This Act of Parliament being founded in humanity, we ought not on any account to put such a construction on it as to render it useless even if its expressions were doubtful...". He concluded that the Africans died a "natural death" within the meaning of the statutes and not through "perils of the sea". Lawrence J. said: "I do not know that it was ever decided that a loss arising from a mistake of the captain was a loss within the perils of the seas. There was a case (a) [*Gregson v Gilbert*], where a ship mistook Jamaica for Domingo, and it was decided not to

304–305; Lobban, "Slavery, Insurance and the Law", p 325.

[318] *Gazetter and New Daily Advertiser*, 3 May 1796; Shyllon, *Black Slaves*, p 208.

be a loss within the perils of the seas."

Navigation and the Longitude Problem

Sailors at the time of the *Zong* voyage had an adequate method of finding latitude, and had done for a long time. They used a quadrant or sextant to find the height of the sun above the horizon at noon. With the aid of tables they could then calculate how far north or south the ship was relative to the equator. At night they could make a similar calculation using stars. Finding longitude at sea, that is, how far east or west the ship was relative to a given starting point, was a much more difficult problem.[319] In fact, it was the greatest scientific problem of the eighteenth century.

In 1707 the fleet of Admiral of the Fleet Sir Cloudesley Shovell[320] was returning from Gibraltar in bad weather. The fleet was thought to be sailing safely west of Ushant, an island off the coast of Brittany. However, due to a combination of bad weather and the mariners' inability accurately to calculate longitude, the fleet was off course and approaching the Scilly Isles instead. Before the mistake could be corrected, the fleet struck rocks and four ships were lost. Some 2,000 sailors, including the admiral, lost their lives.[321] This prompted the British government to pass the Longitude Act 1714.[322] It announced a number of prizes up to £20,000, a huge sum at the time, for a reliable and practical method of finding longitude at sea. It also created the Board of Longitude to assess the proposed solutions.

As is well-known, the ultimate solution was the marine chronometer, developed by John Harrison, the self-taught English clock-maker.[323] This allowed ships to carry with them a device giving the time at a

---

[319] There were methods of finding longitude on land, such as observing the moons of Jupiter through a telescope, invented by Galileo, or the lunar distance method, which measured the distance between the moon and given stars. These were effective if the telescope was on a stable mount, but that was not available on a moving ship: Richard Dunn and Rebekah Higgitt, *Ships, Clocks & Stars: The Quest for Longitude*, London, Royal Museums Greenwich, 2014, pp 45–57.

[320] John B Hattendorf, 'Shovell, Sir Cloudesley (bap 1650, d 1707)', ODNB, 2004; online edn, May 2015 [http://www.oxforddnb.com/view/article/25470], accessed 13 January 2016.

[321] N A M Rodger, *The Command of the Ocean: A Naval History of Britain, 1649–1815*, London, 2004, p 172.

[322] (1713) 13 Anne c 14, 9 St Realm 927. The Act received the royal assent in July 1714.

[323] Dava Sobel, *Longitude: The True Story of a Lone Genius Who Solved the Greatest Scientific Problem of His Time*, London, Fourth Estate, 1998.

given point of known longitude, Greenwich Observatory being generally used, and then to compare it to the time on board the ship at noon, ie, the highest point above the horizon reached by the sun, each day, which was found using a sextant. Each hour, east or west, by which the time on the ship differed from Greenwich Mean Time represented 15 degrees of longitude.

Harrison's fourth chronometer, known as H4 and which resembled a large watch, had a successful trial in 1765, and a further refinement, H5, was approved in 1773. A practical solution required, however, that simpler and less expensive chronometers could be produced by other watch-makers. K1, based on H4, was made by Larcum Kendall, and was used successfully by Captain James Cook on his second voyage (1772–1775). K2 was lent to Captain Bligh for the voyage of HMS *Bounty*.[324] The *Zong* set sail from St Thomas (São Tomé) on 6 September 1781. Affordable chronometers in sufficient numbers only became generally available after about 1783, some years after the voyage of the *Zong*, although given the chaotic organisation of the voyage it is doubtful whether the owners would have supplied a chronometer even if it had been available.

Before marine chronometers became generally available and affordable, the method of estimating longitude at sea was dead reckoning.[325] In dead reckoning, a fix or starting point was taken from a point of known longitude. Readings were then taken at regular intervals, perhaps several times a day, estimating the ship's speed, using the log method. The log method was to tie a piece of wood – the log – on the end of a length of twine or thin rope with knots at intervals along it, usually at 8 fathoms distance from one another (47 feet 3 inches), throw it over the side and count the number of knots that passed through the sailing master's hand in a given time, usually 30 seconds, using a sand glass. Hence, "knots" became used to refer to nautical miles per hour. The word "log" came to be used also for the book in which the readings were recorded, as in "the ship's log" or "recording it in the log". At best this could estimate the speed of the ship relative to the surface of the water, but currents meant that the surface itself was moving, either slowing or speeding up the ship, leading to inaccuracy. Direction could be estimated using a compass,

---

[324] It was taken by the mutineers to Pitcairn Island and only returned to England in 1840. It is now in the National Maritime Museum, Greenwich, as are all of Harrison's "sea-clocks".

[325] Dunn and Higgitt, *Ships, Clocks & Stars: The Quest for Longitude*, London, Royal Museums Greenwich, 2014, pp 22–25.

but currents and winds could affect the estimate of direction as well as speed. The method was far from ideal or accurate. Any errors made at a previous fix or point were carried over to the next fix and therefore accumulated.

Since longitude could not be measured accurately at sea, the standard practice for reaching a destination of known latitude was to sail north or south until the latitude was reached, and then sail along the line of latitude, east or west, until the destination was reached.

Did it Really Happen?

In the course of researching the *Zong* case, I learned that Dr Nicholas Rodger, the distinguished naval historian of All Souls' College, Oxford, had expressed doubts as to the truth of the account of the *Zong* massacre as related by Stubbs and Kelsall.[326] I therefore contacted him by email and what follows is a brief account of his views based on his replies to me which he has kindly given me permission to reproduce.

In Dr Rodger's opinion, the account of the navigation error is difficult if not impossible to believe. Using the dead reckoning method, as described above, the *Zong* would have sailed up from the coast of Africa to reach the latitude of Jamaica, and then sailed westwards along the line until she reached her destination. The island of Hispaniola lies east of Jamaica on virtually the same latitude. Kelsall and Stubbs maintained that the captain had mistaken Jamaica for Hispaniola, in other words, that he had failed to sight Hispaniola at all. This is hardly credible. If they were on the correct latitude for Jamaica they would have passed within a few miles south of Hispaniola. Kelsall maintained that they had passed about 27 miles south of what they thought was Hispaniola. Dr Rodger points out that:

> In trade-wind latitudes high islands are invariably topped by a permanent cloud, which is visible much further off than the peak – you can see St Helena almost 100 miles away. Both the Blue Mountains in Jamaica and the Morna la Selle in Hispaniola are higher than that, and could certainly have been seen in that way at 27 miles. This, however, does not make Kelsall's story more plausible. It means that it would be very hard for even the most incompetent

[326] Dr Rodger had apparently mentioned his doubts in a conversation with the late Professor Martin Dockray and this was related to me by Dr Ruth Paley, Editor of Archives at the British Records Association.

(or drunken) navigator to pass to the southward of Hispaniola and Jamaica in turn without being aware that they were there, unless he were so far to the southward as to have sunk even the clouds below the horizon – say 120 miles. That is two degrees of latitude, when even the clumsiest navigator ought to have been able to fix latitude to about ten minutes.

Dr Rodger explains further:

> "Making the land", however, usually means making a landfall,[327] approaching the land near enough to identify it and fix a position, which they clearly did not do if the evidence is to be believed. The West India Pilot makes it clear that nobody used the high, cloud-wrapped peaks for navigation. All the seamarks[328] and landfalls are features along the coast, the most notable for navigators running their westing[329] down from the Windward Isles being the prominent island of Alta Vela off the southernmost point of Hispaniola, and Morant Point on Jamaica. Kelsall says they took a departure (meaning the last fix of land) from Tobago, and two days later on 20th or 21st November were in about 12–13°N, 63–64°W, say 120 miles to leeward of the Grenadines, having almost certainly passed within sight of Grenada. The usual easterly trade was blowing then and for three days afterwards. On 27th Kelsall claims they sighted something which they took for Hispaniola but did not identify. ...coming downwind from the eastward, the only possible point on Hispaniola which they could have sighted from a distance without subsequently closing the land (if not hitting it) would be Alta Vela, and it is extremely likely that that is what they meant to do, as it is the obvious, if not indispensable landfall for Jamaica. They must have been much closer than 27 miles, as it is only 500 feet high, but they would have taken care to keep just to the southward since the coast of Hispaniola thereabouts is mostly cliffs with little shelter. From there it would be a

---

[327] "The point at which the deep-sea navigator meets or intends to meet the coast." Rodger, *The Command of the Ocean*, p 757.

[328] "A beacon, tower or other prominent object serving to assist the navigator to fix his position in relation to the coast." Ibid, p 764.

[329] "Distance run or made good to the westward." Ibid, p 770.

Introduction

simple run of two or three days to Kingston nearly dead to leeward, making careful observations for latitude morning and evening because Morant Point lies low.

You will see why I think it virtually impossible that any navigator coming from the Windward Isles could have sighted Jamaica without first having made a landfall in Hispaniola, almost certainly Alta Vela. Nor does it seem remotely plausible that anywhere on the Jamaican coast could have been mistaken for Alta Vela. Still less can one believe, as James Walvin suggests, that they thought they were seeing Cape Tiburon. It seems to me inescapable that the story is a clumsy falsehood, meant to cover up for some activity which could not be acknowledged in court.

If the navigation error is not to be believed, there must be an alternative explanation as to how it came about that the *Zong* arrived in Jamaica at least a month late and with 142 slaves fewer than they were supposed to have. Dr Rodger provides a possible explanation:

> If the ship did not make Jamaica, she was doing something else which the owners were not anxious to talk about. The evidence, as I read it, was more than equivocal, the chief witness (the master) was dead, Kelsall was conveniently absent, and the log was missing in highly suspicious circumstances. No-one familiar with the slave trade, then or now, would have any difficulty in guessing what the *Zong* might have been doing in that unexplained month in the vicinity of Jamaica. British slavers were accustomed to supply French and Spanish planters,[330] contrary to French and Spanish law, and British law as well in wartime. The profits were large, and the chances of detection low. The obvious suspicion is that the *Zong* slipped into one of the small ports on the south coast of St Domingue – Jacmel or Les Cayes, perhaps – and sold her cargo for a good price. Alternatively it could have been somewhere in Sto. Domingo or Cuba. No-one would have suspected anything had the owners not been greedy, decided to double their money

---

[330] The island of Hispaniola was divided into two colonies, one French, Saint Domingue, and the other Spanish, Sainto Domingo. After the successful revolt by slaves and free people of colour, Saint Domingue became the Republic of Haiti in 1804. The Dominican Republic became independent in 1821. In 1781 both France and Spain were at war with Great Britain.

with an insurance fraud, and thus attracted a vast amount of unwelcome publicity.

Dr Rodger has clearly raised serious doubts as to the plausibility of the navigation error. The alternative explanation of what actually happened is, as Dr Rodger acknowledges, pure speculation and is unsupported at present by any direct evidence. British slavers certainly supplied Spanish and French colonies in the Americas in the eighteenth century.[331] This would have been more risky in wartime, but French and Spanish owners of slave plantations were no doubt not fussy about who supplied their needs and had the resources to bribe local officials to turn a blind eye. If any evidence exists that the *Zong* put into Saint Domingue or Sainto Domingo and sold slaves there, it would have to be in archives in Haiti or the Dominican Republic. Haiti suffered a catastrophic earthquake in 2010 so if any records had survived to that point they might then have been destroyed and the present author has no knowledge of archives in the Dominican Republic.

For anyone who has read about or written about the *Zong* massacre, Dr Nicholas Rodger's doubts make uneasy reading. Yet a scholar who knew of them but chose to ignore them would be doing a disservice to the practice of history, especially in view of the eminence of the source. What is one to make of them? No one at the time seems to have doubted the truth of the shocking story. The story also played an important part in raising the awareness of the English public against slavery and that was surely all to the good whether it was in fact true or false. The abolitionists such as Granville Sharp and other believed it to be true. They did not practice any deception. Also, as has been pointed out, there were many other instances of enslaved Africans being thrown overboard from slave ships, although none so blatant or on such a scale as in the case of the *Zong*. No seamen familiar with navigation in the vicinity of Hispaniola or Jamaica expressed doubts at the time about the account, which is odd. In his answer, prepared for the abortive proceedings on the Court of Exchequer, James Kelsall stated that:

> [37]...Saith that having made Land the twenty seventh of the said Month of November which the Captain taking for Hispaniola but which was actually Jamaica distant from it

---

[331] David Richardson, "The British Empire and the Atlantic Slave Trade 1660–1807" at pp 458–459. in P J Marshall ed, *The Oxford History of the British Empire*, vol II, "The Eighteenth Century", Oxford, OUP, 1998.

> South nine [38] Leagues they steered their Course as for Jamaica which was as this Defendant believes the Occasion of the *Zorg* [sic] getting to Leeward of the said Island of Jamaica but this Defendant cannot attribute that Mistake either to Unskilfulness Ignorance or any sinister Intent as many regular bred Seamen Captains in [39] the African Trade from Liverpool have imperceptibly got to Leeward of that Island by Mistake as this Defendant has heard and believes...

If that was so, then any evidence of similar mistakes, if it exists, may lie in ship's logs or journals in the TNA or elsewhere; however, this is beyond the scope of this volume.

TRANSCRIPTIONS

Jonathan Strong

Gloucestershire Archives D3549/13/3/28.

Granville Sharp

[1]

An Account of the Occasion which compelled Granville Sharp to study Law, and undertake the Defence of Negroe Slaves in England

One Morning in the Year 1765 as Granville Sharp was going out of the House of his Brother Mr William Sharp (then an eminent Surgeon in Mincing Lane and afterwards in the old Jewry) he saw a poor Negroe Boy about Sixteen or Seventeen years of age, standing at the Door, with other poor sick People, waiting for advice; the appearance of the Boy was so extremely distressful (as he seemed ready to drop down) that GS thought it right to go back again and speak to his Brother, that immediate Relief might be given to him, tho['] it appeared afterwards by the Boys own account that he had been relieved a Day or Two before by Mr William Sharp. The Boy was sent immediately by Mr William Sharp to St Bartholomew[']s Hospital, where he was confined above four Months before he was fit to be discharged after which having no place to go to, he apply'd again to Granville Sharp for relief, who recommended him to Mr Brown a Surgeon and Apothecary in Fenchurch Street as an Errand Boy to carry out Medicines with whom he lived in that Capacity about two Years, was paid Wages, had a Livery given to him, and grew to be a good looking, Stout, Young Man.

On Saturday the 12th Sept'r 1767, Granville Sharp received a Letter dated from the Poultry Counter[1] signed Jonathan Strong imploring protection from being Sold as a Slave. GS did not recollect the name, but went the next Day (Sunday 13th Septr 1767) to the Prison and demanded to see Jonathan Strong who being called up, GS immediately recollected Him, and enquired what he had done to be thus imprisoned? The Lad said, He had not been guilty of any Offense whatever but that his former Master, David Lisle Esqr, who brought him

---

[1] Ed. Poultry Compter (also sometimes known as Poultry Counter) was a small compter, or prison, run by a Sheriff of the City of London from medieval times until 1815. It took its name from a section of Cheapside called Poultry, from the produce that was once sold in street markets.

from Barbadoes and had cruelly beat and ill treated him so as to occasion the miserable condition and Sickness (for which He was sent to Bartholomew[']s Hospital about Two Years ago) had seen him behind a Hackney Coach attending his Mistress and followed him Home to Fenchurch Street, that he might know where to find him and that he had sold him to a Jamaica Planter, and put him into the Counter until a West India Ship should be ready to sail. GS charged the Keepers of the Prison not to deliver up the said Jonathan Strong to any Person whatsoever until he should be lawfully carried before a Magistrate. After this GS accompanied by his Brother James Sharp, waited on the Lord Mayor (Sir Robert Kite) and requested that all Persons who pretended to have any claim on the Person of Jonathan Strong might be summoned before his Lordship. When the appointed time was come David Lisle Esqr. did not appear, but only Mr William Macbean a Notary Publick as Attorney for James Kerr Esqr, a Planter of Jamaica, and David Laird, Captain of the ship *Thames*, bound to Jamaica, both claiming the Negro as the Property of the said Planter by virtue of a Bill of Sale, which they produced, signed by David Lisle Esqr. By this extraordinary demand of Mr William Macbean and Captn. David Laird, the poor Negro was put into extreme fear and anguish they being, both of them, absolutely unknown to him, as well as the name of the Person for whom they asked. [2] Nothing can be more shocking to Human Nature than the case of a Man or Woman who is delivered into the absolute Power of Strangers to be treated according to the New Masters Will and pleasure; for they have nothing but misery to expect; and poor Jonathan Strong, who was well acquainted with West India Treatment seemed to be deeply impressed with that extream horror which the poor victims Of the inhuman Trafic generally experience. After much dispute between Mr Macbean and GS (during which the poor trembling Negro seemed ready to sink down with fear) the Lord Mayor was pleased to discharge Jonathan Strong from his confinement telling him he was at liberty to go where he pleased: Upon which the West India Captain (David Laird) laid hold of him by the arm saying he would secure him as the property of Mr Kerr; but the Coroner of London (Thomas Beach Esqr) having prompted GS by coming behind him and whispering in his Ear the words "Charge him" GS immediately told Captn. Laird that he would charge a Constable with him for an assault if he presumed to take Jonathan Strong. The Captain thereupon withdrew his hand; and all the parties retired from the presence of the Lord Mayor; and Jonathan Strong departed also, in the sight of all, in full Liberty, nobody daring afterwards to touch him. Some little time afterwards James and Granville Sharp were served with Copies of Writs to answer to the aforesaid James Kerr Esqr. in a plea of Trespass, and where charged with £200 damages. They employed an eminent Attorney of the Lord Mayors Office to defend them, who shewed to GS a Copy of an Opinion dated in Jany. 14th 1729 signed P York and C Talbot the former being at that time Attorney General, and the other Sollicitor General, and who afterwards became much more eminent and celebrated under the Titles of Lord Hardwicke and Lord Talbot both of them being afterwards elevated to the dignity of Lord Chancellor of England and yet they delivered a Doctrine in the said joint Opinion entirely opposite to the Ideas which induced Granville Sharp to liberate Jonathan Strong.

> "We are of the Opinion" (said they) "that a Slave by coming from the West Indies to Great Britain or Ireland, either with or without his Master, doth not become free; and that his Master's Property or right in him, is not thereby determined or varied; and that Baptism doth not bestow freedom on him, nor make any alteration in his temporal condition in these Kingdoms; We are also of Opinion that the Master may legally compel him to return again to the Plantations (signed P York, C Talbot, Jany 14 1729."

This Opinion so intimidated the Attorney, that he assured James Sharp and G Sharp that their Case could not be defended, that the Court of Kings Bench, especially, had confirmed that Opinion, by the Chief Justice (Lord Mansfield) in several Instances, and therefore he advised a Compromise so that GS who could not believe that the Laws of England were really so Injurious to natural Rights as so many great Lawyers, for Political reasons, had been pleased to assert, was compelled in defence of Himself and Brother to search through the Indexes of a Law Library lately purchased by his Bookseller, for whatever the Books might afford in opposition to the Opinion of the Attorney and Sollicitor General tho['] he had never before opened a Law Book in his Life. But GS was still more surprised and astonished at the absurdity of the Law Proceedings, Writs, and Declarations, against his Brother and himself which he strongly expressed in Remarks upon them which he drew up, for his Attorney to lay [3] before Council, intituled the Case of James and Granville Sharp as far as they are concerned with James Kerr Esqr. The Writs were dated the 8 July 1767 viz. near two Months before the pretended Trespass could possibly have been made Mr Kerr having only a Secondary claim founded merely on the pretended Right of David Lisle By virtue of a Bill of Sale, which did not bear date until the 7th Setr. following. The Declaration still more absurdly set forth, that

> "J and G Sharp maliciously intended wrongfully and unjustly to injure and aggrieve him the said James Kerr and to deprive him of the Service of his Negro John Strong (mistaking his Name) on the first Day of June 1767, and also that they received and entertained One other John Strong and refused to deliver him up the requested on the same Day and Year by the P. James Kerr to do so, and also that they enticed [-] one other John Strong, his Negro Servant to depart and absent himself on the same Day and Year; and also that they received and entertained one other John Strong his negro Servant and refused to deliver him up tho requested the same day and Year [-]".

Thus (it was remarked in the Case) J and G Sharp are charged not with one Negro but with Four and these as distinct and different from each other (according to the Express Words of the Declaration) as "One Person" may be said to be from One other Person; and yet not one of the Four bears the name of the Negro whom they really relieved. The Common Excuse for Erroneous Writs and false Declarations (he remarked) is that "they are mere matters of form" so indeed they might be considered (said GS) if Mr Kerrs Attorney had drawn them up in the name of John Doe and Richard Roe, his Pledges to prosecute for with these fictitious Names alone, they might have been innocent enough Perhaps; but by inserting also the Name of his Client, Mr Kerr, he added an Air of authenticity to his own Inventions which rendered them highly injurious. GS reprobated the Corrupt Custom which had been permitted to prevail in England, viz that, even in the very commencement of what ought to be an Examination into Truth the most vague and unjust accusations should be permitted to be exhibited in the form of a declaration with so much impunity, that they scarcely seem even to aim at the truth &c. That instead of making a modest and true Declaration of their Clients complaint they are allowed to spread as it were a large Nett of Falsehood to enable them to catch a little Truth or rather to ensnare the Truth that they may make their own advantage of it, howsoever innocent and justifiable it may be in itself. That the very first Principle of controversial Law between Man and Man vizt. "Thou shalt not bear False Witness against thy Neighbour" is spurned at and affronted under the Pretext and excuse of "mere matter of Form". And he earnestly exhorted the Gentlemen of the Law to procure some proper Judicial censure of this Attorney's Proceedings, that Writs, Declarations, and other Instruments (originally intended to procure a fair and equitable examination and Determination of Private Differences) may no longer seem as if they had been rather calculated to set even Law and Justice themselves at variance. GS, afterwards, collected from the Law Books very ample Authorities to oppose the Opinion which he had undertaken to answer. Amongst these he cited from the learned Dr (afterwards Judge) Blackstones' [sic] Commentaries an Opinion of Judge Holt recorded in Salkelds Reports – that "as soon as a negro comes into England, he becomes free" &c. This was cited from the first Edition of the Commentaries, but unluckily for GS the 3rd Edition was then published wherein no such Opinion appeared, the learned Author having been [4] induced (as it is said) by the Sentiments of Chief Justice of the Kings Bench (Lord Mansfield)[2] to withdraw that opinion. As soon as GS was informed of this alteration he sent his Attorney to retain Dr Blackstone as one of his Council, in addition to the Recorder of London (now Lord Chief Baron Eyres[3] [sic]) and he then sent to Dr Blackstone the Answer he had Drawn up to the Opinion of the Attorney General and Solicitor General, and waited upon him a few Days afterwards. He had the satisfaction [to] find that the learned Commentator had no objection to make to this Answer, but only warned him that "it would be uphill Work in the Court of KB" and he desired that a Consultation might be held on the Case with the Sollicitor General (then Mr Dunning afterwards Lord Ashburton).[4] The consultation was appointed to be held at the Sollicitor General's Chambers W[h]ere GS attended with his Attorney, and had some discourse with the Recorder and Dr Blackstone before the Sollicitor General came in. Dr Blackstone said that the Case of the Boy may be considered in the Nature of an Apprenticeship, that it was a contract implied, the Service having been Due to the Master in the West Indies it was imply'd to be due also here" (agreeable to the Doc-

---

[2] Ed. There does not appear to be evidence that Blackstone was persuaded to alter his opinion by Mansfield, although it may have been the case.

[3] Ed. Douglas Hay, 'Eyre, Sir James (bap. 1734, d 1799)', ODNB, 2004; online edn, Jan 2008 [http://www.oxforddnb.com/view/article/9032], accessed 5 April 2016. Eyre was created serjeant-at-law, knighted, and made a baron of the exchequer on 6 November 1772, becoming chief baron on 26 January 1787. He became chief justice of the Common Pleas on 11 February 1793.

[4] Ed. The same John Dunning who was to argue the case for Thomas Lewis, and later to infuriate Sharp by appearing on behalf of the the slave owner in *Somerset v Stuart*: above, page 3, below, page 129.

trine laid Down in his 3rd Edition in Conformity to that Prejudice in the Court of Kings Bench which had induced him to expunge his former Just Opinions). But GS immediately answered that "a Contract could not be implyed without implying at the same time the free Consent of both Parties to the making of the Contract, which free Consent was impossible in the Case of A Slave, because being held in Captivity or Prison during the making of a Contract is deemed duress which annuls all Contracts". Afterwards when the Sollicitor General came in he opened the business in Form, and declared the same Doctrine exactly which Dr Blackstone had Stated – vizt. that it was a Contract "implyed" &c to which GS made no further answer at that time, being no Speaker, but reserved himself till he could have Opportunity to state accurately in writing his Objections to that Doctrine, which he afterwards added to his remarks. GS did not dare to print his Answer whilst the Action subsisted against him (which was pending about two years) but had about 20 Copies of them in MS which he lent for perusal, amongst his Friends, and particularly amongst the Professors of the Law, which had the desired Effect, for it intimidated the Plaintiffs Lawyers from proceeding in their Action till they were nonsuited, and obliged to pay the Costs, after which in 1769 GS printed and published an answer to the Opinion of the Attorney and Sollicitor General, and set at Liberty every Negro that complained to him, recovered several from on Ship board, and compelled their quondam Masters to quit the Kingdom to avoid Prosecution for Damages on the Habeas Corpus Act. In the case of Thomas Lewis (who in the year 1770 had been recovered from on board a Ship in the Downs by Writ of Habeas Corpus which GS obtained for him) Lord Mansfield, on the 20th Febry. 1771, openly avowed his former Doctrine that "Negroes continue to be Slaves in England", and declared from the Bench that "he had many times granted Writs of Habeas Corpus to take Negroes that had been pressed into the publick Service and restored them, as Private Property to their respective Masters". GS afterwards drew up a full declaration of the illegality of such proceedings, as being contrary to the fundamental Principles of the Law, prefering [sic] private to Public advantage, pecuniary or sordid Property, as that of a Master in a Horse or Dog to inestimable Liberty and abusing a noble Statute intended for the "freedom" of injured subjects from [5] imprisonment, to render it on the contrary, an instrument of Oppression for delivering up poor Innocent Men in to absolute unlimited Slavery, dragging them, even, out of the Public Service against their Will to deliver them up like Horses or Dogs to a Private Individual as mere Property! But notwithstanding these Declarations of the Chief Justice in favour of Slavery the Poor Negro Thomas Lewis obtained a Verdict of the Jewry [sic] in his favour, but Lord Mansfield never could be prevailed on to give Judgment upon it, though Motions were regularly made in Court in Four successive Terms to demand it. However in the next Year when the Case of James Somerset (who was removed from on board a Ship by Writ of Habeas Corpus) was brought forward by GS for a legal Determination in the Court of Kings Bench, the Chief Justice thought Proper to alter his former Opinion and gave a clear and decided Opinion in favour of the Negro, absolutely denying the claim of Mr Stuart his Master, Saying that "in a Case so odious as the Condition of Slaves must be taken strictly, Tracing the Subject to natural Principles, the claim of Slavery never can be supported. The Power claimed by this return" (ie the Masters Plea in answer to the Writ of Habeas Corpus) "was never in use here. No Master was ever allowed, here, to take a Slave by force to be sold abroad because he had deserted from his Service, or for any other reasons whatever. We cannot say the Cause set forth by this return is allowed or approved of by the Laws of this Kingdom, and therefore the Man must be discharged". On the 18 February 1772 GS wrote to Lord North (the Premier) stating the monstrous indignity of the Colonial Laws for tolerating Slavery. That "immediate redress was necessary, for to be in power, and to neglect, even a Day, in endeavouring to put a Stop to such monstrous injustice and abandoned wickedness must necessarily endanger a Man's eternal Welfare, be he ever so great in temporal Dignity or Office". On the 22nd June 1772 GS received a Letter from Mr Anthony Benezet of Philadelphia dated 14th May 1772 on the Subject of Slavery and the Slave Trade together with several Copies of his Tract against the Slave Trade to which he had added an Extract of the greater part of G Sharp's answer to the attorney and Solicitor General printed in 1769. The said Letter was answered by GS on the return of the same Ship. This answer principally related to the Mode of Petitioning to be adopted by the Colonists, whether against the Slave Trade in General, or against Slavery in the Colonies, wherein a material distinction was to be observed viz. that in the former Case, they should address themselves to the King and British Parliament, but not in the Latter Case: for it was clearly explained in this Letter, as also in the Letter to Lord North (a Copy of which was sent at the same time) that the British Parliament has no right to interfere with the Acts of the Colonial Assemblys, if such acts are not inconsistent with natural Justice and the general Laws of the Empire. This distinction was not inserted with any Political View, but merely to promote petitions in the Proper Channel ag[ains]t the Slave Trade, and to urge the Colonists to petition their own Assemblies against the Wickedness of their own Legislative Acts for tolerating slavery in America. And Mr Benezet's answers shew, that the Doctrine of this Distinction about Colonial Rights of Legislation was more and generally communicated in America than could easily have been conceived. Mr Benezet answered – "I have made out several Copies of such parts of this Letter as were likely to promote the good end proposed. These were sent to Virginia, South Carolina, and Maryland, to such Persons as had this Matter at [6] Heart; with all the additional Strength in my Power in order to encourage their taking the most Effect" and he added that "a Lawyer had undertaken to Draw up Models of Petitions" also "we have pushed" (said he) "the point amongst ourselves" (meaning the People of Pensylvania [sic]) "by our handing about extracted Copies of thy Letter, of the Virginia Petition (vizt. a Petition to the King against the Slave Trade) and of a publication which our Agent Benjamin Franklin had made in the London Chronicle of the 20 June last. One of our Assembly Men, representative for this City" (Philadelphia) "who had requested Copies of these Papers caused them to be Published in 2 of our Public Papers &c. "I have also sent" (says he) "the Extract of thy Letter, of the Virginia Petition, &c to some weighty Members of three Different Counties in New York Government, and the same to two Counties in New Jersey's requesting they would also take in Consideration the necessity of uniting in the same measure with us, of petitioning their Assemblies to remonstrate to the King and Parliament against a Continuation of the Slave Trade. The New Yorkers approved well of the Measure but the Session of their Assembly was so far gone they thought it improper to put in a Petition at this time, but from the Representation now made to their Representatives it was proposed to augment the Duty upon Slaves imported". All these transactions seem to have been in the Latter end of 1772, The Philadelphia Petition has no Date, Several other letters from Mr Benezet declare the wide Circulation of These Papers into every Part of America so that the Doctrine of the Separate [sic] Rights of the Colonial Assemblies was most extensively cultivated and it is very remarkable that a humble endeavour to oppose domestic Tyranny and Slavery, without any other view should be the means of communicating throughout America a Warning to the colonists of the Natural Independance [sic] of their several Assemblies, with respect to the British Parliament. In Mr Benezet[']s Letter to GS, dated 5th April 1773 among other Things he says "I am glad to understand from my Friend Benjn. Franklin that you have commended an acquaintancy and that he expects you will in future act in Concert in the Affair of Slavery". The Declarations of the Peoples Right to a Share in the Legislature printed in 1774 in defense [*sic*] of the Injured Americans, could not possibly have been Undertaken by the Author had he not been previously compelled to Study the Principles of Law and Legal Freedom in his own Defense [*sic*], when prosecuted for having liberated the Poor Negro Boy, Jonathan Strong, an event which has had very extensive Effects.

King (Lewis) v Stapylton

Proceedings in the Court of King's Bench

20 February 1771

MS in New York Historical Society,
Manuscript Collections Relating to Slavery:
Granville Sharp collection, 1768–1803.

[1]

No 1

The Proceedings in the Cause of
The King on the prosecution
of Thomas Lewis a Negro   Plaintiff
against
Stapylton and others   Defendants

by Indictment for Assault and Imprisonment of the said Thomas Lewis with Intent to transport and sell him as a Slave. upon which Indictment the several Defendants were found Guilty.

— tried —

In the Court of King's Bench before Lord Mansfield on Wednesday February 20th. 1771 [2]

Jurors – by whom the Cause was tryed

1. Richard Glover
2. Charles Grooby
3. Peter Taylor
4. Daniel Bower
5. Wm Stainbank
6. John Coates

7. Job. Bearley
8. Samuel Foxlove
9. Willm Evans
10. Daniel Jennings
11. Wm Barlow
12. Christopher Golding

Council for the Crown
Mr Dunning[5]
Mr Davenport
Mr Lucas

For the Defendants
Mr Walker

[3]

Mr Davenport. Please your Lordship and you Gentlemen of the Jury[:] This is an Indictment upon the prosecution of Thomas Lewis against Robert Stapleton John Maloney and Aaron Armstrong. The indictment states that they seized and intended to Transport Lewis the Prosecutor abroad to the Island of Jamaica and to sell & dispose of him there; It likewise states that upon the 2d day of July in [the] 10th year of the Reign &c in the year of our Lord 1769 at the Parish of St Luke Chelsea in the County of Middlesex with force & arms & upon the Prosecutor then & there did make as assault and there seize him, & drag him, & put him into a Boat then floating in the river Thames & then & there Gagged his Mouth & against his Will & consent put him in prison for 2 or 3 days – to which charge the Defendants have pleaded not Guilty whereupon the Issue is joined – [4]

Mr Dunning. Please your Lordship and you Gentlemen of the Jury I am likewise of Council [sic] for the prosecution of the several Defendants Robert Stapylton, John Maloney and, Aaron Armstrong who are brought before you to answer to a Charge of a very Gross and outra-

---

[5] Ed. John Cannon, 'Dunning, John, first Baron Ashburton (1731–1783)', ODNB, 2004; online edn, May 2006 [http://www.oxforddnb.com/view/article/8284], accessed 27 February 2015.

gious [sic] assault upon the person of the Plaintiff accompanyed with the Actual Imprisonment of his person for the space of 76 hours, and with a Great deal of Malice and Outrage and the Indictment likewise charges it to be with a purpose which is still Worse than the Action complained of Namely with a purpose of Conveying the person of the Unhappy Prosecutor where only such persons as the Defendants ought to live, into such a country where from the right one [5] man has over the person of another and by the Laws of that Country they are to be engaged to what ever purpose they think proper to employ them.

Gentlemen[,] Thomas Lewis the prosecutor has the Misfortune as he finds it to be in point of Colour a Black and upon the Ground of that Discovery made by them, his having a Darker Complexion than the now defendants[,] they have taken it into their heads to say he was not under the protection of the Law of this Country and that they have a right to treat him as their property or whether or not their property they had a right to treat him as a Horse or a Dog to carry him where they pleased and do what they pleased with him. But I trust by your Verdict they will find themselves mistaken. For by the Laws of this Country they have no such right.

Gentlemen[,] the Prosecutor so far as he gives [6] the Account of himself is the Son of what is called a Free Negroe born on the Gold Coast[.] his Father was Free[.] after his Father[']s death he lived with an Uncle[.] after he left his Uncle he was sent to Santa Cruz and divers other places and he will give you an account of his being brought to England and from his Infancy it appears he was friendless and fatherless and has been in the service of different persons at different places and has also been in the public Employment of a Sailor in the Course of which Employments he became acquainted with the Defendant Robert Stapylton. I think he sailed with him two or three Voyages and lived with him in England and at present the Defendant was at an Ale house at Chelsea[.] the other two Defendants are sailors or Boatmen or Watermen of his acquaintance.

Gentlemen[,] the Prosecutor when he came to [7] England knowing nobody in it but this Stapylton renewed his Acquaintance and lived with him some part of his time and was [a] waiter I believe or Drawer at this public house[.] he had likewise lived in England with other persons but when he was in no other place he looked upon this man as his Friend and went to him. In '69 the Transaction happened which is now intelligible enough though not so at the time it happened[.] this young man accompanyed with Stapylton found himself to be inveigled and put on board a Ship and from thence intended to be conveyed away to some of our plantations but he escaped at that time by the Vessel in which he was being lost and he was among the few survivors who escaped to shore.

Gentlemen[,][6] I was stating to you that some time before this transaction which is the immediate subject of the present Indictment the present [8] prosecutor found himself on board a ship inveigled for the same purpose (which I shall more particularly state to you presently) of making a pecuniary advantage of but he was as I observed before saved by the ship being lost and so he Escaped for that time and either not suspecting this Stapylton[']s intention or though suspecting him not knowing where better to goe he returned to his House and there remained till the latter end of June or the beginning of July last, when Stapylton formed a Design of Getting this Lad into a Boat for the purpose of carrying him to a ship in which he was put on Board for the purpose of selling him and thence conveying him to a certain place where these things are thought innocent.

The Boy was brought to a place some where [9] near the Water[.] he was conveyed into a Boat for the purposes I before mentioned and The Boy knowing or suspecting what was to happen tryed to Alarm the neighbourhood with his Cries and so far he succeeded in it that he was very distinctly heard by some persons on the shore but however they tyed him neck and Heels in the Boat and they found a method to silence him by cutting some sticks and forcing them into his mouth to make it impossible for him to make any resistance either by his mouth or Limbs and in a Dark night they rowed him down to the place where the ship was to sail from[.] when they got him there they delivered him to the Captain of the Vessell for the purpose that was particularly stated by me at the outsett[.] the Defendant thought fit as he called it to sell the Boy and for that purpose delivered him to the Captain[.] you will hear more particularly from the Witness's [10] how much he was to get for him:

Gentlemen[,] the Captain who had or was to pay this money was ex-

---

[6] Ed. An interval of time seems to have elapsed before the following passage, since counsel repeats what he said.

ceedingly unwilling to part with his pretended property and application was made to a Magistrate from whom a Warrant or Summons was brought[.] this the Captain disregarded and refused obeying by not delivering up the Boy[.] But the humanity of some person whose residence was near the Water and near the place where the poor Boy was put in the Boat hearing his Outcries induced somebody to apply to this Court for a Habeas Corpus in consequence of which the Captain not thinking fit to expose himself to the Chance or hazard of disobeying thought proper to bring him up again by which means the prosecutor once more recovered his Liberty:

Gentlemen[,] this Indictment is brought for a Violent Outrage done to the Laws of your [11] Country in the person of this Unfortunate prosecutor Thomas Lewis, and I am give to understand that it is insisted the prosecutor is the property of some or one of the Defendants or somebody or other belonging to them[.] In the first place it does not exist in my Idea as applicable to this cause how it can be supported, but if so, I shall have leisure and opportunity to insist before you, or in any Court wherever they think proper to support it that the Laws of this Country admit of no such property; I know nothing where this Idea exists; I apprehend it only exists in the minds of those who have lived in those Countrys where it is suffered; and where the nature and situation of the place may require such Laws. Gentlemen[,] upon the Habeas Corpus being issued the Boy was delivered from his confinement and since that time there has been frequent attempts by [12] Defendants to remove the Prosecutor that he might not give evidence against them and no longer ago than Yesterday some of the party had him seized on and impressed.[7]

Lord Chief Justice[:] you cant go into that[.] if you could bring it home to them you cannot go into it[.] I will not try any thing but this indictment[.] we have business enough –

Mr Dunning[:] My Lord I trust with regard to the punishment for this offence it would be of Material influence for the Jury to consider of the transaction I was going to state.

Lord Chief Justice[.] that will make no difference now[.] it may come in another shape[.]

---

[7] Ed. See below, note 28 on page 117, and note 72 on page 150.

Mr Dunning[:] My Lord So far it may make a Difference that these people should understand and I hope will be made to understand that whatever Idea they may have the prosecutor would be [13] Safe in coming into this Court to give testimony for no longer ago than Yesterday fresh experiments were made to prevent his coming here to give evidence[.]

Lord Chief Justice[:] The Court will be open to any sort of Complaint[.] if they do any thing of that sort they will take it at their peril and take the Consequences the same as if it was done to any body else. the Court will not suffer any body coming here to give evidence to be impeded[.]

Mr Dunning[:] My Lord it is certain it is not the subject of the present complaint.

Gentlemen[:] I have in General stated the Outlines of this case[.] I shall prove it by the Boy himself and by others that conveyed him down to the Ship and by other Witnesses to that part of the Transactions and when they have proved it I make no doubt of your finding the several Defendants Guilty and though I have intimated that difference of right and property [14] which I have talked to you about, I believe I shall not hear about that sort of Defence which if I do I shall have an oportunity [sic] to reply to it.

Thomas Lewis sworn. Examined by Mr Lucas

Q. Where was[8] you born?
A. Upon the Gold Coast Sir.
Q. What is the name of the place?
A. The name of the place I can't remember Sir.
Q. Do you remember any relations of yours?
A. I remember a little of them.
Q. Do you remember your uncle?
A. Yes Sir.
Q. Who brought you up?
A. When my fader [sic] died my Uncle brought me up.

---

[8] Ed. It is noticeable that both counsel and Lord Mansfield use "was" for the second person past tense of the verb, rather than the modern "were".

Q. Who was your Uncle?
A. He is a Gentleman in our Country.
Q. That is he was a Freeman?
A. Yes Sir. So was my Fader.
Q. Now what time did you leave your Uncle?
A. I leave him when I was between 6 or 7 years of age. [15]

Lord Chief Justice: You don't prove his being free by himself.

Mr Dunning: My Lord I have nobody that was bye that can give any other accounts.

Lord Chief Justice: you can't prove by himself. You will see how they prove the Contrary.

Mr Dunning: This Boy has always understood himself to be free.

Lord Chief Justice: I shall presume him to be free unless they prove the Contrary[9] –

Mr Dunning: My Lord you will hear from his evidence how he came into this Country and how they deluded him away.

Mr Lucas
Q. to Lewis: Who did you go to live with upon the death of your Uncle?
A. My Uncle was not dead when I came over[.] I lived with my uncle when my fader died.
Q. When your Father died you lived with your Uncle[?]
A. I did not live with him long, but about 12 months[.] [16]
Q. Who did you go to live with when you left your Uncle?
A. I have been with the General and Governor of the place[.]
Q. You was a servant of the General?
A. Yes. when the General came away after my father died he come to receive my fader[']s Estate[.] when he come I went to him[.] He could speak English and he ask me if [I] should like to go abroad. if I did I should learn the Language[.] I said I should like it very well because he understand and I did not understand it. So far he gave me leave to

[9] Ed. Note that this is the first occasion that Lord Mansfield clearly states that a person is presumed free until proven otherwise, although implied by his previous comment.

go in the first ship and he put me on board a Dean[10] ship[.] when the Captain was going away in this part of the World he went to send me. I went on board when the ship was ready[.] I came away[.] they did not send me on the shore but carried me to Santa Cruz and they gave me to a Dean Captain[11] who died and another took the Command of the ship. [17]

Lord Chief Justice[:] they brought you to Santa Cruz; who was you with there?
There they bestowed me to a Dean[12] Nobleman then after the Nobleman Died I was with the Cooper of the Dean Nobleman's Wharfe and he died[.] then when he died I live a good while with his Clerk[.] after the Dean Nobleman died the Clerk took me to a Merchant[,] an English merchant.

Council[:] Q. What was his Name?
A. his Name is Bob Smith[.]

Lord Chief Justice[:] to an English Merchant[.]

Mr Dunning[:] to an English Merchant of the name of Robert Smith[.]
Q. how long did you live with Mr Smith?
A. I cant say[.] I believe it was about half a Year or more. then I went on board this ship with Mr Smith and then one day I went on board with him to wait upon him[.] after that he ask me if I should like to go abroad with this Stapylton[.] [18]
Q. Mr Smith asked you?
A. Yes Sir. then I told him I should like it very well as I never had been in any parts of the World[.] So accordingly I did and about a week and [a] half between this Staplyl[ton] was coming away to a place called Carolina[.] he sent for me upon shore[.] before I went with a man[.] I cannot tell wither [sic] Stapylton's man was Mullathe[13] or one of the White Sailors[.] when I went to Stapylton we came away there from Santa Cruz to go to Carolina[.] when we came there the brig was taken by a Spanish privateer[.]

---

[10] Ed. From further on, page 115, it appears that by "Dean ship" the prosecutor meant a Danish ship.
[11] Ed. Meaning a Danish captain. See note 26 on page 115.
[12] Ed. Meaning a Danish nobleman. See page 115.
[13] Ed. An Indian personal name.

Lord Chief Justice[:] Q. What Stapylton's Brigg?
A. Yes.
Q. And you went on board the Spanish ship[?]
A. Yes

Mr Lucas
Q. You was taken prisoner?
A. Yes from Stapylton[.] when I was taken they sent Stapylton and 2 men in the Brigg and all the rest on board the ship[.] then they [19] Carried me to Augustine[14] and then to Havannah[.]
Q. How long was you at Havannah?
A. I was I believe four or 5 Weeks.
Q. What did you do at Havannah?
A. I was with the Captain of the Spanish ship who took me by force from Stapylton[.] I was with him[.] then afterwards one of the sailors coming to the Captain, the Spanish Captain's House[,] he told me I have seen the captain of the Brigg and speaking some Spanish Language I did not understand[.] I said nothing[.] then about 2 Days afterwards I come away from the Spaniards[.] then I went to a place called Havanna[15] where was the English Merchant[.] then the English Merchant he took me to a Tavern[.]
Q. What did you do at the Tavern?
A. I wait there.
Q. Then you was a Waiter there?
A. I was there till such time as I could better myself[.] [20]
Q. How long was you there?
A. About 2 or 3 Weeks[.]

Lord Chief Justice[:] At what place?
A. at the Havannah[.]
Q. from Council; had you any Wages?
A. He allow me some money:
Q. Who did?
A. the man I served there[;] the man at the Tavern[.]
Q. What wages did he allow you?
A. He allow me money Victuals and Drink[.]

Mr Lucas[:]

[14] Ed. St Augustine, Florida. See page 132.
[15] Ed. The word is sometimes spelled "Havannah" and at other times "Havanna" in the MS.

Q. Did you wait there till you could better yourself[?]
A. Yes Sir[.]
Q. How long did you stay there?
A. I was there 3 or 4 Weeks then the tavern keeper was out of town and he said [, "]you stay in the Tav[er]n till I come home["".] he left some meat for me to dress for my Dinner then there came in Stapylton and two or three more captains and [21] then when they came in I knowed the buttons upon his Coat and I went and speak to him and he said he did not know me[.]
Q. You scraped acquaintance with him then?
A. Yes Sir[.] he said he did not know me[.] I made myself known to him – I was there till almost night and then he took me away from there and brought me to the Town[.]
Q. What did he say to you there?
A. He said nothing to me but told the Merchant I belonged to him and insisted upon having me away[.] When I came away he put me into a Schooner on board a Ship that was going to Philadelphia[.] I don't know the Captain[.] the next day about 12 or 1 o[']clock he took me away from there and carried me on shore and as he took me on shore[...]

Lord Chief Justice[:] the ship was going to Philadelphia[?]
A. Yes[.] the sloop was going there[.] [22]
Q. Where did he carry you to?
A. He took me to the Captain's house and after that took me to New York[.] then I was on board a week I cant really tell how much[.] it was after that there he carried me to Captain Coffee's house[.] I was there till he came away from Havanna to New York[.] then he put me to one Mr Frazier a Wine Merchant[.]

Lord Chief Justice[:] At New York and at Havanna[.] Where next?
T. Lewis[:] and when he took me to Mr Frazier I was there and as a Servant[.] I used to [23] carry out Wine[.]

Mr Dunning
Q. Did you get any Wages?
A. Mr Frazier used to allow me something[.]
Q. Did you get to Mr Smith afterwards[?]
A. Yes[.] so afterwards Stapylton took me and brought me away to New York[.]

Lord Mansfield[:] Who brought you to New York?
A. Stapylton.-

Mr Dunning[:] he had been at the Havanna's at Philadelphia and then Going to New York.

Lord Mansfield[:] No[.] he had not been at Philadelphia – All this minuteness can never be material.

T. Lewis[:]
from New York we went to Santa Cruz again and then I was two or three days before I went to Mr Smith again[.] I was with him a year and a half and [24] Stapylton come away from there and went to Pensacola and there he was for some time – I lived with Smith till he died[.]
Q. when was that do you recollect?
A. No I don't[.]
Q. where did you go then?
A. the Judge of the place took me to live with him.
Q. Then you was Servant with the Judge?
A. Yes Sir[.]
Q. Had you any wages?
A. he allowed me so much a week[.]
Q. How long did you live with this Justice?
A. I was about 10 or 12 weeks[.]

Lord Mansfield[:] You did not agree for Wages but he allowed you Wages?
A. yes he allowed me Wages[.]
Q. When did you leave him? [25]
A. When I was with the Judge his Hair dresser was coming away[.]
Q. The Judge[']s Hair dresser was coming away.
A. Yes and he wanted me to come away with him abroad.
Q. where did you go to with the Hair Dresser?
A. to New England[.]

Mr Dunning[:] All I wish is to know the Different places where he lived and to shew he had wages and was not a Slave but free[.]

Lord Mansfield[:] It does not shew he was free -

Q. Where did you live afterwards?

112   *Cases on Slavery*

A. At New England[.]
Q. In any body's Service there?
A. I staid [sic] with the Hair Dresser[.]
Q. Did you live with any body else there[?]
A. No Sir[.] I went to Stapylton[']s Sister in Law[.] [26] She keep me in the House and not let me go[.]
Q. How did you come from Pensacola[?]
A. Stapylton came from Pensacola to New York[.] then he took me away with him to sea[.]
Q. Did he take you away with the Consent of the Hair Dresser?
A. He took me away by force from the Hair dresser[.]
Q. Where then did you go?
A. To a place called Carolina to Jamaica and to New York[.]
Q. With Stapylton?
A. Yes[.]
Q. Where then[.]
A. To England[.]
Q. And you have been in England ever since?
A. Yes till they trepan[16] me[.]
Q. Where did you live in England with Stapylton? [27]
A. At Chelsea.

Lord Mansfield[:] Stapylton took you from the Hair dresser[.] where was you then?
A. At Carolina at New York and Jamaica X[17] here[.]

Council[:]
Q. Have not you been cast away since[?]
A. Yes Sir[.] Stapylton trepan[18] me away on board a Ship since I have been in England twice[,] Sir.
Q. Then you escaped by the Ship being wrecked[?]
A. Yes Sir[.]
Q. Have you been since with Stapylton again?
A. He find I come and the Captain was wrecked[.]

Mr Dunning[:] I don't want to know the particulars of the Wreck[.] After that you came to London?

[16] Ed. OED. trepan, trapan, obs. arch. To catch in a trap; to entrap, ensnare, beguile.
[17] Ed. There is an X marked in the MS at this point before the word "here". The speaker is obviously not in Jamaica.
[18] Ed. In the sense of entrap. See page 112 note 16.

A. Yes Sir and he found where I was and sent for me to take me away by force[.]
Q. Since that time you have been in Stapylton[']s [28] House?
A. Yes and he kidnap me again.
Q. Tell us how you were kidnapped this last time?
A. It was between ten or eleven [or] twelve o[']clock[.] I cannot tell what time of night it was one Monday night this last Summer[.]

Lord Mansfield[:] After you was wrecked you came to England and lived again with Stapylton?
A. Yes Sir.

Mr Dunning[:] You was kidnapped about 10 or 11 o clock at night you say?
A. Yes Sir[.] Stapylton one night says ["]I have got["], says he[,] ["]some Gin and tea down by the Water side by Mrs Banks[']s[19] wharfe and I am afraid there is a Custom house Officer has notice and intelligence of it[."]

Lord Mansfield[:] You had not left him? [29]
A. No Sir[.] he said the Custom house Officer had intelligence[.] So says he[, "]you might go and fetch it up from the Waterman[.] but come the back way not through the Colledge for fear the Custom house Officer take it from you as they have notice of it before[".] when I went there he had two men[.]

Lord Mansfield[:] where was it you went to?
A. down by Mrs Banks[,] the Water side at Bull Wharfe[.]

Mr Dunning[:] it is at Chelsea [where] Stapylton lives[.]

---

[19] Ed. Mrs Banks, Sarah (1709–1804), eldest daughter of William Bate and his wife, Arabella, was the mother of Sir Joseph Banks, the naturalist. Mrs Banks owned the house at 22 Paradise Row, Chelsea. Sir Joseph used to stay there when not in Oxford since it gave him ready access to the Chelsea Physic Garden. (The rock garden still contains some Icelandic lava brought to the garden by Sir Joseph in 1772 on a ship named St. Lawrence.) Paradise Row was demolished in 1905 and the land now forms part of Royal Hospital Road. John Gascoigne, 'Banks, Sir Joseph, baronet (17431820)', ODNB, 2004; online edn, September 2013 [http://www.oxforddnb.com/view/article/1300], accessed 11 November 2016; Folarin Shyllon, *Black People in Britain, 1555–1833*, London, OUP, 1977, p 23. Reginald Blunt, *Paradise Row; or, A broken piece of old Chelsea, being the curious and diverting annals of a famous village street newly destroyed...*, London, Macmillan, 1906.

Lewis:
Then when I went down there he sent one man down with me and all this time he had a man coming after me [–] one behind me and the other before me[.] I did not know all this and some Waterman was hiding in a passage there and three men and the Waterman that came out layed hold on me[.]
Q. Do you know who they were? [30]
A. I know 3 of them[.]
Q. Name them[.]
A One was John Malony[,] the other Aaron Armstrong and Richard Coleman[.] When I went there they seized me directly[.] then I began to call out for help[.] I called to Mrs Banks for help[.] I told them the same persons took me away before[,] the same person going to trepann[20] me on board a ship[:] then they began to fight with me and I would not go and I fought about a quarter of an hour with them in the way and at last they drag me about a hundred yards and dragged me upon my back upon the Ground and when I got to the water side they shoved me into the Water instead of the Boat because I would not go and then they put me into the Boat and then put a Cord round my Leg. [31]
Q. from Mr Lucas[:] Did you cry out?
A. Yes Sir[.] I cry out all the time, and then they put a stick across my mouth and Gagg me[.] I struggled and got it off[.] then when I got past Chelsea Colledge then I hold my tongue then[.]
Q. Did any body give directions about tying or Gagging you[?] did you hear any body[?]
A. Yes[.] I heard some people[.] I heard him cry out ["]Gagg him["] says he.
Q. Who cryed out? ["]Gagg him["]?
A. I thought it was Stapylton.
Q. You knew his Voice?
A. Yes Sir[.] he was somewhere upon the side of the shore crying out ["]Gagg him["].]

Mr Dunning[:] Did not you say you knew his Voice?
A. Yes Sir[.] [32]

Lord Mansfield[:] Where was you sent then?

---

[20] Ed. "Trepan" in the sense of entrap, beguile. See page 112 note 16.

A. I was sent on Board the Snow[21] called the Fanny[,] Captain Sawver[22][.]
Q. Where was you carried to first in the boat[?]
A. First to Gravesend[.] Mrs Banks sent down to Gravesend for me: I was put on board the ship there[.] the captain refuse twice to give me up[.]
Q. Who was the Captain?
A. Captain Seaward[,] the Captain of the West Indiaman[.] then when he refuse to give me up the Magistrate[23] come on board[.] they would not deliver me up[.] The Magistrate ask me ["]is it not better to go abroad["].] I said I don't chuse to it.
Q. Did the Captain give any reason why he would not deliver you up?
A. He said he had a Bill of Sale from Stapylton[.] then they take me down [33] to Gravesend[.] Mrs Banks send the Corpus[24] and sent after the Captain and he would not deliver me up till such time as he went on shore and had further notice[.]

Cross Examination by Mr Walker for Defendants[:]
Q. You said you was born at Guinea?[25]
A. Yes Sir[.]
Q. And you was put on board a Danish[26] Ship when you left your Uncle?

---

[21] Ed. "Snow: the largest of all old two-masted vessels. The sails and rigging on the main mast of a snow are exactly similar to those on the same masts in a full-rigged ship; only that there is a small mast behind the mainmast of the former, which carries a sail nearly resembling the mizzen of a ship." Daniel Defoe, *A General History of the Pyrates* (1724) "The Introduction", in Manuel Schonhorn, ed, *A General History of the Pyrates*, reprint, Dover, 1999, p xlviii.

[22] Ed. There seems to be some confusion as to captains' names. Lewis here gives the name of the captain of the snow, the *Fanny*, as Captain Sawver. Later, a few lines down, the captain of the West Indiaman to which Lewis was transferred at Gravesend is mentioned by Lewis as Captain Seaward, but later when the captain gives evidence he is sworn as Phillip [sic] Seaward or Saver, below, page 121.

[23] Ed. Unclear word, as is the same word later in the sentence. May be abbreviated, but "Magistrate" is consistent with Dunning's statement of the facts at the beginning of the MS.

[24] Ed. ie writ of habeas corpus.

[25] Ed. Earlier, in examination in chief, Thomas Lewis said that he was born on the Gold Coast. However, in the eighteenth century the general area or hinterland was known as Guinea, while the coastal region was dominated by forts occupied by European powers. The coastal areas were the Ivory Coast, the Gold Coast and the Slave Coast.

[26] Ed. The prosecutor had earlier referred to a "Dean" ship. This makes clear that he meant "Danish". Above, note 10 on page 108.

A. Yes Sir.

Mr Walker[:] My Lord what I mean to prove is that he was the servant of those people when they sent him away[.]
Lord Mansfield[:] very likely – no thing he has said was inconsistent with that one way or another[.]
Q. What was Stapylton at the time you first came home? [34]
A. he was Captain of a Merchantman[.]
Q. What was he when he came over to England[?]
A. He came over Blind[.]
Q. He continues blind now?
A. Yes Sir[.]
Q. Very old and incapable of carrying on any business[?]
A. Not very incapable[.]
Q. He and his Wife came over to England together?
A. Yes
Q. Have you been out of Order, ill[?]
A. Yes[.] since I came into England[.]
Q. Who took care of you?
A. He did a little time and then got a Letter to get me into Hospital[.] I went and got a letter from Mr Hurst of Chelsea[.] he gave me a letter to go to the Hospital to St Georges Hyde Park Corner[27] [.]
Q. All the time you was in England he took care of you[?] [35]
A. No Sir not always[.]
Q. Only when you was with him? But not when you went away from him?
A. Yes[.] when he used me ill. [H]e always paid for my Victuals when I was with him[.]

Lord Mansfield. Have you any Deduction of property Mr Walker?
W. Walker. My Lord I have a Title under which we can prove him the servant of the Defendant.
Lord Mansfield. I[']ll tell you what I think to do; The general Question may be a very important one, and not in this Shape ever considered as I know of[.] If you have the Title of property; I shall first of all leave it to the jury to find whether he is their property as a Slave and then put

---

[27] Ed. St George's Hospital was opened in Lanesborough House (now the Lanesborough Hotel) at Hyde Park Corner in 1733 and is still in existence, represented by St George's Hospital, an NHS Trust in Tooting, south London. The original hospital moved to Wimbledon in 1859 and to Tooting between 1976 and 1980.

it in some solemn way to be tried - His being black will not prove the property.

Mr. Walker. The only Excuse for this prosecution is, that he is not Stapylton's property, but he was sent as their Servant is what we shall prove.

Lord Mansfield. I have granted several Writs of Habeas Corpus upon Affidavits of Masters for [36] their Negroes, two or 3 I believe upon affidavits of Masters deducing sale and property of their Negroe[.] upon being prest[28] I have granted Habeas Corpus's to deliver them to their Masters; but whether they have this kind of property in England never has been solemnly determined[.]

Mr Walker[:] My Lord we have from Captain Smith a Regular transfer to Stapylton and at all those places he has claimed him[:] at Havannah[,] at New York and Pensacola and he never has denied it.

Lord Chief Justice[:] There is a Great Chasm before you took him at New York – for he was at Santa Cruz with Smith again and then with the Judge there.

Mr Walker[:] From Mr Smith we have him.

Lord Chief Justice[:] No[:] he is twice with Smith[.]

Mr Walker[:] It was in the year [']62 we first purchased him[.]
[37]

Lord Mansfield[:] If you have you [sic[any evidence of the fact you allude to[,] it will acquit them[.] I suppose the fact in dispute is the Kidnapping him and sending him away[.][29]

Mr Walker[:] As to Malony and Armstrong I am not concerned for them[.] I know nothing of them[.]

---

[28] Ed. Grammatically the subject of "prest" is "I" but Sharp in his remarks, page 150, takes it to mean that the black people were impressed and Mansfield granted habeas corpus to deliver them to their alleged "masters".

[29] Ed. The words "if you" are inserted above the line. The second "you" should have been deleted so that the sentence was probably intended to read "If you have any evidence of that fact you allude to, it will acquit them."

Lord Mansfield[:] You can[']t discharge him from them[.]

Richard Coleman sworn.
Mr Walker produced a paper. Look at that paper.
A. I cant read[.]
Q. You cant read it you say?
A. No sir[.] I can[']t read[.] I own I can[']t read[.]
Q. Do you know the handwriting?
A. No Sir[.] I don't know that[.]
Q. Nor you can[']t read?
A. No Sir[.]
Q Nor you can[']t read writing? [38]
A. No Sir[.]

Mr Davenport[.]
Q. Coleman[.] Do you know Robert Stapylton of Chelsea?
A. Yes Sir[.]
Q. Do you know Thomas Lewis the Black before you?
A. Yes Sir[.]
Q. What are you Coleman?
A. a Waterman Sir[.]
Q. Was you applied to at any time by Stapylton concerning this Black?
A. Yes Sir[.]
Q. Tell us when and how[.]
A. I think it was the latter end of Last June about the 29th I think.
Q. What for?
A. They came to me I think to the best of my memory it was on a Friday[.] he came to me and said he should want me[.] I said what is it about[?] he said he should not tell me then [39] but he would come and let me know[.] he came about 9 and said he should not[30] want me that night[.] he came again on Saturday and said ["]I shall want you to night[".] he said ["]do you know what it is upon[?] I said ["]no["].] Says he ["]you can guess can[']t you[?"] Say I ["]I can[']t unless it is to carry the Black down again[.] he — come about 9 o'clock and said I was not to carry him down without the Captain had sailed out of the River to Gravesend[.] on Sunday night they came again[.] I was not to go then[.] then a Monday they came again and sent the Black down to me to fetch some things.

---

[30] Ed. The word "not" is inserted in the line above.

Q. Who did he send him to[?]
A. To me[.] then I was to lay in ambush and they sent a man with the Black under pretence to help him and he was to seize him and put him on board the Boat and then at that time that they seized him I was away at a distance from the shore and I heard a strange noise[.] I judged what it was and went to them[.] I heard him [40] say ["]Mrs Banks come help me for God[']s sake[.] they are going to trepan[31] me and take me on board the ship["] and he hallowed out for the Coachman.—-
Q. Who put him into the boat?
A. One Malony a Redheaded Man, and one Armstrong.—-
Q. In what way was he put on board the Boat?
A. In the hold[.]
Q. Did they put him in the Water?
A. In getting him into the boat they shoved him in. he said he could not swim and he would Jump over board and be drowned[32] sooner than go. I then tyed his leg with a Rope[.]
Q. Was Stapylton there?
A. I did not see him[.]
Q. Did they do any thing to his Mouth?
A. He Hallowed out prodigiously when he was in the Boat[.] there was one man tried to put a Stick in his mouth and was going to put a [41] String round his Mouth but he got that off[.]
Q. Did any body say ["]Gagg him["]?
A. I heard somebody say ["]Gagg him["].
Q. Did you know Stapylton[']s voice?
A. Yes I believe I do[.]
Q. Did you take it to be his Voice?
A. He[33] made such a noise that I could not tell.

Cross Examination

Q. You did not see Stapylton there? You knew him for some time?
A. So far as I see he wore something about his eyes[.] I don't know whether he is blind or no.
Q. Did nobody interpose about their taking him away?
A. One of Madam Banks's servants spoke to me[.]
Q. From Mr Dunning[:] Did they say they had any authority?

---

[31] Ed. See page 112 note 16.
[32] Ed. The words "and be drowned" are inserted above the text at this point.
[33] Ed. ie Lewis.

A. He pulled a paper out of his pocket and said ["]this is a Newspaper we had advertised him in["].]
Mr Dunning[:] Under the pretence of property I [42] understand they said they had a Warrant from [the] Lord Mayor which prevented the people interposing.—

Lord Mansfield[:] Who produced it? Was it Armstrong that said it?
A. No.
Q. Was it Malony?
A. No My Lord[.]

Mr Dunning[:] it was one of those that assisted I suppose[?]-

Mr Dunning[:] Wee [sic] have several people that stood on the shore that saw the transaction of putting him into the Boat but I believe it is sufficiently proved already[.]

Mr Walker[:] My Lord I can say no more in the Defence of my Clients than this[,] that this Negroe has been a Servant and as a Slave abroad sold by Smith to him he has all the accounts to produce in evidence that [43] that [sic] he has been his slave and that as such he brought him into England and as such he has been in England and as such he has Continued ever since he has been in England[.] he has run away from him at times and has been advertised and then he has returned again as his slave and whatever aggravated facts these are he cannot be criminally answerable for them and I can only submit it to the Jury that we can prove him to be the property of the Defendant Stapylton.

Mr Dunning[:] I dispute the fact and the possibility of his being any body['s] property here in England[.]

Mr Walker[:] this paper I have in my hand is to show that he was transferred to Stapylton by Smith, the Black knows it and I can prove by the Witnesses I shall call that he always has acknowledged it[.]

Lord Mansfield[:] Can you call any Witness to prove the Conveyance- [?] [44]

Mr Walker[:] My Lord I cannot for want of the person that made the Conveyance[.]

Mr Dunning[:] Any man may treat his servant then as this man has been treated if this is the Case].

Lord Mansfield[:] to be sure it will be expected you should prove the property very clear in order to make out the question.

Mr Roch called[,] sworn and Examined by Mr Walker.
Q. Roch[,] do you know the Defendant Stapylton[?]
A. I know him very well Sir[.]
Q. You was with him at Santa Cruz?
A. Yes Sir.
Q. Did you know Robert Smith?
A. Yes Sir very well[.]
Q. You know of his purchasing the Black of Smith?
A. I know very well he had a Boy [who] was called August[.] To the best of my opinion his name was August[.] I cannot tell [45] whether it was his name or no.
Q. to Lewis[:] Was your name August?
A. Yes but there was 2 or 3 besides me of the same name.
Council[:] The Habeas is by a different name[.]
Mr Roch. He was thought by every one there that he was his property[.]
Q. That he was Stapylton's property[?]
A. Yes
Q. You don't know the Boy?
A. No I don't know him.

Phillip [sic] Saver or Seaward[34] sworn[,] Examined by Mr Walker –
Q. You was Captain of the Vessel that had this man on board?
A. Yes Sir.
Q. Do you now the Defendant Stapylton?
A. Yes Sir[.]
Q. Do you know his Boy?
A. Yes Sir[.] [46]
Q. In the year [']68 did you know him?
A. No I did not know him till about 3 years ago[.]
Q. Where was that[?]
A. When [I] came out from New York.

---

[34] Ed. The words "or Seaward" are inserted above the text at this point. Since the name of the witness is given by the shorthand writer, he may have confused "Saver", or "Sawver", and "Seaward".

Q. You knew the Defendant then?
A. Yes Sir and before.
Q. You knew the Boy?
A. Yes[.]
Q. Is this the Boy he brought from New York?
A. Yes Sir[.] He came home with my Brother.
Q. How long have you known him?
A. Since last April was 3 years[.]
Q. Who was his Master?
A. Stapylton – he called him his Boy –

Mr Dunning Cross Examination -
Q. From your Name Sir I suppose you was the purchaser?
A. No Sir I was not[.]
Q. Was you the man that Commanded the ship at Gravesend from where the Boy was brought? [47]
A. He was put on board me at Gravesend.
Q. Pray Sir was it not on Board your ship this poor Boy was brought by these people Maloney and Armstrong?
A. He was brought on board by Coleman[.]
Q. For what purpose was he brought on board your ship?
A. To be sent to Jamaica[.]
Q. For what purpose was he to be sent there?
A. As a Servant[.]
Q. What was he to do when he got there[?]
A. Why! he was to be sold at Jamaica[.][35]

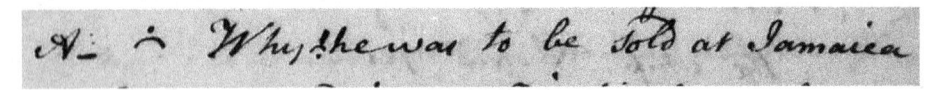

Illustration: The Gulp

Q. Did you find it any Difficulty to bring that out, because you Gulped[36] at it?
A. No Sir.
Q. You undertook to sell him then as a servant?
A. I gave a Bill of lading for the Negroe[.]

[35] Ed. There is an odd mark in the text at the beginning of the line: a circular line like the top half of a circle with a dot above it. It is clear from Dunning's next question that it indicates that the witness gulped at that point. It seems to be an eighteenth century emoticon or emoji.

[36] Ed. Dunning suggests that the witness gulped because he was forced to admit the truth. Dunning refers to the gulp again, below, page 124.

Q. Did you specifie the marks – like a bale of Goods? [48]
A. No I believe not[.]
Q. This Negroe you took a Bill of Lading for and you undertook to sell him at Jamaica – did you receive any money or pay any for him?
A. No I was to sell him[.]
Q. Did not the Mayor of Gravesend apply to you to see the Boy?
A. No Sir[.] It was only the Custom house officer[.]
Q. He wanted him to be carried on shore to the Mayor?
A. No Sir[.] He asked me if I had a boy on board the ship – I said ["]Yes["].
Q. Did you send him on shore?
A. When I got nigh to the town I sent him on shore[.]
Q. On what occasion?
A. By the Habeas. Q. Did nobody else apply to you for him to be brought on shore? [49]
A. Only by the Officer, and he asked if I had this Boy[.] He came to search the ship.
Q. Then did you look upon it that the Custom house officer came to measure him and gauge him; so then nobody applyed to you and you refused nobody[?]
A. I say no body applyed to me but Mrs Banks's servant[.]
Q. And you refused [to] deliver up the Boy, did he not tell you he had an Order from the Mayor?
A. No.
Q. Nor did he tell you he had an order from the Mayor of Gravesend?
A. No he never told me anything about it[.]
Q. [(]Shews a letter:[)] Is this your handwriting?
A. Yes Sir –
Q. Recollect yourself now in this Letter you assure Mrs Banks, you are perfectly innocent [50] of Mr Staplyton's intentions with regard to the Negroe?
A. I do not know what he did with him before he got on Board mee.
Mr Dunning[:] In your Letter you told her you were perfectly innocent of what Capt. Stapleton [sic] had an inclination to do with said Negroe[?]
Capt Saver[:] I knew he had a mind to sell him.
Q. But did you mean to say that when you wrote this Letter[?]
A. I sent the Boy on shore by the Habeas[.]
Q. But what did you mean by this: ["]I am perfectly innocent of what Captn[.] Stapleton had an inclination to do with the said Negroe["]?

Take another Gulp[37] and let us have another rise now – What was his inclination?
A. I told you he said it was to sell him.
Mr Dunning[:] From whence I should conclude you were not perfectly innocent; What did you mean she should understand by it? [51]
A. I did not understand, or mean any thing particular by it -

Miles Stapylton sworn[,] Examined by Mr Walker
Q. What are you?
A. The Defendant[']s brother.
Q. Do you remember the Boy[']s coming with him into England?
A. I came along with them into England.
Q. Who has he lived with ever since?
A. With my Brother except during the time of his Elopement.
Q. When was that?
A. Several times.
Q. At all other times, he lived with your brother?
A. Yes always.
Q. And always acknowledged being his servant?
A. Yes Sir.
Q. You know of his being taken care of when [52] ill in bed[?]
A. Yes[.]

Mr Dunning[:] very well –
Q. You say he always acknowledged being his servant?
A. Yes

Lord Mansfield[:] he means his slave in the capacity of his servant.

Mr Walker[:] You came from Santa Cruz?
A. Yes.
Q. Your brother does?
A. Yes[.]
Q. Was he born there?
A. No Sir but he has lived there all his time but was born in England.

---

[37] Ed. Dunning referred earlier to the witness gulping, above page 122, and here seems to taunt the witness who he has caught out in a contradiction. Captain Saver, or Seaward, in his letter to Mrs Banks had said he was unaware of Stapylton's intention, but has admitted in evidence now that he did.

Mr Dunning[:] To be sure according to their opinion[38] a man acquires a property to a man with a Black face by coming over with him, but when he is white he does not. [53]

Lord Mansfield[:] Mr Walker you are calling all them witnesses to a fact not disputed[.] it is agreed by the Boy and[39] nothing is said by the boy inconsistent if you cant[40] Make out a title to his being a slave[.]

Mr Walker[:] Wee [sic] can prove his being at great Expense on account of the Boy[41] and that he always acted as the Defendants servant[.]

W[illia]m Watson sworn.
Mr Walker Q. Do you know any of this Negroe Boy?
A. Yes Sir[.]
Q. Who did [he] belong to?
A. he belonged to Captain Robert Stapylton at the time I knew him[.]
Q. How do you know that[?]
A. I was acquainted with his brother Briant[42] at Chelsea Colledge some years[.]

Mr Dunning[:] What you said to him or he to [54] them is nothing to the purpose.

Watson[:] S[i]r I'll tell you the point how I know this to be Captain Stapylton's Boy if you please to let me tell you the truth[.]

Mr Dunning[:] he is going on with the Conversation between himself and Bryant Stapylton w[hi]ch is nothing to the purpose[.]

Watson[:] Sir I went and got a letter for the Boy to go into St George[']s Hospital where he was admitted there[.] Gen[era]l Hudson said to me ["]will you give it under your hand that you will take him away if he does well[".] after that I went to see him and heard this Black fellow say he belonged to Mr Stapylton[.]

---

[38] Ed. The words "according to their opinion" are inserted above the line.
[39] Ed. The words "by the Boy and" are inserted above the line.
[40] Ed. The last letter here looks like a smudged "t" but the word might be "can".
[41] Ed. The words "on account of the Boy" are inserted above the line.
[42] Ed. Bryant, ie Stapylton's brother.

Mr Dunning[:] All this would have happened if he had been your son[.]

Watson[:] My son a negro! What! A negroe[,] my son[!][43]

Mr Dunning[:] Don't be angry my friend[.] What is all this ferment about[?] it might have happened to you[.] They [55] never have admitted people into the Hospital in any other way[.]

Watson[:] I cant tell whether they do or not. I went to see him several times and I asked him how he did[.] he was then getting better[.]

Mr Walker[:] Q Who did he belong to?

A. He belonged to Captain Robert Stapylton[.] he always called him Master.

Q. How did he say he belonged to him?

A. As his property and that he brought [him] from abroad[.] when he run away and came to him again he always allowed him to be his Master[.]

Cross Examination

Mr Dunning[:] what have you heard him say when he went away?[44]

A. That he would not do so no more.

Q. Did you ever hear him say he was Stapylton[']s property?

A. Yes Sir I have[.] [56]

Mr Dunning[:] A Thousand times I will give you credit for[.]

Watson[:] I have heard him several times say he was Captain Stapylton[']s property[.]

Q. Do you venture to[45] swear you ever heard him say once that he was Capt[ain]n Stapylton[']s property[?]

A. I heard him say that he was his Master[.]

Q. But not the word property – you want to bring in some other Word?

A. No Sir -

Q. But you shall not bring in no other Word but the truth – Did you ever hear him say he was his property?

A. That he was his Master Sir[.] There was an Advertisement with a Reward in the newspaper[s][46] for him and he always came back to his Master[.]

---

[43] Ed. Dunning seems to have been trying to provoke the witness, and, if so, he got the reaction he was looking for.

[44] Ed. The words "when he went away" are inserted above the line.

[45] Ed. The words "enture to" are inserted above the line.

[46] Ed. The word "newspaper" is at end of a line and the end curves over, so may include an 's'.

James Moneybank called but did not appear[.]

Theobald Burk sworn – Examined by Walker [57]
Q. Look at that paper[.] is that your hand writing? (producing a Bill of Sale.)
A. No Sir.
Q. Is that Captain Smith[']s hand writing?
A. Give me leave to look at it again:
Q. Is that Captain Smith[']s hand writing?
A. I cant say – I cant swear to it[.]
Q. Did you ever see him write?
A. very often.
Q. Do you believe that to be his hand writing?
A. I believe it may be[.] I have often seen him write[.]
Q. Who was Robert Smith?
A. He was for some time a Merchant in Santa Cruz and for some time a Distiller[.] I was well acquainted with him and one of the Executors of his will.
Q. Do you know any thing of this black[?]
A. No Sir[.] [58]
Q. Is your name William Burk[?]
A. No Sir[.] I am not one of the Witnesses to this Paper[.]
Mr Dunning[:] but this Gentleman represents you as if you was -

Bryant Stapylton sworn[,] Examined by Walker[.]
Q. I will ask you one question with regard to his being advertised[.]

Lord Mansfield[:] does that vary it any more than his passing as his Slave[?]

Mr Walker[:] My Lord it is an acknowledgement he belonged to Defendant Stapylton when he came home pursuant to that Advertisement[.]

Q. When this black came home again what have you heard him say?
A. I have brought him home myself[.] I brought him home once[.]
Q. Did you bring him home more than once[?]
A. Only once[.] [59]
Q. Did you ever hear him object to his being your Brother[']s property?
A. No Sir[.] he never denyed it.
Q. He never denyed it?

A. No Sir.
Q. You never heard that black Boy object to his being your Brother[']s property?
A. No Sir.

Cross Examination
Mr Dunning[:] What is that to the purpose[?] -
Q. You are upon your Oath?
A. I am Sir.
Q. Do you mean to speak the truth[?]
A. I mean to say the truth and nothing else[.]
Q. Do you mean to say you heard the Boy call himself your Brother[']s property[?]
A. Where[?] -
Q. In your own house or any where else?
A. Yes Sir I do Sir[.] [60]
Q. A Word more with you Sir if you please – You have been in pursuit of him trying to get him pressed?
A. No Sir, I deny it -
Q. Was it you that put the Press Gang after him[?]
A. No Sir.
Q. Was it not you that sent the Press Gang after him Yesterday to stop his coming here?
A. No Sir[.] I don't know what you mean Sir[.]
Q. Was it not you that sent for those that are ready bye and bye to take him?
A. No Sir – No Sir -
Q. I am told it was you though you pretend to know nothing of it; I am told it was the old Soldier[.]
A. No[,] not one of us[.]
Q. And you know of no such people attending[?] [61]
A. No Sir I do not Sir[.]
Mr Dunning[:] I do not believe one Word you say Sir[.]
A. It is very indifferent to me Sir whether you do or not Sir.

Mr Dunning[:] Gentlemen I believe I need not give you much trouble, but if it had been necessary I should have submitted what my Ideas were upon the existence of this sort of Property. but since they have not proved the fact they endeavoured to prove, it makes it very unnecessary for me now to discuss the Law. There is no proof that he was ever the property of the Defendant, but the Witnesses have proved[,] particularly the last Witness, that the Boy called his brother Master; and he behaved to him as his Master; sometimes he was sent to an Hospital, and was taken care of as this man[']s [62] Servant[.] that is most certainly proved. But I believe it will not be contended, that it is competent in any Master, to convey his Servant into a Boat, to tye his leggs, and Gagg his Mouth there, and then convey him in that Boat from the water side at Chelsea to Gravesend, for the purpose of delivering him into the hands of the Captain (who has been examined upon the side of the defendants) with an express direction to conduct him to Jamaica, and there to sell him as a Slave. I believe it will not, nor has it yet been contended that his Master had a right so to do.

Lord Mansfield[:] The only point is, as to the property, which I shall leave to the Jury.

Mr Dunning[:] I don't in myself see, what the evidence is, upon which that Question can [63] be Construed.

Lord Mansfield[:] Yes there is evidence. I shall certainly leave it to them to find whether he was the Defendant's property or not?

Mr Dunning[:] then if my lord thinks there is evidence sufficient for the question, then I shall submit to you, what my Ideas are upon such evidence, reserving to myself an opportunity of discussing it more particularly and insisting that no such property can exist, which I will maintain in any place, and in any Court in this Kingdom;[47] reserving to myself a right to insist that our Laws admit of no such property.[48] though presuming for a moment there can be such property, Then Gentlemen there is before you no evidence that he was ever their property. I myself do not know, I never have heard any [64] conversation, much less heard or learnt that any man's Ideas ever went further in this Kingdom than is consistent with the names of Master and Servant; with a difference only in point of Duration; pending that du-

---

[47] Ed. The words "in this Kingdom" are inserted above the line.
[48] G#: NB. When Mr Dunning spoke these Words, he held in his hand G. Sharp's Book on *the illegality of Tolerating Slavery in England* (printed in 1769) having one Finger in the Book to hold open a particular part: and yet after so solemn a Declaration he appeared on the opposite side of the Question against James Somerset, the very next year. This is an abominable and insufferable practice of Lawyers to undertake causes diametrically opposite to their own declared opinions of Law and Common Justice!!! [Ed. The title of Sharp's book is in fact *A Representation of the Injustice and Dangerous Tendency of Tolerating Slavery...*]

ration upon no other or different right than any Master has over his Servant, and that which any one man may do to his Servant, another may do to their Servant; and that which they may do to their Servants, you or I may do to our servants;

But this kind of servitude under pretence of property, is said to be a Contract of a longer duration, than those which men term to be a Voluntary duration; I don't yet know what kind of property will admit of (and go to) this sort of treatment; I apprehend it will not, nor has it ever been insisted any Ordinary Master may lay hold of an Ordinary Servant, for the purposes disclosed here, and treat them in the manner this unhappy [65] Boy has been proved to have been treated. (I don't know nor believe the Master has been well advised in forcing him into a Boat, in tying his leggs with Ropes, in Gagging his Mouth to stop his Outcries, and conveying him to Gravesend; there putting him into the Care of the Captain who upon his cross examination told me, it was for the avowed purpose of selling him at Jamaica.) I say Gentlemen if they were not entitled to treat him in that manner, then it seems to me to be Material whether there exists that sort of property or not? but if not, I submit this clear result to you, that the Boy is born as free as any other man, and can never be otherwise than free, but by some Act of those, that have power over another, by Captivity in War, or Circumstances of that sort. xxxxxx![49]

Gentlemen[,] It appears by his own evidence that his Father was a free Negroe, that when his Father was dead, he lived with his Uncle, and after his Uncle[']s death, he was recommended into the service of one, and [66] then to another, and so on in 5 or 6 different places which I need not enumerate to you, then it appears he became acquainted with Stapylton: and the Gentlemen would have foisted upon me, If I had not been a little attentive about it, a paper which they would talk about, as if it conveyed some title; which they had acquired to the Boy; the subject in question; and you therefore as it is not in proof, will not think you have heard a Word about it, not knowing what it contains; & there is no proof that this Stapylton did by deed or paper, (or any other instrument) by which this party could acquire if it were acquirable, any such right to him. but upon the Contrary it is in proof, they did not in fact acquire any right to this Boy. his coming into England, being forced away from the Judge[']s Hair Dresser is proved. The

---

[49] Ed. These "x"s in the text appear to have been added by Sharp.

Boy himself proved it, that he came over with this man in the quality of a Servant, in whose Service it was competent to live if he thought fit, [68][50] but when he did not chuse to stay with him any longer, but talked of going into some other service, then the Defendant thought fit to create that conduct from whence arose the present prosecution;

Gentlemen[,] Is it to be contended or made a question of, that a Sailor by bringing this boy from New to Old England, (or from any other part of the World) his colour being black makes him more his property than if he was white[;] is it to be distinguishable only by Colour that such right is to exist? and with regard to Capacity that it creates property in the one not in the other, or does one tittle of evidence xxxx[51] make it stronger in one, than in the other. It would be very extraordin[ar]y, in this age upon his coming into this part of the World, in company with a man, who upon the single ground of coming here, with him, says you are my property; if that man was to be allowed such right.

It was tryed to be screwed out of the Witnesses [69][52] and the old Soldier was to prove the Boy had acknowledged himself to be a Slave and had said he belonged to him as his property[.] But upon the Cross Examination of their Witnesses, the Conversation held with the Boy imported no more, than this Boy's acknowledging himself to be his servant. but he never used the Word property or Slave. Nor can he be taken any otherwise, than as a person born of the freest parents any man in England can be got by; the Boy ever treated the defendant as his Master, the Master treated him as his Servant. Gentlemen[,] unless you have more regard to what belongs to you, and more feeling for your fellow creatures than to assent to such Ideas as this, supported upon such evidence as this, and upon the Contrary to hold a man free from punishment, and hold [70] no Guilt upon such Conduct, (to which you and I might have been liable had we been the Subject) you will acquit the Defendants, but I trust you will think it the Guilt of the most atrocious kind that can be attempted, and which has been attempted without any colour of Cause, much less proof of the Cause; under pretence of being their property, of which there is no evidence in my opinion, and I will venture to say, you will resent this Conduct, and protect this prosecutor, and not suffer any man in a free Country like this, to be sold and conveyed to the place where he would be

[50] Ed. The pagination in original MS misses out the number 67.
[51] Ed. Four "x"s in the text, apparently added by Sharp.
[52] Ed. The word "Witnesses" is repeated on the next page.

treated like a Horse, or a Dog, or be treated with more inhumanity, than would be applied to a Dog.

Lord Mansfield[:] Gentlemen of the Jury this is an Indictment brought by Thomas Lewis a Negroe against Robert Stapylton and [71] John Malony and Aaron Armstrong for taking him by force and putting him in a boat and then binding and Gagging him and conveying him on board a Ship in order to have him sold[.] the Consequence of it may be different in point of law in case he is or can be his property being here in England or if he is not and therefore one Question first for you to settle as I said before is whether he was the Defendant Stapylton[']s property as a Slave[.] if you are of that opinion I shall recommend if you think proper so to do to find a Special Verdict. I don[']t know whether it will be necessary for if you are of opinion he is not his property you will find the Defendant Guilty[.] There is no question of the ill treatment being proved, if free or a Slave and to be sure it is a very infavorable [sic] [72] Question and therefore he that claims a property in him must prove it Strongly and clearly in order to lay the foundation[.] with regard to this Cause the evidence that is given by the Boy is very material as to his condition from his infancy[.] The Boy says he was born upon the Coast of Africa that his father was what they call a free Negroe[.] When his father died he lived with his Uncle who put him on board a Danish ship and sent him to sea with a Captain who brought him to Santa Cruz and that captain bestowed him upon a Danish Nobleman[.] that Nobleman died and he lived with the Clerk who took him to Smith an English Merchant[.] Smith had him for some time, he went then on board the Defendant Stapylton[']s ship who asked him if he should like to go abroad and he did goe with [73] Stapylton from this Smith being with him[.] he was taken by a Spanish privateer and carried to St Augustine[']s then to Havannah[.] he lived some time with the Spanish Captain and then he went away from the Spanish Captain: Here you see he is taken by a Spanish Captain[.] Supposing he is a Slave he becomes the property of the Spaniard by Capture like other Goods. Supposing him a real Slave and trafficked for in the West Indies the property will be altered by Captured like a bale of Goods[.] When he went from the Captain he waited at a Tavern in Havannah[.] they paid him something[.] Stapylton coming there he made himself known to him and Stapylton said he belonged to him and he took him away and put him with Frazier a Wine Merchant who likewise allowed him something[.] He [74] says he then took him to New York and then back to Santa Cruz and then he lived with him a Year and half and then he went away to Pensacola[.] Smith died and he then lived with the Judge of the place then with the Judge[']s Hair Dresser and he went with him from New England to New York and what is a Material part of the Cause you see he has been with the Judge and with another man at Santa Cruz and afterwards he is with this Hair dresser: He says the Defendant Stapylton when he came to New York from Pensacola took him by force from the Hair Dresser[.] Now whatever the original right of the Defendant Stapylton might be upon the purchase of Smith if there was a purchase from Smith which they set up you see that is gone by [75] the Capture – there is no new Capture but he finds him with the Hair dresser and it is by an Act of force and Violence[,] the taking him from the Hair Dresser[.] He swears positively he took him from the Hair Dresser by force and carried him to Carolina, Jamaica[,] New York and then he brought him over to England. Upon the part of the Defendant there is no evidence of a Bill of Sale[,] no evidence to shew he bought him and no price mentioned[.] Then they prove that he was in the possession of the Defendant and that he Called him Master and the other calling him servant or negroe[.] The Boy owned himself that he was the Defendant['s] servant and as the Defendant[']s Brother said owned himself to be his property[.] [76][53] that is all Material evidence on both sides now upon this state of the Cause[.] If you find he was not the slave purchased with the money of the Defendant Stapylton you will find the Defendants Guilty – If you are of opinion he was his slave and property you will find a Special Verdict and that will leave it for a more solemn discussion[54] concerning the rights of such property here in England but as I said before if you find he is not the slave nor property of the Defendant Stapylton you will find the Defendants Guilty of this Indictment and it will be left to the Court to Judge of the punishment.

The Jury brought in their Verdict in these Words[:]

Wee don[']t find he was his property.[55] [77][56]

---

[53] Ed. Original MS page wrongly numbered 75.
[54] Ed. Lord Mansfield here indicates that if the jury were to find that Lewis was the property of Stapylton, he would refer the point of law to all the common law judges.
[55] G#: Remark*: These were probably the words of the Foreman of the Jury, but there was at the same time a general voice[.]
[56] Ed. Original MS page wrongly numbered 76.

Lord Mansfield[:] Then you will find he is Guilty.

The Jury then brought in their Verdict ["]Guilty]"][.][57]

Lord Mansfield To Mr Dunning[.] You will find more in the question then [sic] you see at present[.]

Mr Dunning[:] my Lord I shall never find any Ideas that could have gone farther than Master and Servant[.]

Lord Mansfield [:] It is no matter mooting it now but if you look into it there is more than by accident you are acquainted with[.] there are a great many opinions given upon it[.] I am aware of many of them but I know that Justice Forster[,] Lord Hardwick[e] and [78][58] Talbot had several discussions concerning the right of property in Negroes and one of them quotes a text of St Paul[59] which I don't Immediately think of that shows their being Christians don't vary the Case – Perhaps it is much better it never should be finally Discussed or Settled – I believe you will find them still slaves after they are Christened – if you will not find they are upon the footing of Contracted Servants in that opinion I am confident you will not[.]

Mr Dunning[:] it is a short opinion here it is my Lord[:]

Lord Mansfield[:] Gentlemen[,] I think you have done very right[.] I should have found the same Verdict[.]

– To Mr Dunning[:] I don't know what [79][60] the Consequence may be if they were to lose their property by accidentally bringing them into England[.]

Again to the Jury[:] I think you have done very right to find him not

---

[57] G#: *Remark: "Again a general voice among the Jury together..." [Ed. The bottom half of the following line is partly missing at the bottom of the folio but seems to contain two words in quotation marks. From Granville Sharp's report of the trial, page 147, they are identified as "No property!", "No property!" See also his introduction to his arguments drafted just before the trial came on, below, page 139.]

[58] Ed. Original MS page wrongly numbered 77.

[59] Ed. The passage usually cited is Ephesians 6.5, in the AV: "Servants, be obedient to them that are you masters...". Modern translations tend to replace "servants" with "slaves".

[60] Ed. Original MS page wrongly numbered 78.

the property for he was not the property and you have done the right – according to the evidence to find it so[.]

Mr Dunning made application then to Lord Mansfield that the prosecutor might be protected from being taken away by a Press Gang who were waiting in the Public Hall without the Court for that purpose at the Instance of the Defendant[.]

Lord Mansfield[:] If anybody dares to touch the Boy as he is going out of the Hall especially now as the Jury have found the Boy not the property of the Defendant tell the officer to take them into [80][61] Custody and bring them before me -

Mr Dunning[:] I have found the opinion here are my Lord.

Lord Mansfield[:] Well am I not right as to my opinion that their being Christians don't take away the right of property[?]

Mr Dunning[:] it does not my Lord[.]

Lord Mansfield[:] I was sure it did not – I hope it never will be finally discussed[,] For I would have all Masters think they were Free and all Negroes think they were not because then they would both behave better[.]

Finis

These proceedings were faithfully taken in short hand and transcribed by me William Blanchard[62] No 69 Fetter Lane[.]

---

[61] Ed. Original MS page wrongly numbered 79.
[62] Ed. William Isaac Blanchard. See Introduction, above, page 2.

Motions for Judgment

MS in New York Historical Society, Manuscript
Collections Relating to Slavery:
Granville Sharp collection, 1768-1803.

[1]

No. 2

The King & James [sic] Lewis
Ag.t
Stapylton & Other[sic]
An Acct. of the 1st & 2d
Motions for Judgement against
Stapylton

[2]

In the King's Bench On Monday June 17th 1771

Upon a Motion by Mr Impey in the Cause of the King against Stapleton[63] & others

My Lord I move that Defendants Stapleton Maloney & Armstrong may be called to receive Judgment.

Lord Mansfield – What is it about?

Mr Davenport – It is about the Black if your Lordship remembers[.]

---

[63] Ed. So spelled here.

The Defendants were called but did not appear[.]

Mr Impey – If your Lordship pleases I move that their default may be recorded and that their recognizances may be estreated.

Lord Mansfield – Ever since that Trial I have had a great Doubt in my mind, Whether [3] the Negro could prove his own Freedom by his own Evidence – When I come to state it more particularly, I will shew how it came about – for ever since the Trial I have had a Doubt about it[.]

Mr Dunning - I don't believe it will come at all before your Lordship[,] for the people do not appear[.]

Lord Mansfield – Then I am glad I mentioned it. He was led on by degrees to give a History that came at last to prove that by which the Jury found him free[.]

I speak from Memory what occurred to me a very few Minutes after the Trial. He was led into the Evidence improperly – at first I started at it but the Council did not make the objection to his giving such Evidence [4] of his own Freedom which came at last to be the only Fact to prove him Free.

There was no manner of Doubt of his having had Wages – That was proved clearly[.] He was taken in the last War and the Capture I thought changed the property[.] The Capture was proved and that the Ship was carried into Port and there was a long Account given of himself when he went to Jamaica and the other Places – I remember I left it to the Jury to find whether he was a Slave or Free and in Case he had been found by them to be a Slave the question would have come properly before the Court. (upon the Special Verdict) as to the Nature of the Prosecution and the Consequences of it and the Jury with that Direction as I gave – with regard to the Capture [5] found him Free.

Afterwards I had a Doubt in my Mind (and as it may be a General Case I am very glad to have this opportunity of mentioning it) whether a Slave may be a Witness to prove himself Free.

Mr Dunning – Supposing the General Question upon the Point of Law to [do] so But in Point of Fact there was no Evidence before the Court that he was the Defendants Property which was the Ground upon which he acted – if he had been any other Person's Slave he was entitled to be protected the same as if he was free.

Lord Mansfield – you say right I looked afterword to the Pleadings and I find they are very [6] particular; I am Glad of an Opportunity of mentioning it as I have a great Doubt in my own mind whether he can be sufficient Evidence of his own Freedom; in your Point it will come out the same; if he was any other Man's property. The Point I left to the Jury was that the Capture made and End of the property of the Defendant in this Cause: and that he could not be there Slave afterwards by seizing him & carrying him to Jamaica, Carolina and elsewhere.

That was proved all by himself and nobody else that was with him at any of those Places.

Mr Wallace[64] – I suppose it is made up if they do not appear.

Mr Doudall – no it is not made up[.] we want them to receive judgement: [7]

Wednesday Evening at almost 10 o'clock.

Mr Dunning made another Motion that Defendants Stapleton and others might be called to receive Judgment there having been an improper Notice given them upon which they were not obliged to attend

It appears that only one answers. Stapleton does appear, they have called the other two who do not appear. I move your Lordship that Stapleton may receive Judgement and that the Recognizances of the other two may be estreated.

Mr Justice Aston – The Judgement must be respited for the other that appears as we have had no report of the cause.

---

[64] Ed. James Wallace (bap. 1729, d 1783), solicitor general, 1778, attorney general, 1780, G M Ditchfield, 'Wallace, James (bap 1729, d 1783)', ODNB, 2004 [http://www.oxforddnb.com/view/article/63083], accessed 10 March 2015.

Granville Sharp's Argument

MS in New York Historical Society, Manuscript
Collections Relating to Slavery:
Granville Sharp collection, 1768-1803.

[1]

THE KING
against
Stapleton & Ors

This Cause was Tried in the Court of King's Bench at Westminster before Lord Mansfield on Wednesday the 20th of February 1771 and the following Arguments (except of few additions and alterations since made) was drawn up in haste at a Coffeehouse near the Hall just before the Trial came on, but there was no opportunity to make use of it, because the particular circumstances of the case were such, that there was no necessity to introduce the general Question concerning property in Slaves which indeed the Court seemed desirous to avoid; for the Lord Chief Justice himself declared in Court after the Trial, that the general Question was a point which never had, and he hoped never would, be determined:- That he would have all Masters believe their Negroes free; and the Negroes think themselves Slaves for the sake of good behaviour on both sides. I cannot assert that these were the very Words spoken by his Lordship, but only that they were to this effect.

As the general Question was avoided, the jury had it not in their power to find a verdict so full and conclusive, for the Honour and Dignity of [2] the Human Species, as could have been wished, or indeed as the honest Jurymen themselves really seemed to intend; nevertheless they unanimously determined without going out that the Defendant Stapleton had no property in the Plaintiff, and they as readily found the Defendant Guilty of the Indictment.

The King agt. Stapleton and others
(for attempting forcibly to carry away Thomas Lewis
a Negro Servant under pretence of private property)

(an argument concerning property in Slaves)

Mr Stapleton[']s defence cannot be grounded on any other point than the Plea of Private Property, and the necessary obligation of the Courts of Law to secure to every Man his own.

Now the Argument against this Plea will lye in a very small compass, when couched in a few approved Maxims of the Common Law. If a Negroe is considered as property in this Country, he falls under the head of Chattels, and must be so esteemed accordingly, I mean so far as the Masters right ought to be considered. [3]

Now the Chattel is *"res Estimabilis"* a thing to be valued, a thing merely of a pecuniary consideration: and the Slaveholder accordingly rates his supposed property in a Man at a base Price not more upon an average than the Value of a good Horse Viz. £30 £40 or £50 to the disgrace of human Nature; whereas on the other hand the Negroe has certainly a superior Right and Title to his own Person, a claim of natural property in himself, which is inestimable, far above all pecuniary consideration; surely his Liberty to him is inestimable; at least the English Law presumes that it is so *"Libertas estres inestimabilis"* Jenk Cent 52[65] Now let the Idea of a Chattel even at the highest price it will bear, be weighed and compared with the subject of the last mentioned Maxim, and let Justice hold the Seale, shall we doubt whether the Estimable or inestimable is to be preferred?

"The Law regards the Person above his Possessions – Life and Liberty most; Freehold and Inheritance above Chattels &c.["] so that Chattels we find are but of a very inferior consideration being ranked only in the Third Degree.

---

[65] Ed. "Liberty is inestimable [in value]": Jenkins' *Eight Centuries of Reports, English Exchequer [1220-1623]*, Jenk 52, 145 ER 39.

"Law favoureth Life, Liberty, and Dower" and cannot therefore give [4] preference to the Masters more mercenary claim of Property without a manifest contradiction to itself and "the Law abhors Falsehood, Variance, contrariety &c" "*Lex angliæ non patitur absurdum.*" 9 Co. 22. "*Lex rejicit pugnantia incongrua.*" Jenkins Cent 140.133.176.[66]

It is true indeed that the Law in this Case suffers a wrong by the Masters losing his right and Property, but if we consider that the admitting such a property would be a want of mercy in the Law, any even an act of Cruelty (which the Law abhors) towards those Persons who have a superior because a natural Interest in the determination of this Question it must appear to demonstration [sic] that the Law doth no wrong when it rejects the lesser claim of property and therefore howsoever the imaginary Proprietor may think himself aggrieved yet the Law is vindicated herein when we consider that every claim of property is absolutely unjust in itself and must necessarily be set aside through the mercy of the law if it interfere or is inconsistent with that natural and equitable claim to personal Security which the Law of this Kingdom hath always favoured for "the Law on England is a law of mercy" "*Lex Angliæ est Lex misericordiæ*" 2 Jno. 315 [5] so that each Slaveholder must still be obliged to allow that the Law (even in this unavoidable Decision against himself) doth injury to no Man. "*Lex nemine operatur iniquum nemini facit injuriam.*" Let the Slaveholder remember also that his being thus deprived of his imaginary property cannot be considered otherwise (let him make the moot of it) than merely as a private Loss, whereas if such unnatural right be admitted without the consideration of the superior personal right of the Negroe a worse Vassalage than the Ancient Villenage would in time be introduced into this free Christian Country by which the publick would be materially injured as well in honour as in Morals and National Safety, therefore the Law will rather endure a particular mischief (the loss of private Property) than a general in convenience. "*Lex citius tollerare vult privatum Damnum quam Publicum malum*" Co. Lit. 152.

Thus stands the common Law with respect to the point in question, and, I apprehend, that it is not in the least altered by Statute Law, and unless the Defendants['] Council can prove that is altered, [6] we may safely conclude with the following Maxim "that whatever was at com-

---

[66] Ed. Jenk Cent 133: "*Lex rejicit superflua, pugnantia, incorgrua*" (Law rejects superfluous, contradictory and incongruous things).

mon law and is not taken away by Statute, remaineth still" Co. Lit. 115.

The learned judge before whom this Cause will come, is said to have given an Opinion, formerly, that Negroe Slaves continue such even when brought to England; or something to that effect. But I have too high an Opinion of his Lordships Justice and good sense to conceive that he will still persist in that Sentiment, if the case is fairly stated and compared with the above mentioned established Maxims: neither will the Council for the Defendant venture to contradict these Maxims because such behaviour would necessarily draw upon them that just censure and contempt which the learned author of the Doctor and Student expresses in his 8th Chapter against all lawyers, without exception to dignity that presume to contradict approved Maxims. "The fourth Ground of the Law of England standeth in divers Principles that be called Maxims the which have always been taken for Law (*semper habita et tenta sunt pro lege*)[67] in this Realm, so that it is not lawfull for any that is learned to deny them; for every one of these Maxims is sufficient Authority to himself." Thus for the Translater: but we may gather from the Words of the excellent Author himself that Men who deny these Maxims are no longer worthy to be talked with; for he adds "*intanto quod cum negantibus ea (Vizt. maxima) non est ulterius arguendum,*[68] *Quantum fundamentum Legis Angliæ stat in diversis principiis quæ a peritis Legis Angliæ Maxima, quæ semper habita et*[69] *tenta sunt pro lege in hac [?] Regno Angliæ quibus non est licitum alicui legis perito contradicere quia unum quodque maximoram illorum sibi ipsi fides in tanto quod cum negantibus ea non est ulterius arguendum.*"

A more modern, but not less respectable Author, has furnished us with a Maxim nearly to the same effect Vizt. ["]Those that let go the Law of

---

[67] Ed. [Christopher Saint Germain] *Doctor and Student* (First edition, 1518; 17th edition, London, 1787), Introduction, Chapter 8, p 26; *Doctor and Student* (T F T Plucknett and J L Barton, eds) (1974) 91 Seld Soc p 57.

[68] Ed. (1974) 91 Seld Soc p 59: "to such an extent that it is fruitless to argue with those who deny them." The Latin phrase in 91 Seld Soc p 58 is in square brackets and does not contain the words "(Vizt. maxima)". Sharp then to goes back to the beginning of Chapter 8 of *Doctor and Student* ("the fourth Ground of the Law of England...") to quote what follows from this point, ending with the same phrase he just quoted.

[69] Ed. The word in the MS appears to be "and" rather than "et", but presumably this was a slip.

the Land deservedly incur from thence a perpetual Stain of Infamy"
"*Legem terræ amittentes perpetuam infamiæ notam inde merito incurrunt*".
Sr. Ed. Cook. 3.Inst.221.

(Copy)

Granville Sharp's Remarks on the Case

MS in New York Historical Society,
Manuscript Collections Relating to Slavery:
Granville Sharp Collection, 1768–1803.

[i]

A Report of the Case
of Lewis (a Negro) ag[ains]t Stapylton,
With remarks by G. Sharp.

Memorandum

These Remarks are merely intended to prevent this Trial from being quoted as a precedent, and not to injure the character of the Judge; and therefore, as these remarks are only in the hands of the Council for James Somerset, the Author requests that they may not be mentioned or shown to any person, not immediately concerned in this clause, unless the same reason should and make it absolutely necessary: for the Severity of the Censures, herein contained, could not be avoided when the facts of such a nature were mentioned; and therefore, as the point in question is a publick cause, the Author would be extremely sorry that there should be the least appearance of private resentment by making these remarks more public than is absolutely necessary for the purpose intended[.]

[1]

Report of the Case of Lewis against Stapylton

King's Bench 20th February 1771

Before Lord Mansfield

The King on the Prosecution of Thomas Lewis a Negroe against Robert Stapylton, John Maloney And Aaron Armstrong	Plaintiff Defendants

The case was stated in the Indictment to the following Effect.

> "That the Defendants seized and intended to transport Thomas Lewis, the Prosecutor, abroad to the Island of Jamaica, and to sell and dispose of him there.
>
> That on the 2d of July at Chelsea in Middlesex they with Force and Arms in and upon the said Prosecutor, did make an Assault, and seize him and drag him, and put him into a Boat on the River Thames, and there gagged his Mouth, and without his Will and consent, put him in Prison [2] (on Ship Board) for 2 or 3 Days."

This Indictment was found by the Grand Jury of Middlesex (without the least doubt or demurrer either on Account of the Plaintiff's Complexion or any Idea of private property) and was removed by Certiorari into the Court of King's Bench. When the Trial came on, Maloney and Armstrong, did not appear, but only Stapylton the Master.

Towards the beginning of the Trial Ld. M_l_d[70] declared "I shall presume him free unless they prove the contrary": and, on summing up

---

[70] Ed. Lord Mansfield. Sharp uses this abbreviation, or thinly disguised reference to the judge, in what follows, although he has stated the name at the beginning of the report.

the Evidence, his Lordship allowed that, "upon the part of the Defendant, there is no Evidence of a Bill of Sale; No evidence to shew he bought him etc. - so that, it is manifest, they did not prove the contrary." The Charge in the Indictment was clearly proved by several Witnesses; and Ld M_l_d observed in his Charge to the Jury - "There is [3] no Question of the ill treatment being proved, if free or a Slave; and to be sure it is a very unfavourable Question and therefore he that claims property in him must prove it strongly, and clearly, in order to lay the in order to lay the Foundation. With regard to this Cause the Evidence that is given by the Boy is very material, as to his Condition from his Infancy", &c.

The Verdict of the Jury consisted of 2 Parts - viz. 1st:– "We don't find he was his Property" (and the general Voice among the Jury was "no property" -"no property") Thus (said Ld M_l_d) "You will find he is guilty". Upon which the Jury brought in the 2d part of their Verdict, "Guilty". Ld M_l_d, afterwards, addressed himself to the Jury, saying, "Gentlemen, you have done very right; I should have found the same Verdict". And, soon after, he said again; "I think you have done very right to find him not [4] the property, for he was not the property and you have done the right, according to the Evidence, to find it so."

From the Proceedings, therefore, of this Day, every person present must necessarily conclude that the poor Negroe had gained a Clear and decisive Determination in his favour. But in the following Term on Monday 17th of June 1771 when Mr Impey moved for Judgement, Ld M_l_d said; "Ever since that Trial, I have had a great Doubt in my Mind, whether the Negro could prove his own Freedom by his own Evidence."

This he repeated (or nearly to the same Effect) several times, but assigned no Grounds for his Doubt.

On the Wednesday Evening following, (19th June about 10 o'Clock) Mr Dunning, appearing, moved once more for Judgment against Stapylton and that the Recognizances of the other two, who did [5] not appear, might be estreated: but Ld M_L_d not being in Court, Judge Aston said; "The Judgment must be respited for the other that appears, as we have had no report of the Cause."

Michaelmas Term 1771

On the last Day of Michaelmas Term (28th November. 1771) Mr Dunning moved Ld M_l_d, that Stapylton might be called to receive the Judgment of the Court; to which his Lordship replied:

"I am surprised, that Stapylton was brought up! I did not expect they would bring him up again! I was in great doubt, and so were my Brother Judges, and many of the Council, whether the Black could be a proper witness of his Freedom, he being the only Witness; and I wish any Body could satisfy me of that Doubt. But I did not think they would have brought him [6] up; and I should advise the Prosecution not to bring him up, as she has got the Black in her Possession."

Then the Recognizance was ordered to be respited till further Orders.

Remarks

Now, though Ld M_l_d declared, that he would presume the Boy free, unless they proved the Contrary, – yet, it is plain, his Lordship was willing to presume, likewise, that the Idea of the Master's property in the Boy was sufficient to justify such a violent outrage, if it could have been proved; otherwise, the question and Examination, on that point, had been unnecessary.

The indictment was for a violent Assault, Gagging, False Imprisonment &c –; [7] against which outrages, there are many clear and positive Statutes, besides the Common Law and Customs of the Land.

These Laws and Customs ought therefore to have been obeyed, unless Ld M_l_d could have shewn, that there is any exceptions, express or implied, in any of these Laws, whereby Men may, with impunity, assault imprison and export those unfortunate persons, whom they are pleased to call their property.

But, if no such exceptions can be produced, the plea of private property is nugatory, and never ought to be admitted, or even named, in an English Court, by way of Justification for the like Outrages.

Nevertheless Ld M_l_d, without alleging any such exceptions, has absolutely refused to give Judgment on a clear verdict, which was [8] 3 times publickly approved by himself!

He seems to think the bare mention of "A Doubt in his mind" - a sufficient excuse, without assigning any, the least, probable Grounds to justify an Arrest of Judgment. A Practice this, which must render all Trials at Law useless and trifling; and must consequently reduce and annihilate the practice Gentlemen, who profess the Law; because Men will be obliged to seek some other means of settling their differences, when the uncertainty of Determination (already too great) is increased: for every reasonable person will carefull[y] shun the Expense of a Contest at Law when the issue of it depends, merely, on the Will and pleasure of one Man.

Nay, His Lordships Behaviour would not have been justifiable, in the present Case, even if he could have produced any such legal exceptions [9] to the general Laws of Protection, or even an Act of Parliament, made expressly for the purpose of holding such unnatural kind of property in this Kingdom; for, as the supposed property was not proved by the Defendants, the Negroes own Evidence, about his own freedom, stood unimpeached, and ought, without a Doubt, to have been admitted; because, it is, and ever has been, the constant practice of the Courts of Law to allow, even to a Felon, the Benefit of his own Evidence in his own Cause.[71]

For, though a Malefactor is already Indicted, by one Jury, upon a sufficient Evidence, yet, he may plead "not Guilty"; and to the Court must of Course presume, that he is innocent, and the 2d. Jury must acquit him accordingly, unless the contrary is clearly proved. What [10] room, then, could there be for "a Doubt" in the Case of this innocent Negroe with respect to "his own Evidence" in behalf of his own Liberty! For his plea of Freedom ought, certainly, to be much more favoured in Law, than the "not Guilty" of a Malefactor, especially, as there are no Laws in this Kingdom to justify so notorious an Outrage even if the property had been clearly ascertained.

The boy, therefore, had, undoubtedly, a right to a Determination in his favour; and, he more especially, as the Pretenders to property in his Person really failed in their Proofs: for, under the like Circumstances, he must have been entitled to a Judgement in his favour, even in the most tyrannical Court of the West Indies.

---

[71] Ed. This was not quite the case. Before the Criminal Evidence Act 1898 there was no general right of a defendant in a criminal trial to give evidence in his or her own defence, although certain statutes gave such a right.

If the Conduct of Ld_M_l_d in this Case should be alleged as a precedent [11] for such proceedings and opinions for the future, I must be obliged to protest against it, not only is being without the least foundation, either in Reason, Equity or Law; but, also, as being absolutely, contrary to many clear & positive Laws, wherein there are no exceptions whatever, that can, in any way, be [unclear] to justify such a doubt; &, consequently, that the refusal of Judgment, in this Case, is so far from being a proper precedent, that it ought to be esteemed an open Contempt of the Legislature, as well as a notorious Breach and perversion of the Laws.

I am the more solicitous to protest against this precedent, because I had the Mortification to hear the same Judge, upon the same Trial, quote some precedents of his own making, which are equally contradictory to the Spirit and meaning of the English Laws.[12]

"I have granted" (said he) "several Writs of Habeas Corpus upon Affidavits of Masters deducing Sale and property of their Negroes upon being prest.[72] I have granted Habeas Corpus's to deliver them to their Masters."[73]

Now the intention of the Writ of Habeas Corpus is, certainly, to relieve from false Imprisonment; and not to deliver up a poor wretch, against his Will, into the Hands of a Tyrannical Master, who rates him merely as a Chattel, or pecuniary property, and not as a Man.

There are no Laws, indeed, to justify Pressing,[74] as it is commonly

---

[72] Ed. Mansfield's exact words are "upon being prest I have granted Habeas Corpus's to deliver them to their Masters", above, page 117. Sharp here assumes that "prest" refers to the alleged slaves, which accords with Dunning's allegation, although as Mansfield pointed out, it was not in the indictment, above, page 105 and n 73, below.

[73] Ed. It is stated in the Proceedings that attempts were made on several occasions to impress Lewis and that the day before he had been "seized on and impressed" by the defendants or those acting on their behalf, page 105, in an attempt to prevent his giving evidence. This had only been foiled by the habeas corpus. The Recruiting Act 1756 (29 Geo II, c 4) was restricted to men who did not 'follow or exercise any lawful calling or employment or have not some other lawful and sufficient support'. See Kevin Costello, "Habeas Corpus and Impressment, 1700–1756" (2008) 29:2 *Journal of Legal History* 215–251.

[74] Ed. Sharp also opposed the practice of impressment as a form akin to slavery. The Gloucestershire Archives, Granville Sharp Papers, contains an MS (GA D.3549

practised, &, therefore, the Writ of Habeas Corpus is, certainly, a very proper Relief from that illegal oppression: so far, then, the precedent of Ld M_l_d in granting the Writs is good, and may, certainly, be esteemed a clear [13] acknowledgement from his Lordship of the illegality of pressing. But, if it should appear, that the said Negroes (though pressed) preferred the publick Service to a State of abject Slavery under a private person (which is more than probable,) then, it must be allowed, that the Writ of Habeas Corpus, contrary to its known use and design, was rendered the instrument of oppression, and ought so to be esteemed, rather than the Press Warrant: which latter is only allowed & submitted to in Consideration of a supposed exigency of Public Affairs; and therefore, the mere pecuniary private interest of a 3d. Person, not personally injured, is not to be set in Competition with the publick necessity; especially, if the person pressed has years of discretion to judge for himself, and is desirous to continue in the Public Service: because, no private Interest, that is merely pecuniary [14] ought to be preferred to the Public Good.

The Judge, therefore, who grants a Writ of Habeas Corpus to force a Man, against his Will, from the King's Service is manifestly guilty of a threefold Injury.

1st. He injures the King & and the Publick by depriving them of a usefull Sailor (for the Negroe must be supposed Capable of the publick Service, otherwise he would not have been pressed; (and, indeed, it is well known, that Negroes, in general, turnout able & handy Sailors, when a little inured to the Service) -

2dly – He cruelly injures the very person, whom this Writ of Liberty ought to favour, (the poor Negro himself,) by dragging him from the King's Service (in which he was content) in order to deliver him up, against his will, into the Hands of a cruel private Tyrant.

3dly – He notoriously injures the Laws & Customs [15] of this Kingdom, by perverting a constitutional Writ to a purpose entirely opposite to its original use, meaning, & intention! For what can be more oppo-

13/6/4) of the pamphlet Granville Sharp, *The Sailors Advocate*, 1727–8; republished as *The Sailors Advocate: first printed in 1727–8: to which is now prefixed, some strictures, drawn from the statutes and records, relating to the pretended right of taking away men by force, under the name of pressing seamen*, London, Printed for B White ... and E and C Dilly, 1777.

site to the meaning and use of the Writ of Habeas Corpus, (which was certainly intended as a Relief from all oppression, and false imprisonment) than to use the same as an Instrument for delivering Men into the most absolute Slavery?!!!

If such a Latitude in the interpretation and use of Laws be allowed, what Salutary Statute may not be perverted to the very worst of purposes?

My Indignation, however, is merely against the practices and Opinions here mentioned, & not against the promoter of them; wherefore, I hope, these Remarks will never [16] be produced, unless there should be an absolute necessity, for the honour and Vindication of the Law: for I really wish for the Amendment, rather than the punishment or Shame, of those who do wrong; and so far from having any personal resentment, in the present Case, that, if the Gentlemen whose Conduct I have now been obliged to censure, should even be injured in any particular point wherein I might happen to have it in my power to vindicate him, I sincerely profess, that I should be is anxious to serve him, for the sake of strict Justice, as I am now anxious to prevent the oppression of the poor helpless Men, in whose vindication these Remarks were drawn up.

Granville Sharp

Somerset v Stuart

First Hearing in the Court of King's Bench, 7 February 1772[75]

Arguments of Serjeants Davy[76] and Glynn[77]

Court: Lord Mansfield CJKB
Mr Justice Willes[78]
Mr Justice Ashurst[79]

MS in New York Historical Society,
Manuscript Collections Relating to Slavery:
Granville Sharp Collection, 1768–1803.

---

[75] Ed. The report is of the earlier first hearing which is not reported in Lofft: *Somerset v Stewart* (1772) Lofft 1, 98 ER 499. The MS is undated but the date given here is that given by Shyllon. See Introduction, page 4.

[76] Ed. J H Baker, 'Davy, William (d 1780)', ODNB, 2004 [http://www.oxforddnb.com/view/article/7320], accessed 22 February 2015.

[77] Ed. Peter D G Thomas, 'Glynn, John (bap 1722, d 1779)', ODNB, 2004; online edn, October 2006 [http://www.oxforddnb.com/view/article/10841], accessed 27 February 2015.

[78] Ed. Matthew Kilburn, 'Willes, Edward (bap 1723, d 1787)', ODNB, 2004; online edn, January 2008, [http://www.oxforddnb.com/view/article/63079], accessed 11 February 2015; Foss, *Judges of England*, 8.401.

[79] Ed. [sic] Douglas Hay, 'Ashhurst, Sir William Henry (1725–1807)', ODNB, 2004; online edn, January 2008 [http://www.oxforddnb.com/view/article/784], accessed 21 February 2015.

[*ii*]

[Handwritten note on inside cover:]

"E[x] libris Granville Sharp"

with a bookplate of
James Chaffin

[*iii*]

[Handwritten note on first (recto) page:]

> This celebrated case which was brought forward by Granville Sharp first made him known to the public, and is always granted as deciding that a Slave becomes free on reaching English ground.
> The negro was, during a fit of sickness in London, turned off by his master to perish, but he claimed him again as his property, when he had been restored to health by the benevolence of Mr Sharp and others. The law, however, rescued Sommersett from the power of Charles Stuart, and finally settled the question.

[Pasted in under the note is a cutting of an extract from a printed auction catalogue or advertisement for sale of the MS:]

> "MANUSCRIPT- A most interesting Manuscript, containing the Report of the Proceedings in Court, with Documents, in the Affair of James Summersett [*sic*], the negro, whose wrongs being made known to Mr Granville Sharp, that Gentleman warmly espoused his Cause and obtained a legal dictum declaring Slavery to be illegal in this Country, 4to, bds, uncut,
>
> "'E Libris Granville Sharp' is written inside the volume; an inscription which adds considerable interest, as there is every reason to believe that the report was taken in Court for him."

[1]

Upon the Motion of Mr Serjeant Davy
The Court ordered the Return to the Habeas
Corpus to be read in Court – which was
accordingly read – as follows -

I John Knowles Commander of the Vessel called the *Ann and Mary* in the Writ hereunto annexed Do most humbly certify and Return to our present most Serene Sovereign Lord the King That at the time hereinafter mentioned of bringing the said James Summersett [sic] from Africa and long before there were and from thence hitherto there have been and still are great Numbers of Negro Slaves in Africa and that during all the time aforesaid there has been and still is a Trade carried on by His Majesties Subjects from Africa to His Majesty's Colonies or Plantations of Virginia and Jamaica in [2] America and other Colonies and Plantations belonging to His Majesty in America for the necessary supplying of the aforesaid Colonies and Plantations with Negro Slaves and that Negro Slaves brought in the Course of the said Trade from Africa to Virginia and Jamaica aforesaid and the said other Colonies and Plantations in America by the Laws of Virginia and Jamaica aforesaid and the said other Colonies and Plantations in America during all the time aforesaid have been and are saleable and sold as Goods and Chattels and upon the Sale thereof have become and been and are the Slaves and property of the purchasers thereof and have been and are Saleable and sold by the proprietors thereof as Goods and Chattels.

And I do further Certify and return to Our said Lord the King that James Summersett in the said Writ hereunto annexed named is a Negro and a Native of Africa and that the said James Summersett [3] long before the coming of the said Writ to me to wit on the 10th day of March in the Year of our Lord 1749 was a Negro Slave in Africa aforesaid and afterwards to wit on the same day and year last aforesaid being such Negro Slave was brought in the Course of the said Trade as a Negro Slave from Africa aforesaid to Virginia aforesaid to be there sold.

And afterwards to wit on the first Day of August in the Year last aforesaid the said James Summersett being and continuing such Negro Slave was sold in Virginia aforesaid to one Charles Stuart Esq. who then was an Inhabitant of Virginia aforesaid.

And that the said James Summersett thereupon then and there became and was the Negro Slave and property of the said Charles Stuart and hath not at any time since been Manumitted, Enfranchised, Set free or Discharged.

And that the said James Summersett so being the Negro Slave and the [4] property of him the said Charles Stuart. And the said Charles Stuart having occasion to transact certain Affairs and business of him the said Charles Stuart in this Kingdom he the said Charles Stuart before the coming of the said Writ to me to wit on the first Day of October in the Year of Our Lord 1769 departed from America aforesaid on a Voyage for this Kingdom for the purpose of transacting his aforesaid Affairs and Business and with an Intent to return to America as soon as the said Affairs and Business of him the said Charles Stuart in this Kingdom should be transacted and afterwards to wit on the 10th Day of November in the same year arrived in this Kingdom to wit at London that is to say in the Parish of St Mary le Bon in the Ward of Cheap.

And that the said Charles Stuart brought the said James Summersett his Negro Slave and property along with him [5] in the said Voyage from America aforesaid to this Kingdom as the Negro Slave & property of him the said Charles Stuart to attend and Serve him the said Charles Stuart during his Stay and abiding in this Kingdom on the occasion aforesaid and with the intent to carry the said James Summersett back again into America with him the said Charles Stuart when the said Affairs and Business of the said Charles Stuart should be transacted which said Affairs and Business of the said Charles Stuart are not yet transacted -

And the intention of the said Charles Stuart to return to America as aforesaid hitherto hath continued and still continues.

And I do further certify and return to Our said Lord the King that the said James Summersett did accordingly attendance serve the said Charles Stuart in this Kingdom from the time of his said Arrival until the said James Summersett his departing [6] and absenting himself from the Service of the said Charles Stuart hereinaftermentioned to wit at London aforesaid in the Parish and Ward aforesaid and that before the coming of this Writ to me to wit on the first Day of October in the Year of Our Lord 1771 at London aforesaid to Wit in the Parish and

Ward aforesaid the said James Summersett without the Consent and against the Will of the said Charles Stuart and without any lawfull Authority whatsoever departed and absented himself from the Service of the said Charles Stuart and absolutely refused to return into the Service of the said Charles Stuart and serve the said Charles Stuart during his Stay and abiding in this Kingdom on the occasion aforesaid. Whereupon the said Charles Stuart afterwards and before the coming of this Writ to me to wit on the 26th Day of November in the Year of Our Lord 1771 on board the said Vessel called the Ann and Mary then and [7] still lying in the River of Thames to wit at London aforesaid in the Parish and Ward aforesaid and then and still bound upon a Voyage for Jamaica aforesaid did deliver the said James Summersett unto me who then was and yet is Master and Commander of the said Vessel to be by me safely and securely kept and Carried and Conveyed in the said Vessel in the said Voyage to Jamaica aforesaid to be there sold as the Slave and Property of the said Charles Stuart.

And that I did thereupon then and there to wit at London aforesaid in the Parish and Ward aforesaid receive and take and have ever since kept and detained the said James Summersett in my Care and Custody to be carried by me in the said Voyage to Jamaica aforesaid for the purpose aforesaid and this is the cause of my taking and detaining [8] the said James Summersett and whose Body I have now ready as by the said Writt I am Commanded.

Mr Serjeant Davy – My Lord Mr Wallace will shew your Lordship why they have penned the Return in that manner and by what right it is they claim a right to this Man as their property.

Lord Chief Justice – You must make your objections to the return to be sure as they put it upon property in the return – it seems accurately drawn.

Mr Serjeant Davy - My Lord this is as great a Question and perhaps a Question of as much Consequence as can come before this or any Court of Justice. And it is a true genuine Question of Liberty in which no party is concerned – about which there can be no political disputes and which I may be at Liberty (without the possibility of incurring any sort of resentment from any Sett of Men) [9] to discourse as I shall do of my own native Sentiments of the Subjects improved if they have been improved but they have not been altered by any thing I have been able to read or hear upon the Subject since that time allotted me to speak to it – I should have been glad had it been suitable to general Convenience to have had an opportunity of considering it in the Vacation after the Circuit to argue it in the next Term – because I know there have been Writers upon this Subject – General Writers of Law lately – some of which I have a little averted to but which I have not been able to search or look into so minutely and particularly within the time I have had as I could have wished – I had some reference to the Museum and enquiring for a Book there which has been [10] searched for diligently but there that Book cannot be found -

The proposition I shall endeavour to maintain before your Lordship upon this occasion is, that no Man at this Day is, or can be a Slave in England.[80] When I have troubled your Lordship with what I have to urge upon that Head – I shall consider the Nature and Ground of the present dispute in behalf of this Man who is claimed by Mr Stuart as I consider this as his Affair and consider the Nature and Ground upon which this Man is supposed to be the Subject of property – I shall then submit to your Lordship such observation as have occurred to me considering the opinions which had been delivered upon this occasion in and out of Court -

My Lord I said when[81] I laid down my proposition that no Man can at this day be a Slave in this Kingdom, I do by that mean to be understood that there [11] has been a time when Slavery was understood to exist in this Kingdom – But that was a great while ago indeed - Villenage[82] [37] remained in this Country after all Ideas of Slavery in it were lost – as I can only throw out a few Hints upon the occasion from the Authorities I shall submit to the Consideration of the Court that very early indeed and long before the Extinction of Villenage in this Country the Word Slavery which had been adopted by the Law Writers very early changed it's [sic] name – and there was a distinction afterwards as though there ceased to be any such thing as Slavery – though there was Villenage - My Lord the Origin or Commencement of Villenage

---

[80] Ed. In the left margin of the MS at this point there is drawn, one assumes by G#, a small hand with the finger pointing at this line: ☞ the text of which is also underlined.

[81] Ed. There may have been an interval of time between Serjeant Davy's opening statement and what follows.

[82] Ed. This is the spelling used throughout the MS, except in the case of a quotation from *The Mirror of Justices*, below, page 160.

in this Country is not perfectly known at this Day[:] whether it was as Sir William Temple[83] supposes introduced by the Saxons usurping their Authority [12] over the poor remnant of Britain after some retired to Gaul in the Wars there and others to Wales or Cornwall – and the poor few unarmed Defenceless Creatures were as he supposes made to be Hewers of Wood and Drawers of Water[.] – Whether that was the Commencement of it or whether as some Writers supposed it was a Danish Transaction in which ever of these Ways it came about I don't find there is a perfect understanding of the matter to be found or whether it was as the Mirror[84] says as your Lordship will observe – whether the Origin of making Slaves of those that where Infidels was introduced upon the first introduction of Christianity – your Lordship will see bye and bye I will account for the Mistake of that Point. – In which ever of these Ways it was there was at sometime or other a Set of Men who were called [13] Slaves in England who afterwards were succeeded by a much larger Body of Men who were called Villeins[85] and those again were very much increased by another Set of Men who themselves were not Villeins but held Lands in Villein's Service. – It is necessary to preserve the Distinction between these three Sorts of Men Slaves, Villeins and those who held Lands in Villein's service – My Lord whatever was it's [sic] Origin at whatever time it commenced this I will venture to say of it, its commencement be it by whom or when it may was Tyranny and Oppression and it was a Usurpation upon the natural rights of mankind – It was the Effect of Power which was resistless but will never alter Lawfully the natural Condition of the Subject[.]

My Lord when one reads the Authors upon this Subject that speak of Villenage and of the State of these Men – One sees but two [14] Sorts of them when there is Light thrown into the Subject – I mean down from Littleton's time[86] and that was Villeins regardant and Villeins engrossed – The first of Those were not in such a miserable State at first and so much in the power of the Lord as the others for they were not subjected to do any Duty or perform any Subjection out of the Manors to which they belonged – The Villeins in Gross were those who had

---

[83] Ed. Sir William Temple, 1st Baronet (25 April 1628 – 27 January 1699, English statesman and essayist), *An Introduction to the History of England*, London, 1708, p 176.

[84] Ed. *The Mirror of Justices* (W J Whittaker ed) 7 Seld Soc (for 1893).

[85] Ed. The spelling "villein" is used throughout the MS.

[86] Ed. J H Baker, 'Littleton, Sir Thomas (d 1481)', ODNB, 2004; online edn, May 2007 [http://www.oxforddnb.com/view/article/16787], accessed 1 March 2015.

been severed from the Manor and became absolute Villeins though I cannot call them property for at no time do I understand the Man himself was the Subject of property – his Service was the Lord[']s but his Person was his own though he was subject to great inconveniences imprisonment and so on to make the Hardships little distinguishable from the absolute State of Slavery – I speak now of a poor Villein in Gross -

My Lord [15] one thing is clear upon that Subject that there was but two ways in which it was possible to shew a Man a Villein by Prescription or by Confession upon record – My Lord that of Confession upon record will resolve itself into the following Considerations for Confession upon a Record amounts to no more than this[:] an Admission that he was a Villein. But my Lord with regard to prescription that proves this that no new families of the Man could ever be made Villeins – that no new Race of Men coming from where they may, being what they may Christians or Infidels for that time they knew of no other Sort but Saracens and Infidels – be whom they may or come from where they may whatever was their Condition in their Native Country they never could become Villeins here for they must all be derived from the common [16] Stock of Villeins – no new Family could ever be introduced into the State of Villenage in this Country – for My Lord it was necessary to prove a Man a Villein to shew that he had been in his Stock and had been a Villein beyond all Memory - My Lord it struck me by reading Littleton at first – and gave some Offence to me upon reading the Words[.] He speaks how a free Man might become a Villein – I began at first to imagine there was some Mistake in the Printing of the Word Freeman – for that is in the same way as saying how a Man may become a Felon by Confession – because if he confesses it is proof he was a Slave or Villein – but how Freeman will become a Villein will not apply that way – because an honest Man cannot confess himself to be a Felon neither [17] is it to be supposed a Freeman will confess himself to be a Villein – He speaks how a free Man may become a Villein by Confession upon record – I find I was mistaken when I imagined it was a Misprinting because I find this distinction that after such Confession the Children born after should be Villeins but the Children born before should be free – therefore I find it considered by that, that it could not by their Confession throw him into the same Condition and State of Villenage that he would have been in upon Proof of his being before a Villein and if he maintains the Description whether all his Progeny will be in a State of Villenage also was the point. But it seems as if it was the Alteration of the State and Condition of the Man from the State of Freedom to that of a Villein or from a Villein to that of [18] absolute slavery -

My Lord that goes some way towards refuting the Argument for it proves a Man cannot by Contract make himself a Slave - But when your Lordship considers the Wisdom of the Law in guarding against any possible inconvenience upon that Subject – it will shew you not only that no such Contract ever should be implied – but also that no such Contract should ever be binding but in one form only that of a Confession upon Record in a Court having Jurisdiction of the matter in the Court – it is expressly laid down by Littleton and Lord [sic] Coke[87] upon it there must have been an Action depending in the Court and the Court must have Cognizance of the matter and have a Jurisdiction to [19] take such Confession by Record and that was the only possible way of doing it.-

Your Lordship observes that as these were the only two ways by which a Man could be a Villein by the Law and had not only guarded against the possibility of his becoming a Villein by any implication of a Proof therefore it is clear a Man never could be proved to be a Villein by Prescription – My Lord it is in Proof not only that Courts of Law never would suffer a Man in any other Form to become a Villein but upon the Contrary a Thousand Devices and thousand Modes of Manumitted them by Implication were devised by the Lawyers from time to time[.] There are a vast Number of them in all Ages as far back as we can go – Any one Act done by the Lord towards his Tenant [20] incompatible with the Idea of the State of Slavery was an implied Manumission – the Master giving him a Bond or granting an Annuity - or giving him any permanent Estate and many other ways they devised – then they laid hold of all possible devices to Enfranchize the Man and set him free from the Bonds of Villenage.

My Lord it is observable too (and it is very possible) that as soon as we hear of a State of Villenage we hear of its decline if we go as far back as we can in our Enquiry into a State of Villenage and the first Accounts of it one meets with those devices and Shifts in Order to reduce the Number and it is very observable they have been now for a great Number

---

[87] Ed. Co Lit 122b, s 185. Allen D Boyer, 'Coke, Sir Edward (1552–1634)', ODNB, 2004; online edn, January 2009 [http://www.oxforddnb.com/view/article/5826], accessed 1 March 2015.

of Years and as far back [21] almost as Edward the 6th endeavouring to effect that purpose – And it is a question whether there were Men (I believe I have seen somewhere a Note of it) remaining at the restoration in the State of the Villein – but supposing that it now appears that of the vast quantity there were Originally all [in] this State became totally Extinct and Annihilated without the Assistance of a Single Act of Parliament – and there never was any Statute in this Realm or Act of Parliament which at all Assisted much less encouraged such a State – That is something more than a curious Enquiry and will do Honour to this Country and perhaps be of Service to this Country – and resist new feeble Arguments upon the Subject whence were the Causes of that Extinction of Villenage – I place it [22] first to the Account of Humanity – I do presume that Many Men merely upon the Account of the feelings of Human Nature – from the Condition to which Men were reduced – incapable of possessing property – and absolutely at the Will of the Lord to be disposed of and dealt with as they please, to be beat, scourged, imprisoned and treated as the Lord thought proper without any possibility of redress – where no Civil Suit will lay – and no Appeal of Mayhem – for the instant he recovers Damages of his Lord he pays them and the moment the Man has them he takes it from him again – and this was their miserable Estate – and there was no way of prosecution but an Appeal of Death[88] or an Appeal of Rape – no mode of Redress pointed out by Law for Wrongs and Injuries done – therefore [23] I can impute the reducing the Number of these people in some Measure to the Humanity of the Laws – much more may be said for the Wisdom of the Laws, and I could wish all such as hold Slaves would profit a little upon that Consideration and they would be as wise as the Lords of Villeins have been formally in this Country – For they saw their Estates were most wretchedly managed by Slaves, they saw but little profit from them and how could it be otherwise – for the Work of a Freeman and the Slave are very different. the[89] Work of a Person compelled or the voluntary Work for Hire and Reward is very differently conducted[.] The one is done against a Man's Will[:] the other with all his Heart –

---

[88] Ed. A primitive survival in the common law by which an heir or widow of a deceased could bring an "appeal" and force prosecution, after 1215, before a petit jury, even if prosecution by indictment had resulted in a conviction for manslaughter or an acquittal. It was thus contrary to the modern notion of double jeopardy, but could also force compensation on the part of survivors. It was abolished in 1819. Daniel R. Ernst, "The Moribund Appeal of Death: Compensating Survivors and Controlling Jurors in Early Modern England" (1984) 28:2 *The American Journal of Legal History*, pp 164–188.

[89] Ed. Lower case in MS.

My Lord, seeing this, the Lords found it would be their Interest to better these [24] Men's Condition a little – not to give them a direct Enfranchisement immediately but let them continue in their Estate to make them understand at least that they and their families should live quietly for they would not divest them of their Liberty and they were to remain in Peace & Order to give them Encouragement at first though the Estates were held at Will and according to a Custom of the Country which introduced that way – but in many places there was Computation made of what these people should have for doing such Service – or giving them a Sum of Money for such certain Service – and that Enfranchises them – and there was divers modes made use of to enfranchise them from time to time and none to continue them in a State of Slavery – [25]

With regard to their being Christians it is a very different Consideration – for Christianity is Irreconcilable to a State of Slavery as applied to the Considerations of Enfranchising them as it respects the Honor [sic] of Christianity and the liberal System of Religion and the interference of Christianity with the Civil Rights of Mankind – when I speak of Christianity I don't mean the Christianity of the Proprietors to use the Word properly. – It is said, My Lord, upon the Dawn of the Protestant Religion in this Country Wyckliffe[90] and his followers in the Reign of Hen[.] 4 – in speaking of opening the minds of Men upon the Subject it was by first teaching them to think upon the Subject and not to take every Opinion from mere Authority. – [26]

They inculcated the Opinion of Liberty – as being most consistent with a Christian State and it was that which every Man advised since (& I don't mean the Papist Clergy[91] but others[)][92] who spake upon the Subject of Religion warmly inculcated in the minds of People an Opinion it was more for the Service of the Christian Religion that Men should be made free than remain Slaves and religious Motives might be more attended to by enfranchising them – What is most striking in the present Enquiry is that the people themselves and the Interpreters

---

[90] Ed. Anne Hudson, Anthony Kenny, 'Wyclif, John (d 1384)', ODNB, 2004; online edn, September 2010 [http://www.oxforddnb.com/view/article/30122], accessed 27 February 2015.

[91] Ed. Wyclif was in fact a Catholic priest, although a dissident one and regarded as a forerunner of the Protestant religion.

[92] Ed. There is no end-bracket in the MS.

and Oracles of the Law – who were the Judges – they in all Ages seem to have revolted against Villenage and endeavour by every Subterfuge by every Art and Chicane and by every possible Contrivance though they [27] were not able to contradict the Laws, such was the interpretation of the State of them – that they contributed by their Manumissions most wonderfully in favour of the Subject against Slavery - I beg leave to insist before your Lordship that I consider the Commencement of Villenage to be entirely an oppression and I consider the Extinction of it to be nothing more than a general Assertion of the natural Rights of Mankind, according to the Temper, Disposition, and Spirit of the People of this Country, it's [sic] Climate, the Genius of the People and the Soil all which I look upon to be the Ingredients to make up the English Constitution. –. My Lord Slavery was upheld by the Power of great Men of those Times and how far they would have carried it is very obvious when one Considers that Statute [28] of the 9th Richard the 2d.[93] and another Statute which upon another occasion I shall take Notice of by and by in the Reign of Edward the 6th[.] That of Richard the 2d. was one of the severest Blows to Freedom the most cruel and tyrannical wicked Act of Parliament that ever was made or the Laws ever founded – That under the Head of Villenage takes Notice that many Villeins in the Country had rebelled against their Lords – and insisted upon their Enfranchisement on Account of the Lands they held and offered to prove that their Lands were not Villeins Lands by Doomsday Book – that is recited in the Act – Therefore without considering the Man's right or property – Commissioners are to go into the Country at the request [29] of the several Lords to imprison all these Men without Bail or Mainprize unless the Lords interfere in it and desire otherwise[.] So it was in the absolute power of the Lords to send many Men to Gaol[94] and to make it still Worse Doomsday Book should not be admitted in Evidence to prove these Men had a right to their Enfranchisement –

My Lord that was itself an Act [which] as it were created Villeins — but that Act of Parliament did not last long[.] It was very soon repealed – it shows however the use they intended to make of it was to fullfill [sic] at that time the strong desire of the great Lords who themselves were almost the Government by having the Power in their own Hands – thus the poor people were ground to Death – in this State and

---

[93] Ed. In St Realm the statute is 1 Ric II c 6 (1377), St Realm ii.2.
[94] Ed. Spelled "Goal" in MS.

Condition they are found to remain [30] for some Ages in this Country – And as I said to your Lordship just now All this great Business of Tyranny was destroyed by the Genius of the People –

I mentioned your Lordship just now and I introduce it at present merely as it stands in order to give more Liberty to speak to matters for your Lordships Consideration afterwards [as to] that other Statute of the 1st of Edwd. 6th[.] It is the only Act of Parliament that has the Word Slave in it. it is 1st of Ed 6 Chap. 30.[95] That is the only Act of Parliament that ever attempted to introduce Slavery into this Country – it States That all Idle Vagabonds should be made Slaves and those slaves to be the property of the Person who should apprehend such and carry them before a Justice of the Peace - that they should be [31] fed upon Bread and Water and refuse Meat – that they should wear a Ring of Iron round their Necks or Arms and in Case they did not find that answer so well they were to be markt with a hot Iron upon the Breast with the Mark of a Villain[96] [sic] and that he was to be the property of those that presented him to the Justice of the Peace. - And all this was to be done not in pursuance of any Conviction by Tryal by a Jury but this was to be done by two Justices of the Peace.–

This was the 1st of Edward 6th and your Lordship will see in the 3d & 4th of Ed. 6 Ch 16[97] that Act of Parliament repealed - it was repealed and in the recital of that of the 3d and 4th it was a Repeal of the former Act upon Account of its Severity – so my Lord from that Act of the 1st to the 3d [32] of Ed 6. when there was such a thing as Slavery in this Country; even then those were Slaves only who fell under the Title of Rogues and Vagabonds but however my Lord it was a State which in English Mind revolts at – the English Constitution could not bear that any Set of Men under any Circumstances should be put in such a State

---

[95] Ed. In St Realm 1 Edw VI c 3, 1547, St Realm, iv.5. Section 1 provided for a "vagabond" on conviction by two justices of the peace to become the slave of the person offering him or her work, for two years, and to be marked with a "V" with a hot iron. If the slave absented himself or herself within the two years for a period of fourteen days then two justices could order him or her to be burned on the cheek or forehead with an "S" and to be a slave of his or her master forever. If he or she ran away a second time, he or she was to be deemed a felon. The status was to cease if the slave came into property of his or her own. John Reeves, *History of the English Law, from the Time of the Saxons, to the End of the Reign of Philip and Mary*, 4 vols Dublin, 2nd edn, 1787, iv.451–52.

[96] Ed. More likely "V" for vagabond.

[97] Ed. 3 & 4 Edw VI c 16, 1549–50, St Realm iv.115.

in this Country – I have heard very grave and good Men speak upon the Subject who have said they could wish there were fewer Capital Punishments in this Country and those that forfeit their Lives could be made usefull instead of being put to Death – with regard to that Objection It would be very unfit to familiarize such Objects to our View it would be unfit to be seen in this Country. [33]

It is the Pride of this Country that it looks upon all other Countries in a bad Light – as this is the only Country where they are free – I should be glad to know whether it absolutely ceased before the Restoration or whether there was a few Villeins at that time – I do presume there is such an Account – but we have heard nothing of that State since that time – not since the Restoration – I would be very glad to know whether the people of this Country would now endure or whether the Judges would now endure a State of Villenage to exist. – Let it be for this purpose I imagined by way of humour upon the Subject – let me suppose any Name – a Mr Buckhorse – if he should say ["]give me Half a Crown [34] I will confess myself a Villein["] the Person whom he thus addresses should say ["]with all my Heart but put it upon record["] – I should be glad to know what the Court would say of it – if the Learning Council [sic] or Serjeant very gravely and sagaciously (as in the Common Pleas it must be a Grave Serjeant – with a Grave that is to say with a Sad Countenance) was to move the Court that Mr Buckhorse's Confession might be admitted upon record – My Lord I don't know what the Judges of the Court of Common Pleas would say but I am sure they would stare at it – I do believe it is impossible for any Sergeant to be found to make such a move – if they did they must do it with a very sad Countenance indeed – But I am sure it would have a very sad [35] Effect – for it is impossible any Judge would hear more of it – they would be told that all England would revolt that it – that the Genius of the People would not suffer it, that there could not be any Man that would dare to introduce such a Record into any Court – But yet there is no Law against it – why? - why not? Why should not the Man be a Villein – where is the Law? where is the Statute? where the Distinction? where is the Common Law? show the Book if you can that forbids it! – No such Book can be found, but there is the Law written in the Hearts of Men of this Country – That is the Law – it is the Constitution – For the Constitution of this Country requires it when that is not found in a particular Book it is growing out of [36] the Hearts of Men, I am not talking of Licentiousness nor in the Sense some understand it - But true genuine Liberty is the Birth Right and

Inheritance of the People in this Country – that Liberty being governed by certain Rules[.] If a Man could be a Slave he must be subject to the Will and Caprice of his Tyrant Master and he is under no Laws then but the arbitrary pleasure of his Master – That I desire to be understood is no other Liberty but that of being governed by certain Laws as making a part of those people - by Statute Magna Charta Lib. Hom. were not to be imprisoned but by Judgment of their Peers[.] That I suppose there was a Sett of Men at that time who were not Lib. Hom. &c your Lordship will please to observe that [37] in all Ages during the time of Villenage there is no Law providing what is to become of them or what is to become of the property or Estates given them or when the Lord of the Villein should cease to take them into his own Hands – or how many Provisions are made (speaking of the Relation of the Lord & Villein) there is not one Word to be found in any of these Writers of the State of Slavery – it would have been extraordinary among all the Writers if there had been such a thing as Slavery in this Country for none of them to have written of what was the Law with regard to it.-

I will now tell your Lordship what the Mirror[98] says of that – in the Edition I have upon the Title Villeinage[99] – some Mistakes might arise because the Word Villein and the Word Cerf [sic] is indiscriminately used in it – These Cerfs [38] were the ancient Cervi – I apprehend I shall be found right upon Enquiry – it appears by the Mirror there were Slaves who were not Villeins and there were Villeins who were not Slaves – If the Mirror is accurately attended to – I mention this in general – The Mirror endeavours to shew the Origin of Villenage and I don't know whether he's mistaken or no, very possibly he may because he supposes (as he goes up so far as the Flood about it – and speaks of Shem, Ham and Japhet)[100] he supposes from them was the Origin of all the Villeins – in another Passage he talks of Villeins the Christians may give away – and your Lordship will find by and by he calls these sort of Villeins Slaves - He says that Baptism will Enfranchize them – [39] he is right when understood – because the sort of Slave that becomes such merely upon Account of not being Christians but Infidels and Subjects of an Infidel Prince in which State and Condition only the right of Slavery had attached upon them, if there was such a sort of People as these the instant they were Baptized they

---

[98] Ed. *The Mirror of Justices* (W J Whittaker ed) 7 Seld Soc (for 1893), pp 76–80.
[99] Ed. This is the only example of the spelling "villeinage" with an "i" in the MS, presumably because it is quoted from The Mirror, "villenage" being used elsewhere.
[100] Ed. *Mirror of Justices*, p 77.

ceased to be Infidels and were then out of the State and Condition from whence their Slavery accrued - but that never applied to Villeins – I believe it was upon a Mistake of this kind that some of the Entries upon this Subject where they have spoken of Negroes and Slavery they speak of them as Infidels and the Subjects of an Infidel Prince – their being so has no relation to the Subject of our Enquiry – but under the Notion that Baptism might possibly free them out of Slavery – [40] I agree it would if the right of Slavery attached upon them merely upon Account of their being Infidels – if Slavery was the Effect from their being Infidels - if removed by Baptism he ceases to be a Slave – but to shew the Mirror does not apply to that your Lordship will find in the next Section it treats of Villeins – Now there must be another Species of Villeins who were not Enfranchised by receiving Holy Orders from the Ordinary – it would be inconsistent if Baptism emancipated them and Holy Orders did not.- They returned to their former State and nothing but entering entirely into Religion would hinder their State of Slavery and in that Case an Action would lye – when he speaks of that he says (these are the Words) Villeins became free [41] many ways, some by Baptism as that removes them from their State of Infidelity – in which State were those Saracens who were taken by Christians and brought by Grace to Christianity – In that he cannot be understood to speak of Villeins in general or Slaves in general – I shall have a particular reason for speaking of that by and by – I don't pretend that Baptism makes any alteration for I am afraid that the Idea has hindered many of those Poor Men from being instructed in the Religion of this Country – so I renounce the Idea of Baptism making any alteration in Slavery in this Country -

The Mirror says all Villeins are not Slaves for, says he[,] Slaves are still regardant – Your Lordship will observe he speaks of two Species of Men, those in the State of Villenage in [42] this Country and those reduced to it by Slavery as the Saracens and other Infidels[.] Though it is most certain that besides the kind I am now speaking of their was Villeins till the 11th of Elizabeth[101] – which I find in Noy[102] – there is some Notice taken of the Disputes between the Lords and the Slaves and that the Judges by some device or other freed the Men - in every one of these Accounts I don't find a Man ever come into Court

---

[101] Ed. 1568/9.
[102] Ed. Probably refers to *Pigg* v *Caley* (1617) Noy 27, 74 ER 997, H 15 Jac I, thought to be the last case in which it was alleged a person was a villein regardant. See also *Fleyer* v *Crouch* (1568) 3 Dyer 283b, 73 ER 636.

and went out of Villein in any Case for these 2 or 300 Years past – in the instance I alluded to the Man did not go out again Villein – it is mentioned in the Second part of the 1st Volume of Rushworth's Collection[103] page 458 or 468 – it is said there that the Managers of the House of Commons not Mr Lilburne – though the Book says so – but in that Affair of the [43] Impeachment in the House – in the Judgement against Lilburne – the Judges cited a Case in the 11th of Elizabeth[.] The Case was this – One Cartwright[104] (which your Lordship sees is an English Name) – One Cartwright brought a Slave from Russia and would scourge him for which he was questioned - (Cartwright was) And it was resolved that England was too pure an Air for Slaves to breathe in[105] – that was in the 11th of Queen Elizabeth – My Lord about that time the People at large were not so considerable I mean in their Collective Capacity they were not so considerable as they have been since – the House of Commons were treated then in a very different manner to what the Crown would presume or dare to treat them now – and when Monarchy held its Head so very high in this Country as [44] it did in the Reign of Queen Elizabeth it was resolved that England was too pure an Air for slaves to breathe in – I hope, my Lord the Air does not blow worse since – I hope it is not but unless there is a Change of Air I hope they will never breathe here. for that is my Assertion. The moment they put their foot upon English Ground that moment they become free – there are subject to the Laws and they are entitled to the protection of the Laws of this Country, and so are their Masters thank God. My Lord another thing upon the State of Villenage in the worst State of it in this Country even pure Villenage they was not their property – No Lord of a Villein could dare to say what this honest Gentleman says here by this return – it would not have been endured That he was his property – his Slave – [45] that he was going to transport him and sell him abroad - that never should nor ever could be asserted by any Sett of Men in this Country according to the Old Books –

[103] Ed. Rushworth, *Historical Collections of Private Passages of State*. Volume 2: 1629–38 (1721), pp 461–481. [http://www.british-history.ac.uk/ rushworth-papers/vol2/pp461-481], accessed 9 March 2015.

[104] Ed. Ibid. "In the Eleventh of Elizabeth, one *Cartwright* brought a Slave from Russia, and would scourge him, for which he was questioned; and it was resolved, That England was too pure an Air for Slaves to breath in." Above, page 22.

[105] Ed. In the left margin of the MS at this point there is drawn, one assumes by G#, a small hand with the finger pointing at this line: ☞ the text of which is also underlined.

But my Lord it seems that as we have extended our Commerce and got into America a New Species of Tyranny is set up to prevail in this Country – and that is a Species of Slavery that is created entirely by Colony Government – and here I am afraid of fighting the Air not knowing precisely upon what ground it is they will insist upon the prevalence of the Colony Laws in this Country[.] I will say nothing my Lord therefore by way of Anticipation upon that head – when the Gentlemen have stated the Ground upon which they set up that Claim – [46] I hope I shall have an opportunity to revert upon it - but my Lord my Argument is to prove that when any Man of what ever State and Condition – I don't speak now of Ambassadors for that is quite a different Consideration therefore those I mean to be excepted that are protected by the general Laws of Nations.

But all the People that come into this Country immediately become subject to the Laws of this Country – are governed by the Laws, regulated entirely in their whole Conduct by the Laws of this Country and intitled to the protection of the Laws and become the King's Subjects – (That is to say) when they come here they are a part of the Body of the People called the Lib. Hom. Angliæ – either this man [47] remains upon his Arrival in England in the Condition he was in abroad in Virginia or he does not – He does or does not so – If he does so remain the Master's Power remains as before – If the Laws having attached upon him abroad are at all to affect him here it brings them all, either all the Laws of Virginia are to attach upon him here or none – for where will they draw the Line? – they may say what Power has his Master over him in Virginia which he has not here - but what will of the Master[']s is the Servant bound to obey there which he is not bound here – how is his Dominion to be affected upon his Arrival in this Country if not totally affected – all these matters belong to them to State, and when that is done I shall know in what manner to answer them. [48] At present I will meet them here – All I can say therefore in the meantime upon that Head is - That the Laws here makes [sic] no difference between the State and Condition of One Man and the State and Condition of another – it did not at the time of Magna Charta because I can understand a particular sort were then existing – when it says no free Man shall be imprisoned and so on – but by the Judgement of his Peers or the Law of the Land - no free Man – because at this time there was a Sett of Men in the Country under the Denomination of Villeins who were not free Men - that we may observe from the Language of it – No free Man – as if they were only a part of the People and not the whole – but that has never been used in any Act of Parliament for several hundred [49] years last past – in the Case of Villenage here People either Men or Women Villeins All were the King's Subjects without Distinction the Condition of one Man and the Condition of another they are all equally bound and all equally affected by the Laws – both the Laws to punish and the Laws to protect.

My Lord I have stated in general upon the Subject of the liberty of this Country, the right of Liberty which every Man setting his Foot upon English Ground has – I will now with submission to your Lordship beg leave to consider the Nature and ground of the present Claim – of Mr Stuart over this Man. I observed by the return they state first (in the substance of it they say) that in Africa there are Slaves and that this Man was [50] a Slave in Africa – they then state the Trade that is carried on – and a wicked Trade it is God knows – the Trade carried on between Africa and the Plantations abroad to serve the Colonies – That he was brought from Africa being a Slave and Sold in Virginia – Now my Lord these are two distinct matters – his having been a Slave in Africa – and his having been a Slave in Virginia – for by the Laws of Virginia his having been a Slave in Africa does not at all affect the question here – nor his being a Slave in Virginia effect his being a Slave in Africa - I have looked in the Virginia Laws and I find there are two Laws the first is in Charles the 2d 34th[106] which was repeated by the 4th of Queen Ann[107] which is the present [51] Act now in force and descriptive who should be Slaves and it creates the Slaves in the Country – it is That all Servants brought into this Country by Sea or Land except Turks and Moors in Amity with Her Majesty and Negroes and others that cannot make due proof of their being free in England or any other Christian Country – for the *Onus probandi* is entirely upon the Man throughout all the Virginia Laws - I say you are a Slave[;] prove you

---

[106] Ed. Virginia, 34 Car II, Act 1 (1682):

> ...it is Enacted, That all Servants, not being Christians, being imported into this Country by Shipping, shall be slaves...

Acts of Assembly, passed in the colony of Virginia, from 1662, to 1715. Volume I. London, MDCCXXVII. [1727] [Eighteenth Century Collections Online: Range 5711], p 139.

[107] Ed. Virginia 1705, Act No 22:

> All Negro, mulatto and Indian slaves... within this dominion... shall be held to be real estate...

Acts of Assembly, Virginia, Volume I, p 261.

are free - "All Negroes and others that cannot make due proof of being free in England or in any other Christian Country shall be accounted as Slaves and as such be bought and sold notwithstanding their being converted to Christianity["] -[108] afterwards they seem to have entertained some Doubts [52] about their Baptism making them free – But it is the Law as it now stands in Virginia as a Repeal of the Statute of 34 C. 2d –[109]

Therefore as that is the Law there your Lordship sees his having been an African Slave has nothing to do with it – If he had been an African Prince[,] as Oroonoko[110] was[,] he is as liable to be made a Slave in Virginia as any other Man - so if any Man in Africa had been inveigled and carried by any Man on board a Ship to another Place if a Man comes here and claims his Liberty by Our laws – No says Mr Wallace you have been a Slave once and an African Slave and so you are here a Slave though you were transported from Africa here – so your Lordship sees the Gentlemen have unnecessarily introduced his being a Slave in Africa – [53] as that is a distinct Consideration and nothing to do with his becoming a Slave in Virginia - "In Africa there are Slaves. and this Man was a Slave here in England". I don't understand that Logic. Why if a Man in Africa or in any other Country escapes from a State of Slavery and comes into this Country in Order to be free – to add to the Service of this Country by such Liberty or contribute to the

---

[108] Ed. This section is contained in the 1682 Act: Acts of Assembly, Virginia, Volume I, p 140.

[109] Ed. Serjeant Davy appears to make the point that the 1705 Act of Virginia did not repeal the 1682 Act generally, but provided that baptism, at least if they were not Christian when they arrived in Virginia, did not make black people, etc free.

[110] Ed. The reference is to the short novel *Oroonoko: or, the Royal Slave* by Aphra Behn (1640?–1689), published in 1688. Behn was one of the earliest women writers in English. She was also a supporter of the abolitionist movement. The novel concerns the Coromantin grandson of an African king, Prince Oroonoko, who falls in love with Imoinda, the daughter of the king's top general. "Coromantee people" were Akan people brought as slaves from present-day Ghana. Janet Todd, 'Behn, Aphra (1640?–1689)', ODNB, 2004 [http://www.oxforddnb.com/view/article/1961], accessed 23 October 2012. There was at least one case of a person of princely rank being sold as a slave to America: Abdul-Rahman Ibrahim Ibn Sori (aka Abdul-Rahman) was a prince from West Africa who was a slave in the United States. After spending forty years in slavery, he was freed in 1828 by order of President John Quincy Adams and Secretary of State Henry Clay after the Sultan of Morocco requested his release: Terry Alford, *Prince among Slaves*, New York, London, c 1977. A film was made based on the book: "Prince Among Slaves", PBS Documentary film, 60 min, premiered Monday, 4 February 2008. [http://www.pbs.org/programs/prince-among-slaves/], accessed 2 February 2014; Unity Productions Foundation, PBS Home Video DVD.

general good of the Nation because it is rich and assisted by the Number of Inhabitants – I should be glad to know whether any Man has a right to say that Man is his Slave – his coming with another or without, or any Man having antecedently exercised Authority over him or not they are different Considerations – the [54] right of property in one Man and the right of Liberty in another -

Then with regard to the Laws of Virginia do they bind here? Have the Laws of Virginia any more influence, power or Authority in this Country than the Laws of Japan? – The King makes Laws for Virginia, alone if he pleases – if he is thought proper to introduce a particular form of making Laws in that Country, or the Assembly makes them under the power of the Crown - as he might have granted such a Charter or any other – but he cannot make Laws here without the Consent and Authority of the two Houses of Parliament – suppose instead of this Man's coming from Africa he had come from Turkey – now suppose [55] a Christian Slave brought from Turkey here or suppose a Bashan[111] came into this Country with half a Score Circassian[112] Women Slaves for his Amusement suppose they should in this Case think proper to say to this Bashan ["]Sir we will no longer be the subject of your Lust["] – I believe he would make but a miserable figure at the Bar of the Old Bailey upon Indictment for a Rape -

With regard to their being Infidels or Christians it makes no difference at all for that cannot affect the Question – suppose a Man in Poland or any other country whatsoever where they are Slaves if they come into this Country there are entitled to the protection of the Laws – unless in the Case of an Embassador [sic] [56] governed by the general Laws of Nations for I am not now supposed to be speaking of a Man coming in a Publick Capacity as the representative of a Prince respecting any Man's assuming a Dominion over the Person of another Man – be he Christian or not bringing them in this Country I insist this Man is free and they are all free that are brought here – if the Gentleman should ask what is their Enfranchisement I answer the Soil and the Air is their Enfranchisement and their Arrival here make them free.

---

[111] Ed. "Bashan, country frequently cited in the Old Testament and later important in the Roman Empire; it is located in what is now Syria." *Encyclopaedia Britannica*.

[112] Ed. "Circassian, Russian Cherkes, or Cherkess, plural Cherkesy, member of a Caucasian people speaking a northwest Caucasian language." *Encyclopaedia Britannica*.

I will now trouble your Lordship with a Word or two upon the Ground of Expediency or Inexpediency on this Subject as perhaps that Consideration might have [57] introduced some Opinions upon the Subject from some great Authorities and most respectable Names perhaps that have been mentioned, I apprehend your Lordship will not be governed by such opinions but to provide against any Arguments that may be insisted on and to prevent such Arguments from having any Effect upon the minds of any Body here, I desire to trouble your Lordship with the Word or two upon the Subject – first with regard to the Inexpediency on either side of the Question – let the Claim which is set up in this return be allowed and what hindrance would there be to a West Indian owner of an Estate in this Country stocking his Farm with Negroes[?] – then what a Sweet Race of Men we should [58] have among us – and then instead of the Farmers who now drive his Plan he would say call out a Hundred of my Fellows and set them to the Plough - and go to the Ironmongers for half a Score of Tortures to make them do it the better – I have one at home though I did not think it so proper to bring it down to shew your Lordship –

Another great Argument[:] suppose a West Indian coming here with half a Million in his Pocket builds a fine House but is served entirely by Negroes, here is one upon his Coach Box and half a Dozen behind – some at the Plough[,] some at the Carts[,] some at serving others reaping and so on – If that is to be the Case, in God's Name let us have an Act of Parliament [59] to prevent the abominable Numbers of Negroes being brought here by those West Indian Planters – and as there is no Law at present in this Country for it – before we have an Importation of them I hope we shall have a Law to prevent the abominable practice of bringing them over in such Numbers – for if there is not such a Law passed I don't know what our Progeny may be[,] I mean of what Colour - a Freeman of this Country may in the Course of time be the Grandfather of a half a Score of Slaves for what we know - and I think it would be an immediate inconvenience in this Country[.] I think it would not be a pleasant Sight nor would be endured but would occasion a great deal of Heart Burn. [60]

Then with regard to the inconveniency upon the other Side – how can that be? – A Man brings his own Slave into this Country, the Consequence of which is the Man's Manumission – Why then keep him where he was before! – There are sufficient Laws in all the Plantations to prevent Slaves being brought over – there can be no danger of a

Man's Escaping and so coming into this country – none at all – and perhaps it would be full as pleasant and usefull to us if these Gentlemen did not bring over so many of them and I fancy they will not – at least after this Question has been discussed – if I am so happy as to prevail in any Argument – Suppose what could not possibly be the Case but suppose Sugar [61] and Tobacco were immoderately dear from it[.] Suppose the Plantations could not be so well worked without them – that would be avoided by their staying there – I do remember an Author on the Spirit of the Laws[113] in speaking of this Subject – says what would be his Argument supposing he was an Advocate in favour of it – (and against what I am now contending for[;] he tells the reader what would be his Argument) and he is rather pleasant on the Subject – it is Ironical the whole of it - Sugar would be dearer therefore for God's sake let these Men be slaves – That is a ridiculous Argument – But I will take up another Argument – suppose these Men cannot have Souls – he concludes in saying at least these are not Men that they are divested of all [62] Ranks of Humanity[.] For if these are Men I am afraid we shall stand much in danger of losing our own Character as Christians – I believe he concludes in that manner – But I have read in a very ingenious Author on the Conveniency -

Lord Mansfield – Have you any Account how many Planters were persuaded to that by Montesquieu[?]

Mr Serjeant Davy – Oh Planters – I will tell your Lordship about the Laws made at that time – I could not have time to find all. I have endeavoured to search for them but God knows I have not been able - but I have turned to Posthlewayte['ls [sic] Dictionary[114] and tumbled it over from one Title to another – at last I stumbled upon the Title America and the different Treasures to be found - [63] The Rivers – Towns – Situations &c and then speaking of the Natives of the Country – my Lord this Essay is very ingenious and sensible and seems to

---

[113] Ed. Montesquieu, *The Spirit of the Laws*: Charles de Secondat Montesquieu, baron de, *De l'esprit des loix...Nouvelle edition, avec les dernieres corrections & illustrations de l'auteur*, Edinbourg, G Hamilton & J Balfour, 1750.

[114] Ed. Savary des Brûlons, Jacques (1657–1716) (Malachy Postlethwayt, trs) *The universal dictionary of trade and commerce*, translated from the French of the celebrated Monsieur Savary, Inspector-General of the manufactures for the King, at the Customhouse of Paris: with large additions and improvements, incorporated throughout the Whole work London: printed for John and Paul Knapton, in Ludgate-Street, 1751–55. Note: Eighteenth Century Collections Online lists volume 1 of 2 only, but the text is in fact of volume 2 only.

be very well considered – who was the Author I don't know that it is an Argument to prove it would be much more beneficial to this Country to Civilise these people than carry on this way of Slavery – and that the Business of the Plantations would be carried on much more effectually and more for the benefit of the Planter and consequently for the Mother Country if they could be worked by the Freemen as Covenant Servants – how much more profitable it would be – at least equally – but indeed more when applied to the Plantations alone – but it would be infinitely more advantageous for [64] the Mother Country – but upon the head of convenience another answer might be given to the Gentlemen – let this be understood that it is a distinction I don't very much contend for – I only throw it out for your Lordship's Consideration – If the Owner of a Slave from Africa or America was to bring him into this Country – if he comes with his Master into this Country the Master himself Manumitts him – But if he escapes and comes here not being brought by his Master – it should not have that operation – it would totally answer all the inconveniency to the Master – he knows the Terms on the Effects of bringing them here and it becomes his Act if the Man does not escape and come [65] here himself – if he had it not in his Power to alter his Condition – supposing I was right in that part of the Argument but the Master himself has brought him here and consequently made him free – so much for the Doctrine of the Convenience and Inconvenience[.] But I could wish them not to be brought here for now and then we have some Accidents of Children born of an Odd Colour - which is owing I supposed to the Difference of Colour between the Fair and the Negroe – for I cannot suppose any other reason – for the Children not being quite so white as their fathers or the Origin of the Mothers[.] I have just touched upon those Matters of Convenience[.]

I will if your Lordship will give me Leave just take Notice of the Opinion which the Colonists themselves [66] entertain upon the Subject – My Lord it seems by that Act of the Assembly I last mentioned your Lordship of Queen Ann as if they had entertained the Idea that the Slave coming into this Country had a Manumission while he was here and was Enfranchised while he was in England therefore they provide for that Case – and it is inserted in their Law if such a Slave afterwards returns to Virginia he shall then return back to that State in which he was before his coming into England – the Words of it are these – by

6th Section of the Act 4 of Ann[115] it is provided that a Slave being in England should not be sufficient to discharge them from their Slavery without other Proof of his having been Manumitted there – [67] My Lord it means that the Opinion of the Legislature of that Country[,] the Assembly of that Country[,] was that his being in this Country gave them a Manumission or Freedom during his Residence here – "But if that Man should happen to return there it should be considered only as a Local or Temporary Enfranchisement["] during his being here which will not operate upon his returning to that Country where Slaves are allowed – I mentioned your Lordship just now that if these People came into England – they must come under the Idea of the Laws of Virginia which having once attached upon them and so having attached upon them they bring as it were the Virginia Laws with them here – [68] My Lord if that was to be the Case there is a great Difficulty in drawing the Line - it would be is the most absurd of all propositions to say that All the Laws of Virginia are to Operate upon them here for instance the moderate punishment in Case a Man should attempt to escape of cutting off half their Foot with an Ax and such other kind of little Punishments – but to be sure the right of Chastisement must belong to them[.] If we speak now of moderate Chastisement how is that to be determined[?] – My Lord it is determined by the Act of Assembly – I find this Act of Assembly there - "That if any Slave.[..]" now your Lordship will see what is the Idea of Chastisement by the Owners of Slaves – And the Master or Slave Holder don't change from their Habits of thinking [69] by their Arrival in this Country: your Lordship will see what their Habit of thinking is, – it is in the 21st of Charles 2d No 1 "That if any Slave resist his Master or others by his Master's Orders correcting him and by extremity of Correction they should Chance to die".[..] and it and very frequently happens "such Death shall not be accounted Felony by the Master or that other Person appointed by the Master to inflict the Punishment but they shall be quit from Molestation the same as if it was no Offence at all" they acquit from it.

The reason assigned in that Act of Assembly is this – since it cannot be presumed that propense Malice which alone makes a Murder Felony should induce any Man to destroy his own Estate – Now I do [70] presume the Steward or Master or any others belonging to them have not

---

[115] Ed. Acts of Assembly, passed in the colony of Virginia, from 1662, to 1715. Volume I, London, MDCCXXVII [1727] [Eighteenth Century Collections Online: Range 5711]. See also above, note 107 on page 172.

changed their Mode of thinking – their powers are not Changed – and I humbly insist if they are not changed totally they cannot be changed at all that I insist upon the Consideration of the Cases which have happened upon the Subject – I will mention to your Lordship in the Order of time[.] One of them in Butts & Penny[116] in 2 Levings [sic] 201 in the 29th of Charles the 2d – there was an Action of Trover brought for 100 Negroes and upon a Not Guilty it was found by Special Verdict that the Negroes where Infidels the Subjects of an Infidel Prince – (which Idea prevailed then) – and they are usually brought and sold as a Custom of Markets there – and Plaintiff bought [71] them and was in possession 'till the Defendant took them – & = [sic] Thompson argued no property could exist in Villeins but by competent Jurisdiction by a Court: but the Court held that Negroes being usually bought and sold amongst Merchants and also being Infidels (what is part of the reason assigned) but no Judgement upon the Contrary given there might be a property sufficient to maintain Trover and therefore gave Judgement for the Plaintiff. Nisi Caus.; – and upon the Prayer of the Attorney General the Day was given until next Term – and then I find it in Keeble [sic] 3d 785.[117] Nothing is said there but after their becoming Christians they were Enfranchised – he tells you what the Court said upon that Head – but I find there was no Judgment of entered in this Case – [72] and your Lordship will see by and by in a Case afterwards that search has been made for the Judgment but no Judgment could be found that was ever entered –

The next Case in Order time that happened was the Case of Chamberlain and Harvey in William the 3d. That Case is cited in two Books

---

[116] Ed. *Butts v Penny* (1676) 2 Lev 201, 83 ER 518, Court of King's Bench. "Trover for 100 negroes". "Thompson argued, there could be no property in the person of a man sufficient to maintain trover, and cited Co Lit 116. That no property could be in villains but by compact or conquest. But the Court held, that negroes being usually bought and sold among merchants, as merchandise, and also being infidels, there might be a property in them sufficient to maintain trover, and gave judgment for the plaintiff, *nisi causa*, this term; and at the end of the term, upon the prayer of the Attorney-General to be heard as to this matter, day was given until next term."

[117] Ed. *Butts v Penny* (1676) 3 Keb 785, 84 ER 1011, Court of King's Bench: the report speaks of a "special verdict in trover" for "10 negroes and a half"(!) and continues "and Thomson, on 1 Inst. 116, for the defendant, said here could be no property in the plaintiff more than in villains; but per Curiam, they are by usage *tanquam bona* [as if goods], and go to administrator untill they become Christians; and thereby they are infranchised: and judgment for the plaintiff, nisi".

but best Cited in 5th Modern[118] begins at 182 and goes on for several Pages afterwards all at Large – and at 1st Lord Raymond 146.[119] My Lord that was an Action of Trespass for taking & keeping a Negroe of the Plaintiff's of the Value of £100 and upon a Not Guilty the Jury found a Special Verdict at the Guildhall and the Verdict finds that one Edward Chamberlain was seized in the Fee of a Plantation in [73] Barbadoes and certain Negro Slaves – I should have told your Lordship in Virginia as well as Barbadoes Negroes are part of the Estate – it appeared that the Negro in question was born in Barbadoes of Negro Parents – they find by an Ordinance of their Government that they were entitled to the Inheritance of their Negroes – They find he died seized of some Negroes and 3 came to Mary his Widow as her Dower and the Reversion of &c came to the possession of the Son and Heir – it states that Mary the Widow being so seized was married to Sir John – and in her right – he was seized &c – and being so seized – he in the 32 of George 2d[120] brought this Negro into England where he continued in the [74] Service of Sir Jno – several years – he was Baptised here[.] They thought it material but your Lordship sees that I in my Opinion give that Point up – after the Death of Mary Sir John turned this Negroe out of his Service – and then all this right of Dower which belonged to the Plaintiff was gone – The Negro afterward served several other Masters here and at the time of [sic] the Trespass was supposed to be committed he was in the Service of Defendant and had for Wages £6 a year – but there the whole is left to the Judgment of the Court and I see my Lord by Lord Raymond in his Report of it and in the 5 Modern he says the Council was Sir Bartholomew Shower and Mr B – I suppose Sir B – S - [75] was for the Plaintiff – there are 3 Conditions made by the Plaintiff's Council[.] the first was whether upon this finding there was any Legal Property vested in the Plaintiff and 2dly - if any such property be vested in them whether his bringing these Men into England

---

[118] Ed. Sub nom *Chamberline v Harvey* (1701) 5 Mod 182, 87 ER 598, Court of King's Bench.

[119] Ed. Sub nom *Chamberlain v Harvey* (1696) 1 Ld Raym 146, 91 ER 994, Court of King's Bench: "Trespass will lie for taking of an apprentice, or *hæredem apparentem*. An abbot might maintain trespass for his monk; and any man may maintain trespass for another, if he declares with a *per quod servitium amisit* [by which he lost service]: but it will not lie in this case. And per Holt Chief Justice, trover will not lie for a negro, contra to 3 Keb. 785, 2 Lev 201, *Butts v Penny*." NB The point appears to be that the writ alleged only that the person was a "negro", which did not disclose a cause of action, and not that he was a servant, which would have done, ie "negro" did not imply servant.

[120] Ed. 11 June 1758 – 10 June 1759.

be not a Manumission and 3dly whether an Action of Trespass will not lye for taking a Man of such a Value perhaps it was £100 – I don't find any Opinion was given upon the first of these positions – but it lays upon the last whether the Trespass will lay - the Judgment was given in Hilary Term afterwards – it underwent great Consideration – it began in Michaelmas and in Hilary Term Judgment was given for the Defendant – that Trespass would not lay - [76] for the Court were of the Opinion that no Action of Trespass would lye upon taking away a Man – in the general Sense of the Word but there might be for taking away a Man Servant – Lord Raymond adds more to that in 5 Modern: & p[er] Holt Chief Justice Trover will not lay for a Negro – which is contradictory to Butts and Penny – and there are your Lordship sees Lord Chief Justice Holt held that the Opinion which had been given in the Case of Butts and Penny was not Law[.][121] It appears the Case itself was never decided for upon the prayer of the Attorney General[.] it was ordered to stand over 'till he could be heard and no Judgment was given -

In the Case of Smith and Gould[122] in 2 Lord Raymond 1274 that was in the Michaelmas the 4th of [77] Queen Ann[.] Your Lordship will take Notice that Act of the Assembly of Virginia was made in this very year – but whether it was made before or after that determination does not appear but it might appear if narrowly looked into – This was an Action of Trover for a Negro and several Goods[.] The Defendant let Judgment go by Default[.] That was before Lord Chief Justice Holt in London[.] the Jury (I suppose by his direction) gave separate Damages as to the Goods and Negro[.] A motion was made as to the Negro upon Arrest of Judgment and it was determined no Trover would lye for a Negro. Now your Lordship sees like Butts and Penny it was directly before the Court – For the Plaintiff it was argued [78] that the Negro was a Chattel by the Law of the Plantations and Trover would lie – and by the Levitical Law they was property but it was determined by the whole Court per Totam Curia - All the 4 Judges concurred in Opinion – the Chief Justice declared that Opinion "That such Action does not lye for a Negroe no More than any other Man for the Common Law takes no notice of Negroes being different from other Men"[123] - "by the Common Law no man can have a property in another." – This was

---

[121] Ed. Above, page 180.
[122] Ed. *Smith* v *Gould* (1706) 2 Ld Raym 1274, 92 ER 338; (1705) 2 Salk 666, 91 ER 567.
[123] Ed. (1706) 2 Ld Raym 1274, 92 ER 338: "...for the common law takes no notice of negroes being different from other men."

said by the Lord Chief Justice in Concurrence with all the rest – No Man can have a property in another but in especial Cases[,] so if they are taken in War they do not kill them but Sell them or Ransom them [79] for there is no such thing as Slavery by the Law of England - There was a Case put by Lord Chief Justice Holt[.] If A takes B a Frenchman Captive in War – he cannot maintain an Action for it – but the Court denied the Opinion of the Case of Butts and Penny - That was upon the 2d time of arguing – and therefore Judgment was given for the Plaintiff for all but the Negro – That is the Case of Smith & Gould[.]

My Lord there is another Case and that is the only remaining Case in the Printed Books of Smith against Brown and Cooper[124] [.] That is in 2d Salkeld 666[.] That was an Action Indebitatis assumpsit for a Negroe sold in London – there was a Motion for Arrest of Judgment in that Cause and upon that Argument Lord Chief Justice [80] Holt held as soon as they came into England they became free - One maybe a Villein in England but not a Slave[.] Mr Justice P-[Powell] says the Law takes no Notice of a Negro - Then Lord Chief Justice Holt puts them in a way to set it right – you should have averred in the Declaration (says he) that the Negroe was in Virginia by the Laws which Country Negroes are Saleable and then he directed it to be amended – That the Sale was in London of a Negro in Virginia – that would have been right. - But here it is stated it was for a Negro Sold in London so that was not the Question whether the Man upon being in London could be sold – I insist no he cannot but in Virginia he might be sold because they are Saleable there – they might Sell him being there in London – it was [81] stated to the court that in Virginia Negroes were Inheritance[125] and transferrable [sic] by Deed so there was no other way of selling the Slave but by the Laws of Virginia[126] - that was the whole of that Case -

Lord Chief Justice[:] in truth and in fact the Slave was sold in London – was not he[?]

---

[124] Ed. *Smith v Brown and Cooper* (1705) 2 Salk 666, 91 ER 566, Court of King's Bench.
[125] Ed. ie they were not only property, but real property, above note 107 on page 172.
[126] Ed. By the 4th proviso to the 1705 Act, no person selling a slave "shall be obliged to cause such sale or alienation to be recorded, as is required by Law to be done upon the alienation of other real estate, but that the said sale or alienation may be made in the same manner as might have been done before the making of this Act..." The point of making slaves real property was therefore so that they should descend as real estate, ie in fee simple, or could be the subject of a settlement creating life estates or entails: see page 268 note 217.

Mr Serjeant Davy – Yes but the Slave himself was in London and Sold in London.-

Mr Justice Willes – The Slave himself in London and Sold in London[?]

Mr Justice Ashurst - So it was as a fiction merely judged so, to give Effect to the Sale that the Slave was in Virginia – when in London at the same time.

Mr Serjeant Davy – Nothing else – Oh! I beg Pardon it was not to give a fiction – the truth of the Case was that he was in Virginia – [82] (I see now) If he was in England he dare not be sold[,] No more than me or you or any Man – he could not be sold in England not being the Subject of private property – and being no Slave but if he was in Virginia there he might be the Subject of property – he might in London contract for the purchase of a Plantation and Slaves abroad – they might be Slaves abroad but not here -

These are the Cases in the printed Books – I have been favoured with a Site of a Paper in which was a Note of Mr Justice Forster[']s: it is in Easter Term the 21st of George the 2d – I was suffered to take an Extract of the Note – one of your Lordship[']s – I know has it likewise [sic] – this I have is a very short Note and I mention it with setting out the [83] Case to prevent any Argument being derived from it as a Case of any Authority against the Cases I have mentioned – All the Note speaks of it is [that] an Information had been granted – The Plaintiff had brought his Action and applied to the Court here for an Information which was granted upon his undertaking not to proceed upon the Action – it being an Action for Assault and taking away his Negro Slave – I suppose there was particular Circumstances of violent proceedings – but having brought his Action it was objected to – I suppose by the Council[127] – that they ought not to proceed by Information too – the Court therefore would not file an Information but upon his undertaking not to proceed in the Action and afterwards the Act of Grace passed which [84] Discharged the Defendant from prosecution by Information – upon this the Plaintiff applied to the Court for leave to proceed in his Action (which he could not do without the Court's Leave) which the Court granted but ordered to be struck out a little part of it which was for the Assault and then gave him leave to

---

[127] Ed. Meaning, by counsel? Counsel is often spelled "council" in the MSS.

proceed in his Action. There the Note stops - What was done in that Action or whether it was before the Court to consider the propriety of the Action concerning the taking away the Negro Slave[,] That does not seem to have entered into the thoughts of any Body – with regard to this Subject they gave him leave to proceed but not in that part of the Injury done by Violence – that was struck out – [85]

Mr Justice Ashurst - What was the Name of it.[?]

Mr Serjeant Davy – It was Wager and Webb[128] Easter the 21st of George 2d.

Mr Justice Willes – The Action was brought by the Master of the Slave[?].

Mr Serjeant Davy – Yes for beating him and taking away his Negro Slave[129] - but the Note is totally Silent whether the Negro could be the Subject of property.

Mr Justice Aston[130] - I have that Note – and Master Burroughs lent me his Book likewise – it is put down in Forster's Note – nothing was done in it – he says in his short Note of it this – If the Matter had been tried and determined a New Action could be brought – but let the Plaintiff be at Liberty so far as the retainer of the Negro but he cannot maintain that part of Assault and Imprisonment – [86] so let that be struck out. I borrowed Mr Burrough[s]'s Book which is taken very fully[.]

Mr Serjeant Davy – Nor does it appear whether this was an Action of Trespass – but it is most clearly so – where it claimed the Negroe as property – the Negro may be a Servant – so may a White Man and any Man may serve or Enter into Service for Life - But this I beg leave to say the absurdist [sic] of all Contradictions is, for a man to sell himself as a Slave – but the Contrary Argument is, If a man was to sell himself for £100 the moment he receives it the Master may take it from him – it is a Contradiction in Terms to suppose such a Contract – it would be a Contradiction to the Idea of Slavery – a Man may hire himself for [87] 7 Years or for Life as I said before but a person in the Condition of

---

[128] Ed. No citation. Not traced.

[129] Ed. It would seem that the action was brought by the original master against someone else who held the black person as his slave and beat him.

[130] Ed. James Oldham, 'Aston, Sir Richard (1717–1778)', ODNB, 2004 [http://www.oxforddnb.com/view/article/826], accessed 21 February 2015.

Slave is incapable of having any property - the reason I cite this for is – a Sheet of Paper very fairly wrote by Mr Justice Forster which I have seen upon the Subject of Slavery - it consists of 2 Parts[:] the first is the state of temporary Servitude – stating it from the Levitical Law in Exodus 21st Chap[.][131] a Servant being bought with his Master's Money was to serve so long a time – and then to shew that Our Saviour and the other Planters of the Christian Religion his Disciples that they did not at all abrogate[,] if I may so say[,] the moral obligation or deny the rights of the Master – and then there is the Epistle by name particularly stated - that is a Gospel Argument to [88] shew Christianity did not interfere with Men's Civil rights – certainly they did not – it is no Legal Argument – further to shew it would be absurd to say it was assisted from the same authority and that passive obedience and non resistance was a Gospel Dispensation and that it was a Damnable Doctrine to hold the Contrary – it is remarked that that Chapter I think it was the Romans – it was wrote in the time of Nero and speaking of the power of Nero over him he must be obedient for Conscience sake – It was not the business of the first or any writers upon the Christian Religion to touch Civil Rights at all – If that was wrote with a View to refute the Ideas arising from Baptism making them free – [89] I give it up – I cannot too often repeat it for the sake of the Bye standers – I should be glad to have it understood that it does not affect the Temporal Right he has over his Slave – (if he has any such right over his Slave) I wish to remove any idea to the Contrary – for the sake of these poor Wretches that they may have the Benefits of the Christian Religion and be baptised – If that Argument means to shew that Slavery is compatible with Christianity in a general Sense I beg leave humbly to deny it – for my Lord I do assent with a great Deference to your Lordship – that the Doctrine of Christianity opens the Minds of Men and teaches them as Doctor Sherlock[132] has proved, it has enlarged the Ideas of Natural

---

[131] Ed. Exodus 21.2: 2 (AV): "If thou buy an Hebrew servant, six years he shall serve: and in the seventh he shall go out free for nothing." Many modern translations say "slave" instead of "servant". See also Deuteronomy 15.12: "And if thy brother, a Hebrew man, or a Hebrew woman, be sold unto thee, and serve thee six years; then in the seventh year thou shalt let him go free from thee."

[132] Ed. Thomas Sherlock (1678–18 July 1761), master of St Catharine's College, Cambridge and vice-chancellor of the university, dean of Chichester, bishop of Bangor in 1728, Salisbury in 1734, and London in 1748. His published works include *The Use and Interest of Prophecy in the Several Ages of the World* (1725), *The Tryal of the Witnesses of the Resurrection of Jesus* (1729) and his collected *Sermons* (1754–1758). Colin Haydon, 'Sherlock, Thomas (1677–1761)', ODNB; online edn, May 2009 [http://www.oxforddnb.com/view/article/25380], accessed 16 September 2013.

Religion –[90] where it is taught – It will be a Benefit resulting from Christianity to open the mind of Men this Day, so largely, that they do renounce all Idea of Slavery in this Country for Englishmen will never suffer it -

There are some other Cases of a later Date – there was a Case of Hylas and Newton[133] which was a special Verdict when the State[134] [sic] was Stated – it came on before Lord Chief Justice Wilmot[135] in Dec. 1768 – Nothing was done upon it, no opinion so far as I can understand ever dropt from the Lord Chief Justice which I can the more readily believe because I know he very rarely ever dropt any inclination of an Opinion upon any Subject that deserved Consideration that was left for future consideration[.] nothing [91] was done in it respecting the present Question therefore I need not trouble your Lordship with the particular Circumstances of that Case – There was an Act of Parliament made in the 5th of George the 2d for the recovery of Debts in the Plantations in America[.] it is 5 Geo. 2 Chap 7 Section 4[136] [.] all the Act says upon it is – It was enacted that the Houses, Lands, Negroes, Estates, of &c. (further part of what they had in England) the Houses, Lands and other Hereditaments situate or being within any of

---

[133] Ed. See page 377, York Minster Library COLL1896/1.

[134] Ed. Seemingly an error for "case".

[135] Ed. Sir John Eardley Wilmot (1709–1792) CJCP from 20 August 1766 to 26 January 1771. James Oldham, 'Wilmot, Sir John Eardley (1709–1792)', ODNB, 2004 [http://www.oxforddnb.com/view/article/29624], accessed 28 February 2015.

[136] Ed. *An Act for the more easy Recovery of Debts in his Majesty's Plantations and Colonies in America*, 5 Geo II, c 7, 1731, s 4:

> IV. And be it further enacted by the Authority aforesaid, That from and after the said twenty-ninth Day of September one thousand seven hundred and thirty-two, the Houses, Lands, Negroes, and other Hereditaments and real Estates, situate or being within any of the said Plantations belonging to any Person indebted, shall be liable to and chargeable with all just Debts, Duties and Demands of what Nature or Kind soever, owing by any such Person to his Majesty, or any of his Subjects, and shall and may be Assets for the Satisfaction thereof, in like Manner as Real Estates are by the Law of England liable to the Satisfaction of Debts due by Bond or other Speciality, and shall be subject to the like Remedies, Proceedings and Process in any Court of Law or Equity, in any of the said Plantations respectively, for seizing, extending, selling or disposing of any such Houses, Lands, Negroes, and other Hereditaments and Real Estates, towards the Satisfaction of such Debts, Duties and Demands, and in like Manner as Personal.

the said Plantations belonging to any Person shall be liable and chargeable with Debts – they shall be Assets for Satisfaction of Creditors in the manner personal Estates are in this Country &c. – I mention that only as throwing it out – that where they are Saleable and are liable [92] to payments of Debts as they are in Virginia they should be sold and liable to payment of Debts in England. – There is no Doubt of it – from their being Saleable there they may by that Act contract for them here in England - They may buy a Plantation here in England – and they may buy a Slave here who is in America – while they are in America they are Slaves any where[:] that is not at all the Question – but they are reasons that occurred to me upon this Subject from the Cursory View which I have had time to bestow upon it – If there are any other Cases or Accounts upon the Subject I am sure they have not yet occurred to me in the very short time I have had to search for them. [93]

Mr Serjeant Glynn – May it please your Lordship to favour me upon the same side, and after the Apology my Brother Davy has made for himself I will make the same from myself – as this matter has now been so lately put into my Hands and any preparation therefore I have been able to make cannot be sufficient for the present purpose – but I have received great Satisfaction from the Gentlemen who have gone before me - to find this matter has gone thro' so thorough a research.

As I cannot take upon me to add to that research to produce any fresh Argument much less to produce any Authorities that have not been already stated to your Lordship – I hope that important as this Question is I shall not be under the necessity of taking up much of the time of [94] the Court – My Lord the Question as it appears now before your Lordship is whether Mr Stuart is intitled to the detention of this Man which your Lordship will infer from the present Plea. – The dominion of Mr Stuart upon the pretension he has set up in his Return – That this person is a Native of Africa – by the Colony Laws (the Laws of America) a Person being a Slave in one Place can be a Slave in another – That he has a Right to exercise the Dominion of a Master over his Slave in the Kingdom of Great Britain – My Lord this is the Return made by Mr Stuart and this is the Return we are called upon to answer – I trust little preparation will be necessary to support any Man whatsoever to gain a good and sufficient Judgment against the Return of this Sort. [95] Whatever might have been the ancient Laws this Kingdom – Whatever the degree of Slavery might have been tolerated in it and whatever barbarous Customs in remote Ages have prevailed. Yet I will avert even to those remote Ages and with some Confidence say in the remotest time of Our History – no such return as this was ever admitted by the Court – I daresay the Claim of Mr Stuart would have been heard with much more favour & attention then than with Justice to the Times it will be heard now – but no time could this Claim of Mr Stuart ever be endured by a Court of Justice - Mr Stuart I perceive has Stated to the Court this remarkable repugnancy in his Return – he has stated the Person he claims as Goods & Chattels to be a Man breathing the Air of England, [96] and having stated that, he has in the Sentence he asserts confuted his Claim.

With respect to this Question now before your Lordship it is truly stated to be a Question of Liberty not only the Liberty of an Individual but it would be injurious to == [sic] affect the General System – but my Lord of this Claim cannot be supported without violating one of the most fundamental Principles of that Constitutional Liberty – and I do submit your Lordship it will be productive of Consequences prejudicial to the Peace and dangerous to the Liberty of the Kingdom if once introduced. – if it did not interfere so far as to captivate the Affections of the People – if the People of Our Country did not fall in love with them – it is too much to be feared that some people might [97] be too well pleased with Dominion and from Habit and use it might [...][137] their Sentiments – but if that did or no there would be a Numerous Attendance of Persons in the Condition of Slaves – and under the absolute Dominion of their Masters – if that Condition was one subsisting it is too much to be feared the Objects would be multiplied and the Consequence of it is too apparent to need pointing out – with respect to the Colonies and the Point of Convenience I will once mention it for the purpose of dismissing it out of this cause – As your Lordship is now to determine a Question of Law of the utmost Consequence – If the Colonys find a convenience from continuing their arbitrary Laws which are productive of Scenes too Shocking to be allowed in this [98] Country – obtaining only in barbarous times – for in the Ideas of Civil Times it was found not only repugnant to Humanity but repugnant to all Principles of Sound Policy - If the Columnists have found any Convenience in this Traffick – this I am sure – the Convenience must terminate there – for the people of this Country will find a great inconvenience in extending it here and the Convenience must be in keeping

---

[137] Ed. The text is continuous in the MS, but a verb seems to be missing.

these Negroes within the Limits of their Colonies and not in pointing out inducements to Men to bring them into other Countrys – I do apprehend no principle or Consideration at this time will induce the Court or prepossess your Lordship with any undue influence in this Cause because I apprehend it would be as repugnant to the Principles of Policy [99] on which that Traffic is admitted as against the general principles of Law and Liberty in this Kingdom – if admitted -

A great deal has been said to your Lordship upon the State of Villenage as it was subsisting in this Country formally – My Lord that Subject has been thoroughly sifted and most thoroughly examined – that I shall say to your Lordship but a very few Words upon it because I do not conceive that the Laws respecting Villenage has any other application to this question than the principle attempted to be borrowed upon it – that the Laws of this Country did it sometimes terminate Villenage in a State of qualified Servitude – there is no other purpose that Villenage can be [100] adduced for or applied to the present question but thus much I am called upon to say since it has been introduced – That Villenage though it has subsisted in this Country and though it was like the other Customs held as having had the Sanction and Countenance of the Law. but never in Courts of Justice can it prevail – The Judges who were the most enlightened part of those antient times – then looked upon it as contravening the Principles of Law and only as a Custom to encourage the Cultivation of Land – However my Lord as it grew to be a Staple Servitude which had permitted before I believe it wore out by the Intervention not of positive Laws but the disposition of the Principles of Policy – that kind of Servitude in [101] those antient Demesnes rendered such a Subversion of Liberty they was not suffered to be continued. All sorts of Subterfuges were taken in favour of Emancipation – and the Non Suit of one was the Non Suit of the whole – it was more peremptory - though in no other whatsoever – if a Man by Accident brought an Action against his Villein he was instantly enfranchised – so my Lord from thus much we must conclude the State of Villenage to be contrary to the Genius and Temper of the Times – even in Antient times much less will it be endured in the present times -

Thus much I must observe upon Villenage as it wore itself out and became exploded without the interposition of positive Laws - if it ever occurred to [102] the Legislature of those times there existed such a Claim there would have been no doubt of their making then (which has not been done) a positive Law to prevent it – If Villenage was so discountenanced and thrown out of Doors formally by all Courts whatsoever – if there had been a Condition of any other Species of Slavery they must not have had this Question now to be considered[;] it must have been decided by the Legislature - it never could have been admitted to exist – if it could be admitted in any degree an infinite Number of Regulations would have been necessary to it's [sic] existence – it is proved it never was considered by the Legislature that there could be such a State –

In times when the Law endured such a State of Slavery it endured it with [103] great reluctance and there were but three ways in which it had ever been considered – there was but 3 Grounds in which it was ever contended that a Man could be in any Degree in the State of Slavery in this Kingdom – and but those 3 that ever found their way or got admission into the Course of the Administration of Justice or that was recognised by Courts of Justice – and all in the most oblique way – if by Judicial Determination it was with other Subjects they might be obliged to take Notice of – I take this as my Ground there never was in this Kingdom any other way of claiming a Man but by declaring against him as his Villein of one Species or other either Slaves, Villeins or those who hold in Villeins service except what might have been said [104] of very ancient times – when by a State of Captivity that might [have] existed but such Claim and proceedings of that time cannot be adduced now – it would be impossible at this time of Day according to the established Notions of these times – then it was if they took another in War and warrantable Hostilities then he might keep or Sell him as a Slave but that is a Notion which cannot be endured at this time but if enduring or not these are the 3 sorts in which it was possible in those times for a Man to have Dominion or Power over another that was ever admitted into England. – But that Argument lays upon the other side – when we have stated him to be a Man and a strong presumption any human Creature living in England is intitled [105] to the protection of the Laws of England. – most certainly I am authorized to call upon the Gentlemen to show that there either did exist another Species of Servitude besides those I mentioned[;] if not it falls under one or other of these Denominations. He must be *eo nomine*[138] a Villein of one Species or other – is there any pretence of a prescription from the Father and Son beyond the time of memory the Claimants exer-

---

[138] Ed. Italics supplied. Under that name, explicitly.

cised a power over this Man[?] – for that will be necessary to support such a Claim as this – is there any pretence that any Hostilities began and were lawfully carried on between Great Britain and any other Power and that this Man was taken in the Course of War[?] – Could he be claimed as a Captive[?] – if he could that must be [106] in the place where they are held in a State of Slavery – that Captivity must be confined under the Dominion of the Realm that took him and never permitted to go abroad and no one proof or instance can be found in which at any time such Conditions are more favoured than they are in England – that the Man was ever claimed as a Captive there is no pretence or that he was ever taken in War between this and other Nations – and he is come from that Nation who were not at War with the power in which he was taken – no such power can ever therefore be set up – he cannot be claimed as a Captive for he was not a Captive[:] he cannot be claimed as being originally his Slave – and he cannot be claimed as [107] a Slave here – because this is not the Place where he was taken.

What has been observed to your Lordship might be material that the Laws of England[,] however Slavery was tolerated[,] had discountenanced it and has checked it in its progress and opened every Door for Escape of people from the Condition of Slavery and shut every Door from coming into it – If that Question is introduced to know what is the Condition of a Villein – we know how he came into it and how he came out of it and we have the Comfort to know he never can enter it again – though if we know not who may be the objects of it and how far it may obtain. - Is it confined to Complexion[;] is it confined to a particular Quarter of [108] the World – upon what Principle is it[?] – can a Man become a Dog for another Man[?] if he ceases to be a Human Creature why not the Inhabitant of any other Country do the same.[?] How far then must it go necessarily – How is it considered in antient times[?] in antient times there was antient Remedies adapted to it – but no right adapted whatever to the Claim of Slave – and under what Regulations, Restrictions and limitations he is[,] so no person can say if his Condition is not understood – how is he to be delivered from it except by express Manumission or any other way – but that is too idle to say how he should get out of that State because no body knows how he got into it. [109]

With great Submission to your Lordship I insist there can be no pretence for saying the Man now before the Court can be a Slave – If he is a Slave he must be a Slave in one of these particular Modes as no other Denomination of Slavery ever obtained in this Country – with respect to what was said of Saracens, Infidels and those under the Government of an Infidel Prince – Your Lordship knows there never was any other Writ but that of the *De Naturo Habendo*[139] thought of – but this your Lordship knows, that Ancient Opinion of Villenage was overthrown by the more enlightened times – The Saracens and Infidels were to be considered as an Alien, Enemy, and perpetual Enemy so consequently not to have the [110] Benefit of the Laws of England – they were worse[140] than Villeins because they were not only at the mercy of one Man but that the mercy of every man. – but your Lordship knows that sort of Slavery is exploded and these Men are Testimony to be received and entitled to all the priviledges [sic] any Man in England would be entitled to – Let the Gentlemen prove (this Man if this return is to be supported) that this Man is a Slave – prove him a Slave in the way the Laws of England ever at any time allowed when they granted a Toleration of Slavery – Granting there was such a Toleration let them prove him a Villein – prove him a Captive – Your Lordship sees there is no such pretence in the return – I must now take Notice what are the particular Grounds set forth in [111] the Return – They have set forth in the particulars of the Return, That the man was a Native of Africa and a Slave there – that the Man was afterwards sold into Virginia and became the Slave of Mr Stuart there and came with Mr Stuart into England and he (Mr Stuart) adduces the consequences That he is a Slave here[.] Now if your Lordship will take notice of the Laws of Africa and the small State of the Coast of Africa and how far they do go – you will[141] find those are Laws entirely repugnant to Humanity – But the Slave in Africa if he had been so and immediately come to England there is no pretext for saying he could be a Slave here. I was very glad to find there has been such a very diligent research into this point by [112] my Brother Davy – who adduced one Case very much to the purpose – was the Case of the Russian Slave[142] where it was resolved that England was too pure an Air for Slaves to breath in so in that Case we find in the 11th of Elizabeth that Slavery was reprobated – Let me put the Case seriously what is the point upon which you are to draw the Line – If you admit a Right acquired in prejudice of Liberty – the Claim a Man derives from common Nature – if you permit them

---

[139] Ed. Italics supplied.
[140] Ed. ie worse off.
[141] Ed. Error in MS: "fill".
[142] Ed. *Cartwright*, note 104 on page 170.

to raise up & bring here the Laws of one Country I don't know but we must go round the Globe to find all their Laws – Suppose Galley Slaves were brought here – would the Master be allowed to exercise that power over them[?] – should they when they set their Foot upon [113] English Lands be allowed that Authority which in other Countrys where Servitude is in it's [sic] full extent allowed[?] – where the Slave is in the most wretched State and absolutely at the mercy of his Master – suppose they were to bring their Slaves into England would the Courts permit him to exercise that power over them – if not Then to what degree will they restrain him[?] – The Right of Arbitrary Correction is as I apprehend the Essence of Slavery - Arbitrary Power and Arbitrary Correction is the definement of it – The Laws of this Country did not long suffer that – By the Laws of Villenage they were to be Corrected – but they had a right to appeal to the Laws – and they would recover satisfaction for their Lashes and with it their Liberty likewise – [114] Therefore considering it in this manner suppose from any of those Dominions where Slavery is endured in it's [sic] full extent and immoderate Correction used – they were to brings a Slave and make use of the same Correction here – Your Lordship would certainly not permit it - Yet in not permitting it you contradict the Idea of Slavery - for by restraining Correction the Courts are under a necessity of saying he is not a Slave but stands in some other relation – And the Court cannot find out in what relation he does stand.

I shall now consider upon what general Grounds they pretend a right of Slavery accruing from the Laws of other Countries – I submit that a Man as soon as he arrives here ceases to be a Slave – [115] and his Master cannot keep and exercise that power over him – If he could he must exercise it in the way he claims to exercise a power over the Slave – If it is Correction it must be by some Rule that in England negatives the Assertion of that Man being a Slave – and that he is in some other Condition and therefore not in a Slave's - Therefore with respect to the Laws of Virginia for that must be the other Ground of Mr Stuart's Claim – That being a Branch of the British Empire this Man was a Slave by the Laws of Virginia – I am under a Difficulty of comprehending how such a Description can operate here – but this I conceive was not inserted for nothing[.] I conceive some Argument is to be built upon it – That he was a Slave in Virginia – [116] and the Conveyance as they assert from bringing him here is that he is his Slave in England – Does this Consequence follow[:] shall the Legislature of a Province extend it's [sic] operations and Acts to this Country[?] shall they have it in their power to supersede not only the Laws of this Country but to affect Them in the Vitals and Heart of them as those Men by [their] coming into England by such residence should enjoy their Liberty and not have it taken from them[?] – I presume the contrary can never be contended for[.] therefore whatever the Acts of Virginia are if they are Contradictory to the Fundamental Laws of this Country – it is not my business to examine what effect they have there – This much I will say of the Laws of Virginia[:] they cannot [*117*] come to England - so they cannot affect our good and principal Maxims – for by our Laws they cannot be Slaves here, such Servitude cannot be acquired here and the Laws of Virginia can have no possible Effect upon our Laws here - If a power was given to the Legislature for the better government of Virginia – they can never make such Laws operate here that exist in that Country and therefore I conceive there can be no pretence or Colour of Argument drawn for those Virginia Laws.

That this being the Colour of the Men Slavery must be there Condition and Quality when he arrives here because those Laws are the particular Laws of those Colonys – founded from their necessity I presume originally but they need not by any reasoning be extended further [*118*] because it was for their interest if the State of the Colony required it – that the Land should be Cultivated by them - it is therefore for their interest they should not be carried out of it – Therefore I should conceive and upon no Ground is there a Colour or pretence to say Mr Stuart had a right to exercise Dominion over the Man now produced before your Lordship – I am now speaking by way of Anticipation of the Arguments for every thing properly lays upon the other Side – but I will consider whether in any other way a Man – a Planter if he comes into England he can maintain that power which he could in the Colonys over any other Man in England for by the same Law he may over one Man as over another – I am now considering whether when he arrives [*119*] in England – by any other principle than those we mention he can maintain that power[:] we cannot by any principals tolerate Slavery as originally – because they must bring them within one Denomination or other of the different modes that was ever tolerated in this Country – without they find out a Construction of Servitude of a different sort of Slavery and more qualified can be permitted in this Country permitted, I will not say because Servitude may be permitted – as a Man by a Voluntary Act becomes an Apprentice or a Servant for a Term but I should suppose when a Claim is not for a Term but for Life it is not one of those favourite claims in the Idea of the Law that by fiction is to be assisted that the Court would raise a presumption there must have been a Contract which [120] gave a right to exercise that Power – If upon express Contract – When was that Convention made? there is no pretence for that – If made in Virginia there is an End of the matter[.] the Master who has an absolute power over the Slave can never contract with that Slave – The Contract would be void because there is a Despotick Violence held over the Man at the time he entered into it – If there was an express Contract made there I should apprehend with Submission to your Lordship that would be deemed to be invalid by the Courts of England because though permitted there the Man has no Assent – No Will of his own but the other exercises an absolute power and Dominion over him – and the Man in that Condition would certainly not be permitted to contract with him. [121] It would be like being in the Hands of Highwaymen or Banditti or the Hands of any persons that exercise Violence and Duress upon the Person of Men[.] their Actions would undoubtedly be void – My Lord it is not here as it is in Virginia - If the Laws permit it yet still the Man has no Will – while the other has dominion over him and such as is repugnant to the Laws of this Country and I submit to your Lordship an express Contract there will not do when he comes to England – is there any Ground or principle of Law upon which that implication can be founded[?] there is no Ground but upon a Principle that must be taken as repugnant to it – and the principle must be stopt in the place where he came from – It should be necessary for any [122] Contract to bind that it was free and voluntary; I do apprehend there can be no principle that ever does raise by Construction and implication in any one Man a power over another and give One Man any such right to the Service of another as his Slave - There is no such Doctrine or Opinion upon an implied principle or implied Service[.] the time of implied Servitude must be determined by the express Act of the Person who enters into that Servitude – In no Case whatsoever can be found there ever was such an Idea entertained as a presumptive Construction of Servitude for any time whatsoever much less for Life – and therefore there is no Ground for that in this Particular instance because I apprehend all the Circumstances [123] militate most strongly the other way – My Lord supposing it – and taking it for granted any Man could by presumptive Construction gain a right to the Service of any Man – does that justify the Return now before your Lordship[?] The Return is an implied Servitude – that he has a right of Dominion over the man and he has therefore laid him in Irons – if it was to be considered as a Servitude arising by express or implied Contract is it to be found that it arises by Convention then an Action must be founded on that Convention – that will be test to the whole of this Doctrine for supposing the Action to be brought upon it could or would the Action be maintained in that Case – would not the Court require an express Proof of that Contract the Master alleges for [124] the Ground of his Action – Suppose an Apprentice or any other Servant if he was to be understood to be a Servant undoubtedly this is not the way in which a Servant is to be treated – sent in this manner on Ship Board loaded with Irons for the purpose of sending him into another Country and there sold[.]

L[or]d Mansfield – There is nothing of Irons mentioned in the Return.

Mr Serjeant Glyn[n] – It appears from the Affidavit my Lord[.] But they sent him on Ship Board for the purpose of sending him out of the Kingdom[.] where is the Contract to be implied – that gives such Authority[?] let him justify that! with great Submission to your Lordship he cannot – there can be no such Contract – and nothing short of the most express of all Agreements can ever Justify a Man in [125] exercising such a power as that – When I say Agreement – it never can justify it – because no Breach of Agreement does Warrant such immediate Violence to be used by one Man over another – that must not be the way Men are to be treated with great Submission to your Lordship – As I said before in every way considering this Case there appears to be no ground whatsoever for such a Claim[:] at no time will it be held good – and with much greater Confidence I say at no time will this power Mr Stuart now claims ever be permitted to be Exercised in England – with respect to the Cases upon this Subject I may venture I think to say that Judicial late Opinions are most Uniform – whatever Opinions may have been held - those Opinions that ever appeared to be properly considered [126] do state that no such right or power can exist in England – In the General manner of treating these Cases and these sort of Claims they have no sort of Affinity with Villenage save only that it borders upon such kind of Claim – but certainly nothing of that kind can take place in this Country. -

With respect to the Question how far their Temporal Estate is affected by Baptism these things are entered as ingredients into the Consideration of all these Questions that have been sufficiently discussed by my Brother Davy[.] with respect to Judicial Determination your Lordship perceives there has been by great Authorities Determinations that

Trover or Trespass does not lye for a Negroe – that Determination has been adhered to [127] ever since and there has been no contradictory Determination of that – I have stated that Determination abstracted from the rest though it fell from a Man of great Reputation in the Law the first Judge this Court Lord Chief Justice Holt when he determined and the Action of Trover would not lay - he said the Opinion of Butts and Penny[143] which is the first Case where it was considered that they were a mere matter transferable one to another – Was not Law - but if they were a matter transferable there was no doubt Trespass or Trover would Lye - but the Idea of a Person being disposed of as a Negro and an Action being brought for the loss of the Servant differs – the latter presumes some other Condition besides that of a Slave – [128] that Declaration I am now going to mention – of Lord Chief Justice Holt was that a Person coming from the Colony's [sic] abroad did instantly acquire his freedom here whatever his Condition was abroad - he was a free Man here[.] that was the precise positive Declaration of Lord Chief Justice Holt – I don't apprehend nor does it appear nor is it pretended the learning Judge ever retracted from his former Declarations then or at any other time – and to make him consistent with himself I think it may fairly be presumed that is the true History of that particular Case – I think that Case of Butts and Penny being once reprobated and overthrown – the Judicial decision is trodden down as not Law – and upon that best opinion of Lord Holt[']s [129] a Man cannot be a Slave in England upon any Authority whatsoever – upon these Authorities I submitted to your Lordship and no Determination ever has been made contradictory to Liberty – but all in favour of Liberty I trust I may with great Confidence expect the Court will make a Determination in this Case in favour of Liberty and contrary to the Claim of Mr Stuart – upon the Grounds upon which I have contended it – that this Man is in no Degree a Slave – it lays upon them them [sic] to show under what Denomination he is a Slave – they must prove him to be so under that Denomination - for the General Allegation of Slavery will not do – and no species of Slavery to which the Old [130] Denominations do not apply are to be introduced in this Kingdom.

I do then submit that the Danger great as it may be arising from the Old Denominations becomes infinitely more in a New Species as a General Species of Slavery and Servitude not known nor recognised by the Laws of this Country – and to which they have adopted no Rem-

---

[143] Ed. See notes 116 and 117 on page 179.

edy - which is now set up – I think it requires no Arguments to prove it would be the most dangerous Doctrine that could be set up – therefore if they can prove that Doctrine to hold here – I will give up that advance ground and let them take Choice of the Old Time to show this Man could be a Slave – according to them – and to prove that there are any Authorities upon their Side and [131] then my Lord I shall draw an Inference from that and apply to them – and then they will be obliged to confess it is impossible for this Man in any way whatsoever to be a Slave[.] therefore I submit to your Lordship this Man should not be remanded to the Custody of his Master who avers to have treated him in this manner and to have detained him for the purpose which he avers of transporting him out of the kingdom – but should be now discharged and restored to the full State of Freedom as a Subject of this Kingdom.

Lord. Mansfield – Is there any traces there existed such a Case as that of the Russian Slave[?][144]

Mr Serjeant Davy – I know nothing more of it than what I told your Lordship.

Lord. Mansfield – This thing seems by the Arguments probably to go to a great length – and it is [132] the end of the Term so it will be hardly possible to go through it without stopping it – therefore let it stand over 'till next Term.

---

[144] Ed. Above, page 22 and note 104 on page 170.

Third Day, "Second Hearing" in the King's Bench

14 May 1772

As reported in (1772) Lofft 1, 98 ER 499
Note: page numbers in Lofft are shown in square brackets.

[1]

Easter Term 12 Geo. 3. 1772 K.B.

On return to an habeas corpus, requiring Captain Knowles to shew cause for the seizure and detainure of the complainant Somerset, a negro – The case appeared to be this –

That the negro had been a slave to Mr. Stewart, in Virginia, had been purchased from the African coast, in the course of the slave-trade, as tolerated in the plantations; that he had been brought over to England by his master, who intending to return, by force sent him on board of Captain Knowles's vessel, lying in the river; and was there, by the order of his master, in the custody of Captain Knowles, detained against his consent; until returned in obedience to the writ. And under this order, and the facts stated, Captain Knowles relied in his justification.

Upon the second argument, (Serjeant Glynn was in the first, and, I think, Mr. Mansfield[145]) the pleading on behalf of the negro was opened by Mr. Hargrave. I need not say that it will be found at large,[146] and I presume has been read by most of the profession, he having obliged the public with it himself: But I hope this summary note, which I took of it at the time, will not be thought impertinent; as it is not easy for a

---

[145] Ed. It was in fact Serjeant Davy, not Mr Mansfield: above, page 5.

[146] Ed. Hargrave published his argument as Francis Hargrave, *An argument in the case of James Sommersett a negro, lately determined by the Court of King's Bench: wherein it is attempted to demonstrate the present unlawfulness of domestic slavery in England. To which is prefixed a state of the case. By Mr. Hargrave, one of the counsel for the negro,* London, printed for the author: and sold by W Otridge, opposite the New Church, in the Strand, MDCCLXXII. [1772].

cause in which that gentleman has appeared, not to be materially injured by a total omission of his share in it.

Mr. Hargrave.

The importance of the question will I hope justify to your lordships the solicitude with which I rise to defend it; and however unequal I feel myself, will command attention. I trust, indeed, [2] this is a cause sufficient to support my own unworthiness by it's [sic] single intrinsic merit. I shall endeavour to state the grounds from which Mr. Stewart's supposed right arises; and then offer, as appears to me, sufficient confutation to his claim over the negro, as property, after having him brought over to England; (an absolute and unlimited property, or as right accruing from contract;) Mr. Stewart insists on the former. The question on that is not whether slavery is lawful in the colonies, (where a concurrence of unhappy circumstances has caused it to be established as necessary;) but whether in England? Not whether it ever has existed in England; but whether it be not now abolished?

Various definitions have been given of slavery: One of the most considerable is the following; a service for life, for bare necessaries. Harsh and terrible to human nature as even such a condition is, slavery is very insufficiently defined by these circumstances – it includes not the power of the master over the slave's person, property, and limbs, life only excepted; it includes not the right over all acquirements of the slave's labour; nor includes the alienation of the unhappy object from his original master, to whatever absolute lord, interest, caprice or malice, may chuse to transfer him; it includes not the descendible property from father to son, and in like manner continually of the slave and all his descendants. Let us reflect on the consequences of servitude in a light still more important. The corruption of manners in the master, from the entire subjection of the slaves he possesses to his sole will; from whence spring forth luxury, pride, cruelty, with the infinite enormities appertaining to their train; the danger to the master, from the revenge of his much injured and unredressed dependant; debasement of the mind of the slave, for want of means and motives of improvement; and peril to the constitution under which the slave cannot but suffer, and which he will naturally endeavour to subvert, as the only means of retrieving comfort and security to himself. – The humanity of modern times has much mitigated this extreme rigour of slavery; shall an attempt to introduce perpetual servitude here to this island hope for countenance? Will not all the other mischief of mere utter servitude revive, if once the idea of absolute property, under the immediate sanction of the laws of this country, extend itself to those who have been brought over to a soil whose air is deemed too pure for slaves to breathe in? Not that they cannot actually breathe in it; but the laws, the genius and spirit of the constitution, forbid the approach of slavery; will not suffer it's [sic] existence here.

This point, I conceive, needs no further enlargement: I mean, the proof that our mild and just constitution is ill adapted to the reception of arbitrary maxims and practices. But it has been said by great authorities, tho' slavery in it's [sic] full extent be incompatible with the natural rights of mankind, and the principles of good government, yet a moderate servitude may be tolerated; nay, sometimes must be maintained. Captivity in war is the principal ground of slavery: Contract another. Grotius *de J. B. & P.*[147] [3] and Pufendorf, b. 6. C. 3. §5. approves the making slaves of captives in war. The author of the *Spirit of the Laws* denies, except for self-preservation, and then only a temporary slavery. Dr. Rutherforth[148] in his *Principles of Natural Law*, and Locke, absolutely against it. As to contract; want of sufficient consideration justly gives full exception to the considering of it as contract. If it cannot be supported against parents, certainly not against children. Slavery imposed for the performance of public works for civil crimes, is much more defensible, and rests on quite different foundations. Domestic slavery, the object of the present consideration, is now submitted to observation in the ensuing account, its first commencement, progress, and gradual decrease: It took origin very early among the barbarous nations, continued in the state of the Jews, Greeks, Romans, and Germans; was propagated by the last over the numerous and extensive countries they subdued. Incompatible with the mild and humane precepts of christianity it, it began to be abolished in Spain, as the inhabitants grew enlightened and civilized, in the 8th century; it's [sic] decay extended over Europe in the 14th; was pretty well perfected in the beginning of the 16th century. Soon after that period, the discovery of America revived those tyrannic doctrines of servitude, with their wretched consequences. There is now at last an attempt, and the first yet known, to introduce it into England; long and uninterrupted usage from the origin of the common law, stands to oppose its revival. All kinds of domestic slavery were prohibited, except

---

[147] Ed. Hugo Grotius, *De jure belli ac pacis* (On the Law of War and Peace), Paris, 1625 (2nd edn, Amsterdam, 1631).

[148] Ed. *Institutes of Natural Law; being the substance of a Course of Lectures on Grotius de Jure Belli et Pacis*, 2 vols, Cambridge, 1754–6.

villenage. The villain was bound indeed to perpetual service; liable to the arbitrary disposal of his lord. There were two sorts; villain regardant, and in gross: The former as belonging to a manor, to the lord of which his ancestors had done villain service; in gross, when a villain was granted over by the lord. Villains were originally captives at the conquest, or troubles before. Villenage could commence nowhere but in England, it was necessary to have prescription for it. A new species has never arisen till now; for had it, remedies and powers there would have been at law: Therefore the most violent presumption against is the silence of the laws, were there nothing more. 'Tis very doubtful whether the laws of England will permit a man to bind himself by contract to serve for life: Certainly will not suffer him to invest another man with despotism, nor prevent his own right to dispose of property. If disallowed by consent of parties, much more when by force; if made void when commenced here, much more when imported. If there are true arguments, they reach the King himself as well as the subject. Dr. Rutherforth says, if the civil law of any nation does not allow of slavery, prisoners of war cannot be made slaves. If the policy of our laws admits not slavery, neither fact nor reason are for it.

A man, it is said, told the judges of the Star-Chamber, in the case of a Russian slave whom they had ordered to be scourged and imprisoned, that the air of England was too pure for slavery. The parliament afterwards punished the judges of the Star-Chamber for such usage of the [4] Russian, on his refusing to answer interrogatories. There are very few instances, few indeed, of decisions as to slaves, in this country. Two in Charles the 2d. where it was adjudged trover would lie. *Chamberlayne* and *Perrin*, [sic][149] Will. 3d. trover brought for taking a negro slave, adjudged it would not lie. – 4th Ann. action of trover; judgment by default: On arrest of judgment, resolved that trover would not lie. Such the determinations in all but two cases; and those the earliest, and disallowed by the subsequent decisions. Lord Holt - As loon as a slave enters England he becomes free. *Stanley* and *Harvey*, [sic][150] on a bequest to a slave; by a person whom he had served some years by his former master's permission, the master claims the bequest; Lord Northington decides for the slave, and gives him costs. 29th of George the 2d. c. 31.[151] implies permission in America, un-

---

[149] Ed. *Chamberline (or Chamberlain)* v *Harvey* (1696) 1 Ld Raym 146, 91 ER 994; (1701) 5 Mod 182, 87 ER 598.

[150] Ed. *Shanley* v *Harvey* (1762) 2 Eden 126, 28 ER 844.

[151] Ed. The Act referred to seems to be 29 Geo II, c 35, 1756 (Recruiting North America), *An Act for the better recruiting his Majesty's Forces on the Continent of America, and*

happily thought necessary; but the same reason subsists not here in England. The local law to be admitted when no very great inconvenience would follow; but otherwise not. The right of the mailer depends on the condition of slavery (such as it is) in America. If the slave be brought hither, it has nothing left to depend on but a supposed contract of the slave to return; which yet the law of England cannot permit. Thus has been traced the only mode of slavery ever been established here, villenage, long expired; I hope it has shewn, the introducing new kinds of slavery has been cautiously, and., we trust, effectually guarded against by the same laws.

Your lordships will indulge me in reciting the practice of foreign nations. 'Tis discountenanced in France; Bartholinus *de Republica* denies its permission by the law of France. Molinus gives a remarkable instance of the slave of an ambassador of Spain brought into France: He claims liberty; his claim allowed. France even mitigates the ancient slavery, far from creating new. France does not suffer even her King to introduce a new species of slavery. The other parliaments did indeed; but the parliament of Paris, considering the edict to import slavery as an exertion of the sovereign to the breach of the constitution, would not register that edict. Edict 1685, permits slavery in the colonies.[152] Edict in 1716,[153] recites the necessity to permit in France, but under various restraints, accurately enumerated in the Institute of French Laws. 1759 Admiralty court of France; *Causes Celebrées*, title *Negro*. A French gentleman purchased a slave, and sent him to St Malo's entrusted with a friend: He came afterwards, and took him to Paris. After ten years the servant chuses to leave France. The master not like Mr. Stewart hurries him back by main force, but obtains a process to

---

for the better Regulation of the Army, and preventing of Desertion there.; Chronological Table of the Statutes, HMSO.

[152] Ed. The *Code noir*, which insisted that all slaves be instructed as Catholics and not as Protestants. Jews in the colonies were not pemitted to own property or slaves. It provided for the passing of the status of slavery through the mother and not the father. It establishing harsh controls over the conduct of the enslaved, including prohibitions on them meeting in large numbers. Slaves had virtually no rights, although the code did enjoin masters to take care of the sick and old.

[153] Ed. Sue Peabody, "Slavery in France The Problem and Early Responses", in Peabody, *'There Are No Slaves in France': The Political Culture of Race and Slavery in the Ancien Régime*, Oxford, 1997. It set conditions whereby slave owners could bring their slaves to France without fear of losing them. According to the edict, there were two legitimate purposes for bringing slaves to France: to give them religious instruction or to teach them a trade. But the Parlement of Paris did not register the Edict of October 1716, which created a legal limbo for slaves who came to Paris or other cities within the parlement's jurisdiction.

apprehend him, from a court of justice. While in prison, the servant institutes a process against his master, and is declared free. After the permission of slaves in the colonies, the edict of 1716 was necessary, to transfer that slavery to Paris; not without many restraints, as before remarked; otherwise the ancient principles would have prevailed. The author *De jure Novissimo* tho' the natural tendency of his book, as appears by the title, leads the other way, concurs with diverse [5] great authorities, in reprobating the introduction of a new species of servitude. In England, where freedom is the grand object of the laws, and dispensed to the meanest individual, shall the laws of an infant colony, Virginia, or of a barbarous nation, Africa, prevail? From the submission of the negro to the laws of England, he is liable to all their penalties, and consequently has a right to their protection. There is one case I must still mention; some criminals having escaped execution in Spain, were let free in France.

[Lord Mansfield - Rightly: for the laws of one country have not whereby to condemn offences supposed to be committed against those of another.]

An objection has arisen, that the West India company, with their trade in slaves, having been established by the law of England, it's [sic] consequences must be recognized by that law; but the establishment is local, and these consequences local and not the law of England, but the law of the Plantations.

The law of Scotland annuls the contract to serve for life; except in the case of colliers, and one other instance of a similar nature. A case is to be found in the History of the Decisions, where a term of years was discharged, as exceeding the usual limits of human life. At least, if contrary to all these decisions, the court should incline to think Mr. Stewart has a title, it must be by presumption of contract, there being no deed in evidence; on this supposition, Mr. Stewart was obliged, undoubtedly, to apply to a court of justice. Was it not sufficient, that without form, without written testimony, without even probability of a parol contract, he should venture to pretend a right over the person and property of the negro, emancipated, as we contend, by his arrival hither, at a vast distance from his native country, while he vainly indulged the natural expectation of enjoying liberty, where there was no man who did not enjoy it? Was not this sufficient, but he must still proceed, seize the unoffending victim, with no other legal pretence for such a mode of arrest, but the taking an ill advantage of some inaccurate expressions in the Habeas Corpus Act; and thus pervert an establishment designed for the perfecting of freedom? I trust, an exception from a single clause, inadvertently worded, (as I must take the liberty to remark again) of that one statute, will not be allowed to overrule the law of England. I cannot leave the court, without some excuse for the confusion in which I rose, and in which I now appear: For the anxiety and apprehension I have expressed, and deeply felt. It did not arise from want of consideration, for I have considered this cause for months, I may say years; much less did it spring from a doubt, how the cause might recommend itself to the candor and wisdom of the court. But I felt myself over-powered by the weight of the question. I now in full conviction how opposite to natural justice Mr. Stewart's claim is in firm persua- [6] sion of it's [sic] inconsistency with the laws of England, submit it chearfully [sic] to the judgment of this honourable court: And hope as much honour to your lordships from the exclusion of this new slavery, as our ancestors obtained by the abolition of the old.

Mr. Alleyne - Though it may seem presumption in me to offer any remarks, after the elaborate discourse but now delivered, yet I hope the indulgence of the court; and shall confine my observations to some few points, not included by Mr. Hargrave. 'Tis well known to your lordships, that much has been asserted by the ancient philosophers and civilians, in defence of the principles of slavery: Aristotle has particularly enlarged on that subject. An observation still it is, of one of the most able, most ingenious, most convincing writers of modern times, whom I need not hesitate, on this occasion, to prefer to Aristotle, the great Montesquieu, that Aristotle, on this subject, reasoned very unlike the philosopher. He draws his precedents from barbarous ages and nations, and then deduces maxims from them, for the contemplation and practice of civilized times and countries. If a man who in battle has had his enemy's throat at his (word's point, spares him, and says therefore he has power over his life and liberty, is this true? By whatever duty he was bound to spare him in battle, (which he always is, when he can with safety) by the same he obliges himself to spare the life of the captive, and restore his liberty as soon as possible, consistent with those considerations from whence he was authorised to spare at first; the same indispensible [sic] duty operates throughout. As a contract: In all contracts there must be power on one side to give, on the other to receive; and a competent consideration. Now, what power can there be in any man to dispose of all the rights vested by nature and society in him and his descendants? He cannot consent to part with them, without ceasing to be a man; for they immediately flow from, and are essential to, his condition as such: They cannot be taken from him, for they are not his, as a citizen or a member of society merely; and are not to be resigned to a power inferior to that which gave them. With respect to consideration, what shall be adequate? As a speculative point, slavery may a little differ in it's [sic] appearance, and the relation of master and slave, with the obligations on the part of the slave, may be conceived; and merely in this view, might be thought to take effect in all places alike; as natural relations always do. But slavery is not a natural, 'tis a municipal relation; an institution therefore confined to certain places, and necessarily dropt by passage into a country where such municipal regulations do not subsist. The negro making choice of his habitation here, has subjected himself to the penalties and is therefore entitled to the protection of our laws. One remarkable case seems to require being mentioned. Some Spanish criminals having escaped from execution were set free in France.

[Lord Mansfield - Note distinction in the case, In this case, France [7] was not bound to judge by the municipal laws of Spain; nor was to take cognizance of the offences supposed against that law.]

There has been started an objection, that a company having been established by our government for the trade of slaves, it were unjust to deprive them here. – No: The government incorporated them with such powers as individuals had used by custom, the only title on which that trade subsisted; I conceive, that had never extended, nor could extend, to slaves brought hither; it was not enlarged at all by the incorporation of that company, as to the nature or limits of it's [sic] authority. 'Tis said, let slaves know they are all free as soon as arrived here, they will flock over in vast numbers, over-run this country, and desolate the plantations. There are too strong penalties by which they will be kept in; nor are the persons who might convey them over much induced to attempt it; the despicable condition in which negroes have the misfortune to be considered, effectually prevents their importation in any considerable degree. Ought we not, on our part, to guard and preserve that liberty by which we are distinguished by all the earth! to be jealous of whatever measure has a tendency to diminish the veneration due to the first of blessings? The horrid cruelties, scarce credible in recital, perpetrated in America, might, by the allowance of slaves amongst us, be introduced here. Could your lordship, could any liberal and ingenuous temper, endure, in the fields bordering on this city, to see a wretch bound for some trivial offence to a tree, torn and agonizing beneath the scourge? Such objects might by time become familiar, become unheeded by this nation; exercised, as they are now, to far different sentiments, may those sentiments never be extinct! the feelings of humanity! the generous sallies of free minds! May such principles never be corrupted by the mixture of slavish customs! Nor can I believe, we shall suffer any individual living here to want that liberty, whole effects are glory and happiness to the public and every individual.

Mr. Wallace – The question has been stated, whether the right can be supported here; or, if it can, whether a course of proceedings at law be not necessary to give effect to the right? 'Tis found in three quarters of the globe, and in part of the fourth. In Asia the whole people; in Africa and America far the greater part; in Europe great numbers of the Russians and Polanders. As to captivity in war, the Christian princes have been used to give life to the prisoners; and it took rise probably in the Crusades, when they gave them life, and sometimes enfranchised them, to enlist under the standard of the cross, against the Mahometans. The right of a conqueror was absolute in Europe, and is in Africa. The natives are brought from Africa to the West Indies; purchase is made there, not because of positive law, but there being no law against it. It cannot be in consideration by this or any other court, to see, whether the West India regulations are the best possible; such as they are, [8] while they continue in force as laws, they must be adhered to. As to England, not permitting slavery, there is no law against it; nor do I find any attempt has been made to prove the existence of one. Villenage itself has all but the name. Tho' the dissolution of tile: monasteries, amongst other material alterations, did occasion the decay of that tenure, slaves could breathe in England: For villains [sic] were in this country, and were mere slaves, in Elizabeth. Sheppard's *Abridgement*, afterwards, lays they were worn out in his time.[154]

[Lord Mansfield mentions an assertion, but does not recollect the author, that two only were in England in the time of Charles the 2d. at

---

[154] Ed. William Sheppard, *A Grand Abridgement of the Common and Statute Law of England*, London, 1675, Pt IV, 167: "For villeins, which were bondmen, and was a servile tenure, are long since gone. And therefore of them...we shall say nothing at all."

the time of the abolition of tenures.]

In the cases cited, the two first directly affirm an action of trover, an action appropriated to mere common chattels. Lord Holt's opinion, is a mere dictum, a decision unsupported by precedent. And if it be objected, that a proper action could not be brought, 'tis a known and allowed practice in mercantile transactions, if the cause arises abroad, to lay it within the kingdom: Therefore the contract in Virginia might be laid to be in London, and would not be traversable.[155] With respect to the other cases, the particular mode of action was alone objected to; had it been an action *per quod servitium amisit*, for loss of service, the court would have allowed it. The court called the person, for the recovery of whom it was brought, a slavish servant, in *Chamberlayne's Case*.[156] Lord Hardwicke, and the afterwards Lord Chief Justice Talbot, then Attorney and Solicitor-General, pronounced a slave not free by coming into England. 'Tis necessary the masters bring them over; for they cannot trust the whites, either with the stores or the navigating the vessel. Therefore, the benefit taken on the Habeas Corpus Act ought to be allowed.

Lord Mansfield observes, The case alluded to was upon a petition in Lincoln's Inn Hall, after dinner; probably, therefore, might not, as he believes the contrary is not usual at that hour, be taken with much accuracy. The principal matter was then, on the earnest solicitation of many merchants, to know, whether a slave was freed by being made a Christian? And it was resolved, not. 'Tis remarkable, tho' the English took infinite pains before to prevent their slaves being made Christians, that they might not be freed, the French suggested they must bring their's [sic] into France, (when the edict of 1706 was petitioned for,) to make them Christians. He said, the distinction was difficult as to slavery, which could not be resumed after emancipation, and yet the condition of slavery, in it's [sic] full extent, could not be tolerated here. Much consideration was necessary, to define how far the point should be carried. The court must consider the great detriment to proprietors, there being so great a number in the ports of this kingdom, that many thousands of pounds would be lost to the owners, by setting them free. (A gentleman observed, no great danger; for in a whole fleet, usually, there would not be six slaves.) As to France the case stated decides no [9] farther than that kingdom; and there freedom was claimed, be-

---

[155] Ed. Meaning, could not be formally denied in pleading.
[156] Ed. *Chamberline (or Chamberlain) v Harvey* (1696) 1 Ld Raym 146, 91 ER 994; (1701) 5 Mod 182, 87 ER 598.

cause the slave had not been registered in the port where he entered, conformably to the edict of 1706. Might not a slave as well be freed by going out of Virginia to the adjacent country, where there are no slaves, if change to a place of contrary custom was sufficient? A statute by the legislature, to subject the West India property to payment of debts, I hope, will be thought some proof; another at devests [sic] the African Company of their slaves, and vests them in the West India Company: I say, I hope these are proofs the law has interfered for the maintenance of the trade in slaves, and the transferring of slavery. As for want of application properly to a court of justice; a common servant may be corrected here by his master's private authority. Habeas corpus acknowledges a right to seize persons by force employed to serve abroad. A right of compulsion there must be, or the mailer will be under the ridiculous necessity of neglecting his proper business, by staying here to have their service, or must be quite deprived of those slaves he has been obliged to bring over. The case, as to service for life was not allowed, merely for want of a deed to pass it.

The court approved Mr. Alleyne's opinion of the distinction, how far municipal laws were to be regarded: Instanced the right marriage; which, properly solemnized, was in all places the same, but the regulations of power over children from it, and other circumstances, very various; and advised, if the merchants thought it so necessary, to apply to parliament, who could make laws.

Adjourned till that day se'nnight.

Mr. Dunning – 'Tis incumbent on me to justify Captain Knowles's detainer of the negro; this will be effected, by proving a right in Mr. Stewart; even a supposed one: For till that matter was determined, it were somewhat unaccountable that a negro should depart his service, and put the means out of his power of trying that right to effect, by a flight out of the kingdom. I will explain what appears to me the foundation of Mr. Stewart's claim. Before the writ of habeas corpus issued in the present case, there was, and there still is, a great number of slaves in Africa, (from whence the America plantations are supplied) who are saleable, and in fact sold. Under all these descriptions is James Somerset. Mr. Stewart brought him over to England; purposing to return to Jamaica, the negro chose to depart the service, and was stopt and detained by Captain Knowles, 'till his master should set sail and take him away to be sold in Jamaica. The gentlemen on the other side, to whom I impute no blame, but on the other hand much commendation, have advanced many ingenious propositions part of which are undeniably true, and part (as is usual in compositions of ingenuity) very disputable. 'Tis my misfortune [10] to address an audience, the greater part of which, I fear, are prejudiced the other way. But wishes, I am well convinced, will never enter into your lordships minds, to influence the determination of the point: This cause must be what in fact and law it is; it's [sic] fate, I trust, therefore, depends on fixt invariable rules, resulting by law from the nature of the case. For myself, would not be understood to intimate a wish in favour of slavery, by any means; nor on the other side, to be supposed maintainer of an opinion contrary to my own judgment. I am bound by duty to maintain those arguments which are most useful to Captain Knowles, as far as is consistent with truth; and if his conduit has been agreeable to the laws throughout, I am under a farther indispensable [sic] duty to support it. I ask no other attention than may naturally result from the importance of the question: Less than this I have no reason to expect; more, I neither demand nor with to have allowed.

Many alarming apprehensions have been entertained of the consequence of the decision, either way. About 14,000 slaves, from the most exact intelligence I am able to procure, are at present here; and some little time past, 166,914 in Jamaica; there are, besides, a number of wild negroes in the woods. The computed value of a negro in those parts 50*l*. a head. In the other islands I cannot state with the same accuracy, but on the whole they are about as many. The means of conveyance, I am told, are manifold; every family almost brings over a great number; and will, be the decision on which side it may. Most negroes who have money (and that description I believe will include nearly all) make interest with the common sailors to be carried hitherto. There are negroes not falling under the proper denomination of any yet mentioned, descendants of the original slaves, the aborigines, if I may call them so; these have gradually acquired a natural attachment to their country and situation; in all insurrections they side with their masters: Otherwise, the vast disproportion of the negroes to the whites, (not less probably than that of 100 to one) would have been fatal in it's [sic] consequences. There are very thong and particular grounds of apprehension, if the relation in which they stand to their masters is utterly to be dissolved on the instant of their coming into England. Slavery, say the gentlemen, is an odious thing; the name is: And the reality; if it were as one has defined and the rest supposed it. If it were necessary to the idea and the existence of James Somerset, that his master, even here, might kill, nay, might eat him, might sell living or dead, might make him and his descendants property alienable, and thus transmissible to posterity; this, how high soever my ideas may be of the duty of my profession, is what I should decline pretty much to defend or assert, for any purpose, seriously; I should only speak of it to testify my contempt and abhorrence. But this is what at present I am not at all concerned in; unless Captain Knowles, or Mr. Stewart, have killed or eat him. Freedom has been asserted as a natural right, and therefore unalienable and unrestrainable; there is perhaps no branch of this right, but in [11] some at all times, and in all places at different times, has been restrained: Nor could society otherwise be conceived to exist. For the great benefit of the public and individuals, natural liberty, which consists in doing what one likes, is altered to the doing what one ought. The gentlemen who have spoke with so much zeal, have supposed different ways by which slavery commences; but have omitted one, and rightly; for it would have given a more favourable idea of the nature of that power against which they combate. We are apt (and great authorities support this way of speaking) to call those nations universally, whose internal police we are ignorant of, barbarians; (thus the Greeks, particularly, stiled many nations, whose customs, generally considered, were far more justifiable and commendable than their own:) Unfortunately, from calling them barbarians, we are apt to think them so, and draw conclusions accordingly. There are slaves in Africa by captivity in war, but the number far from great; the country is divided into many small, some great territories, who do, in their wars with one another, use this custom. There are of these people, men who have a sense of the right and value of freedom; but who imagine that offences against society are punishable justly by the severe law of servitude. For crimes against property, a considerable addition is made to the number of slaves. They have a process by which the quantity of the debt is ascertained; and if all the property of the debtor goods and chattels is insufficient, he who has thus dissipated all he has besides, is deemed property himself; the proper officer (sheriff we may call him) seizes the insolvent, and disposes of him as a slave. We don't contend under which of these the unfortunate man in question is; but his condition was that of servitude in Africa; the law of the land of that country disposed of him as property, with all the consequences of transmission and alienation; the statutes of the British legislature confirm this condition; and thus he was a slave both in law and fact. I do not aim at proving these points; not because they want evidence, but because they have not been controverted, to my recollection, and are,

I think, incapable of denial. Mr. Stewart, with this right, crossed the Atlantic, and was not to have the satisfaction of discovering, till after his arrival in this country, that all relation between him and the negro, as master and servant, was to be matter of controversy, and of long legal disquisition. A few words may be proper, concerning the Russian slave, and the proceedings of the House of Commons on that case. 'Tis not absurd in the idea, as quoted, nor improbable as matter of fact; the expression has a kind of absurdity. I think, without any prejudice to Mr. Stewart, or the merits of this cause I may admit the utmost possible to be desired, as far as the case of that slave goes. The master and slave were both, (or should have been at least) on their coming here, new creatures. Russian slavery and even the subordination amongst themselves, in the degree they use it, is not here to be tolerated. Mr. Alleyne justly observes, the [12] municipal regulations of one country are not binding on another; but does the relation cease where the modes of creating it, the degrees in which it subsists, vary? I have not heard, nor, I fancy, is there any intention to affirm, the relation of master and servant ceases here? I understand the municipal relations differ in different colonies, according to humanity, and otherwife. A distinction was endeavoured to be established between natural and municipal relations; but the natural relations are not those only which attend the person of the man, political do so too; with which the municipal are most closely connected: Municipal laws, strictly, are those confined to a particular place; political, are those in which the municipal laws of many states may and do concur. The relation of husband and wife, I think myself warranted in questioning, as a natural relation: Does it subsist for life; or to answer the natural purposes which may reasonably be supposed often to terminate sooner? Yet this is one of those relations which follow a man every where. If only natural relations had that property, the effect would be very limited indeed. In fact, the municipal laws are principally employed in determining the manner by which relations are created; and which manner varies in various countries, and in the fame country at different periods; the political relation itself continuing usually unchanged by the change of place. There is but one form at present with us, by which the relation of husband and wife can be constituted; there was a time when otherwise I need not say other nations have their own modes, for that and other ends of society. Contract is not the only means, on the other hand, of producing the relation of master and servant; the magistrates are empowered to oblige persons under certain circumstances to serve. Let me take notice, neither the air of England is too pure for a slave to breathe in, nor the laws of England have rejected servitude. Villenage in this country is said to be worn out; the propriety of the expression strikes me a little. Are the laws not existing by which it was created? A matter of more curiosity than use, it is, to enquire when that let of people ceased.

The Statute of Tenures did not however abolish villenage in gross; it left persons of that condition in the same state as before; if their descendants are all dead, the gentlemen are right to say the subject of those laws is gone, but not the law; if the subject revives, the law will lead the subject. If the statute of Charles the 2d.[157] ever be repealed, the law of villenage revives in it's [sic] full force. If my learned brother, the serjeant, or the other gentlemen who argued on the supposed subject of freedom, will go thro' an operation my reading assures me will be sufficient for that purpose, I shall claim them as property. I won't, I assure them, make a rigorous use of my power; I will neither sell them, eat them, nor part with them. It would be a great surprise, and some inconvenience, if a foreigner bringing over a servant, as soon as he got hither, must take care of his carriage, his horse, and himself, in whatever method he might have the luck to invent. He must [13] find his way to London on foot. He tells his servant, Do this; the servant replies, Before I do it, I think fit to inform you, Sir, the first step on this happy land sets all men on a perfect level; you are just as much obliged to obey my commands. Thus neither superior or inferior, both go without their dinner. We should find a singular comfort, on entering the limits of a foreign country, to be thus at once devested [sic] of all attendance and all accommodation. The gentlemen have collected more reading than I have leisure to collect or industry (I must own) if I had leisure: Very laudable pains has [sic] been taken, and very ingenious, in collecting the sentiments of other countries, which I shall not much regard, as affecting the point or jurisdiction of this court. In Holland, so far from perfect freedom, (I speak from knowledge) there are, who without being conscious of contract, have for offences perpetual labour imposed, and death the condition annext to non-performance. Either all the different ranks must be allowed natural, which is not readily conceived, or there are political ones, which cease not on change of soil. But in what manner is the negro to be treated? How far lawful to detain him? My footman, according to my agreement, is obliged to attend me from this city, or he is not; if no condition, that he shall not be obliged to attend, from hence he is obliged,

---

[157] Ed. 12 Car II c 24 (Tenures Abolition Act, 1660).

and no injury done.

A servant of a sheriff, by the command of his master, laid hand gently on another servant of his master, and brought him before his master, who himself compelled the servant to his duty; an action of assault and battery, and false imprisonment, was brought; and the principal question was, on demurrer, whether the master could command the servant, tho' he might have justified his taking of the servant by his own hands? The convenience of the public is far better provided for, by this private authority of the master, than if the lawfulness of the command were liable to be litigated every time a servant thought fit to be negligent or troublesome.

Is there a doubt, but a negro might interpose in the defence of a master, or a master in defence of a negro? If to all purposes of advantage, mutuality requires the rule to extend to those of disadvantage. 'Tis said, as not formed by contract, no restraint can be placed by contract. Which ever way it was formed, the consequences, good or ill, follow from the relation, not the manner of producing it. I may observe, there is an establishment, by which magistrates compel idle or dissolute persons, of various ranks and denominations, to serve. In the case of apprentices bound out by the parish, neither the trade is left to the choice of those who are to serve, nor the consent of parties necessary; no contract therefore is made in the former instance, none in the latter; the duty remains the same. The case of contract for life quoted from the Year-Books, was recognized as valid; the solemnity only of an instrument judged requisite. [14] Your lordships (this variety of service, with diverse other sorts, existing by law here,) have the option of classing him amongst those servants which he most resembles in condition: Therefore, (it seems to me) are by law authorised to enforce a service for life in the slave, that being a part of his situation before his coming hither; which as not incompatible, but agreeing with our laws, may justify subsist here: I think, I might say, must necessarily subsist, as a consequence of a previous right in Mr. Stewart, which our institutions not dissolving, confirm. I don't insist on all the consequences of villenage; enough is established for our cause, by supporting the continuance of the service. Much has been endeavoured, to raise a distinction, as to the lawfulness of the negro's commencing slave, from the difficulty or impossibility of discovery by what means, under what authority, he became such. This, I apprehend, if a curious search were made, not utterly inexplicable; nor the legality of his original servitude difficult to be proved. But to what end? Our legislature, where it finds a relation existing, supports it in all suitable consequences, without citing to enquire how it commenced. A man enlists for no specified time; the contract in construction of law, is for a year: The legislature, when once the man is enlisted, interposes annually to continue him in the service, as long as the public has need of him. In times of public danger he is forced into the service; the laws from thence forward find him a soldier, make him liable to all the burthen, confer all the rights (if any rights there are of that state) and enforce all penalties of neglect of any duty in that profession, as much and as absolutely, as if by contract he had so disposed of himself. If the court see a necessity of entering into the large field of argument, as to right of the unfortunate man, and service appears to them deducible from a discussion of that nature to him, I neither doubt they will, nor wish they should not. As to the purpose of Mr. Stewart and Captain Knowles, my argument does not require trover should lie, as for recovering of property, nor trespass: A form of action there is, the writ *per quod servitium amisit*, for loss of service, which the court would have recognized; it they allowed the means of suing a right, they allowed the right. The opinion cited, to prove the negroes free on coming hither, only declares them not saleable; does not take away their service. I would say, before I conclude, not for the sake of the court, of the audience; the matter now in question, interests the zeal for freedom of no person, if truly considered; it being only, whether I must apply to a court of justice, (in a case, where if the servant was an Englishman I might use my private authority to enforce the performance of the service, according to it's [sic] nature,) or may, without force or outrage, take my servant myself, or by another. I hope, therefore, I shall not suffer in the opinion of those whose honest passions are fired at the name of slavery. I hope I have not transgressed my duty to humanity; nor doubt I your lordships discharge of yours to justice. [15]

Serjeant Davy – My learned friend has thought proper to consider the question in the beginning of his speech, as of great importance; 'Tis indeed so but not for those reasons principally assigned by him. I apprehend, my lord, the honour of England, the honour of the laws of every Englishman, here or abroad, is now concerned. He observes, the number is 14,000 or 15,000; if so, high time to put an end to the practice; more especially, since they must be sent back as slaves, tho' servants here. The increase of such inhabitants, not interested in the prosperity of a country, is very pernicious; in an island, which can, as such, not extend it's [sic] limits, nor consequently maintain more than a certain number of inhabitants, dangerous in excess. Money from foreign trade (or any other means) is not the wealth of a nation; nor conduces any thing to support it, any farther than the produce of the earth will answer the demand of necessaries. In that case money enriches the inhabitants, as being the common representative of those necessaries; but this representation is merely imaginary and useless, if the encrease [sic] of people exceeds the annual stock of provisions requisite for their subsistence. Thus, foreign superfluous inhabitants augmenting perpetually, are ill to be allowed; a nation of enemies in the heart of a state, still worse. Mr. Dunning availed himself of a wrong interpretation of the word natural: It was not used in the sense in which he thought fit to understand that expression; 'twas used as moral, which no laws can supercede [sic]. All contracts, I do not venture to assert are of a moral nature; but I know not any law to confirm an immoral contract, and execute it. The contract of marriage is a moral contract, established for moral purposes, enforcing moral obligations; the right of taking property by descent, the legitimacy of children; (who in France are considered legitimate, tho' born before the marriage, in England not:) These, and many other consequences, flow from the marriage properly solemnized; are governed by the municipal laws of that particular state, under whose institutions the contracting and disposing parties live as subjects; and by whole established forms they submit the relation to be regulated, so far as it's [sic] consequences, not concerning the moral obligation, are interested. In the case of *Thorn* and *Watkins*,[158] in which your lordship was counsel, determined before Lord Hardwicke.- A man died in England, with effects in Scotland; having a brother of the whole, and a sister of the half blood: The latter, by the laws of Scotland could not take. The brother applies for administration to take the whole estate, real and personal, into his own hands, for his own use; the sister files a bill in Chancery. The then Mr. Attorney-General puts in answer for the defendant; and affirms, the estate, as being in Scotland, and descending from a Scotchman, should be governed by that law. Lord Hardwicke over-ruled the objection against the sister's taking; declared there was no pretence for it; and spoke thus, to this effect, and nearly in the following words - Suppose a foreigner [16] has effects in our stocks, and dies abroad; they must be distributed according to the laws, not of the place where his effects were, but of that to which as a subject he belonged at the

---

[158] Ed. *Thorne* v *Watkins* (1750) 2 Ves Sen 35, 28 ER 24.

time of his death. All relations governed by municipal laws, must be so far dependant, on them, that if the parties change their country the municipal laws give way, if contradictory to the political regulations of that other country. In the case of master and slave, being no moral obligation, but founded on principles, and supported by practice, utterly foreign to the laws and customs of this country, the law cannot recognize such relation. The arguments founded on municipal regulations, considered in their proper nature, have been treated so fully, so learnedly, and ably, as scarce to leave any room for observations on that subject: Any thing I could offer to enforce, would rather appear to weaken the proposition, compared with the strength and propriety with which that subject has already been explained and urged. I am not concerned to dispute, the negro may contract to serve; nor deny the relation between them, while he continues under his original proprietor's roof and protection. 'Tis remarkable, in all Dyer, for I have caused a search to be made as far as the 4th of Henry 8th, there is not one instance of a man's being held a villain who denied himself to be one; nor can I find a confession of villenage in those times.

[Lord Mansfield, the last confession of villenage extant, is in the 19th of Henry the 6th.[159]]

If the court would acknowledge the relation of master and servant, it certainly would not allow the most exceptionable part of slavery; that of being obliged to remove, at the will of the master, from the protection of this land of liberty, to a country where there are no laws; or hard laws to insult him. It will not permit slavery suspended for a while, suspended during the pleasure of the master. The instance of master and servant commencing without contract; and that of apprentices against the will of the parties, (the latter found in it's [sic] consequences exceedingly pernicious;) both these are provided by special statutes of our own municipal law. If made in France, or any where but here, they would not have been binding here. To punish not even a criminal for offences against the laws of another country; to let free a galley-slave, who is a slave by his crime; and make a slave of a negro, who is one, by his complexion; is a cruelty and absurdity that I trust will never take place here: Such as, if promulged,[160] would make

---

[159] Ed. YB Mich 19 Hen 6 p 65 fol 32b, Seipp 1440.083. (Plaintiff proved defendant was his villein by evidence of defendant's uncles. Newton CJCP told the uncles that they were villeins by confession and so were their descendants.)

[160] Ed. Johnson's Dictionary: "to promulgate, to publish, to teach openly."

England a disgrace to all the nations under earth: For the reducing a man, guiltless of any offence against the laws, to the condition of slavery, the worst and most abject state, Mr. Dunning has mentioned, what he is pleased to term philosophical and moral grounds, I think, or something to that effect, of slavery; and would not by any means have us think disrespectfully of those nations, whom we mistakenly call barbarians merely for carrying on that trade: For my part we may be warranted, I believe, in affirming the morality or propriety of the practice does not enter their heads; they make slave of whom they think fit. For [17] the air of England; I think, however, it has been gradually purifying ever since the reign of Elizabeth. Mr. Dunning seems to have discovered so much, as he finds it changes a slave into a servant; tho' unhappily, he does not think it of efficacy enough to prevent that pestilent disease reviving, the instant the poor man is obliged to quit (voluntarily quits, and legally, it seems we ought to say,) this happy country. However, it has been asserted, and is now repeated by me, this air is too pure for a slave to breathe in: I trust, I shall not quit this Court without certain conviction of the truth of that assertion.

Lord Mansfield – The question is, if the owner had a right to detain the slave, for the sending of him over to be sold in Jamaica. In five or six cases of this nature, I have known it to be accommodated by agreement between the parties: On it's [sic] first coming before me, I strongly recommended it here. But if the parties will have it decided, we must give our opinion. Compassion will not, on the one hand, nor inconvenience on the other, be to decide; but the law: In which the difficulty will be principally from the inconvenience on both sides. Contract for sale of a slave is good here; the sale is a matter to which the law properly and readily attaches, and will maintain the price according to the agreement. But here the person of the slave himself is immediately the object of enquiry; which makes a very material difference. The now question is, whether any dominion, authority or coercion can be exercised in this country, on a slave according to the American laws? The difficulty of adopting the relation, without adopting it in all it's [sic] consequences, is indeed extreme; and yet, many of those consequences are absolutely contrary to the municipal law of England. We have no authority to regulate the conditions in which law shall operate. On the other hand, should we think the coercive power cannot be exercised: 'Tis now about fifty years since the opinion given by two of the greatest men of their own or any times, (since which no contract has been brought to trial, between the masters and slaves;) the service performed by the slaves without wages, is a clear indication they did not think themselves free by coming hither.[161] The setting 14,000 or 15,000 men at once free loose by a solemn opinion, is much disagreeable in the effects it threatens. There is a case in Hobart, (*Coventry* and *Woodfall*,)[162] [sic] where a man had contracted to go as a mariner: But the now case will not come within that decision. Mr. Stewart advances no claim on contract; he rests his whole demand on a right to the negro as slave, and mentions the purpose of detainure to be the sending of him over to be sold in Jamaica. If the parties will have judgment, *fiat justitia, ruat cœlum*, let justice be done whatever be the consequence.[163] 50*l*. a head may not be a high price; then a loss follows to the proprietors of above 700,000*l*. sterling. How would the law stand with respect to their settlement; their wages? How many actions for any slight coercion by [18] the master? We cannot in any of these points direct the law; the law must rule us. In these particulars, it may be matter of weighty consideration, what provisions are made or set by law. Mr. Stewart may end the question, by discharging or giving freedom to the negro. I did think at first to put the matter to a more solemn way of argument: but if my brothers agree, there seems no occasion. I do not imagine, after the point has been discussed on both sides so extremely well, any new light could be thrown on the subject. If the parties chuse to refer it to the Common Pleas, they can give them that satisfaction whenever they think fit. An application to Parliament, if the merchants think the question of great commercial concern, is the best, and perhaps the only method of settling the point for the future. The Court is greatly obliged to the gentlemen of the Bar who have spoke on the subject; and by whose care and abilities so much has been effected, that the rule of decision will be reduced to a very easy compass. I cannot omit to express particular happiness in seeing young men, just called to the Bar, have been able so much to profit by their reading. I think it right the matter should stand over;

---

[161] Ed. As Chater has pointed out, "free" servants in the eighteenth century were not necessarily paid wages. See Introduction, above, page 36. It would be extraordinary if Mansfield did not know that. Did he ignore the fact, as he ignored the fact that slaves were hardly in a position to demand wages?

[162] Ed. *Coventry* v *Woodhall* (1615) Hob 134, 80 ER 284: "...generally no man can force his apprentice to go out of the kingdom, except it be so expressly agreed, or that the nature of his apprentice-hood doth import it, as if he be bound apprentice to a merchant-adventurer, or a sailor, or the like."

[163] Ed. Often, more accurately and poetically translated as "let justice be done though the heavens fall".

and if we are called on for a decision, proper notice shall be given.[164]

---

[164] Ed. For judgment in Lofft's Reports, see page 232.

Lord Mansfield's Judgment

1. The Scots Magazine/Estwick version

Version originally printed in 34 Scots Magazine pp. 298–299, June 1772, reprinted with minor amendments and notes in Granville Sharp, The Just Limitation of Slavery in the Laws of God, Compared with the Unbounded Claims of the African Traders and British American Slaveholders, 1776, Appendix 8, p 65.[165]

[65]

> A Copy of what "is said to be the substance of Lord Mansfield's speech in the case of Somerset and Knowles: ...taken from the second edition of a tract, printed in 1773, intituled, 'Considerations on the Negroe Cause, so called, addressed to the right honourable lord Mansfield, lord chief justice of the court of King's Bench', by Samuel Estwick,[166] A.[sic] M. Assistant Agent for the island of Barbadoes page vii. viz"

We pay due attention to the opinion of Sir Philip Yorke and Mr. Talbot, in the year 1729, by which they pledged themselves to the British planters for the [66] legal consequences of bringing Negroe-slaves into this kingdom, or their being baptized; which opinion was repeated and recognized by Lord Hardwicke, sitting as chancellor, on the 19th of October, 1749, to the following effect: he said,[167]

> "that trover would lay for a negroe-slave: that a notion prevailed, that if a slave came into England, or became a Christian, he thereby became emancipated;but there was no foundation in law for such a notion: that when he and

---

[165] Ed. Also reprinted in Shyllon, *Black Slaves*, pp 108–110.

[166] Ed. Estwick, Samuel (?1736–95), of Berkeley St., London and Barbados, Published in *The History of Parliament: the House of Commons 1754-1790*, ed L Namier, J Brooke, 1964. [http://www.historyofparliamentonline.org/volume/1754-1790/member/estwick-samuel-1736-95], accessed 22 September 2015. Estwick became MP for Westbury and resigned to become "secretary and register" of the Royal Hospital Chelsea in 1783: Jour Ho Com 20 March 1783 p 306.

[167] Ed. The *Scots Magazine* version does not put the following passage in quotation marks.

Lord Talbot were attorney and solicitor general, this notion of a slave becoming free by being baptized pervailed [sic][168] so strongly, that the planters industriously prevented their becoming christians: upon which their opinion was taken; and upon their best consideration they were both clearly of opinion, that a slave did not in the least alter his situation or state towards his master or owner, either by being christened, or coming to England: that though the statute of Charles II.[169] had abolished (*homage*)[170] tenure so far, that no man could be a Villein regardant;[171] yet if he would acknowledge himself a Villein engrossed in any court of record, he [67] knew of no way by which he could be entitled to his freedom, without the consent of his master."

We feel the force of the inconveniences and consequences that will follow the decision of this question: yet all of us are so clearly of one opinion upon the only question before us, that we think we ought to give judgment without adjourning the matter to be argued before all the judges, as usual in the habeas corpus, and as we at first intimated an intention of doing in this case. The only question then is, *Is the cause returned sufficient for the remanding him?*[172] If not, he must be discharged. The cause returned is, the slave absented himself and departed from his master's service, and refused to return and serve him during his stay in England; whereupon, by his master's orders, he was put on board the ship by force, and there detained in secure custody,[173] to be carried out of the kingdom and sold. So high an act of dominion must derive its authority, if any such it has, from the law of the kingdom where executed. A foreigner cannot be imprisoned here on the authority of any law existing in his own country. The power of a master over his servant is different in all countries, more or less limited or extensive, the exercise of it therefore[174] must always be regulated [68] by

---

[168] Ed. The *Scots Magazine* version has "prevailed".

[169] Ed. In St Realm, 12 Car II, c 24 (Tenures Abolition Act, 1660).

[170] G#: See a part of my lord Mansfield's speech printed in Appendix, p. 11 of "a Treatise upon the Trade from Great Britain to Africa, by an African merchant" wherein the word "homage" is inserted.

[171] Ed. The *Scots Magazine* version has "regerdine". It would seem that Estwick corrected it. Interestingly, the *General Evening Post* version has "regerdane".

[172] Ed. *Scots Magazine* version does not put this phrase in italics.

[173] Ed. The phrase "and there detained in secure custody" is not in the *Scots Magazine* version.

[174] Ed. *Scots Magazine* version does not have the word "therefore".

the laws of the place where exercised. The state of slavery is of such a nature, that it is incapable of being now introduced by courts of justice upon mere reasoning, or[175] any principles natural or political; it must take its rise from positive law; the origin of it can in no country or age be traced back to any other source. Immemorial usage preserves the memory of positive law long after all traces of the occasion, reason, authority, and time of its introduction, are lost, and in a case so odious as the condition of slaves must be taken strictly. (*Tracing the subject to natural principles, the claim of slavery never can be supported*)[176] The power claimed by this return was never is use here: (*or acknowledged by the law.*) No master ever was allowed here to take a slave by force to be sold abroad because he had deserted from his service, or for any other reason whatever; we cannot say, the cause set forth by this return is allow-[69]ed or approved by the laws of this kingdom, and therefore the man must be discharged.

---

[175] Ed. *Scots Magazine* version has "inference from" at this point which are not included in the Estwick version.

[176] G#: These additions in Italics between hooks before and after the words "The power claimed by this return was never in use here," are taken from the notes of a very ingenious and able counsellor, who was present when the judgement was given.– The rest of his notes sufficiently agree in substance with what Mr. Estwick has printed.

2. Granville Sharp MS of the Judgment

MS in New York Historical Society,
Manuscript Collections Relating to Slavery:
Granville Sharp Collection, 1768–1803.

[1]

Trinity Term 1772

On Monday 22d June 1772

In Banco Regis

The Court proceeded to give Judgment in the Case of Somerset the Negro before the Court upon the Return of the Habeas Corpus.

Lord Mansfield first stated the Return, then spoke to the following import -

We pay due attention to the Opinions of Sir Philip Yorke and Mr Talbot taken in the Year 1729 whereby they pledge themselves to the West Indian Planters for the legal consequences of Slaves coming here or being Baptised. This Opinion was Solemnly Recognized by Lord Hardwicke sitting as Chancellor June the 9th 1749 to this effect.

> "That there had been a prevailing Opinion in the Colonies that Baptism was an Emancipation of a Negro Slave, and that, in consequence of coming here, such Slave became free. That he was satisfied there was no Ground for the Opinion:- and he and Lord Talbot had so expressed themselves upon a cause referred to them for their Opinions, when Attorney and Solicitor General. They had given it all the consideration that the subject could require, and he was satisfied, that neither Baptism nor coming to England made any alteration in [2] the Temporal State of the Slave. That the Statute of the 12th Charles 2d Ch. 4[177] had abol-

[177] Ed. In Stat Realm: 12 Car II c 24 (Tenures Abolition Act, 1660). The Act was a

ished Villeins regardant, but if a Man was solemnly to confess himself a Villein in Gross, he knew of no Law which could possibly prevent the operation of such Confession."

We have, likewise, paid due regard to the many Arguments urged at the Bar of inconveniences, but we are all so clearly of one Opinion upon the question before Us, that there is no necessity to refer to the 12 Judges. The Question is, whether the Captain has returned a sufficient Cause for the detainer of Somerset? The Cause returned is, that he had kept him by order of his Master with an intent to send him abroad to Jamaica, there to be Sold. So high an Act of dominion must derive its force from the Laws of the Country; and, if to be justified here, must be justified by the Laws of England. Slavery has been different in different Ages and States: the exercise of the power of a Master over his Slave must be supported by the Laws of particular Countries; but no foreigner can in England claim a right over a Man: such a Claim is not known to the Laws of England. Immemorial Usage preserves positive Law after the occasion or accident which gave rise to it has been forgotten - And, tracing the subject to natural principles the claim of Slavery never can be supported - The power claimed never was in use here, or acknowledged by the Law. Upon the whole we cannot say the Cause returned is sufficient by the Law; and therefore the Man must be discharged.

(Copy)

---

re-enactment of the statute of the Commonwealth: *An Act for taking away the Court of Wards and Liveries*, November 27, 1656, Firth and Rait, *Acts and Ordinances of the Interregnum 1642–1660* London, HMSO, 1911, ii.1043, which itself had re-enacted a statute of the Long parliament: *Ordinance for removing the Court of Wards*, February 24, 1645–1646, Firth and Rait, ibid, i.833.

3. Letter to the *General Evening Post*

London June 21–23, 1772.

To the Editor of the General Evening Post.

SIR,
The following is as correctly my Lord M–d's Speech on the Negro Cause, as my memory, assisted by some notes, could make it: it begins after the stating of the return.

Yours, &c.
A CONSTANT READER.

We pay due attention to the opinion of Sir Philip York [sic] and Mr. Talbot in the year 1729, by which they pledged themselves to the British planters for the legal consequences of bringing slaves into this kingdom, or their being baptized; which opinion was repeated and recognized by Lord Hardwicke, sitting as Chancellor on the 19th of October, 1749, to the following effect: he said, that trover would lay for a negro slave; that a notion prevailed, that if a slave came into England, or became a Christian, he thereby became emancipated; but there was no foundation in law for such a notion; that when he and Lord Talbot were Attorney and solicitor General, this notion of a slave becoming free by being baptized prevailed so strongly, that the planters industriously prevented their becoming Christians; upon which their opinion was taken, and upon their best consideration they were both clearly of opinion, that a slave did not in the least alter his situation or state toward his master or owner, either by being christened, or coming to England; that though the statute of Charles II.[178] had abolished tenure so far, that no man could be a villein regerdane [sic],[179] yet if he would acknowledge himself a villein engrossed in any Court of Record, he knew of no way by which he could be entitled to his freedom without the consent of his master. We feel the force of the inconveniences and consequences that will follow the decision of this question. Yet all of

---

[178] Ed. Above, page 224. In St Realm: 12 Car II c 24 (Tenures Abolition Act, 1660).

[179] Ed. The *Scots Magazine* version has "regerdine". It would seem that Estwick corrected it to "regardant".

us are so clearly of one opinion upon the only question before us, that we think we ought to give judgment, without adjourning the matter to be argued before all the Judges, as usual in the Habeas Corpus, and as we at first intimated an intention of doing in this case. The only question then is, Is the cause returned sufficient for the remanding him? If not, he must be discharged. The cause returned is, the slave absented himself, and departed from his master's service, and refused to return and serve him during his stay in England; whereupon, by his master's orders, he was put on board the ship by force, and there detained in secure custody, to be carried out of the kingdom and sold. So high an act of dominion must derive its authority, if any such it has, from the law of the kingdom where executed. A foreigner cannot be imprisoned here on the authority of any law existing in his own country: the power of a master over his servant is different in all countries, more or less limited or extensive; the exercise of it therefore must always be regulated by the laws of the place where exercised. The state of slavery is of such a nature, that it is incapable of now being introduced by Courts of Justice upon mere reasoning or inferences from any principles, natural or political; it must take its rise from positive law; the origin of it can in no country or age be traced back to any other source: immemorial usage preserves the memory of positive law long after all traces of the occasion, reason, authority, and time of its introduction are lost; and in a case so odious as the condition of slaves must be taken strictly, the power claimed by this return was never in use here; no master ever was allowed here to take a slave by force to be sold abroad because he had deserted from his service, or for any other reason whatever; we cannot say the cause set forth by this return is allowed or approved of by the laws of this kingdom, therefore the man must be discharged.

4. Lincoln's Inn, Hill MS version

Hill MS 10 ff. 312–314.

[*313*] ...

Lord Mansfield. We pay due attention to the opinion of Mr Ph. York and Mr Talbot in the Year 1729 by which they pledged themselves to the British Plantations for the legal consequences of Slaves coming into this Country and being baptized: which was repeated and recognized by Lord Hardwicke sitting as Chancellor in October 14, 1749 to the following effect: he said an Action of Trover would lie for a Negro Slave, That a Notion had prevailed in the Plantations that if a Slave became a Christian and was baptized he was from that circumstance made free – That when Mr Talbot and he were Sollicitor and Attorney General they were applied to for their Opinion; and that the notion which had prevailed had been the Occasion of preventing many from becoming Christians; but on the best consideration they could give it they thought there was no foundation for this Opinion either from their coming into England or being baptized; That though the Statute has [*314*] abolished villeins regardant to a Manor, yet if a Man comes into Court and confesses himself to be another's Slave he would be a villein in Gross. –

Many Arguments of convenience and inconvenience have weighed with us but we are all so clear in our Opinions that we think we ought to give Judgment without having it argued before all the Judges which is usual in all those cases of Habeas Corpus for a reason that is obvious. — The only Question is whether the Cause of the detention upon the return be sufficient. If it be sufficient then the consequence will be that James Somerset must be remanded. If it be not sufficient then he must be discharged – The Cause which is alleged is that the said James Somerset absented himself from his Master without his leave and against his consent and refused to serve him whereupon he was put on Board a Ship to be carried to Jamaica and there to be sold.

So high an Act of Dominion and power must derive its Authority from the Law of this Country. A Foreigner can't be imprisoned here on any Law of his own Country.– The power of a Master over his servant is different in different Countries, in some it is more in others – less extensive. It must be regulated according to the Law of the place where it is exercised.

Slavery is of such a Nature as not to be introduced by any inference from principles either natural or political. It must be from positive Law. Its origin in no other Country is derived from any other source.

Immemorial usage has continued Laws, when the Reason occasion and Circumstances that induced them – have long ceased – Slavery is so odious that it must be construed strictly. No master was ever Allowed here to send his servant abroad because he absented himself from his service or for any other Cause. No Authority can be found for it in the Laws of this Country. And therefore we are all of Opinion that James Somerset must be discharged.

5. Lincoln's Inn, Ashhurst Paper Book

Dampier MS, APB 10b.

[1]

Ex Parte Summerset

A negroe slave brought from the West Indies cant be carried back by force for the purpose of being sold as a slave.

Tr[inity] Term 12. G. 3d.

...

L[or]d Mansfield gave the opinion of the Court -
States the Ret[urn]

We pay due att[entio]n to [the] Opinion of York[e] and Talbot 1729 - by w[hi]ch they pledged themselves for the legal consequences of Negro slaves being let into this country and baptized - states opinion recognised by L[or]d Hardwick in a subsequent case [spaces] That did not alter his situation or state with respect to his Master or owner - that though tenures abolished... might make him self Villein by confession

But clear of opinion as to the only Q[uestio]n before us that we think [we] ought to give our Opin[io]n... without refer[rin]g it to all the Judges[.]

Q[uestion][:] was cause ret[urne]d sufficient cause in that [the] slave absconded and departed and refused to return whereupon he was put on Board ship by force to be carried out of [the] realm and sold abroad.

So high an Act of Domin[io]n must derive its author[it]y from [the Law][180] of [the] Country where exercised[.]

[A] man cant be imprison'd here under any authority of the L[aw] of [his][181] own country[.]

---

[180] Ed. Edge of text missing in MS.
[181] Ed. Missing text at left edge.

[The] power of authority of [a] master [di]ffer[s] in diff[erent] countrys[.] [It must]¹⁸² be exercised acc[or]d[in]g to [the] L[aw] of [the] country where [they] inhabit...

Slavery cant be traced back to any other source but positive L[aw]. The power claimed[ed] by this ret[urn] never was in use here - to be sent abroad and sold - for any cause[.]

[The] cause set forth by this ret[urn] is not allowed by the Law of this country and therefore the man must be discharged.

---

¹⁸² Ed. Missing text at left edge.

6. Lofft's Report

(1772) Lofft 1, 98 ER 499.

[18]

Trinity Term, June 22, 1772.

Lord Mansfield – On the part of Somerset, the case which we gave notice should be decided this day, the Court now proceeds to give its opinion. I shall recite the return to the writ of habeas corpus, as the ground of our determination; omitting only words of form. The captain of the ship on board of which the negro was taken, makes his return to the writ in terms signifying that there have been, and still are, slaves to a great number in Africa; and that the trade in them is authorized by the laws and opinions of Virginia and Jamaica; that they are goods and chattels; and, as such, saleable and sold. That James Somerset, is a negro of Africa, and long before the return of the king's writ was brought to be sold, and was sold to Charles Stewart, Esq. then in Jamaica, and has not been manumitted since; that Mr. Stewart, having occasion to transact business, came over hither, with an intention to return; and brought Somerset, to attend and abide with him, and to carry him back as soon as the business should be transacted. That such intention has been, and still continues; and that the negro did remain till the time of his departure, in the service of his master Mr. Stewart, and quitted it without his consent; and thereupon, before the return of the king's writ, the said Charles Stewart did commit the slave on board the *Ann and Mary*, to safe custody, to be kept till he should set sail, and then to be taken with him to Jamaica, and there sold as a slave. And this is the cause why he, Captain Knowles, who was then and now is, commander of the above vessel, then and now lying in the river of Thames, did the said negro, committed to his [19] custody, detain; and on which he now renders him to the orders of the court. We pay all due attention to the opinion of Sir Philip Yorke, and Lord Chief Justice Talbot, whereby they pledged themselves to the British planters, for all the legal consequences of slaves coming over to this kingdom or being baptized, recognized by Lord Hardwicke, sitting as Chancellor on the 19th of October 1749, that trover would lie: That a notion had prevailed, if a negro came over, or became a Christian, he was emancipated, but no ground in law; that he and Lord Talbot, when Attorney and Solicitor-General, were of opinion, that no such claim for freedom was valid; that tho' the Statute of Tenures had abolished villains regardant to a manor, yet he did not conceive but that a man might still become a villain in gross, by confessing himself such in open court. We are so well agreed, that we think there is no occasion of having it argued (as I intimated an intention at first,) before all the Judges, as is usual, for obvious reasons, on a return to a habeas corpus; the only question before us is, whether the cause on the return is sufficient? If it is, the negro must be remanded; if it is not, he must be discharged. Accordingly, the return states, that the slave departed and refused to serve; whereupon he was kept, to be sold abroad. So high an act of dominion must be recognized by the law of the country where it is used. The power of a master over his slave has been extremely different, in different countries. The state of slavery is of such a nature, that it is incapable of being introduced on any reasons, moral or political; but only positive law, which preserves its force long after the reasons, occasion, and time itself from whence it was created, is erased from memory: It's [sic] so odious, that nothing can be suffered to support it, but positive law. Whatever inconveniences, therefore, may follow from a decision, I cannot say this case is allowed or approved by the law of England; and therefore the black must be discharged.

Sharp's Memoranda on *Somerset v Stuart*

York Minster Library COLL1896/1

[185]

Memorandum concerning the Case of James Somerset.

The Writ of Habeas Corpus was granted upon the application of the Friends of James Somerset for his Relief from false Imprisonment so that he is properly Plaintiff in this cause, and yet he has been obliged to find Sureties for his Appearance under penalty of £80 and is put to heavy Charges at the Crown Office on that Account for the renewal of Recognizance from time to time, as if he had been Summoned to answer before the Court as an Offender or Defendant rather than as a Plaintiff.[183] On the other hand he understands that Mr Stuart (who is really the Offender not only against the Plaintiff but also against the Laws of the Land) is nevertheless excused the trouble and expense of any such Recognizance, though he ought (at least while the matter is depending in the Court) to have been equally bound to appear. But at present he may laugh at the form and parade of the Court, in carrying on the appearance of so Solemn an Inquiry, and yet leaving him entirely at Liberty to with draw his Claim and himself from the consequences of this enquiry; whenever matters are likely to go against him. That a Plaintiff should be bound under heavy Penalty to appear without a [186] Defendant (either in Custody or bound in Recognizance to Answer) is a new thing in the English Courts, which cannot easily (I believe) be reconciled with Justice.

When the Plaintiff was first brought up before the Chief Justice who granted the Writ of Habeas Corpus, his Lordship (instead of binding the Defendant to answer for his notorious outrage[)] advised the poor Widow, who had been at the Expense of the Writ, to purchase the Plaintiff of the Defendant; but was answered very properly by the Widow, that the same "would be an acknowledgement that the Plaintiff had a right to Assault and imprison a poor innocent Man in the

---

[183] Ed. Somerset was technically not a plaintiff, but the subject of the writ of habeas corpus. He had been released pending the trial of the issue as to the legality of his detention, but Sharp criticises the court for requiring sureties for his appearance while not requiring them of Stewart who had him detained.

Kingdom", and that she "would never be guilty of setting so bad an Example."

Now the Lord Chief Justice professes to have doubts in his Mind concerning this Question, and yet it is plain, by his advice to the Widow above mentioned, that he has neither Doubts nor Scruple on one side of the Question Vizt. when there is a possibility of favouring the Slave-holders Claim (though the same is entirely without foundation either in the Laws or Customs of this Country) and, consequently, we may fairly presume that his Doubts are confined to these particular Points as on [187] The other side of the Question, wherein there are clear and positive Laws to direct him, I mean the Relief and discharge a poor innocent Man from an unlawfull Imprisonment and unjust oppression.

For when any Man whatever in this Kingdom has been hurried in an outrageous violent manner on Shipboard and there confined in Irons in order to be Transported as a Slave, he is undoubtedly entitled to the Remedies which are clearly and positively pointed out in the Laws of this Kingdom and the authors of the Outrage are certainly liable to all the several Penalties of the said Laws for there is not the least exception or Clause whatsoever in any of the Laws that can justify a Doubt about the Extension of their Influence and protection to any Man whatsoever in this Kingdom, who stands in need of them. If a Man claims a Right to break the Laws of Protection and yet cannot produce some Law or other as clear and as positive as those by which he is restrained what room can there be for a Doubt?

But nevertheless if such Doubts, that is groundless Doubts, be admitted as reasons for excusing a manifest Breach of the Law all the Ties and obligations of Law will be thereby rendered vain and [188] Nugatory and the Judges will be no longer obliged to observe a strict legal discretion (*Discretio est discernere per legem quid sit justrum* 2 Inst 56)[184] in their Judgments (that is *discernere per Legem*) but their Will by such a means becomes the only Law. And whatever tends to render Law subservient to the Will of Judges must necessarily put a final Period to the very Existence of our present distempered Political Constitution!

(Copy)

---

[184] Ed. Meaning discretion is to discern through law what is just.

York Minster Library COLL1896/1

[189]

Memorandum

As Mr. Dunning is retained as Council against James Somerset, the following Anecdote may be worth the observation of Mr. Serjeant Davy Vizt.

In the Trial of the King and Thomas Lewis against Stapleton[185] and others, when my Lord Mansfield proposed to leave it to the Jury "to find whether the Plaintiff was the Defendant's property or not"[.] Mr Dunning replyed "Then if my Lord thinks there is Evidence sufficient for the Question, I shall submit to you, what my Ideas are upon such Evidence, reserving to myself an opportunity of discussing it more particularly, and insisting that no such property can exist, which I will maintain in any place, and in any Court in this Kingdom reserving to myself a right to insist that our Laws admit of no such property."

Thus Mr. Dunning has publickly pledged himself to maintain not only that our Laws admit of no such property; but also that no such property can exist, which is certainly true (with respect to strict justice) if Judge Blackstone[']s Arguments on the three Origins of Slavery are considered, See G. Sharp's Appendix p. [ ][186]

(Copy)

---

[185] Ed. The name is spelled "Stapylton" in the transcript of the trial.
[186] Ed. *An Appendix to the Representation (Printed in the Year 1769) of the Injustice and Dangerous Tendency of Tolerating Slavery, or of Admitting the Least Claim of Private Property in the Persons of Men in England.*, p 14.

Gregson v Gilbert

(The slave ship *Zong*)

The Declaration

in the King's Bench

From: John Wentworth, *A complete system of pleading: comprehending the most approved precedents and forms of practice; Chiefly Consisting of Such as have Never Before been Printed...* London: printed for G. G. and J. Robinson, Paternoster-Row, [1797]-99. 10 vols., vol. 4, pp. 422–425.[187]

[422]

LONDON, ss.[188] W. Gregson, &c. &c. complains of Thomas Gilbert, being, &c. for that whereas the said plaintiffs on the third day of July 1781, at, &c. according to the usage and custom of merchants, caused a certain writing or policy of assurance to be made in the name of the said William, but for the use, benefit and interest, and on the joint account of the said [423] by the said William, as well in his own name as for and in the name and names of all and every person or persons to whom the same did, might, or should appertain in part or in all, did make assurance, and caused himself and them, and every of them, to be insured, lost or not lost, at and from the coast of Africa, and during his trade and stay there, and to his discharging port or ports in the British West Indies, or conquered islands, upon every kind of goods and merchandizes, and also upon the body, tackle, apparel, ordnance, munition, artillery, boat, and other furniture of an in the good ship or vessel called the Zong, whereof was master, under God, for the voyage, [Luke][189] Collingwood, or whosoever else should go for master in the said ship, or by whatsoever other name or names the same ship, or the master thereof, was or should be named or called; beginning

---
[187] Ed. This source was identified by the late Professor Martin Dockray.
[188] Ed. *Scilicet*, that is to say, namely.
[189] Ed. There is a blank space in the text to allow for the insertion of Collingwood's first name.

the adventure upon the said goods and merchandizes from the loading thereof on board the said ship, and upon the same ship, &c. and should continue and endure, during her abode there, upon the said ship &c.; and further, until the said ship, with all her ordnance, tackle, apparel, goods, &c. whatever, should arrive at [blank space] upon the said ship, &c. until she had moored and anchored twenty-four hours in good safety, and upon the goods and merchandizes until the same be there discharged and safely landed; and should be lawful for the said ship, &c. in that voyage to proceed and sail to, and touch and stay at any ports or places whatsoever, without prejudice to that insurance; the said ship, &c. goods and merchandizes, &c. for as much as concerned the assureds, by agreement between the assurers and assureds in this policy, were and should be valued at the sum of [blank space] upon the whole of the ship, and on goods as interest appeared, valuing slaves at thirty pounds sterling per head, &c. without further account to be given by the assured for the same, touching, &c. insurance twenty pounds per cent; and in case of loss, which God forbid, the assurers not to make up any average loss under five pounds per sent, unless general. In witness whereof, they the assureds had subscribed their names and sums assured in Liverpool: and, by the said writing or policy of assurance, corn, salt, fish, fruit, flour, and seeds, were warranted free from average, unless general, and the ship was stranded; and by the said policy of insurance it was warranted to make up no average loss by trading in boats under ten pounds per cent, and by insurrections under three per cent, as by the said writing or policy of insurance, reference being thereunto had, will more fully and at large appear; of which said writing or policy of insurance the said Thomas afterwards, to wit, on the same day and year last aforesaid, at, &c. had notice: and thereupon afterwards, to wit, on the same day and year aforesaid, at Liverpool, to wit, at London, &c. in consideration that the said plaintiffs, at the special instance and request of the said defendant, had then and there paid to the said defendant the sum of forty guineas, of, &c. as a premium and reward for the assurance of two hundred pounds of and upon the premises aforesaid, mentioned in the said writing or policy of insu[424]rance, and had undertaken, and to the said defendant then and there faithfully promised to perform and fulfil all things contained in the said writing or policy of assurance, on the part and behalf of the insured to be performed and fulfilled, the said defendant undertook, and to the said plaintiffs then and there faithfully promised, that he the said T. would become an assurer for the said sum of two hundred of and upon the premises aforesaid, in the said writing or policy of insurance mentioned, or contained on his part and behalf as such assurer as to the said sum of two hundred pounds to be performed and fulfilled, according to the form and effect of the said writing or policy of assurance, and then and there subscribed the said writing or policy of assurance as such assurer for the said sum of two hundred pounds.

And the said plaintiffs further say, that the said ship or vessel called, &c. after the making of the said writing or policy of assurance, to wit, on the sixth day of September in the year aforesaid, was in good safety at the coast of Africa aforesaid, and was then and there loaded with divers negro slaves, to wit, five hundred negro slaves of great value, to wit of the value of fifteen thousand pounds, for his[190] said voyage.

And the said plaintiffs further say, that the said writing or policy of assurance so made in the name of the said W. G. was made for and on behalf, and for the use, interest, and benefit, and on the joint account of the said plaintiffs; and that the said plaintiffs, at the time of making the said writing or policy of assurance, and from that time, until and at the respective times of the damages, loss, and misfortunes hereinafter mentioned, were interested in the said negro slaves so loaden on board the said ship or vessel called the Zong, to a large value, to wit, to the value of all the money by the said plaintiffs ever insured or caused to be insured thereon.

And the said plaintiffs further say, that the said that the said ship or vessel called the Zong, with the said negro slaves so loaden on board her as aforesaid, and so being in good safety as aforesaid an having on board a reasonable and proper quantity of water for such a voyage as aforesaid, afterwards, to wit, on the said sixth day of September 1781, departed and set sail from the coast of Africa aforesaid towards the island of Jamaica in the British West Indies; and the same ship, with the same negro slaves so loaden on board her as aforesaid, sailing and proceeding on her said voyage from the coast of Africa towards the island of Jamaica aforesaid, and before her arrival there, to wit, at divers times before her said arrival there, by the perils of the sea, by violent and contrary winds, currents, and other misfortunes, was rendered foul and leaky, and was delayed, hindered, and retarded in her said voyage; and by reason thereof so much of the water on board the said ship for the said voyage was necessarily consumed and spent on board the said ship, that afterwards, and before the arrival of the said ship or vessel at the said island of Jamaica aforesaid, in her voyage afore-

---

[190] Ed. "His" appears to refer to the ship, but a seaman would refer to "her".

said, to wit, on the twenty-ninth day of November 1781, a sufficient supply or quantity of water did not remain on board the same ship or vessel for preserving the lives of the master and ma- [425]riners belonging to the said ship and on board the same, and of the said negro slaves so loaded and being on board her as aforesaid, for the residue of the said voyage; and by reason thereof afterwards, during the said voyage; and before the arrival of the said ship or vessel at the island of Jamaica aforesaid, to wit, on the said twenty-ninth day of November 1781 aforesaid, and at divers other days and times between that day and the arrival of the said ship or vessel at the island of Jamaica aforesaid, divers, to wit, sixty of the said negro slaves, then being on board the said ship or vessel, perished and died for want of water for their sustenance and support, and were wholly lost to the said plaintiffs; and divers others, to wit, forty other of the said negro slaves so loaded and being on board the said ship or vessel, for want of water for their sustenance and support, and by extreme thirst and phrenzy occasioned thereby, were compelled to throw themselves, and did throw themselves, into the sea, and thereby perished and were drowned, and totally lost to the said plaintiffs; and the master and mariners, for the necessary preservation of their own lives and the lives of the residue of the said negro slaves on board the said ship or vessel, and which, by reason of the said insufficiency of water, occasioned by the means aforesaid, they could not have otherwise preserved, were obliged to throw overboard into the sea divers, to wit, one hundred and fifty other of the said negro slaves, whereby the said last mentioned negro slaves perished and were drowned in the sea, and were totally lost to the said plaintiffs, whereby a loss above five pounds, to wit, fifty pounds by the hundred for every hundred of the value of the said negro slaves, so loaded on board the said ship or vessel, and insured as aforesaid , accrued thereon to the said plaintiffs, of all which premises the said defendant afterwards, to wit, on the first day of January 1783, at London aforesaid, in the parish and ward aforesaid, had notice; and by reason thereof, then and there ought to have paid to the said plaintiffs a large sum of money, to wit, the sum of one hundred pounds, in respect of the said sum of two hundred pounds, so by him insured as aforesaid, according to the form and effect of the said writing or policy of insurance, and of his said promise and undertaking in that behalf made as aforesaid.
(Count for money had and received.)

Proceedings in the Court of Kings Bench[191] on a Motion for a New Trial

Wednesday 21 and 22 May 1783

National Maritime Museum
MS REC/19

Court:
Lord Mansfield
Mr Justice Willes[192]
Mr Justice Buller

Counsel for the Insurers:
Mr Davenport
Mr Pigot
Mr Heywood

Counsel for the Slave Dealers:
Solicitor General[193]
Mr Chambre

---

[191] Ed. The report *Gregson* v *Gilbert* (1783) 3 Doug 232, 99 ER 629 is an abbreviated version of the arguments and the judgment differs in a number of respects from the National Maritime Museum MS reproduced here, which was commissioned by Granville Sharp, taken down in shorthand and then transcribed. In the NMM MS G# marked as "Voucher No 2" the present proceedings on a motion for a new trial. He marked as "Voucher No 1" the bill drawn up for the later abortive proceedings in the Court of Exchequer: see below, page 311. See G# comments, below, page 293.

[192] Ed. The judge's name is spelled "Wills" without an "e"in this MS. Above 153.

[193] Ed. John Lee. Below, note 203 on page 254.

244   *Cases on Slavery*

[1]

(Voucher No 2)[194]

In the Kings Bench

Wednesday May 21 1783

Gregson and others against Gilbert and others

Earl of Mansfield. This is the case of a Policy of Insurance upon the ship *Zong* at [space left blank] & from the Coast of Africa from her discharging [space left blank] Port or Ports to Jamaica Island, there is but one Witness examined upon either side, but it is a very singular Case, I don't see the Ground upon which they went, they called a Witness one Stubbs, he says he was bred to the Sea[,] that he was upwards of Forty years in the Service, that he was afterwards appointed to the Government of Annamabo[195] & he took his passage on board the *Zong* for Jamaica[.] there were 442 Slaves on board. Then he gives an Account of the particulars of the Voyage that there was a great Scarcity of Water, & the reason why they did not go into Tobago was, it was then [2] taken by the French & from their Mistaking on the 28 of November Jamaica for Hispaniola which carried them out of their Course[.] they had a Scarcity of Water, some of the Negroes died – They were forced, as the Captain in Consultation said & they approved of all the Captain did, from the Necessity he was under to save the rest they were forced to throw several of the Negroes over Board[.] there was above 64 Slaves that died, there was a Number thrown over board on the 29th of November, he was Cross examined as to, whether the Captain had taken Water enough, whether he might not have got Water, & according to his Judgment the Captain did what was right, he was under that Perilous Necessity[.] they all apprehended they should have died from want of Water if they had not thrown the Slaves overboard to preserve the rest, in short there was an absolute Necessity for throwing over the Negroes & in fact the great Misfortune arose from mistaking Jamaica for Hispaniola which carried them out of their Course, the Jury found

---

[194] Ed. Text in red. Text in red ink in the MS was evidently inserted by Granville Sharp (G#), including his footnotes.

[195] Ed. Anomabu (also known as Anomabo and Annamaboe), is a town on the coast of modern-day Ghana, 72 miles west of Accra.

Gregson v Gilbert

for the Plaintiffs to the value of the Number of Negroes thrown over board to save the rest.

The Matter left to the Jury was, whether it was from necessity for they had no doubt (though it shocks one very much) the Case of Slaves was the same as if Horses had been [3] thrown over board[.] it is a very shocking Case.[196] The Question was, whether there was an Absolute Necessity for throwing them overboard to save the rest, the Jury were of opinion there was - We granted a Rule to shew Cause from the Novelty of the Case. I don't know the Ground they went upon.

Mr Davenport. Your Lordship ordered a Rule for a New Trial with Liberty to move in arrest of Judgment. my ground was, that Stubbs's Evidence was no proof of the Existence of that absolute necessity which was made the Ground of the Cause & of the Verdict. There certainly was no proof of the existence of actual Necessity & if there was that this is no necessity within the Scope or Condition of the Policy.

The supposed necessity in proof from Stubbs was their having sailed from the Coast of Africa & upon Examination of the Casks of Water they had it was found by the Mate that when they were in a Latitude which would have enabled them to have gone to Tobago which at that time in fact was taken by the French[,] though not known to be so by the Crew of the Ship[,] she might have gone either into Barbadoes or St Lucia, that appears perfectly new in this Cause. [4] He said they did not go in because upon examining the state of the Casks though it turned out afterwards, though they were then taken for full Casks[,] some of them were 7 or 8 inches short; Upon that Examination there appeared to be sufficient Water to carry them to Jamaica[.] That that Water though found in the Ship afterwards in that state was sufficient to carry them to Jamaica appeared pretty clear because they had not began [sic] to find any deficiency or want of Water till they are supposed to have missed Jamaica by mistaking it for a part of the West end of Hispaniola – That was the Evidence this Man gave. – I will ask this single Question, had there been any short allowance of Water upon the 29 of November[?], because I take it that turns the whole Cause – Had there been any short allowance or had they been put to a Quarter Allowance or half Allowance or any Proportion whatever,

---

[196] G#: Shocking indeed! but more shocking that a Judge and Jury should be so indiscriminate.

My Lord if they had not there would not exist on the 29 of November that inevitable Necessity, because he proved there were then 3 Butts of sweet Water though not quite full & two & an half of what they call the Gang Casks,[197] Old round Casks, Spirit Casks in which Water was put which is of Course sower [sic][.] it is not agreeable to the taste, but it is certain that would preserve Life. It is put for that very purpose[:] it is known by Sea faring People[.] they [5] do drink it[.] they put it on Board for the very Purpose not having enough of Sweet water & to avoid all that Possibility of Distress from want of Water & they do not of Course go to the bad Water while the sweet remains. – My Ground is there did not exist on the 29th of November any actual Necessity for throwing the Slaves overboard[.] therefore in my Opinion the Verdict is ill founded. If three Butts is admitted & supposing them not full of Sweet there must be two and an half, those Casks contained 180 Gallons each, but, my Lord, there were 442 Slaves and about 17 Whites some of them Sick, the Captain is described to have been a Doctor that had never been [on] a Voyage in his Life as Captain, he was sick from the time they were put on Board & never able to command during the whole of the time – If there was, as proved there was, a Loss by Death of about 60 of these People[,] it would reduce the number to about 364 or 5, then, my Lord, 180 Gallons if there was but one Butt, would be 2 Quarts a Man upon that 29 of November.

Mr Justice Wills. How soon did she get into Port after that 29 of November[?]

Mr Davenport. The 17th or 18th of December.

Lord Mansfield. In December she got into Jamaica.– [6]
All your Observations the Witness Stubbs denied and spoke fully to necessity[.] you made all those Observations to the Jury and that there was but one Witness. I remember now it comes back to my Mind about that Stinking Water.

Mr Davenport. He swore to a necessity that did not exist. the Grounds upon which he swore are Grounds upon which the Verdict ought to be construed, that is the Grounds upon which the necessity is to be taken. He states there was but 3 Butts of Water[:] I will agree with

---

[197] Ed. OED, "gang-cask Naut. 1867, Smyth, Sailor's Word-bk., 'Gang-casks, small barrels used for bringing water on board in boats... usually containing 32 gallons.'"

him, I will suppose there was but one, the actual necessity does not exist[.] he might have given every Person on Board two Quarts a Day, don't every Body know one Quart for a Day or one Pint for a Day has for many & many Cases been sufficient in certain situations – Crews have been preserved without Water for 7 or 8 Days & There was one very remarkable instance of Peoples [sic] going without Water 10 Days but there is no doubt about it but there was 5 Casks of Water & they might have caught Rain before the 21st Day of December.

Lord Mansfield. If not for that accident and the Water had fell[,] he swore they would all have Perished.

Mr Davenport. My Lord I say, if that necessity did not exist & if it is not within the Terms of the Policy[,] there are other reasons upon which it ought to be [7] tried[.] my anxiety was if I could to have avoided any Discussion in Arrest of Judgment or in any error upon such a Record as this by excluding that necessity of the Verdict of the Jury, I wished for the sake of the Country & of the Parties that it might never come to the Question in Point of Law as it must inevitably do if another Jury persist in the same Verdict or this new Trial is refused. My anxiety was knowing the extent of the Trade and the immence consequence it is to the Country, I would rather while there was a chance refer it to the Consideration of the Jury to consider & weigh over & over their Verdict before they give way to a necessity that has not the most indisputable footing. It was upon that Account[,] though the Witness swore there was an absolute necessity, I ground myself upon two short facts. They never were at short allowance for a Moment at the time they first threw the Slaves over nor afterwards & that alone is an Answer, & there was no Insurrection not a Murmur amongst them.

Lord Mansfield. I take it their allowance was very small.

Mr Davenport. No my Lord, they had full Allowance to the very moment & upon Gauging the Casks two Quarts a Man then remained, supposing there was but one Butt of Water but I have no doubt at all either when that [8] Log Book was produced that Mate or any Body but that Witness the only one that knew Nothing but what he heard from the People & upon the supposed Gauge that he could collect, but we wanted satisfaction of the evidence of the Officers of the Ship and the other people on Board the Ship, though he computed them at 2 Quarts a Man & two & an half of sour Water he does not in that Evidence state how long that Water lasted. I stated it would have lasted two days till the Rain fell[.] they might have waited every Hour every minute & every moment 'till the actual necessity arose from an Insurrection of the Slaves on Board or the Whites dropping down & perishing, then they might say some necessity arose, was there one single Slave that had not had his full Allowance of Water when thrown over Board, why not keep him 'till he had his chance or could get Water[.] 'tis not stated nor could Stubbs say any Slave or other Creature on board had had less than their full allowance of Water up to the very moment they were thrown over[.] no Man could state it truly. Stubbs the Witness has not said that any Man was put to short Allowance or dreamt of short allowance[.] I put it to him[.] I thought it an answer that would intitle me to a Verdict when he said there never was a Moment of short Allowance [9] for that is the only thing that I call actual necessity – then one easily sees why Slaves are to go first & why the Sick ones are to go or those that would sell for the least Money are to go before the more Healthy & Valuable[.] one easily sees when this Captain had missed Jamaica. I should say rather from his own Ignorance or want of Skill that the Underwriters do not answer for. When he missed Jamaica and thought the Market gone[,] as there was no doubt it was, at least in appearance to him[,] it was then the time to make the underwriters pay for a bad Market. The second Point is, this is within no Peril nor within the Declaration that states it to be within the Peril of the Policy. it states by Perils of the Sea[,] which I take to be Violent & Contrary Winds & then by other Misfortunes was rendered foul Leaky delayed & retarded their Voyage[.] the Evidence upon that and the Account upon that part of the Evidence Mr Stubbs gave was that they had a long Passage by uncertain Weather, various Winds and by Calms but no one Peril. Would any Captain of Prudence suppose there was not Meat enough on Board (is that inscribed by the underwriter) Rice or Bread or Biscuit enough on Board, then he says he has not [10] Water enough on Board at the time[.] when did any Peril of the Sea whatever either prevent his getting sufficient Water or was there any Peril of the Sea that reduced them to this Necessity or any thing but Ignorance Unskilfulness or Blunder of some sort,[?] if they did not Gauge their Casks properly no doubt they ought to have gone into Barbadoes into St Lucia or Tobago after they had missed Jamaica. I shall shew why they did not by & by.

There could be no doubt of any Body that could look upon the map but can see at once the Moment they had missed Jamaica[.] if they had been Sailors at all they might have gone to Islands within 24 or 30 Hours of the outside where they would have had as Plenty of Water as they would in England they could have gone to the Grand Camanes[198] or the Isle of Pines[199] all of them within less than 30 Hours sail[.] at the very time they missed Jamaica the wind was then blowing easterly as it does constantly unless in Hurricanes at that time of the Year[.] this happened in November[.] there is a constant Trade Wind that would have carried them in less than 30 Hours, but say they[,] & here is their Point, ["]I did not know how soon I could beat my way on to Jamaica against that Wind nor could any Man say that["], therefore says he ["]if I am to be a Month or three weeks out then I lose my Market at Jamaica, I have missed Jamaica, I don't [11] know when I can work my Way up to Jamaica, I may be three weeks or a Month["], No Man that was a Sailor would have told the Court there was any necessity that could not be remedied in 30 Hours[.] if he had gone to any of these Islands he might have had full Quantity of Water, but though they had got full Water they would not have goten [sic] back to Jamaica then he had lost his Market & would not wish to go for Jamaica, ["]I can get enough Water for the Whites but I will send the Sickly part of the Crew over board["] – No Sailor will deny that any one of those 3 Islands might have been fetched with that Wind & they were more in Course than any other though it might be true he might have went [sic] back again under a fortnight or three weeks[.] It seems he did in three weeks get into Jamaica but during that time he did not chuse to risque the Death of the Slaves which in that case would not be charged to the Account of the Underwriters but the owners but says he ["]we will take Advantage of it before it happened in Strictness & before I am driven to it, I will take advantage of this Necessity & charge the underwriter.["] My Lord, I state there is not one Peril within this Policy that could give any Ground for the Recovery, not one Peril[,] no danger of the Sea has happened, the underwriter don't underwrite against [12] a long Voyage or against a Short or longer Passage, if he did he would insure the Market of Slaves, but he does not insure that. he insures only the Perils of the Sea or any Thing that hinders the Voyage from being performed.

Mr Justice Wills. There general Words in the Policy ["]all other Perils loss or Misfortune that shall come to the hurt detriment or damage of the Goods or any part thereof.["]

---

[198] Ed. Grand Cayman Island.
[199] Ed. Former name for *Isla de la Juventud* (Isle of Youth), Cuba.

Mr Davenport. I forbear touching upon any Thing but the fact constituting the Verdict[.] the Power they have to do it remains upon Record[.] there must be Judgment[.] I therefore avoid everything of that sort, but I state if they had been good sailors they would not have missed Jamaica.

Mr Justice Buller. Will not the Question you are now speaking upon appear upon the Record whether it is or not a Peril within the Policy[?].

Mr Davenport. I will tell your Lordship why not[.] there is no proof of those perils which they state & which if true they are not within the Terms of the Policy[,] namely violent & contrary winds or perils of the sea no contrary winds Violent or bad Winds to render the Ship foul & leaky none. That they had had calm weather which was not good for the Voyage, but the Underwriter don't underwrite against that, or that it should not be a [13] Voyage of three Months though it is usual in two Months because the Captain & owners trust to proper People[,] if it happens to be a long Voyage[,] to put in with Liberty to touch at any Port or Place if by their Blunder they have not done it to get more Provision or Water or whatever the supposed or probable want may be that is a blunder[,] a Mistake[,] the Ignorance of those with whom the Ship was intrusted [sic][,] but it is not a Peril within the Policy[.] it falls to the Lot of the owner & is not to be charged to the underwriter. I enquired for the Log Book, there, was none – Reckoning none – Compass none[:] Nothing that common Prudence[,] ordinary Prudence & requisite Prudence to Produce, to charge an underwriter, but a Gentleman that happens to be a Passenger is brought – no other person [-] many are alive though the Captain died, the Mate is out of the way at Present though he may be in London in a day or two[.] Mr Wallace said he had tried to get them but could not & it was no fault of theirs, Some person of the ship should have been produced to have shewn what happened.

Lord Mansfield. There was nobody, if I recollect right, in England. [14]

Mr Davenport. The Mate had been brought from Liverpool & was seen two days before the Trial & brought up by them, when we enquired we were told he was gone to London[.] I have proof here he was seen here within two Days in London. Upon which Mr Wallace said he had slipped out of the way, that they could not get him though he was under Subpoena. I have proof that he was brought up & seen in London within two days, then a Passenger is picked up who knows nothing of the Matter, who is not entrusted with the management of the Ship for when they called this Witness he knew nothing of the proper Management of the Ship or the true reason why they did not go in for Water to any of the Islands which I state they might before they arrived at Jamaica, that they did not go to any of the Islands after they were driven from Jamaica where they might have had Water. I can find they had no reason for it but that which no doubt is the reason of the Case they meant to saddle a bad Market upon the Underwriters instead of the owners, As to the point of Missing Jamaica & being at the distance of the West end of Hispaniola to[200] Jamaica[,] it is impossible that mistake could have happened to the Sailors[.] whether they thought they had better take the Chance with such a Crew on Board in trying still to get to Jamaica & not going to any of the Islands for Water, that is not what the Underwriters are to be accountable for & that they did not reach Jamaica at first is a Blunder we [15] are not answerable for[,] that if the Doctor went out Captain [sic] who was never in a Ship before as Captain cannot tell Hispaniola from Jamaica[,] are the underwriters to pay for his Mistake, if they put a Man on Board who don't know by reckoning what latitude[201] he is in & the form of the Islands when they present themselves to him[?], it seems in that part of the Case such a Negligence as well as in the Antecedent part not going to Tobago after he had missed Jamaica, not going with a Wind the fairest of all others & as I say exepting [sic] Hurricanes always blowing that would have carried them in 30 Hours as I stated before & before any Soul on board could Perish for want or have gone to the Grand Camanes or the Isle of Pines – where they would have had full as fine Water as in any Island upon the face of the Earth, this was so great a Blunder[,] so much Ignorance and Mistake upon this part of the Case that the supposed loss is not fairly imputable to the Underwriters upon the Peril of this Policy[.] if it is not[,] there can be no doubt in the very Nature of the Transaction it ought to undergo a Second Trial[.] I am perfectly sure it astonished the Court after your Lordship's summing up, that the Ver-

---

[200] Ed. The words "Hispaniola to" are inserted above the line.
[201] Ed. "Reckoning" seems to be used here in a general sense. Latitude was found by use of a sextant. "Dead reckoning" (Introduction, above, page 82) was used before the introduction of marine chronometers to estimate longitude, ie to estimate the position east or west of Greenwich. The main mistake in this case was as to longitude, since, by mistaking Jamaica for Hispaniola, they were further west than they thought they were.

dict should be found for the Plaintiff for it was stated to the Jury in express terms that if it was Ignorance Mistake or Blunder occasioned it, the Underwriters were not liable[.] if upon the Wish that I expressed & the anxiety I then felt & now feel & [16] which made me weigh every Part upon the Trial especially upon the fact of necessity at the time to avoid going into the Question of necessity if not arising from Ignorance or Blunder upon which I thought it impossible the Plaintiffs could maintain their action upon this Policy. In order that the Question might never arise in this Country to give an Alarm to the whole Trade what its Merits or Demerits are is nothing to the Question certainly it is greatly in use & the practice of other Nations[.] it may be necessary for this & the other Country where the Slaves are carried, but I wished much to have avoided that Question being put for many Reasons while there was a chance as I thought of doing it[.] I thought there was no Gentleman of the Jury that ever heard of the Places being mentioned or named could have doubted the Ship could have made either of those 3 Islands I mentioned before she came to Jamaica.

Lord Mansfield. Before they apprehended any Scarcity.

Mr Davenport. The scarcity I am correct in Stating existed when they passed these Islands, if it be true that the Butts which by the Mate were taken to be full were not so therefore that is Blunder[,] Ignorance & Mistake of his[.] He thought they had Water enough & it turned out in fact there was [not][.] upon the 28th they were driven past Jamaica, upon the 29th they had two Quarts of Water & what I call 4 days provision & what any Man would call 4 days provision in that situation. [17]

A second Ignorance accrues the Moment they are at Jamaica they mistake that for Hispaniola[.] the third more capital one is doubting they should meet Jamaica again in Time & if they did with a Sickly Crew they would make but a bad Market & then thinking that bad Market had better have been thrown upon the underwriter & their not going to either of the three Islands.

Lord Mansfield. They had no apprehension of distress when you say when they might have gone there, you asked Captain Stubbs to that he said they could not get into any of them.

Mr Davenport. If I had asked any of my learned Friends or any other

Passengers they would have known nothing of it, I am talking of Sea faring knowledge.

Lord Mansfield. You are talking out of the Cause.

Mr Davenport. No[,] in the Cause, the Captain or Sea faring Men must have known[,] if they can keep any reckoning[,] they could have fetched Tobago in 30 Hours & have had Water enough.

Lord Mansfield. You asked the Grounds & he said they could not.

Mr Davenport. He said to his Judgment they could not.

Lord Mansfield. Stubbs said positively they could not.

Mr Davenport. I asked him his reason he said they did not know where they was. [18]

Mr Justice Buller. There is no other Evidence but his.

Lord Mansfield. He is the only Man Existing.

Mr Davenport. Be it so.

Lord Mansfield. You cannot go out of the Cause[.] you asked if he could have gone into any of those Islands[.] he swore he could not.[202]

Mr Davenport. Yes he did, but he gave this reason, he did not know where he was.

Lord Mansfield. May be so.

Mr Davenport. Then the Underwriters are not liable, for if they had been Seamen they must have known. –

Lord Mansfield. Stubbs was a passenger only.

---

[202] G#: Yet surely the Probability of his Evidence was to be weighed & examined; it ought not to be indiscriminately received, when there was just exception.

Mr Davenport. There is no Sailor with Compass or Reckoning but must have known where he was.

Lord Mansfield. They certainly did not know where they was, if they had they never could have mistaken Jamaica for Hispaniola.

Mr Pigot. I am upon the same side with Mr Davenport in this Case, this Case in itself is properly new from the beginning of time to the time of this action there [19] never was an Action of this Sort brought before & besides being new in Specie the Circumstances of it are of such an Extraordinary Nature I should be much better pleased to hear Mr Sollicitor [sic] General[203] upon the other side who is as full of Humanity as his head is full of Law[.] I take it, I am astonished how this Verdict was obtained[.] I take it when this is looked into it never can stand a Moment, If your Lordship is of Opinion I should & if Mr Sollicitor thinks it can stand an Enquiry after what Mr Davenport has said I will go on.

Lord Mansfield. You had better go on.

Mr Pigot. That this should not be the Subject of another Discussion must give Pain not only to me but every Body that hears me from a Consideration of this Circumstance that 130 of our Fellow creatures were plunged alive into the Ocean without (as I shall contend before your Lordship) any such necessity as could Justify such a very extraordinary Transaction or if it did exist it was solely brought on by the Negligence Ignorance and want of Conduct of those whom the Plaintiffs in this action employ & for whom they are Answerable. The Declaration States after stating the Policy that so many of the Slaves died on that Passage for want of Water & therefore without recurring to any Motion in Arrest of Judgment I do presume [20] to contend before your Lordship that the Evidence in this Case certainly does not maintain the Declaration and does not warrant the Verdict given[,] which Verdict affirms that the Slaves died & perished for want of Water. My Lords[,] I might certainly say that this is not any Peril the Underwriters

---

[203] Ed. John Lee, KC (6 March 1733–1735 August 1793). He became a king's counsel in 1780, and was appointed Solicitor General for England and Wales in the second administration of Lord Rockingham. He sat in parliament for Clitheroe and subsequently for Higham Ferrers which he represented for the rest of his life. G M Ditchfield, 'Lee, John (1733–1793)', ODNB, 2004; online edn, January 2008 [http://www.oxforddnb.com/view/article/16294], accessed 21 January 2015.

have insured against[.] I might say that upon some Ground because amongst all those persons acquainted with & conversant in this Trade I believe no instance can be produced by any one of them in which the Underwriter has been made liable for the Mortality of Slaves in the Passage & whatever cause that Mortality is to be attributed to it would be attended with consequences so horrid & dreadful & of so great an Inconvenience to that Trade if the Underwriters were made liable to this Mortality it would be such an inlet of Fraud & Oppressions upon those Person least capable of Protection & it never was from the beginning of the Trade till this moment that the Underwriters were ever called upon to pay the loss arising from the Mortality of Slaves.

Lord Mansfield. Since the trial I was informed if they die a Natural Death they do not pay but in an Engagement if they are attacked & the Slaves are killed [21] they will be paid for them as much as for Damages done for goods &c it is frequently done, just as if Horses were killed, they are paid for in the Gross, just as well as for Horses killed but you don't pay for Horses that die a Natural death.

Mr Pigot. Independent of the Enemy & the Consequences of Capture[,] if my learned Friend knows of any Instance in which the Mortality of Slaves has been charged to the Underwriter however that Mortality is caused, I am content to give up this Business[.] is it to be conceived knowing what your Lordship knows & sees of this Trade every day[,] knowing the sort of Vessels employed & how employed[,] is it possible to conceive from the beginning of the Trade to this Moment no slaves have ever Perished for want of Provisions or Water, is that to be supposed, that from the time the Portugeze discovered them to the present time no Slaves have ever Perished for want of Provisions or Water in a Voyage or is it to be conceived that those who have insured have been so indulgent in no Case whatsoever have they called the Underwriters to pay that loss[?]-That is not to be conceived – Then I may venture to say this is not a Point upon which the Underwriters are answerable to the insured - But when it comes to this Point I am not surprized the Captain Mate & no other Mariners [22] were produced at the Trial[.] I am not surprized they were not here[.] I venture to predict they never will be here, they never will be seen -That this loss should have happened & new in its nature – Extraordinary in its circumstances for which the Insured meant to bring an action, that they should suffer the Captain Mate & every Mariner to go out of this Kingdom when they ought to be tried for Murther in another place &

depend upon a Gentleman in the character of a Passenger to explain the whole of this Transaction, it is very extraordinary when the Evidence comes to be looked into what it is. They sailed[,] I am willing to suppose[,] with Water enough[.] I don't suppose before they left the Coast of Africa it was any part of their design these Slaves should fail[.] no doubt it was not their Interest[:] I don't charge them with it but it is what passed during the Voyage which I collect from the Copy I have of Governor Stubbs Testimony[.] which Governor Stubbs I understand is now in Court, what I collect from that testimony of the only Witness produced it is which induces one to say, if I don't demonstrate as little as I know of navigation this necessity was not an Impending Necessity such as to Justify what has been done or if it were it was a Necessity brought on by [23] Ignorance & want of conduct of those that had the charge of this Ship I desire never to be trusted upon any occasion again. My Lord they were bound to Jamaica.

Lord Mansfield. Have you a copy of it[?].

Mr Pigot[.] I have a copy of Governor Stubbs Evidence that he was formerly Governor of Annamabo.

Lord Mansfield. Is it taken in short Hand[?]

Mr Pigot. No.

Lord Mansfield. Then it will not answer the Purpose.

Mr Pigot. To examine into the State of their Water Provisions with a Retrospect of the Time they should be in regaining Jamaica again after they had mistook it[,] then it was they began to apprehend danger from Want.

Lord Mansfield. They did not apprehend danger only for the Captain said there was an absolute necessity therefore they could not do wrong.

Mr Pigot. They saw Tobago in the Passage & at the time they thought they saw Tobago they said they wanted Water[.] they thought they could see it.

Lord Mansfield. That is right[,] the Mate having reported. [24]

Mr Pigot. It afterwards turned out there was a Mistake in Gauging the Casks[.] here is one fact to be attended to, in Point of Fact they had not a sufficient Quantity of Water, for the Slaves from the Casualities [sic] that Voyage is liable to it might be expected as a Common Accident to which a Ship in that Passage was liable she should fall to the Leward[204] of Jamaica, if it was a Common Accident it should have been provided against when the Fate of so many Men depended upon it or it should depend upon strong Evidence to shew it was Accident and not Negligence[.] they passed Jamaica by a mistake[:] whose mistake was it? It was a Mistake of the Mate or Captain; who is liable for that Mistake? Certainly the Assured who employs these Persons & who in so very essential and important an Article as Water is to sustain 400 & odd Slaves, that was the Number on Board the Ship besides the Crew of it[,] is Answerable in so important an Article & a Mistake so terrible in its Consequences if it should happen, who is answerable for that Mistake? Not the Insurers – they go on however in their Voyage & did not stop at Tobago having no notice Tobago was in the Hands of the Enemy,[205] they go on from Tobago & proceed, they might have [25] seen other Islands, whether they did or not I don't know[.] we have no other part of this History until we are told they found themselves to the Leward of Jamaica & here it is[,] I beg your Lordships['] attention[,] they found themselves to the Leward of Jamaica having mistaken Jamaica for Cape Tiberoon[206] – All vessels keep their reckoning & calculate by throwing a Log,[207] in a Way the Gentlemen know

---

[204] Ed. Common contemporary spelling of "leeward". OED, Transportation, 1679–88 Secr Serv Moneys Chas & Jas (Camden) 16 "To the Bishop of London, for transportac'on of three Chaplains to the Leward Island..." See nautical pronunciation "looard", OED leeward, a. (n.) and adv.; "'And he's farther down to looard, too,' supplemented Bush." C S Forester, *Hornblower and The Hotspur*.

[205] Ed. From 1672 Tobago had been in British occupation, but the French invaded in 1781.

[206] Ed. Cape Tiburon, or the Tiburon Peninsula is a region of Haiti which includes all of Haiti's southern coast.

[207] Ed. ie to calculate longitude. OED: "Log", II 6, "An apparatus for ascertaining the rate of a ship's motion, consisting of a thin quadrant of wood, loaded so as to float upright in the water, and fastened to a line wound on a reel." Hence, OED: II.7.a "Short for log-book. A journal into which the contents of the log-board or log-slate are daily transcribed, together with any other circumstance deserving notice." OED: "knot", 3. a.I.3.a Naut. "A piece of knotted string fastened to the log-line, one of a series fixed at such intervals that the number of them that run out while the sand-glass is running indicates the ship's speed in nautical miles per hour; hence, each of the divisions so marked on the log-line, as a measure of the rate of motion of the ship (or of a current, etc.)".

extremely well, it is subject to Mistake by Vessels in a long Passage sometimes they are many Leagues a Head or a Stern[208] still they keep the reckoning as a guide to them reckoning – When they saw the land at Tobago, which the Map shews us is not a very great Distance, when they saw Tobago they had an opportunity of correcting their reckoning & they must have taken as all Navigators do from the known land, a fresh Departure from Tobago they come towards Jamaica & what do they do[?] they fall to the Leward of Jamaica & they mistake the Westernmost Point or Leeward Point of Jamaica for Cape Tiberoon which is the Westernmost Part of St Domingo or Hispaniola. My Lord what is the distance between these two places[?] I believe upon looking at the Map the distance between the Leeward end of Jamaica to the Leward of which they were & Cape Tiberoon the Western [26] Point of the other Island where they supposed themselves to be is not less than six or seven degrees – Your Lordship will see if you look at this Map Cape Tiberoon is in 74 & the Westernmost Point of Jamaica they conceived themselves to be so much to the Leward of is in 80[209] there is no less mistake in running from Tobago a Windward Island to Jamaica – these skillful Navigators with the Lives of 400 Men in their Hands made such a Mistake as 6 Degrees of Reckoning it is monstrous & it will require a Degree of Evidence, I will venture to say Merchants & navigators of Ships would have required an Evidence too strong to give the Counsel on the other side an opportunity of standing up to explain the circumstance to account for & explain the fact of tossing into the Ocean alive 130 Men, Women & Children – In the Name of God let these Men account reasonably for having mistaken the West Part of St Domingo & the West part of Jamaica[.] let them account for that enormous Transaction, do they take no latitude no departure, is that the way that Men navigate with Common Cargoes with things that are put on board a Ship must less with the lives of People[,] is this to be

---

[208] Ed. For dead reckoning, see Introduction, above, page 82.

[209] Ed. Cape Tuberon, or the Tuberon Peninsula, Haiti, extends between 72°W and 75°W on either side of longitude 74°W. The central part of Jamaica is between longitude 77°W and 78°W: *The Times Comprehensive Atlas of the World*, Eleventh edition, London, 2003. Longitude 80°W is to the west of Jamaica, approximately between Jamaica and the Cayman Islands. Pigot's point is that the error was as much as 6 degrees of longitude: see the next few lines below. The magnitude of a degree of longitude in the northern hemisphere depends on how far north it is of the equator, ie on the latitude. The further north, the shorter is the distance between lines of longitude. Taking Port Royal, Jamaica as an example: Port Royal is on latitude 17.94°. At that latitude a degree of longitude is 57.2 nautical miles or 65.83 statute miles. Six degrees of longitude would therefore be approximately 343 nautical miles, or 395 statute miles.

tolerated or endured? – Then there is to the Leward of Jamaica an Island called the Grand Camanes another Island called the Isle of Pines [27] another called [space left blank][.] were these not to be fetched before this Happened, with respect to what happened on board this Ship I wished to draw a Veil over it[.] 60 perished between the time of her leaving the Coast & the 29 of November[.]

Mr Justice Buller. Was the Verdict for all that Perished[?].

Mr Sollicitor General. Only those that were thrown overboard.

Mr Pigot. That is so much the better for us. Mr Stubbs said that before they were thrown overboard they had a full allowance of Water[,] that Slaves are always allowanced when coming from the African Coast – They are not allowed to take as much Water as they chuse[.] they have a particular Quantity allowed them[.] they had 3 Butts and 1/2 of good Water & 2 Butts that were not sweet which I suppose might have sustained the Life of a Man in this Situation, they began by throwing over these People[.] My Lord[,] then here is not any want of Water but the apprehension of a want of Water arising in the Way I am explaining to your Lordship it did arise. With Islands within 30 Hours Sail to which they might have resorted reasonably & easy where they might [have] had any quantity of Water – The Water had not actually failed but apprehending a Scarcity would immediately arise [28] from the small Quantity they had they determined to thin the Cargo of these Slaves they being insured at £30 a Man they threw over this part of the Cargo that is the fact. – This having been done[,] is this a Thing to be justified by any Man coming into a Court of Justice & talking about it, is it such a necessity that every Man who hears me will say, ["]Good God it is inevitable["] – Another thing[,] is it to be done at all? Were they in such a Calamitous situation that it could not be avoided, what is the Law upon the subject[?] the life of one Man is like the life of another Man whatever the Complexion is, whatever his colour[.] if there was a scarcity he would be intitled to that which remains & to a fair Chance for his life, is this Court or any Court of Jury [sic] prepared to say, these Gentlemen under these Circumstances had a right to drag the one & the other & throw overboard 130 persons who were alive into the Ocean[?] suppose the Exigency existed as long as any remained to be divided. I bottom myself upon the Rights & essential Interest of Humanity. I do contend before your Lordship that to their share of that Thimble full if it was no more these Men were as much entitled & have as good a Right [29] as that Captain that did it or that Governor that advised it or any Man whatsoever. Does the necessity appear – What happened to Captain Inglefield[210] in the *Centaur* when she was lost[?] he quitted his Ship in the midst of the Ocean with 12 Brave Men, they had a 2 Quart bottles of Water or very little more & food in proportion to the Water. Captain Inglefield distributed that Water as long as it lasted equally – Did they even upon the footing of equality cast lots for their Lives? No, they trusted, I don't say to the Partial Interposition of Providence[,] I don't know that Providence ever does any Thing Partially, they trusted to the Interposition of Providence that makes the Rain, it Rained, & they collected Water[.] Captain Inglefield trusted to the Heavens & him that made them & he got Water, they existed for 16 Days – the water they took in lasted 5 out of the 16 but one Man only perished[.] Captain Inglefield lived to see his friends & receive the applause of everyone of his Countrymen – Now see what is the Conduct of this humane Captain of an African Trader, if this thing takes place, I know a little of those Gentlemen & the People concerned in that Trade[.] you consign over whole Nations to those Men who are the last in the world to be [30] trusted with any Power that can possibly be avoided[.] I trust for the sake of Humanity your Lordship will be of opinion it should at least undergo the Revision of another Jury.

Mr Heywood. I am likewise of Council upon the same side. I shall make no Apology for adding a few Words in this Case to what has been said by the Gentlemen who have gone before me. I never felt

---

[210] Ed. John Nicholson Inglefield (1748–1828). Inglefield was captain of HMS *Centaur* (74 guns) which he commanded in three actions against the French, culminating on 12 April 1782 in the Battle of the Saintes. When sailing for England with the convoy under Rear-Admiral Sir Thomas Graves, his ship along with the others was struck by a hurricane. The *Centaur*, an ageing ship, was severely damaged. She eventually foundered despite the efforts of Inglefield and the crew over several days. Inglefield and eleven others escaped aboard the pinnace, while the ship's complement of some 600 men was lost. Subsisting on a few bottles of French cordials, some spoilt bread, ship's biscuit and rainwater collected in a bailing cup, the survivors successfully navigated to Faial Island in the Azores after sixteen days of terrible privations. One of the men died the day before they reached land. On returning to England and the court martial usual in such cases, the survivors were acquitted. Inglefield published his letter to the Admiralty giving a factual account of the incident as *Captain Inglefield's narrative of the loss of the Centaur, in 1782: Being a literal extract of his letter to the admiralty, written from Fayal in 1782*, London, 1813. J K Laughton, 'Inglefield, John Nicholson (1748–1828)', rev P L C Webb, ODNB, 2004; online edn, October 2007 [http://www.oxforddnb.com/view/article/14396], accessed 19 January 2015.

a more serious impression upon my Mind upon the introduction of any Cause whatever in this Court than I do in the Present[.] that it is a new Cause is allowed upon all hands & I hope for the Honor of Humanity & mankind in general it will be the last. That in point of Importance it is the greatest that ever came before this Court cannot well be disputed. – We are not now before your Lordships merely defending the Underwriter from the £660 each obtained against them[.] I cannot help thinking that my Friends who went before & myself upon this occasion appear as Council for Millions of Mankind & the Cause of Humanity in general[.] for the present I shall put out of the Question all that Mr Pigot as well as Mr Davenport have said with regard to the manner in which that Water however small it was ought to have been dispensed with in Case of absolute necessity, I think hereafter if we [31] should be driven to a Motion in Arrest of Judgment that will be the time to take up that Idea, but the Point is now whether there is that inevitable indispensable necessity to oblige your Lordship contrary to your own feelings to say these men were compelled to be thrown overboard – That they were compelled to do it whether they would or no[.] the point before your Lordships it is said was not occasioned by Peril within the Policy but a Blunder a Mistake of the Captain[.] Lord Bacon says the law charges no man with a default where the Act is compulsatory & not voluntary & where there is no Election or Choice[.] – This must be compulsatory and not voluntary. – I am at a loss on hearing the Evidence given today to see where the compulsion laid or that Danger should be so pressing at the Moment these People should have found themselves obliged or compelled to take the horrid step of causing 132 fellow creatures to be drowned in the Ocean[.] that will carry us to the Consideration of the facts in this Case to shew your Lordship no apprehension would be sufficient in such a Case as this to destroy the life Man. There is a Case in Lord Hobart 149[.][211] That is the argument of Lord Hobart himself he says [space left blank][212] [32] which shews there must be extreme necessity, then at the time when the Act

---

[211] Ed. *Colt & Glover* v *Bishop of Coventry & Lichfield* (1612) Hobart 140 at 159, 80 ER 290 at 307:

> ...when you may perceive the case brought to extreme necessity then when the act is done, the law permits you not to kill him that assails you, when you draw near your last refuge, because you foresee that you shall be driven to it, but you must forbear 'till that necessity be at his full period, for 'till then it may be otherwise prevented or remedied.

[212] Ed. Possibly to put in the quotation later.

is done the Law permits you not to kill him that Assaults you when you are driven near your last resource because you think you foresee it[.] you must see that necessity[.] it must be at its full period for you to see if it could be otherwise prevented or remedied. He could not more strongly express the Law upon that subject – His Case went to the Jury & was put upon the same Foundation by your Lordship, this is clear your Lordship was pleased to say to the Jury it must be occasioned by inevitable Necessity, that is most clear – To say that wontonly [sic] or by Ignorance a Captain may throw 132 lives overboard is a Proposition that shocks Humanity[.] I will put the case of a ship that is wrecked where two Persons get upon the same Plank, in such a Case as that the Laws of Humanity or nature would say if that Plank is sufficient to support them Both the one is not justified in throwing off the other, but if one feels the Plank sinking & he is stronger that the other there is no man living but would think himself perfectly justified in throwing off the other – I will now advert to the facts, for there is nothing more material upon this occasion or stronger than the state of the facts themselves – They sailed from St Thomas's[213] on the 6th day of September 1781. That they [33] had on Board 459 People[.] in 10 Weeks & 3 days they Passed by Tobago & arrived at Jamaica. That on the 18th of November they report they had 20 days Water – On the 27th of the same Month[,] 9 days afterwards[,] they did pass Jamaica[.] On the 29th they threw overboard part of the Slaves[,] about 60[.] upon the 30th more of them were thrown overboard; – I beg your Lordship to recollect that 60 had died by Mortality on Board & the Slaves were reduced in their Number of Course[.] the 29th of November when this took place there were not so great a number by almost a Sixth of the whole on board – Upon the 1st of December (two Days after) the rain was Caught & after this 1st of December when this Providential Shower was sent from the Heavens, this Man threw over 26 more of the Slaves after the rain was caught. I shall take the opportunity of observing upon Mr Stubbs['] evidence with regard to that though the discovery was not made till after the Calculation upon the 21st December the time when the Ship arrived at Jamaica. – I will beg leave to call upon your Lordships attention to the Number of People on Board & the Quantity of Water to subsist upon though Mr Stubbs undertook

---

[213] Ed. São Tomé, the larger of the two islands in the Gulf of Guinea that now make up the Democratic Republic of São Tomé and Príncipe. The island was named by Portuguese explorers, who found the islands uninhabited, when they arrived about 1470 on St Thomas's Day (21 December). They subsequently populated them with large numbers of slaves and introduced sugar cultivation.

to Swear there was but one day[']s Water on Board[.] I would sooner trust [34] to his [space left blank] than take for Granted what he swore upon the subject. Upon the 29th of November when they had got 459 Souls on Board Stubbs in his Evidence with regard to the Water swore at the time this Dreadful Catastrophe took place there were six Casks of Water on Board which wanted 7 or 8 Inches of being full & three Casks of Sour Water which had been Rum Casks[.] he said also those Casks though they must have run out had 120 Gallons a piece in them when they wanted 6[,] 7 or 8 Inches they contained about 140 Gallons apiece[.] Having got that for I will give you the Sum of those 3 Butts of Water at 140 each or 420 Gallons which will subsist [space left blank] Men & more at 2 Quarts for a Day, Stubbs is a little bold in swearing the Quantity of Water was too little on Board the Ship[.] he swears upon this that the African ships always calculated 2 Quarts a Man per Day[.] we had evidence to contradict him there[.] we did not go into that the fact we were told was that one Gallon a piece was the Usual Quantity[.] in fact the 420 Gallons of sweet Water was enough for 3 Days & at this time there was 3 Casks & 1/2 of Rum Water on Board that was enough for 3 days more[.] therefore there could be no Want on Board the Ship[.] they took upon themselves to say there was that inevitable Necessity existed so as to [35] give them power over the Lives of these People whom they ought to have protected & guarded[.] there were 5 Day[']s Water on Board & before they had deprived so many People of their Existence they should have seen what they could have done at half Allowance[.] then there was at that time this took place Water enough for 10 Days, Then upon the 1st of December 6 Casks of Rain was Caught which was 11 more Day[']s full Allowance so that upon half Allowance there was sufficient for 23 days & they were but 21 in all[.] After this[,] before they arrived & after they had got all this Rain Water on Board which was enough for 11 Day[']s at full Allowance & enough for 20 at half Allowance[,] they had the cruelty to throw overboard 26 Slaves more[.] If we should fail upon that part & your Lordship should be of opinion that any inevitable Necessity did exist prior to the Rain after they had got 6 Casks on Board if they had been put to half Allowance it would have been sufficient to have lasted – Mr Stubbs evidence struck me as something very remarkable[.] I could not have a great opinion of the Humanity of that Man who[,] notwithstanding his declining to assist in the Consultation of the Officers or assisting himself in throwing the Slaves overboard[,] went down into the cabin & amused himself with seeing them out of the Cabin [36] Windows Plunging in the Sea[.] he swore he counted about 50 of them[.] surely he was not set by those above deck to be Evidence when this Cause came on[.] Surely he was not sent down having nothing to do himself to see & count the Number they had disposed of[.] It makes an Impression upon my Mind that the Man that could calmly & coolly commit such an Act as that & not remonstrate & endeavour to prevent it is not deserving of much Credit here or in any other Court of Justice. I mentioned 26 being thrown over after the Rain when there could be no Scarcity[.] I am told now it was 36[.] ten are stated to have jumped over board who expected to be thrown overboard[,] that 36 were thrown overboard after the Rain fell[.] Mr Stubbs most wisely omitted to give any Evidence about it. I see in my Brief I was obliged to make a Marginal Note of it on the Place where the rest of the Evidence was given with regard to the Number thrown in I took when they had given the Verdict[,] when they could not account for 90 & odd, Mr Wallace was obliged to ask Mr Stubbs the Number again[.] he went over them again after the Verdict[.] then Stubbs was obliged [37] to bring out this truth which he had endeavoured to conceal[.] Mr. Stubbs swore after this Event had taken place the Captain became delirious[,] the Mate was incapable of doing Duty[,] that he himself was obliged to take command of the Ship, thus after the Rain fell[,] after there was no necessity[,] this humane Man took the Command with the Mate & without any Consultation whatever, none appears upon the Evidence[,] the Mate took the Liberty of casting 26 more into the Sea. These circumstances surely do not intitle Stubbs to a vast deal of credit upon the Occasion – Let us see their situation upon the 29th of November – Let us see how the necessity pressed them to that Moment, prior to the 29th of November there is not a single word said in Evidence[.] there was no short Allowance at the Moment these Slaves were thrown overboard till that Moment[.] if they had full Allowance of meat & Drink what could appear to impress the Whites at that Moment with any Apprehension of Danger so strong that they were in Apprehension of Losing their Lives or that death stared them in the Face but for some Days at least they themselves, if there had been short Allowance they might all have been put to short [38] allowance for some time which is what other Ships used to do when there is a Chance & when they were within 60 Leagues[214] to the Lee-

---

[214] Ed. OED, League. "a. An itinerary measure of distance, varying in different countries, but usually estimated roughly at about 3 miles; app. never in regular use in England, but often occurring in poetical or rhetorical statements of distance. marine league: a unit of distance = 3 nautical miles or 3041 fathoms." Sixty leagues on that basis would be 180 nautical miles, nearly half that based on Pigot's statement that the

ward[215] of Jamaica they were within 3 or 4 Leagues of the Grand Camanes & within 4 or 5 days of getting there when they might have had Water enough or 5 or 6 days from another Island the Island of Pines & within two or three days of reaching the Continent of America when they might have had Water enough, My Lord such is the Conduct of those to whom it is the Misfortune of this Country to give up the Government & direction of these Slaves a Commerce which it is true is Authorized by Act of Parliament they it is who are to have the Command of our fellow Creatures – that was the Conduct of Captain Inglefield as Mr Pigot mentioned upon that occasion of the loss of the *Centaur*[.] I dont mention this to shew the Water should have been divided as near as could be but to shew that Captain Inglefield who acted I think with great Humanity did not think himself Authorized[,] in Circumstances of Distress much Stronger than this[,] Authorized [sic] to throw any of the brave Men overboard that the rest might Survive. This my Lord, was the Situation in which Captain Inglefield was with those brave men that were with him – ["]When we left the *Centaur* we were 12 [39] in Number in a Leaky Boat & one Gunnel stove in nearly in the Middle of the Western Ocean["] without Compass Quadrant or Sail all thinly Cloathed in a Gale of Wind a great Sea rolling over them with 2 Quarts of Water & one Biscuit divided into 12 Morsels sufficed then for Breakfast & Dinner with the neck of a Bottle Broke off served them for a Glass which filled with water was the Allowance for 24 Hours each Man with 6 Quarts of rain Water which they caught afterward they kept up their spirits for 16 Days, when they all arrived safe but one, he did not think himself Authorized under the impression of inevitable necessity. In that case Captain Inglefield acted like a Man of humanity but these Men acted like men who had forgot the feelings of Men, where then are we to find this inevitable necessity which alone can set at nought all Human Laws & Controul [sic] all Divine[.] It is a Crime of the Deepest & blackest Dye[.] I am at a loss to find out[,] when they had in their power full allowance for 10 days more after it had rained[,] why they threw the others overboard when they had subsisted for 21 days, when they had missed Jamaica though they could have got there in a fortnight from the time the rain fell[,] when they were within 60 Leagues to the Leward of it[,] when they were within 3 or 4 Leagues of the Grand Camanes [40] & with 6 or 7 days of reaching the Isle of Pines & within 3 or 4 of reaching the Grand Continent of America where they

---

error could have been as much as 6 degrees of longitude, but still a considerable error.
[215] Ed. So spelled in this instance.

might have had Water enough[.] I will upon this Head of necessity say no more Judging your Lordship will be of opinion here was no necessity as could justify them throwing these Slaves overboard – As to its arising from the Blunder of the Captain & not the Peril of the Sea[,] that is not within the Terms of the Policy – Your Lordship was pleased to say in your direction to the Jury the question is this – Whether it is inevitable necessity within the Perils of the Policy[.] the Point is whether it was through inevitable necessity through the Dangers of the Policy – If they had been lost through the attack of a Privateer they might have been paid but the want of Skill in a Commander is not a risque which the Underwriters are answerable for they know nothing of it. Your Lordship will recollect what Stubbs Swore with regard to Collingwood[.] he said he came upon the Coast as Doctor. I don't know there is anything in the profession of Physick or Surgery which could enable Collingwood to act as Captain in fact [41] he swore also that he knew nothing of the Sea[,] that he had never been a Captain before that & he knew nothing of the Sea & this dreadful Catastrophe is sworn to be expressly owing to the Captain & Mate[']s mistake[.] these are the words of Stubbs in his Evidence, ["]with proper care[",] he said, ["]we might have reached Jamaica[".] If your Lordship can be of opinion they were justified by inevitable necessity at that time which I contend never existed amongst them I hope your Lordship will grant a new trial upon this Ground[.] nothing is more clear that this Loss arose from Danger not within the Policy but arising from the Mistake or Blunder of that Captain whom the Underwriters have no Controul over[,] whom they did not appoint[,] whom the owners at their Peril appoint & who was found perfectly insufficient & improper for it. My Lord[,] this comes under Circumstances too Novel and Singular if it had been impossible for us to make out our Grounds so well as we have done[,] I apprehend your Lordship will be inclined to let us have a new Trial where the abuse of Power has been so great[.] if your Lordship was to determine in favour of these owners [42] I dont know but Millions of our fellow creatures may hereafter fall a Sacrifice to this very Decision & I think I hardly say too much when I say it is a Case of that sort & of the first Impression that your Lordships[,] without stating any reason upon Earth[,] even without stating the Mistake of the Captain[,] will grant a new Trial.

Mr Davenport. My Lord there was no proof in Evidence of any Insurrection[.] on Board the Slaves were all Hand cuffed under the hatches & Brought up in order to be thrown overboard hand cuffed[,] now[,] if they had been suffered to die under the Hatches[,] the loss would have been the owners not the Underwriters[.] this haste to get them overboard was, if they died on board upon short Allowance[,] that it would fall upon the Owners.

Mr Sollicitor General. I profess myself I never was more fully persuaded than I am at the present instant of the inevitable necessity there was in this Case, It is very much to be wished that when a great deal of Eloquence is employed care should be taken there should be some foundation for it in truth & in fact – If my learned friends whose Candour will not permit them [43] wilfully to misrepresent any thing had recollected some of the Circumstances[.] your Lordship will remember in the Cause a great Deal of the most passionate Eloquence of my learned friend Mr Pigot who would have been spared that Expression in particular in which he said the Shame & the Scandal was that the Captain of this Ship & the Mate of this Ship should be suffered to go out of this Kingdom that he ought to be tried for Murther in another Place[.] The Evidence was this poor Captain died seven days after he came to Jamaica of this very miserable starving[.] he died very soon after he came to Jamaica[.] that is stated in the Case[.] the poor man never was seen here nor came at all[.] The Mate which Mr Davenport said that we had subpoenaed but that we dared not produce him[.] I happen to know the contrary of that fact. My Lord I should not have stated or gone out of the Case & Report[,] but I am led & forced to do it when it is stated I attended the Consultation with my Friends[.] [44]

Lord Mansfield. At the Trial you know nothing of it.

Mr Sollicitor General. At the Trial we desired every Soul existing that could be come at might be called in the Cause[.] accordingly we had determined if there was time for it to have postponed the Cause to have had them but says Mr Wallace why, if they think there is anything in it Mr Stubbs is here a Passenger who will give the Account –[216] I happen to have in my hand a Protest of the Mate confirming in every respect Mr Stubbs's Evidence[.] I mention that as a reason to shew if we could have had him here & Subpoenaed him we should have produced him[,] therefore in saying we should not do it they are unfounded[.] I dont mean that Mr Davenport knew it but I knew that the Mate was at Liverpool, it was so stated – It was said he had been

---

[216] G#: NB [Ed. in red in text].

seen at London – nobody then said he had been Subpoenaed by us, not one knew that he was. – so much for that – The Cause therefore was tried upon the Testimony of Mr Stubbs & he was the only Witness produced – There is no Question I Believe between my learned friends & me – I should think not but it seems all their Argument goes to Combat a proposition which whether [45] ill of well founded is not for me to dispute, It would be too large a field – It has exercised much greater Abilities than mine & the Point is decided[,] namely That a part of our fellow Creatures of the Negro Cast are (wisely or unwisely) made the Subject of Property by our Law there is no doubt about it – I am not prepared to say that all this was, Unwise, Foolish, Bad, Tyrannical, or Wicked upon the whole whether it is or not justified upon Principles of Utility[.] I am not bound to contradict the fact Your Lordship knows they are real Property & part of a descendable Inheritance in the Provinces belonging to us in the West Indies[217] & this Policy assumes it[.] It is very odd that all the Argument has gone to Combat what the Policy assumes that they are Property, I presume it would be perfectly ridiculous for a Man to insure so high upon human Creatures unless it was upon the Idea they are not only Property but of the Specific Value of 30 £ a head[.] to be sure this Cause is a Cause that has called for great Attention. I am sure my learned Friends need not have pressed it so far[.] it would be great injustice to your Lordship not to say [46] that great Attention was given to it to excite infinite Caution in the Minds of the Jury upon that head for your Lordship stated an Account of the Mischief to which in fact these kind of things might lead if not narrowly watched[.] they ought to be clearly satisfied of the

---

[217] Ed. Slavery was recognised in the West Indian colonies by local statute. Slaves were held not only to be property but real property. Hence, they were subject to the doctrine of estates and could be held for a life interest or entailed: *Beckford* v *Beckford* (1783) 4 Bro 38, 2 ER 26, concerned the will of William Beckford, the father of the more famous William Thomas Beckford, by which he devised all his "manors, plantations, slaves, lands, tenements, hereditaments, and real estates whatsoever" in Jamaica to his son William Thomas Beckford "and to the heirs male of his body", ie in fee tail. William Thomas spent the vast fortune his father had made from the proceeds of slave labour on building Fonthill Abbey, one of the earliest examples of Gothic revival architecture, most of which subsequently fell down or had to be pulled down. William Thomas was also author of the Gothic novel *Vathek* and was also a noted connoisseur and collector. The database project, *Legacies of British Slave-ownership*, set up by University College London, lists William Thomas Beckford as owning 660 slaves in Jamaica. In *Vernon* v *Vernon* (1837) 2 My & Cr 145, 40 ER 596, a father, tenant for life, and son, tenant in tail, of a plantation and slaves, suffered a recovery and resettled the property. Slaves were only "chattels" before they "adhered to the realty", and of course could be "severed", as when sold to other plantation owners.

most dire necessity[,] no fiction[,] no exaggeration in the Case[,] that it was what it pretended to be; that kind of severe Visitation which in the Mind of any Body that could think at all dictated the Act & so justified it. Your Lordship pressed that exceedingly & seemed sollicitous the Verdict should be such as would give that Impression upon every body that heard it[.] Your Lordship directed them to consider whether there was or not such Circumstances in the course of this Voyage at the time the event happened as obliged these Persons for to commit a Murther[.] all these are the words of your Lordship[.] Your Lordship sees the thing in dispute was Whether it was Murther, if that were wanting[,] if there was no danger or that the Danger was not tremendous[.] if the People had any doubt whether they must have perished or an evil happened which would have been greater were the fact not done which being whether it would be Murther [47] or Man slaughter according to the Circumstances of the Case but if I am right or Mr. Stubbs is right who knows far better than I[,] or any of my learned friends with all their declamation on the Subject[,] if he was right and he had a Sufficient opportunity of informing himself on the Subject he represented a Number of People between 4 & 500 to be reduced to a degree of distress that had brought about a great Mortality on[218] Board the Ship[.] Mr Stubbs swore it & I durst say your Lordship reported it accurately that at the time of the first throwing overboard they had but one day[']s Water[.] Your Lordship will observe this is the Case of Chattels[,] [48] of Goods[:] it is really[,] so it is[,] the case of throwing over goods[219] for to this purpose & the purpose of this Insurance they are goods & property & whether Right or Wrong we have Nothing to do with it. -This Property[,] the Human Creatures, if you will, have been thrown overboard but whether or not for the Preservation of the Residue that is the Question[.] Mr Stubbs stated before a single Man was thrown overboard they [49] had but one day[']s Water at 2 Quarts a day[.][220] he said that was the proper & necessary Al-

---

[218] G#: This did not appear[,] neither was it true: Mr Stubbs allows that the Mortality was begun & 64 Negroes & 7 Whites actually dead before the scarcity of Water was ever thought of.

[219] G#: But at the same time it is also the Case of throwing over living Men & though in one sense they may be considered as goods, yet this does not alter their existence & actual Rights as living Men; so that the Property in their Persons is only a limited property, limited I say by the necessary consideration of their human Nature, &c therefore the Argument of the Solicitor General is grossly indiscriminate & void of Foundation.

[220] G#: But there was 4 days['] Water & 1 pint per Day each which as they had plenty of other provision was sufficient to prevent them from perishing & the Rain fell on the

lowance[,] that they had but one day[']s Water[,] at their subsequent throwing over there was but two days[',] that he says & that in this Case of Dearth every Moment they formed an Apprehension that otherwise they must all perish[.] to say that this Captain[']s Interest was not affected was perfectly absurd[.] your Lordship will see that his Interest went against it[.] your Lordship knows this Man was to be paid & Constant Habit & Practice of the Trade is he is to be paid a Commission in proportion to the Quantity of Cargo[221] & every Man that [50] was thrown overboard by his Act or suffered or died was so much against his Interest[,] whether it was a Pound[,] a Crown or half a Guinea[,] the Man was acting against himself & nothing could suggest it but the Preservation of himself & others from Perishing[.] In this situation[,] says this Gentleman[, "I do declare solemnly in my Apprehension nobody had any doubt about it[.] I was a Passenger[.] I had no particular hand in it["],] says he. ["]I thought it necessary, I was myself a Sufferer[.] I had four of my own Slaves thrown over[,] some of them that had been bred with me & lived with me many Years. [There] were amongst some of them[,] such was the Distress & Misery[,] I never knew whether they were dead or living till we got to Jamaica but they were thrown overboard such was the Misery of the Ship["],] says he[,"]they were starving & dying in their last Agonies["].[222] Such was their distress I did not know till I came to Jamaica I had lost even my own Servants[.] I knew that the whole of that Cargo could not be carried without a diminution in that Way without endangering the lives of the rest of them; to what purpose is it to speak of Captain Inglefield [51] or any other Captain[?], you might cite Cases from Romance[.] I wish you could find them in common Life of a Man chusing to die himself to let another Man be sustained[.] does it follow that because Heroism may exist in a single Instance in our knowledge that is to be laid down as a rule of Conduct amongst Men[?], if these men could not but be persuaded[,] if some of these Men did not die, themselves must, That if an hundred did not die in this way 200 must

1st December on 2 days afterwards when several Butts of Water was added to their store; so that they were so far from any actual necessity that they might have used one Quart each day per Man in the intermediate time

[221] G#: Here was the temptation! Those that died of distemper (& 64 had actually died of distemper even before they found out that there was Scarcity of Water) were a loss to the proportional Profits of the Captain; but the Sick that were cast alive into the Sea were to be paid for by the Insurers; here then was the pecuniary temptation to the Captain.

[222] G#: If they were in their last agonies they could want no more water; so that there was not necessity on that account[.] the other reason therefore is manifest.

in another[?] That is necessity[,] that is Wisdom & Utility that directs them, this Mr Stubbs said nobody doubted there was an Universal opinion they could not do otherwise & I cannot help thinking after all the declamation I have heard upon the Subject though your Lordships are provoked almost & invited almost to a degree of provocation[,] if any Man of them was allowed to be tried at the Old Bailey for a Murther I cannot help thinking if that charge of Murther was attempted to be sustained & Mr Stubbs adduced to prove the Evidence & the facts it would be folly & rashness to a degree of Madness & so far from the Charge of Murther laying against these People[,] there is not the least imputation, of Cruelty[.] I will not say but of impropriety not in the least. It is very easy for Persons sitting at their ease to fancy that this or that [52] Circumstance don't call for this or that Exertion[.] It may be that I may feel myself weaker than others but I do think myself[,] I thank God[,] I am not likely from my Habits in the Profession to be in such a Situation[.] it would be a great Misfortune to be in such Dangerous Situations[.] I have no conception I should have Heroism of Mind to act otherwise without taking Notice of Black or White because God has made them so[.] I hope there is no such prejudices existing but black or white I could not suffer another Man to live when the single Question was whether I should prefer my Life to his[.] I fear I should not[.] there is no Human Law calls for any preference[.] My learned Friends don't say that in the Nature of the Case it is Murther to throw People overboard then what is all this Vast Declamation of Human People being thrown overboard[?] The Question after all is[,] was it Voluntary or an Act of Necessity? who says it was not an act of necessity[?] does Mr Stubbs[,] who was present himself[,] not know it[?] All who had any Interest upon the Subject that were present declared & every body that knew the Circumstances of the Case must concur with him by declaring the greater evil was avoided by doing the Less, they avoided that greater evil by doing that which if they had not done in a few hours [53] there must have been such an Insurrection All the blacks would have killed All the Whites.[223]

Mr Davenport. There is no such Evidence.

Mr Sollicitor General. Mr Stubbs said it was to prevent such rising, if they had they must have overpowered them as it was suggested.

---

[223] G#: If the Blacks were in a Capacity or able to make an Insurrection they needed not the incitement of the Want of Water[.]

Mr Davenport. Quite the Contrary. I asked the Question[.] he said there was no Insurrection. [Remark See Page 42][224]

Mr Sollicitor General. I did not state there was. Mr Stubbs said so[.] I am sure he stated it. the necessary consequence of it was that if a Man acts upon this Idea the Men perished just as a Cargo of Goods perished[,] not that the same degree of necessity will justify throwing Human Creatures overboard[,] the same as throwing an Iron Gun overboard[.] I don't mean to state that[.] your Lordship stated that if the Jury were of opinion anything else was mixed with the Consultation of Necessity they ought to watch it so narrow that this Case ought not to be encouraged for if not traced [54] properly it might lead to bad Practices[,] a great deal of tyranny, Oppression & Cruelty. The Jury upon the Consideration of the whole of the Circumstances of the Case found that which your Lordship directed & they must find[.] they did so because they could not do otherwise[:] no cruelty[,] no oppression[.] 'twas a most piteous case[,] a most necessary Case & inevitable! It has been said this is all Ignorance[,] all Stupid[,] all Folly. That was flatly contradicted by the Evidence of Stubbs[.] he said there was no Ignorance[,] that this was an experienced & able Navigator that had gone 9 or 10 or 11 Voyages[.] this Captain[...]

Mr Pigot. As a Doctor.

Mr Sollicitor General. That he had been a Surgeon I know was said & true[,] but that he had gone eleven or nine Voyages[,] I am not sure which was proved. The Journal as I understand is accurate[.] I believe it was there & produced[,] I am pretty sure[,] at the trial to give an Account whether they were at this Place or any other at a particular time mentioned[.] it was open to the Inspection of my Friends the Counsel or Witnesses (if they had any) & their supposed mistake of taking the Coast of Hispaniola for Jamaica was declared by Captain Stubbs not only to be no mark of Ignorance at all but had actually happened in two instances that very [55] Year[,] so there was no imputable Negligence of any sort & at the very time they had done so your Lordship will observe this arose out of Circumstances at the beginning of it. very particular & hardly ever known, for the Average time of the Voyage is

---

[224] Ed. Square brackets and words enclosed within them are in red ink and by G#. Mr Davenport on MS page 42 (above, page 266) remarks that there was no evidence of insurrection and that the slaves were all in chains.

6 Weeks & I think it was in this Instance three times as many[:] Eighteen Weeks in performing that part of the Voyage which is usually performed in Six, this was owing to such accidents as variable Weather[,] accident or the like, the usual time is six Weeks[.] it was in this instance 18 & if it had not been for this they had an Abundant Plentiful Supply of Water for want of which the Whole Crew would have perished if this melancholy event had not happened – What is the Evidence when a Gentleman that knows the Sea himself & has been several Voyages declared there was no Ignorance[.] all was accident & not a common thing[.] Your Lordship finds it happened by the mere circumstance of an unavoidable Peril such as would happen for Instance in Hazy Weather[.] Suppose a Man not before there in his Life & did not know Jamaica from Hispaniola will your Lordship[,] if he is a skilful [sic] Navigator[,] Suppose that is such a Circumstance of Ignorance that is not liable to the Perils of the Policy[?] if these men were at short allowance & it became inevitable Necessity there is no pretence for its not being within the Perils of the Policy. If this Man had [56] passed the Navy board & as accurately as any Captain of a Man of War & it was not imputed to him for Ignorance having passed Jamaica & took it for Hispaniola found themselves in Peril for want of Water that the whole of the Crew[225] could not be saved[,] what could Nature do[?] was it not better that a small part should perish to preserve the rest – that is all as to the Circumstance[.] respecting the Mate[,] to take off any imputation as if we had kept back the Evidence we were able to produce[.] I say it & I know & they know it from the Circumstance of the Protest of the Captain who is dead & we could not produce him though Mr Pigot challenges us to produce him[.] the Mate confirms him in his Evidence[.] the Mate lives at Liverpool[.] they knew he was there[.] does you Lordship believe if they had conceived the Mate would have done any good they would not have had him there[?] they knew he had made an Affidavit corresponding with Mr Stubbs.[226]

Mr Pigot. Not a word [57]

Mr Sollicitor General. One is forced after that & I will read this declaration upon oath of this James Kelsal of Liverpool Mariner[.] [Here Mr

---

[225] G#: All the Whites were but 17 & were never put to short allowance, so that this Man[']s Declamation is entirely wide from the real Case.
[226] This affidavit of Kelsall has not been traced at the present time.

Sollicitor stated the Affidavit of Kelsal][227] And lastly Dep:t[228] saith that unless some Mode had been taken to lessen the Number of Slaves on board the Ship immediately upon the discovery of the reduced Stock of Water every Person on Board must have Perished on Board the Vessel & the Cargo have been lost & no other means or expedient could be suggested or thought of for the Preservation of Life[,] Ship & Cargo but throwing the Slaves over as asserted[,] which appeared less cruel than suffering them to expire by degrees when every Possibility of escaping Destruction is at an end – This Mate was never in London that we know of[.] I wished to have him[.] he confirms Stubbs in every particular[.] he goes the whole length of what the Evidence can have reported & therefore in my Apprehension[,] not that I wish the Cause to be tried again after a Verdict found upon Satisfactory Evidence[,] I should be very sorry to hear Mr Stubbs or this Man give a different Account at the distance of two or three Years than that they gave upon the Spot when it was recent[.] it would look as if there was some tampering in the Business; This is upon Oath if there is any truth in it there is no Law in the Case[,] no Question about it when a person [58] insures Slaves as Property[,] which he assumes they are[,] he values them at £30 a Head[.] they are thrown overboard from necessity as any other irrational Cargo or inanimate Cargo might be[.] whether he is entitled to recover the Value[,] there seems to be no doubt about it[.] All the arguments come to this[:] all our Law is foolish Arbitrary & Tyrannical[229] which make Human Creatures the subject of Property[.] What has your Lordship to do with it? Nothing. This Trader in Human Flesh that chuses to Value them in his own Policy at £30 a Head[,] it is not much against him to say they are Property[.] the Underwriter says ["]I consent to have them valued thus & if they are lost I will pay for them £30 a Head[."] One of the Gentlemen says ["]Alack a Day[,] why undertake that[?], they were all Human Creatures[.] the moment you Value them at £30 a Head you consign to Infamy & Disgrace Millions of People[."][230] if the Law was [that,] [59] they should have no Slaves[,] you never could recover any thing for them but as the Law stands at Present it cannot bear a Moment[']s Argument further. My

---

[227] Square brackets and text within them are in MS. The affidavit has not been traced as yet.

[228] Abbreviation presumably for "Deponent". Not used elsewhere.

[229] G#: Surely it is so. Whilst we have such unfeeling Professors of it that will undertake to defend any cause for a paltry fee[.]

[230] G#: vizt. [Ed. Alternative abbreviation for viz., videlicet, that is to say, namely] If the insurers pay for those that are wilfully destroyed! This fair Argument the callous Solicitor endeavours to pervert[.]

Apprehension of the Case is this the Men were come to a situation in which they were without the Fault of any one, by the Providence of God[231] by the Winds & Weather & the degree of their Distress was such as to make this dreadful Calamity unavoidable as it is sworn by the Witness & Mr Haywood[232] put it upon the best Ground[.] if his Ground is Tenable this Verdict ought not to stand, if Mr Stubbs who was the only Witness was entitled to no credit the Verdict cannot stand I admit it – It really concerns me to hear Mr Heywood give such a representation of the Man exhibiting himself at the Windows[.] says he ["]I went up[.] I had nothing to do with it["]- says he ["]I saw those poor Creatures that were thrown overboard[.",] says he[, "]I did not see the act of throwing but I saw them swimming in the Sea["] & I think he says ["]I heard some of the Shreiks [sic] of some of them.["] Mr. Heywood says he was amusing himself with it – This Gentleman gave his Evidence with as much apparent Sympathy & as great tenderness as I ever saw in my Life & he must have been a Brute if he had not then shewn it. [60]

Your Lordship sees instead of this being fiction & mere Invention & nothing to be set against it & his amusing himself with it[.] your Lordship sees the Evidence of a Grave Man meaning to speak correctly & circumstantially[.] if his Evidence is true no Man can doubt of the inevitable necessity.

Lord Mansfield. This must stand over till tomorrow[.] there is some other Gentleman upon the same side I suppose[?]

Mr Chambre. I am upon the same side[.]

Lord Mansfield. There is only two Points, the one mentioned before he came in, therefore I don't wonder at it, the other is since -That before he came in is this -That in the Declaration you lay the Peril of the Sea to Wind & Storms & Currents which made the Ship foul & leaky which was the Cause of the Impediment of the Voyage[.] That is not the fact upon the Evidence – It was by Calms not by Storms[,] neither was the ship foul & leaky – The next thing mentioned by Mr Haywood is a fact which I am not really apprized of, that is, there was 36 Slaves added to the Number for which you recovered after Mr Stubbs gave

---

[231] G#: Were they cast into the Sea by the Providence of God?
[232] Spelled with an "a" here and further down.

Evidence by his adding to the Jury upon casting up the Figures that were thrown over [61] a Day after the Rain[.] I am not aware of that fact[.] I did not attend to it[.]

Mr Haywood. Some days after I believe between 7 & 10 Days.

    Cause adjourned till next Day.

[62] [blank]

[63]

(Voucher No 2 Continued)[233]

Continuation of Proceedings in the Case of
Gregson & others against Gilbert & others

May the 22d 1783

Mr. Chambre. I will trouble your Lordship with a few additional observations in support of this Verdict – There were two points slightly touched upon in the Argument upon which I do not mean now to give the Court any Trouble because the objections so alluded to are objections which appear upon the Face of the Record[.] it will be proper for the Consideration of the Court upon a motion in arrest of Judgment if the Gentlemen should think fit to make such a Motion -The Question is whether this sort of loss in its Nature is a loss within the meaning & intention of the Parties to this Policy – The Policy is upon Record & it will be open to the Gentlemen upon the motion in arrest of Judgment.

Lord Mansfield. I doubt not for there is part of the Fact in it they alledge [sic] in the Declaration it was by Wind & Weather[,] Wind & Storms which made the Ship foul & leaky. [64]

Mr Chambre. I mean to touch upon that part but I mean to touch upon the loss of the Slaves thrown overboard as a sort of Loss within the meaning of the Policy. The other objection upon the Necessity if they could Justify the Act done then that would throw the loss upon the Underwriter[.] that is a Matter equally open upon the Arrest of Judgment.

The two Points I shall trouble your Lordships with are whether in point of fact the inevitable Necessity did exist to justify the Act done – The next is if it did exist[,] whether that necessity was brought about by the Accident of the Voyage or that sort of Mistake Ignorance & Misconduct of the Master of the Ship for which the assured & not the Underwriters are responsible? My Lord[,] an observation was made pre-

[233] Ed. Text in red.

vious to the Examination of the particular Circumstances of the Evidence actually given in this Case upon the nonproduction of Witnesses whom we might have called & whom they say it was our duty to have called – That Observation I trust will be found to have no foundation in fact & no sort of Application to the Question now before the Court – My Lord[,] the Captain who was said [65] to have the Command of the Vessel is proved to have been dead[.] one of the Mates is likewise dead, a great many of the Crew are dead & the only person that was suggested there was a possibility of our calling to support the Plaintiff's case[,] except the Person we did call[,] was another of the Mates whose Name was Kelsall[.] it did not appear upon the trial we knew where Kelsall was or that we had any means of procuring his Testimony – It did appear by the acknowledgement of the Gentleman of the other side that they knew where he was & they might have produced him if they thought his Evidence would have been of any Service to us – If Kelsall had been within our reach we certainly would have produced him[.] we meant to have done it if he had been in Court to have produced him though I trust it would not have been necessary so to have done[.] the Case we made out we proved by a most unexceptionable Witness that could possibly be produced[.] The witness we called was a Passenger in the Ship unconnected totally with all the contending parties[,] no connection with the Owners[,] no connection with the Underwriters[.] he was the only person on board the Ship who had nothing to do with the act the present subject of enquiry & therefore the only person [66] that could be said to be perfectly disinterested in this Question, he was applied to for his Advice it so appeared in Evidence, He was applied to upon the dreadful occasion by the Captain of the Ship for his Advice[.] he declined giving any at first saying he was a Passenger[.] he recommended him to consult his own Crew & they should Act for themselves according as they thought the Necessity of the Case required[.] he was likewise a Man of great experience & described himself as being bred to the Sea, he had been in actual Service upwards of 40 Years[,] had been Master of a Man of War & frequently gone in the particular Voyage this Ship went upon & certainly was a Witness beyond all Exception whatsoever[.] considering the treatment of this Gentleman to whom the preservation of the Ship was owing after the disaster happened, the Master was taken so ill he was incapable of acting & the Mate in the same situation & of necessity this Gentleman towards the latter end of the Business was obliged to take the Conduct of the Vessel & give directions for the Sailing[.] if he had not the Vessel & every Soul must have perished & there is no Question the Underwriters would have been in that case liable to the whole Amount of the Sum [67] insured for no Man would have been alive to have given an Account of the loss that happened or the Manner it did happen & it is not a very greatful [sic] return for this Gentleman[']s Services to make that sort of Observation we have heard & impute to him any Circumstances of Cruelty – Namely because he saw & heard these Things which he could not avoid without shutting his Eyes or Ears[.] these Acts of Wanton Cruelty[,] as they are called[,] he had no Share in[.] he declined giving his Advice as he told you before. If this Gentleman is to meet with the treatment he has met with if it is liable to the Sort of Observation made upon it what would have been the Treatment Mr Kelsal[234] the Mate would have met with – Mr Kelsal if he had been called would no doubt have confirmed Mr Stubbs's Testimony. It tallies with it in every particular[,] his Affidavit does[.] if he had been present I should have thought there would have been no impropriety in calling him[,] but I should have expected instead of addressing him upon the Question upon the facts fairly delivered by the Witnesses[,] I am pretty certain nothing more would have been heard from the [68] Gentleman with respect to Mr Kelsal but declamation addressed to the Passions & not to the Judgment of those who were to decide upon the Question.

Now we come to the real Points for Consideration of the Court[.] It is imputed to us by the Gentleman upon the part of the Defendant the Act committed was not an Act of indispensable Necessity but of Fraud & Wanton Cruelty – Undoubtedly an Act of Violence which destroys the Lives of 122 persons or upwards cannot be described or spoke of without exciting in those that hear it some degree of Horror[,] but there are two Points of View in which this Act is to be considered & examined, If the Act which was so done was for the Preservation of twice that Number of People & if the forbearance of doing that Act would have destroyed not only all those that were saved but even the persons that was destroyed it became justifiable & the Question for the Consideration of the Court is whether in Law all the Circumstances that were proved in this Case this Justification does arise to the Party? Now I own from the Circumstances of this Case it does appear to me if possible for a Case of Necessity to justify the Act to exist[.] it did exist in this Instance[.] at the [69] time when the Mistake was discovered the Ship is described by Stubbs to have been a great Number of

---

[234] Spelled with a single "l" here and from now on.

Leagues to the Leward of Jamaica & their return to that Island must have been retarded & prevented by a very strong Current[.] he says that the shortest period of time in which there was a Possibility even in all the most fortunate Circumstances that could occur in which there was a possibility of regaining the Island was between three Weeks & a Month & it was within two or three Days of a Month before the Vessel was able to regain the Island of Jamaica. A Survey of the Water was taken at that time. A Minute examination of every vessel[,] every Water Cask on Board the Ship was gauged & examined with all the accuracy possible & the whole Quantity of Water found on Board the Ship at this Period of time was one day[']s full allowance of two Quarts to a Man[,] was the whole of the Water that remained on Board and this was to sustain this very large Crew for near a Month or near two or three days of a Month, what is to be done under these Circumstances[?] Mr Pigot says there were other Places which the Ship might have got to sooner than they could reach the Island of Jamaica[,] some Island that he called the Grand Camanes & the Isle of Pines [70] and the possibility of their reaching any other Harbour than Jamaica though an Enemy's Port they should have steered & endeavoured to gain it, this is an Argument from the Map & not from the Evidence in the Cause[.] I dont wonder Mr Pigot made use of that Argument[.] he was not by & did not hear the Evidence actually given; it will be in your Lordship[']s recollection I was not in Court to hear you Lordships Report of the Evidence therefore in stating my Evidence from recollection & a Note from a Gentleman not in the Cause but who took a Note from Curiosity[,] I am pretty certain what I state is accurate & consisting of the Evidence. Your Lordship will recollect I am sure upon this particular point[:] the Witness we called was extreamly [sic] pressed by Mr Davenport upon his Examination[.] It seemed to be material to the Defence & he proved beyond all Contradiction it was absolutely impracticable to reach those Islands or any other Place so soon as Jamaica.

Lord Mansfield. He certainly did, there is no Question of that, but then they say it is because they did not know where they were. [71]

Mr Chambre. My Lord[,] they did not know then where they were & steered a proper Course from that Period the Vessel conducted in the best manner possible[.] The Witness proved it was impossible to gain the Grand Camanes or the Isle of Pines or any other Place but Jamaica from the Winds that prevailed at that time[.] Mr Davenport stated the fact in that respect was materially varied from what he expected[:] if it turned out as he expected he had material Persons experienced Captains to have contradicted Stubbs & shewn the Want of Skill & Judgment[.] none of those were examined & from a North east Wind that prevailed at that time it was impossible & impracticable to reach any of those places or any other Place sooner than there was a probability of their reaching Jamaica[.] that circumstance therefore may be entirely laid out of the Question[.] then it is for Consideration what the Crew could possibly do with such a supply of Water only, for such a Voyage it was sworn to be but one day[']s Allowance at full Allowance, this is a matter that does not depend upon any thing but facts – The subsequent facts will prove the Case beyond any Argument that can be used arising from the Quantity of the Water then on Board the Ship or any other Quantity of Water [72] that would have served on Board other Ships upon particular occasions[:] no Inferences can be drawn from that unless Circumstances are Similar. This was a Ship in one of the Hottest Climates[.] it had on Board not only a Sufficient Number of Men to Navigate the Vessel but it was loaded with a Human Cargo[,] Loaded with Slaves that must necessarily be kept Pent up, the want of Water to such a Crew as that must necessarily be greater than there could be any necessity for in any other Circumstances[,] in many other Voyages where there are a smaller Number of men on Board & where there is a Difference of Climate. It was said by the Gentlemen that they did not make use of even the Water they had that there was a great deal of Water in Rum Casks that was represented as having been spoiled. I am sure your Lordship will recollect the Witness was much pressed upon that Point[.] In answer to all the Questions put to him upon that Subject he said every possible experiment was tried to make use of that Water[,] that they boiled their Beans in it[,] they boiled their Victuals in it[,] they tryed to Boil their beans in it & when they were taken out of the Water they were in such a miserable [73] State that they were harder than when they went in[.] they tried the same with Corn & found it impracticable to use the Water – when taken inwardly it produced a Sickness in the Men & they found it totally impracticable to make any Use of it whatever under these Circumstances[.] the Crew consult & find it impossible to sustain the whole of the Crew[,] to sustain the lives of the whole that are on Board[,] but[,] says Mr Pigot[,] that while there is a Gallon or Quart on Board every Man has an equal share to his right of that Water[.] it ought to be equally distributed[.] you have no right to make a distinction between black & white People[,] they are all of the Human Specie with respect to the

Rights of Existence[.] they are all upon the same footing[.] they make no distinction between one & another & while there was any Water on Board every Person on Board has a Right to an equal distribution of it[235] let us see how that will hold[:] we dont make any distinction between peoples complexions who are white or Black[.] what [74] would have been the Consequences of an Equal Distribution[?] ever[y] person on Board must have perished[.][236] it would have been the Destruction of those that had perished & every one else if there had been this equal Distribution[.] there is not a pretence that any one Person could have survived it to have told the disaster at Jamaica[.] Captain Inglefield was in a situation similar as has been alluded to I have no doubt Captain Inglefield did every thing which became a Brave & humane Man to do[.] let us see whether any advantage could arise to Defendants from the Comparison of the Defendants' Circumstances they were in[.] Captain Inglefield saved himself with 12 Men in a Boat[.] according to Mr Pigot's Argument every Man on Board the Man of War had an equal right to the Boat[.] if every Person had exercised that Right the whole would have perished[.] if it was put upon the Argument of Wise or experienced[,] if they had an equal right to it[,] they might have cast lots for it[.] no, he took his opportunity[.] he got on Board the Boat in the most secret & wise manner he could[.] if every Body had followed[,] the Boat would have overset & every man would have perished[.] with respect to what happened afterwards [75] the Cases are not at all Similar[.] there was but a very small allowance both of Water & Provision for the Captain & 12 men[.] the Captain had authority over the rest but if the Captain had proposed to have thrown any overboard the most probable conjecture is he would have been the first Man they would have thrown overboard[.] the Man who had made such a Proposal would have been the first to be sent overboard[237] Captain Inglefield could not have resisted them.

Lord Mansfield. It is not at all applicable to this Case[.] You are not sure that Captain Inglefield did not push two or three people into the Water that laid hold of the Boat & wanted to get in[.][238]

---

[235] G#: All this is surely true[.] no Doctrine of necessity can be admitted against it[.]
[236] G#: All this is manifestly false even by the Evidence of Stubbs himself for it is allowed they were relieved by a Supply of Rain before the Casks were empty[.]
[237] G#: And very justly.
[238] G#: Such a suggestion is unworthy to be uttered; especially by a Judge, unless he had some Evidence of the fact[.]

Mr Chambre. Certainly. he had a Right.

Lord Mansfield. No Question of it[.] he could not do otherwise[.] The Question was whether all should be saved or some.[239] [76]

Mr Chambre. There is the strongest instinct of self Preservation implanted in every Human Breast[.] when some must perish each one endeavours to take care it shall not be themselves. In this Case they did not determine any should Perish till the Event was absolutely unavoidable – It was said 26 Men were thrown overboard by the Evidence of Mr Stubbs after they had a Supply of Rain, there is no Evidence at least that I recollect to warrant such an Assertion.[240] In the first place as to Mr Stubbs himself he never gave any Orders at all.

Lord Mansfield. I don't know whether you was here when Mr Heywood mentioned it, it is new to me[.] I did not know any Thing of it. He said after the Cause was over & the Verdict brought in[,] upon casting up how much it came to at so much a head for the Negroes[,] they then added 26 which were thrown overboard by the evidence of Stubbs after the Rain had fell several Days & there was 10 jumped overboard. [77]

Mr Chambre. No[,] the Contrary is true[:] we expressly disclaimed damages on account of those that threw themselves overboard & the Attorneys were to settle the Computation amongst themselves if it was wrong.

Lord Mansfield. I did not attend to settling[,] what Quantity of Money it came to. Mr Heywood mentioned it.

Mr Heywood. My Lord, I beg leave to say three words upon Stubbs Evidence. I mentioned the different Sums[.] your Lordship will see the different Number supposed to be proved[.] it is impossible to make out the Number without the 36[,] ten of whom jumped overboard[,] that were thrown overboard after the rain fell within a Week or 10 Days after, after all the Number of Slaves to make out the Verdict was

---

[239] G#: The case so ungenerously supposed of Captain Inglefield having pushed 2 or 3 people into the Water that laid hold of the Boat is a very different case from artfully casting people overboard with their hands tied.

[240] G#: Mr Stubbs own written account proves the fact & thus he made up the Number to be paid for.

not yet proved[.] I stated 64 died to make out the Number as they stand upon the Verdict. On the 29th he swore there was 50 thrown overboard[,] upon the 30th he mentioned 40, 10 more he stated to have jumped overboard & after that 26 more which came out upon a Calculation of the whole to make out only 126 in Number[,] [78] so that after all upon this Trial only 126 were proved instead of 132[.] that is the way in which it stood.

Lord Mansfield. What is the Verdict[?] 122[?].

Mr Heywood. 132. There jumped overboard 10[.] that is the only Mistake I have been guilty of[,] taking them exactly as Mr Stubbs gave his Evidence[,] but then Mr Stubbs mentions 26 that were thrown overboard after the Rain fell[.] My Lord, he has stated that he was in the Cabin Window[.] The Witness says that he saw through the Window the Slaves plunging & heard them in the Water[,] that he saw upwards of 50 that night (meaning the 29th)[,] that afterwards they threw out 40 or upwards[.] when he came to make up the Precise Number he could not do it without those were reckoned who were thrown overboard after the Rain fell.

Mr Chambre. If there is any Error in the Computation of the Damages that is a matter that can very easily be rectified indeed[.] it is necessary for the Attorneys to adjust it. [79]

Lord Mansfield. That is a Material Circumstance unaccounted for, how they came to throw any overboard after they had Water from the Rain.

Mr Chambre. I dont know how that was proved.

Lord Mansfield. I recollect so far the Water supplied by the Rain went but to a certain Degree only what they could catch.

Mr Chambre. According to Mr Stubbs's Evidence none were thrown overboard without the most extream [sic] necessity[.] I appeal to your Lordships recollection for that.

Lord Mansfield. That is certain he did.

Mr Chambre. Notwithstanding the Providential Assistance of the Rain[,] notwithstanding all the Number of those thrown overboard[,] there was not half the Quantity or a Quarter the Quantity of Water to carry them to the End of their Voyage[.] the Rain continued but a Day or 2[.] the Quantity that fell was very far from being adequate to the supply of the Ship[.] your Lordship will recollect the Circumstances & Situation of the Whole Crew as described by Stubbs[.] at the time they reached Jamaica Stubbs [80] gave in Evidence to your Lordship that so far from throwing too many overboard for the preservation of the rest[,] when they arrived at Jamaica there were 30 of the Negroes laying dead[241] upon the deck[,] actually lying dead upon the deck from famine & no other cause & therefore whatever supply they received from the Rain[,] nothing can be clearer or more demonstrable than the Supply was not adequate to the Crew[.] your Lordship will recollect not only the state of the negroes but of the Crew[,] this dismal situation of the whole Crew that consisted of 17 persons who had the Power in their Hands[.] they had spared so much of the Water for the support of [81] the remaining Slaves on Board when the Crew arrived at Jamaica [that] they were reduced to the utmost necessity & distress when they arrived at Jamaica[.] they were so thin their Bones actually pierced though their skin, seven of them were so far reduced they could not be recovered by Medical assistance & during the short space of time Stubbs remained on the Island seven died & died merely from famine. Then what becomes of the Idea of Fraud, It is supposed they threw the people overboard with a view to the Insurance & to make the Underwriters liable, Why Mr Stubbs told your Lordship he believed not a Man on Board knew there was any such Thing as an Insurance[,] but if that was their object why suffer 30 or 40 to die of Famine on board the Ship why not throw them all overboard[?] if they had not been particularly attentive to the Preservation of the crew[,] why did they abridge themselves so much as they appear to have done for the preservation of the Cargo[.] it is clear & manifest out of 17 they sacri-

---

[241] G#: About one third of the Negroes in a Slave Ship commonly die of the Jail Distemper by being stowed too close through the avarice of the Traders, and it appears by Stubbs['] own evidence that 64 Negroes actually died of distemper even before the want of Water was known & it is very unlikely that not a single Man should die afterwards of the same distemper. This clearly proves that none but the sick & such as were likely to die were cast over alive & it is therefore very probable that the remaining 36 which are said to have died for want of Water were really distempered & died of disease & ill treatment for it is not likely that such a Mortality assigned in the Ship during the first part of the Voyage should stop all at once in the latter part of it so that not a single Man should die of the same disorder.

ficed 7 of their own lives,[242] can this be called a Case of Fraud or any thing [82] else but the most absolute necessity[.] it seems impossible to put it in any other Point of View & to use any other Arguments to support the necessity of the Case would be but a Waste of time but no argument can speak so strongly as they do, then the necessity of this Conduct is established[.] it remains to be considered whether it was the Consequence of any such Gross mistake as could discharge the Underwriter & make the Assured only liable to the loss[.] for this purpose two Mistakes are insisted upon, the first was a Mistake that was committed when they came off the Island of Tobago. Now[,] My Lord[,] the Captain upon that occasion did that which became him[,] the Voyage being unusually long & when he came off the Island of Tobago he thought it necessary for a Survey to be made of the Water Casks that he might judge whether it was necessary to go into Tobago for Refreshment[.] the Survey was made & a Report made to the Captain[.] there was Water allowance for 20 Days[.] Mr Stubbs supposes there was a Mistake in it, most probably there was a Mistake[.] whether the Mistake was made in gauging the Casks or any improper Consumption of the Water afterwards does not appear[,] but most probably there was a Mistake[.] What was that Mistake? It was not a Mistake [83] fatal at all to the Voyage[,] not a Mistake that could have produced any ill consequences, if a subsequent mistake had not happened for Mr Stubbs told the Court the length of that Voyage from Tobago to the Island of Jamaica was a Voyage of 10 Days or 8 days though the Quantity of Water was not stated[.] in truth or in fact there was a Supply of Water & full Allowance for a longer Voyage as they supposed, they had been out 11 Days before the Examination of the Water was made[.] during that 11 Days there was a full allowance[.] the mistake at Tobago was not fatal to the Voyage[.] you may say if the real state of the Water had been communicated to the Captain he would have put into Tobago but not gone forward to Jamaica. No doubt 10 days full allowance might have served 20 Days or 3 times the Period of time in which the voyage was compleated [sic][.] that Circumstance therefore may be entirely laid out of the Case[.] then it remains to be considered what was the effect of the subsequent Mistake according to the account given by Stubbs of that[.] I conceive there cannot be imputed any thing criminal in Neg-

---

[242] G#: If any Whites died it was not through want of Water, for it does not appear that they were ever put on short allowance & they carried a quantity of Water into port. See Page 6 of the account delivered to the Court of Exchequer wherein it appears that the 7 Whites here mentioned by Mr Chambre actually died before any want of Water was known.

ligence or Ignorance of the Captain but it is one of those unavoidable accidents which will not discharge the Underwriters or at all vitiate the Policy – In the usual course of [84] the Voyage the Practice is to Sail from Tobago very near the Island of Hispaniola[.] The Captain did not do that for a very good reason & the purpose for which he acted is clearly & manifestly much as for the purpose of the Underwriters as his Employer that being then in the Enemy's possession & the Coast being there infested with by Cruizers[243] of the Enemy he held & properly held it most adviseable [sic] to keep at a Distance from that Island of Hispaniola. There is this Circumstance further in the Evidence of Stubbs[.] That the Currents had set in stronger than usual & he meaning to keep in view of Hispaniola at that sort of Distance necessary for the safety of the Ship, but the Currents that then were set in they were carried to a greater distance than they had any reason to expect – The Distance from Hispaniola to Jamaica was a Day & an half or two days sail[.] in 10 Days they came to the sight of land the first they had seen they being at a considerable distance from it they had no doubt it was the Island of Hispaniola they continued sailing two days longer & then & not till then they suspected they might have missed Jamaica[.] when that became the doubt that moment the examination was made & with great deference to the Court I do submit the Underwriters are not discharged [85] by every possible mistake in the course if a Voyage[.] the Assured did not undertake the Captain they employ & the Crew they employ shall in every Circumstance & at all events do that which is most beneficial & proper to be done[.] they only undertake that common care & common diligence shall be used & common attention – in this Case there was a great Degree of attention paid by the Captain. there was no instance of criminal inattention to discharge the Underwriters nor gross negligence to subject the Captain himself to a suit by his employers. The Captain acted like a prudent cautious Man keeping at that distance from the enemy's port he conceived necessary for the preservation of the Ship[.] the accident that happened in consequence of that arose from the Currents setting in more violent than usual or that he had any reason to expect & I hope the Court will be of opinion upon this Ground the defence is totally unfounded. Your Lordship mentioned another circumstance that was urged by the Gentlemen that the loss which has happened is not a loss of that Nature which is described in the declaration[.] My Lord[,] I conceive & sub-

---

[243] Ed. Johnson's Dictionary: "Cruiser: One that roves upon the sea in search of plunder."

mit to the Court with great deference it is sufficient if the Declaration substantiates the cause of the loss[.] it is not necessary that every fact in the Declaration be [86] be proved[.] for instance[,] if it was alledged [sic] in the declaration by lightning[,] violent storms & tempest the Ship was destroyed[,] shattered & bulged[,] the declaration would be sustained though it was not proved any lightning happened[,] if it was proved the Ship was destroyed by tempest.

Mr Justice Buller. In that case you state 2 or 3 things and one of those are misstated[,] if you say by storms & tempests[,] lightning if you please[,] if you prove the loss happened by one of them that Declaration is proved.

Mr Chambre. That I say.

Mr Justice Buller. But that is not this Case.

Mr Chambre. Then taking it for granted the Declaration does contain that fact how the loss happened I should conceive in a Declaration of this Sort there need not be greater certainty than in an Indictment for Murder[.] If a Man is indicted for murdering another it is sufficient to shew that he died at the time specified & by his means – In the warrant of Insurance if it should be alledged the Ship was destroyed by lightning & it is proved the Ship was cast upon a rock it would be [87] a very different kind of loss it would not substantiate it[.] but here the loss is proved which does correspond with the averment in the Declaration, the declaration states by Perils of the Sea contrary Winds & Currents & other Misfortunes the Ship was rendered foul & leaky and was retarded in her Voyage & by means of her being so retarded in her Voyage the Water on Board the Vessel was consumed so that enough did not remain on Board for the subsistence of the Cargo, it was stated the loss happened by the Consumption of Water occasioned but the delay from the Weather – that is the substance of what was proved[.] It is stated in the Declaration the Ship was rendered foul & leaky[.] I believe no questions were asked of the Witness in that respect – It does appear by the protest that was the Case & the Voyage was retarded from what happened even before the reaching [of] Jamaica but as no questions were asked of the Witness with respect to the ship being foul[,] as he did not prove that fact[,] I am content to consider that fact as not proved but no objection was made at the trial in this Business[,] but suppose it not proved foul and leaky[,] it is proved she was delayed & retarded in her Voyage nay it is farther proved that Delay was occasioned by the Currents[.] that was a fact Captain Stubbs [88] in his Evidence expressly proved by the Currents she was carried so far from Hispaniola she lost sight of that Island[,] the Consequence of which was it was retarding the Voyage for near a Month – If this is not stating in substance the occasion of the loss I really dont know what is & it so seemed to be considered by the Gentlemen upon the part of the Defendants no sort of objection was taken upon that Ground – I trust therefore upon the whole of this Case the Court will be of Opinion that inevitable necessity did exist[,] that there was no gross mistake committed by the Captain to transfer the loss that happened from the underwriter to the Assured[.] the attention of the Jury were [sic] particularly directed to that Fact[.] your Lordship pointed out that Consideration to them & they found it was not owing to any gross mistake of the Captain but the Perils of the Voyage – Upon all these Grounds I hope your Lordship will be of opinion there is no sort of foundation for this application for a new Trial – The Matter has undergone all the examination & investigation it was capable of and there is no ground at all for this application for a new Trial. [89]

Lord Mansfield. It is a very uncommon Case & I think very well deserves a reexamination and there is great weight in that objection which has now been made which was not made at the Trial[,] that is you alledge in the Declaration risques of the Sea to have been the Cause of this Necessity contrary to the truth of the Case for you Charge in your Declaration That by reason of the Currents & Contrary Winds the ship became foul & leaky & being foul & leaky was the cause of her being retarded in her Voyage & that occasioned the consumption of their Water & her being reduced to so much Distress & scarcity - they never asked the Question about her being foul & leaky[.] most undoubtedly that was not the cause of the Delay of the Voyage – the Cause of the Delay was his mistaking Hispaniola for Jamaica[.] the Current would not have affected them if they knew where they were, If they had not made the mistake they would have been in no necessity whatsoever & to be sure what Mr Heywood has observed is a very material Circumstance if in taking the Verdict they had taken for so many Negroes thrown overboard after the rain came without any account how they came to do it the contrary of that [90] fact is averred and it is so uncommon a Case I think upon the Ground of reexamination only it ought to go to a new trial but it must be upon Payment of Costs.

Mr Justice Willes. I am of the same opinion.

Mr Justice Buller. I am of the same opinion the declaration most clearly does not any part of it specify the accident that occasioned the loss[.] As to what Mr Chambre put of an Indictment for Murder you must state the cause of the Death & prove the death of that Nature described[.] if you state the death to be caused by some Instrument you must prove the stabbing & the cause of the Death is to be proved but in this Case it would be attended with serious consequences if we were to overrule the objection to this declaration[.] I will suppose the Law clear for the Underwriters are not liable for a mistake made by the Captain[.] you don't understand me giving any opinion upon this particular Case but for the purpose of the Argument I mention it[.] If this objection was not allowed & upon his Mistake [91] the Plaintiff was to recover that would be allowed for the loss by the Perils of the Sea & the Defendants would have no redress[.] It is stated upon the Record what is not true in point of fact & by this manoever [sic] he would be prevented from coming to the question of Law and arguing that the Evidence of the loss is substantially different from that stated in the Declaration & it does not seem to me in any Way this Evidence can support this Declaration.

Lord Mansfield. Take the Rule upon Payment of Costs.

Letter from Granville Sharp to the Admiralty

National Maritime Museum REC/19

[93]

Copy of a Letter
To the Lords Commissioners
Of the Admiralty dated
2 July 1783

With an Account of the Case - - p.99
And 2 Vouchers - No. 1 - p. 117
No. 2 - p. 1

[94] [blank]

[95]

(Copy of a Letter to the Lords Commissioners of the Admiralty)

My Lords
Old Jewry London 2 July 1783

As the cognizance & right of Enquiry concerning all Murders committed on Board British Ships belongs properly to the Admiralty Department[244] I think it my Duty to lay before your Lordships two Manuscripts Accounts, wherein are stated from unquestionable Authority the Circumstances of a most inhuman & barbarous Murder committed by Luke Collingwood the Master, Colonel James Kelsal, the Mate, & other persons, the Mariners or Crew of the Ship *Zong*, or *Zurg*, a Liverpool Trader freighted with Slaves &c. from the Coast of Africa, which Master Mate, & Crew, on pretence of Necessity lest there should be a want of Water, wilfully & deliberately destroyed 122 poor Negro Slaves, by casting them alive (as it is deposed) into the Sea with their hands bound or fettered, to deprive them of all possibility of escaping! Having been earnestly solicited & called upon by a poor Negro for my assistance to avenge the blood of his Murdered Countrymen, I thought it my duty to share neither labour nor expence [sic] in collecting all the Information concerning this horrible transaction that I could possibly procure for the sake of national Justice, that the Blood of the murdered

---

[244] Ed. The Court of Admiralty had criminal jurisdiction over death or mayhem on the high seas and on ships "below the bridges of great rivers", dating back at least to a treatise at the time of Edward III, *De Officio Admiralitatis*, from which the quoted phrase comes. *Black Book of the Admiralty*, Cambridge UP, 2012, i.221; By the statutes 27 Hen VIII, c 4, 1535–6 and 28 Hen VIII, c 15, 1536 offences of piracy, robbery and murder done at sea or within the admiral's jurisdiction were to be tried in such places as should be limited in the king's commissions, directed to the lord admiral, his lieutenant and deputies and other persons: Jacob, *Law Dictionary*, 1811, i.43; Sir James Fitzjames Stephen, *A History of the Criminal Law of England*, 3 vols London, 1883. ii.17–31. A K R Kiralfy, *Potter's Historical Introduction to English Law*, London, 1958, p 192. The jurisdiction included piracy at common law affecting anyone, but other criminal offences committed on the high seas were within the jurisdiction of the court only where the accused was a British subject. The Admiralty proceedings were originally according to the civil law, and so had no jury, although there were apparently exceptions made: Stephen, ibid, ii.17. Dissatisfaction with this led to the statute 1535–36 by which cases were to be tried by jury (s 2).

may not rest on the whole Kingdom, which already labours under too awful a load of Guilt, in tolerating the iniquitous Slave Trade, whereby amongst other evils, this most inhuman and diabolical Deed was occasioned.

One of the Manuscripts marked Voucher No. 1, is an authentic Copy from the Office of the Court of Exchequer, of a Bill or petition presented to that Court last Hilary Term, in behalf of Thomas Gilbert & others Underwriters & Insurers of the said Ship *Zong* or *Zurg*, Plaintiffs, against Messrs William John & James Gregson & others, Merchants of Liverpool, & Owners of the said Ship & Cargo, who obtained a Verdict in the Court of Kings Bench on the 6th March last against the said [96] Underwriters for the value of the Murdered Slaves rated at £30 per head, though alledged to be wilfully drowned by the Agents & Servants of the said Owners, so that this most abominable Iniquity has been notoriously favoured and encouraged in that solemn Court but on what principle is not easy to be conceived!

The other M. S. Book, marked Voucher No. 2, contains a Copy of Minutes, taken in short-hand, the last Term (on 22nd & 23d May 1783) of the Proceedings in the Court of King's Bench on a Motion for a new Trial of the Cause of Gregson & others against Gilbert & others (the same parties as are mentioned above) concerning the Value of those Murdered Negroes! - Thus the Contest between the Owners & Insurers of the Ship, though a mere mercenary Business, amongst themselves, about the pecuniary value (& not for the - Blood of so many human persons wickedly and unjustly put to death) has, nevertheless, occasioned the disclosure of that horrible transaction which otherwise, perhaps, might have been known only amongst the Impious Slave Dealers of Liverpool, and have never been brought to light.

It will, however, be necessary for me to add to those Vouchers a brief state (which is inclosed) of the principal Circumstances - of the Case, because the two Manuscripts are much too long for the perusal of your Lordships, except in the way of Reference to particular parts, as to Vouchers of the facts; & it is necessary also to add to the inclosed State, some remarks in answer to the Arguments & Doctrine of a very eminent & learned Lawyer[245] who, to the dishonour of his profession,

---

[245] G#: Memorandum. John Lee (or Lea) Esqr. A Yorkshire man, who spoke very broad in the provincial dialect of that County which has seldom been so grossly profaned as by this Lawyer! – This name was not inserted in the original Letter.

attempted to vindicate the inhuman Transaction! Thus it was unhappily demonstrated that there is nothing, howsoever gross & absurd, which some Professors of the Law, accustomed to Sophistry, & hackneyed in the prostitution of their oratorical abilities for hire, will not undertake to justify, relying on their studied powers of perversion [97] like those "doublehearted Men of Old" who said, "with our tongue we will prevail – Our Lips are with us, who is Lord over us?"[246] But, if we must one day "render an Account of every idle word," how much more awful will be the condemnation of that perverse Oratory, which patronizes and defends the most violent of all oppression, even wilful Murder, the superlative degree of unrighteousness!

As there is some variation in the two Accounts, respecting the number of persons murdered, it is necessary to remark that it appears, upon the whole Evidence, that no less than 133 of the unhappy Slaves on board the Zong were inhumanly doomed to be cast into the Sea (Voucher No. 1 p. 2 & 3) and that all the other numbers mentioned in the several Accounts, are to be included in that number, vizt. the 122, mentioned in the beginning of this Letter, who were cast alive (as the owners & witnesses assert) into the Sea with their hands fettered; also ten poor Negroes, who being terrified with what they had seen of the unhappy fate of their Countrymen, jumped overboard in order to avoid the fettering, or binding of their hands, & were drowned; & one Man more that had been cast over hung from the Ship into the water, & there without being perceived, regained the Ship, secreted himself & was saved: So that the whole number drowned (or at least asserted to be drowned according to the Evidence produced) amounted to 132, the number charged to the Insurers by the Owners (Voucher No. 2 p. [blank])

The reallity [sic] of the fact, according to the Evidence produced, was testified upon Oath in one of our highest courts of Justice & was notoriously admitted by both the contending parties - Mr Robert Stubbs, late Governor of Annamaboe &c is a living Witness to a part of the Transaction, & is now in Town vizt. at No. 75 in King Street Westminster - he told me himself that he saw several [98] of the poor Creatures plunging into the Sea that had been cast overboard; though he alledges that he did not see, who cast them over, for, he says, he was only a

---

[246] Bible (AV), Psalms 12.4: "Who have said, With our tongue will we prevail; our lips are our own: who is lord over us?"

passenger in the Ship, & had nothing to do in the transaction; but remained below at the times the poor Creatures were cast over; – Also the Officers & Crew of the Ship William (Richard Hanley, late master) & the Owners of the said Ship vizt. Messrs Gregson, Cave, Wilson, & Aspinal of Liverpool, Merchants (mentioned in Voucher No. 1 p.1) can probably give sufficient Information where the guilty Crew of the *Zong*, whom they employed, are to be found, as also their Names &c. And Mr – – , who defended the Cause of the said Owners has attended their consultation, & was in possession of the Evidence or Deposition of Colonel James Kelsal, the Chief Mate of the *Zong*, (Voucher No. 2 p. [blank]) will be able to confirm the notoriety of the fact; & so, also, will the Attornies [sic] employed in the Cause on both sides [of] the question vizt. Messrs Brograve & Lyon for the Owners of the *Zong*, & Mr Townley Ward for the Insurers.

Informed of all these particulars, your Lordships will now be enabled to judge, whether there is sufficient Evidence for a Criminal prosecution of the Murderers, vizt. Colonel James Kelsal (the Chief Mate) & the rest of the Crew of the said Ship *Zong* or *Zurg* before the Grand Jury at the next Admiralty sessions.

Luke Collingwood the Master of the *Zong* is reported to be dead, as also Richard Hanley, the Master of the Ship William, above mentioned.

P.S. To avoid delay I have sent my original Vouchers without preserving Copies of them, & as they are valuable (the 2d alone having cost me £12.[0].4.) I must request your Lordships to give Orders that they may be returned to me as soon as the Business is concluded.-

I am with the greatest respect
My Lords
Your Lordships most obedient
& most humble Servant
(signed) Granville Sharp

An Account of the Murder of 132 Slaves

National Maritime Museum REC/19

[99]

An Account of
The Murder of 132 Slaves on Board
The Ship *Zong*, or *Zurg*; with some Remarks on the Argument of an eminent Lawyer, in defence of that inhuman Transaction inclosed in the Letter 2d July 1783 to the Lords Commissioners of the Admiralty.

[Granville Sharp]

298   *Cases on Slavery*

[*100*]

An Account of the principle Circumstances stated in a petition to the Court of Exchequer in Hilary Term 1783 (See Voucher No. 1) & in the Arguments on a Motion last Trinity Term in the Court of Kings Bench, for a new Trial in the case of Gregson & others against Gilbert & others, (See Voucher No. 2, being a Copy of the proceedings taken in short hand) respecting the Murder of 132 Negro Slaves, by the Master Mate and Crew of the Ship *Zong* or *Zurg*; to which are added some remarks on the Arguments of an eminent Lawyer who attempted to justify the inhuman Transaction.

[*101*]

The Ship *Zong* or *Zurg*, Luke Collingwood, Master sailed from the Island of St Thomas on the Coast of Africa the 6th September 1781 with 440 Slaves (Voucher No.1, p.2) or 442 Slaves & 17 Whites on Board (Voucher No. 2 p.13 & 22) for Jamaica, & on the 27th November following she fell in with that Island; but, instead of proceeding to some Port, the Master, "either through ignorance or a sinister Intention ran the Ship to leeward" (V.1 p.2) alledging that he mistook Jamaica for Hispaniola (V.2 p.1)

Sickness and Mortality had by this time taken place (which is almost constantly the case on board Slave Ships, through the Avarice of these most detestable Traders, which induces them to crowd or rather to pack too many Slaves together in the holds of their Ships) so that on board the *Zong* "between the time of her leaving the Coast of Africa & the 29th November 1781 Sixty Slaves & upwards & seven white people died & that a great number of the remaining Slaves on the day last mentioned were sick of some disorder or disorders & likely to die or not live long" (V.1 p.4)

These Circumstances of Sickness & Mortality are necessary to be remarked; also the consequence of them vizt. that the dead & dying Slaves would have been a dead loss to the Owners (& in some proportion also a loss to the Persons employed by the Owners) unless some pretence or expedient had been found to throw the loss upon the Insurers (V.1. p.4) (V2. p.8.14.) as in the case of Jetsam or Jetson i.e. a plea of necessity to cast overboard some part of a Cargo to save the rest.

These Circumstances I say are necessary to be remarked because they point out the most probable inducement to this enormous wickedness. [102]

The Sickness & Mortality on Board the *Zong*, previous to the 29th November 1781 (the time when they began to throw the poor Negroes overboard alive) was not occasioned by the want of Water, for it was proved that they did not discover, till that very day, the 29th November (or the preceding day) that the Stock of fresh Water was reduced to 200 gallons (as Mr Stubbs has informed me) yet the same day, or in the Evening of it, before any Soul had been put to short allowance (V.2 p.5.6.18 & 52) & before there was any present or real Want of Water, "...the Master of the Ship called together a few of the Officers & told them to the following effect, that if the Slaves died a natural death, it would be the loss of the Owners of the Ship; but if they were thrown alive into the Sea it would be the loss of the Underwriters" &c (V.1 p.4.) and to palliate the inhuman proposal he said Collingwood pretended that it would not be so cruel to throw the poor sick Wretches (meaning such Slaves) into the Sea, as to suffer them to linger out a few Days under the Disorders with which they were afflicted, or expressed himself to the like effect." (ibid) To which proposal the Mate (whose name is Colonel James Kelsal [sic] (V.1 p.3) objected, it seems, at first, & said – "there was no present want of Water to justify such a measure" - "But the said Luke Collingwood prevailed upon the Crew or the rest of them to listen to his said proposal, & the same Evening & 2 or 3 or some few following days the said Luke Collingwood picked or caused to be picked out from the Cargo of the same Ship 133 Slaves all or most of whom were sick or weak & not likely to live, & ordered the Crew by turns to throw them into the Sea, which most inhuman Order was cruelly complied with." - (V.1 p.5) - vizt. on the 29th[.] He (meaning Mr Stubbs late Governor of Annamaboe) "swore there was 50 thrown overboard & upon the 30th he mentioned 40" (V.2 p.49 & 22) but the learned Counsellor, to whose speech, in the Voucher, I have here referred must [103] mean only the round number mentioned by Mr Stubbs: for I am informed by Mr Stubbs himself, as also by a Memorandum from the Deposition of Kelsal, the chief Mate, (one of the Murderers) that 54 Persons were actually thrown overboard alive, on the 29th of November, that 42 more were also thrown overboard on the 1st December or rather their meaning (I apprehend) is that after the 2d time of throwing overboard which seems to have been on the 30th

November (See V.2 p.22) they counted the remaining Slaves (which Mr Stubbs acknowledges he did after each throwing over) & found by the decreased number of Slaves, the next morning (vizt. on the 1st December) when they counted them, that 42 more Slaves had been thrown over, not that they were then (on the 1st December) thrown over, but only in the praeterpluperfect time, had been - vizt. at the 2d time of throwing over on the preceding day. This I take to be their meaning. And on this very day the 1st December 1781 before the Stock of Water was consumed there fell a plentiful rain, which by the confession of one of their own Advocates "continued a day or two" (V.2 p.50) & enabled them to collect 6 Casks of Water which was full Allowance for 11 days (V.2 p.24)[247] or for 23 days, at half Allowance, whereas the Ship actually arrived at Jamaica in 24 days afterwards vizt. on the 22nd December 1781 (V.1 p.2) They seem also to have had an opportunity of sending their Boat for water no less than 13 days sooner vizt. on the 9th December when they "made the West end of Jamaica distant 2 or 3 leagues only," as I am informed by a person who was on board, so that the 6 Casks of Rain Water, caught on the 1st and 2d December (only 7 days before this opportunity of obtaining water from Jamaica) was not only a providential supply but providentially demonstrated the iniquity of pretending a necessity to put innocent Men to death through the mere apprehension of a want – which supposing it had taken place, could not have afforded an admissable [sic] Justification of the horrible deed but which did never really exist or take place at all in their case, because their Stock of Water was never actually consumed. And yet notwithstanding this proof of a possibility that they [104] might perhaps obtain further Supplies by Rain, or that they might be able to hold out with their new increased Stock of Water 'till they might chance to meet with some Ship or be able to send to some Island for a further Supply, they nevertheless cast 26 more human Persons alive into the Sea even after the Rain! (V.2 p.23.24.25, 48.49 & 50) whose hands were, also, fettered or Bound: & which was done, it seems, in the Sight of many other unhappy Sufferers that were brought up upon the deck for the same detestable purpose, whereby 10 of these poor miserable human Creatures were driven to the lamentable necessity of jumping overboard (V.2 p. 24.48 & 49) to avoid fettering or binding of their hands and were likewise drowned!

---

[247] Ed. Page 263, page 35 of the MS.

Thus 132[248] innocent human Persons were wilfully put to a violent death, not on account of any mutiny or insurrection (V.2 p.28 & 34) nor even through the fear of any such (for the Circumstance of being brought up upon the deck with their hands loose, & in so large a number together as more than ten at one time; & also the Circumstance of binding & casting others overboard in their presence which terrified 10 of them into the desperate act of jumping, entirely excludes the least idea of fearing an Insurrection) but merely on a pretended Plea of necessity through the want of Water (as alledged by the Murderers) a Plea of Necessity which is confuted even by the Circumstances of the Evidence produced in favour of it! A want which was so far from taking Place when the Murder was committed, that they had, at least, 200 gallons of fresh Water by their own Confession besides 2 1/2 Butts of what they called Sour Water (V.2 p.3) [105] and that neither the Slaves nor the Crew had been put to short Allowance (V.2 p.5.18.52) so that, even if the Plea of Necessity for the wilful murder of innocent Persons, was at all admissable [sic] (which it never can be) in a case of want or scarcity, yet no such necessity existed in the present case, because it is proved, even by their own Evidence, that the Stock of Water was sufficient to have held out till the time that an ample Supply was actually received. But there never can be a necessity for the wilful murder of an innocent Man (notwithstanding the high Authority of those learned & dignified Persons who seem to have conceived a contrary idea (See V.2. p.2.22.31 & 34) because wilful Murder is one of the worst evils that can happen amongst Men; so that the Plea of a Necessity to destroy a few men in order to save many is not only the adoption of a declared damnable Doctrine ("Let us do evil that good may come") which is extreme wickedness, but is also extreme ignorance for it is obvious that the death of many by misfortune, which is properly in the hand of Divine Providence, is not near so great an evil as the murder of a few or even of one innocent Man; the former being the loss only of temporal Lives, but the latter endanger the eternal Souls, not only of the miserable Aggressors themselves, but the Souls also of all their indiscriminate Abettors & Favourers! God[']s Vengeance is so clearly denounced against Wilful Murder, that it is certainly a *"Malum in se"* of the most flagrant & odious nature, such as cannot, without extreme ignorance of the English Common Law, be admitted in a legal Justification, because our Law supposes that all honest & true Men (*"Probi et*

---

[248] G#: 133 were ordered to be thrown over (V.1 p.2) but one Man was saved by catching hold of a Rope which hung overboard (V.1 p.9).

legales Homine") "have the fear of God before their Eyes" (the contrary being the Preamble to Arraignment & Condemnation) & consequently all [106] Men in all Countries, where Christianity is to be deemed an established part of the Law (as in England) are required not to fear even death, or anything that can "hurt the body, so much as him, who hath power over both body & soul!["] And therefore whenever a man wilfully takes a Life of an innocent man on pretence of Necessity to save his own, in any case, where the Plea of "*Se defendendo*"[249] will not hold [which requires Proof of an actual attack by the deceased (who therefore is not an innocent Man) such an attack must be inevitable by any other means than the death wound] such a man I say is guilty of a felonious Homicide & also of (what is equally cognizable by our Common Law) a gross contempt of God, in being more afraid of Death & temporal Sufferings than of God's eternal Judgment; so that the felonious Disposition which our Law condemns vizt. the not "having the fear of God before his Eyes" is clearly marked upon such an Offender and upon all his Abettors & Defenders! And therefore a learned & dignified Lawyer did certainly place himself, very inconsiderably,[250] under the same felonious description of Mind, when he asserted in behalf of these Murderers, "I could not suffer another Man to live (said he) when the single question was whether I should prefer my Life to his" &c (V 2. p.33). I trust from the general good Character of this eminent Person , that he did not mean what his words express; for a Man who sets so high & over rated a value on Life, independant [*sic*] of all principle of right, & the fear of God, is unfit to be trusted at all in any Society! because the same principle ("I could not suffer another man to live" which implies a disposition to commit any kind of Violence whatever) would prompt a Man to poison, or to swear away the life of another Man, in case his [107] Own life happened to be in such a predicament of danger as to require the iniquitous expedient!

I should not have taken Notice of such an unreasonable Argument, & much less, have troubled your Lordships with it, did not the Official Dignity of the Speaker, & his high Reputation as a Lawyer, compel me to guard against the adoption of his avowed Doctrines in the present

---

[249] Ed. Self defence.
[250] Ed. Meaning "very considerably" or "not inconsiderably"? The MS sometimes appears to omit a negative when one is intended, as above (MS p 104): "...for the Circumstance of being brought up upon the deck with their hands loose, & in so large a number together as more than ten at one time... entirely excludes the least idea of fearing an Insurrection..."

case; lest Precept, as well as Impunity, should encourage the Liverpool Traders to multiply their murders to the disgrace of the English Name, & to the destruction of the human Species! "If any man of them" (said the learned Advocate for Liverpool Iniquity, speaking of the Murderers in the present case) "if any Man of them", (said he), "was allowed to be tried at the Old Bailey for a Murder I cannot help thinking" (said he) "if that charge of Murder was attempted to be sustained, & Mr Stubbs adduced to prove the Evidence & the Facts, it would be folly & rashness to a degree of madness, & so far from the Charge Murder laying against these people there is not the least Imputation of Cruelty, I will not say, but of impropriety not the least"!!!! (V.2 p.33)

This destruction of Living Men he considered, it seems, as if it were merely "the Case of Chattels of Goods:– "it is really so" (says he V.2 p.31) it is "the Case of throwing over Goods; for to this purpose, & the purpose of this Insurance, they are Goods, & Property; & whether right or wrong, we have nothing to do with" – &c - But at the same time he ought not to have forgot the Nature of these Goods or Property; for that is the most material Circumstance of the Case, & yet he either indiscriminately overlooked, or criminally suppressed this most indispensable point of Consideration; vizt. that it is also the case of throwing over Living Men! And that, notwithstanding [108] They are, in one sense, unhappily considered as Goods or Chattels (to the eternal Disgrace of this Nation!) yet, that still they are Men; that their existence in Human Nature, & their actual Rights as Men, nay as Bretheren, still remain! so that the supposed Property in their Persons (which is so highly, so shamefully favoured) is after all, a very limited sort of Property; limited, I say, by the inevitable Consideration (if we are not Brutes ourselves) of their Human Nature; and therefore the Argument of the learned Lawyer, asserting that "this is the case of Chattels of Goods; it is really so" (said he) "it is the case of throwing over Goods &c." whereby he endeavoured to suppress the Idea of their being, at the same time, Human Persons, & the necessary consideration in favour of the Life of Man, which our Law requires, is certainly liable to the Imputation, not only of Cruelty & Impropriety (though he has asserted the contrary) but must also be imputed to the grossest indiscrimination; which is unpardonable in his profession as a Lawyer! Especially when the most obvious natural Right of Human nature is at stake, vizt. the Right to Life itself!!!

The property of these poor injured Negroes in their own lives, notwithstanding their unhappy state of Slavery, was infinitely superior & more to be favoured in Law than the Slave holder's, or slave-dealers iniquitous claim of Property in their Persons, & therefore the casting them alive into the Sea, though insured as Property, and valued at £30 per head, is not to be deemed "the case of throwing over Goods &c" [according to the learned Advocate's indiscriminate Argument "as any other irrational cargo" (says he) "or inanimate Cargo might be &c!!! V.2. p.57] But it is a flagrant Offence against God, & against all mankind! which (so far from deserving the favor [sic] [109] of a Judgment against the Insurers to make good the pecuniary value of the property, as mere Goods & Chattels) ought to have been examined & punished with the utmost rigour, for the exemplary prevention of such inhuman practises for the future; because our Common Law ought to be deemed competent to find a remedy in all causes of violence & injustice whatsoever. "Lex semper dabit Remedium"[251] - "Lex Hominem rebus ejus praefert - vitam et libertatem" (not the Slaveholder[']s property, "et justitiam omnibus"[252] "Lex libertati, Vitae, Pudicitiae et Doti favet. Recto autem in omnibus et ante omnia".[253] Life & Liberty, therefore, are Rights, which demand favour & preference in Law; so that a Right to live ought by no means to have been suppressed in favour of a mere pecuniary claim in the most doubtful Species of Property, the Service of Slaves, the very reverse of what the Law is required to favour, & which it cannot countenance without tincture of iniquity, nor without violence to its own excellent principles! The Learned Lawyer ought not to have neglected these necessary Maxims: but, on the contrary, his Argument was so lamentably unworthy of his dignity & public character, & so banefully immoral in its tendency to encourage the superlative degree of all oppression, wilful Murder! that the Author of it, as well as the indiscriminate Jury (who favoured the horrible transaction by their Judgment against the Insurers) must be considered Abettors & Parties in the guilt at least, of all the Murders of the same kind that may hereafter be promoted by this failure of Justice, & by the lamentable want of distinction between good and evil, – which has been so notoriously manifested in this inhuman Business!

The only Plea of Necessity that can legally be admitted or are worthy of being mentioned in this case, are 1st a Necessity, incumbent [110] Upon the whole Kingdom, to vindicate our National Justice by

---

[251] Ed. The law will always give a remedy.
[252] Ed. The law of man prefers life, liberty and justice for all.
[253] Ed. The law of liberty favours life, chastity and gifts. The right for all, and before all.

the most exemplary punishment of the Murderers, mentioned in these Vouchers, & 2dly the Necessity of putting an entire stop to the Slave Trade, lest any similar Deeds of Barbarity, occasioned by it, should speedily involve the whole Nation in some such tremendous Calamity, as may unquestionably mark the avenging hand of God, who has promised to "destroy the Destroyers of the Earth"!

Old Jewry
2d July 1783

Letter from Granville Sharp to Duke of Portland

National Maritime Museum REC/19

[111]

Copy of a Letter
To the Duke of Portland
Dated the 18 July 1783[254]
(relating to the Murder of the Negroes
On board the Ship *Zong*)

[112] [blank]

---

[254] Ed. The letter is in fact dated 17 July 1783 at the end.

[113]

Copy of a Letter to the Duke of Portland,[255] dated 18th July 1783[256] inclosing the Copy of a Letter to the Lords of the Admiralty, with an Account of the Murder of 132 Negro Slaves on Board the Ship *Zong* or *Zurg* a Liverpool Trader

My Lord

In the Year 1772, when Lord North was His Majesty's first Minister, I stated, in a Letter to his Lordship, some unquestionable proofs of the necessity of abolishing Slavery in the Colonies, & of putting a Stop to the Slave Trade. Since that time, Barbadoes (the wicked Laws of which, I more particularly complained of to Lord North) & other Islands, whose similar oppressions are tolerated, have been blasted by Tempests & Hurricanes far surpassing the ordinary course of Nature even in those Climates; & also the much greater part of our Colonial Dominions have since been severed from the British Empire. But these warnings have effected no reformation. Corruption & Iniquity of all kinds are as unrestrained as ever; nay the most enormous of all our national Iniquities, the Slave Trade is still fostered by parliamentary Authority; & Slavery is still established in the small remains of our Colonial possessions. As a proof of the extreme depravity, which the Slave Trade introduces amongst those that become enured [sic] to it, I have inclosed the Copy of a Letter, which I sent to the Lords of the Admiralty, in the beginning of the present Month, with an Account of the Murder of 132 Negro Slaves on board the Ship *Zong* or *Zurg*, a Liverpool Trader. The original Vouchers are now at the Admiralty, & I have not yet received any Answer respecting them.

The punishment of that Murder belongs properly to the Admiralty Department, & therefore I do not apply to your [114] Grace on that Account; but only wish, by the horrible example related in the inclosed Papers, to warn your Grace, that there is an absolute necessity to abolish the Slave Trade, & the West India Slavery & that "to be in power, &

---

[255] Ed. William Henry Cavendish Cavendish-Bentinck, 3rd Duke of Portland, KG PC (14 April 1738 – 30 October 1809), first administration, First Lord of the Treasury (Prime Minister), April – December 1783.

[256] Ed. The letter is in fact dated 17 July 1783 at the end.

to neglect (as Life [& I may add, the tenure of Office] is very uncertain). Even a day in endeavouring to put a Stop to such monstrous injustice & abandoned Wickedness must necessarily endanger a man's eternal Welfare, be he ever so great in temporal dignity or Office."

This was my warning to Lord North eleven years ago. -

I am with great respect
My Lord
Your Grace[']s
Most obedient & most
Humble Servant
(signed) Granville Sharp

Old Jewry
17 July 1783

His Grace the Duke of Portland

[115] [blank]

[116] [blank]

Bill in the Court of Exchequer

National Maritime Museum REC/19

[117]

(Voucher No. 1)[257]

Hilary Term in the 23rd
Year of the Reign of
King George the 3d[258]

To the Right Honorable[259] William Pitt
Chancellor & Under treasurer of his Majesty's
Court of Exchequer at Westminster - - -
The Right Hon[oura]ble Sir John Skynner Knt.[260]
Lord Chief Baron of the same Court & the
Rest of the Barons there.

Lancashire, Humbly Complaining, shew unto your Honors [sic], your Orators Thomas Gilbert, John Dawson[,] William Bolden[,] John Thompson[,] John Parker & Edward Mason all of Liverpool in the County of Lancashire[,] Merchants & Ellis Bent of Warrington in the same County[,] Merchant Debtors & Accountants[261] to his present Majesty

---

[257] Ed. Text in red. Text in red in the MS was evidently inserted by Granville Sharp.
[258] Ed. 1783.
[259] Ed. So spelled in MS.
[260] Ed. David Lemmings, 'Skynner, Sir John (bap 1723, d 1805)', ODNB, 2004 [http://www.oxforddnb.com/view/article/25700], accessed 12 March 2015.
[261] Ed. The Exchequer was originally an administrative department concerned with the receipt of the King's revenue. The Exchequer of Pleas had developed as a court which dealt with disputes concerning the King's revenue. Originally private persons were therefore not able to bring an action in the court to recover a debt due from another private person, but over time the court extended its jurisdiction, both for its own benefit and that of litigants. At first "accountants to the King" ie people who collected the King's revenue on his behalf, were allowed to bring actions against those

as by the Records of this Hon[oura]ble Court & otherwise it doth and may appear that some time in the Year of our Lord 1781[.]

William Gregson John Gregson James Gregson George Case Edward Wilson & James Aspinal all of Liverpool aforesaid Merchants fitted out a Ship or Vessel called the *William* under the Command of Richard Hanley since deceased on a Voyage from Liverpool for the Coast of Africa & the British West Indies,

That the said Richard Hanley soon after his arrival upon the Coast or during the time he was trading there for Slaves fell in with a Ship belonging to Bristol which had captured & made prize of a Dutch Vessel called the *Zong* otherwise the *Zorg* with a Cargo on board consisting of Slaves & Goods & Merchandizes calculated for the African Market,

Whereupon the said Richard Hanley agreed to purchase from the Master or Commander of the British Ship the said Prize called *Zong* or *Zorg* & the Slaves & other Goods & Merchandizes on board of her[.]

And your Orators further shew unto your Honors that a Sum being agreed upon between the Commanders of the said Liverpool & Bristol Ships for the purchase of the aforesaid Prize & her [118] Cargo the said Richard Hanley (who made the said purchase for & on the Account of the Owners of the said Ship William) drew one or more Bill or Bills of Exchange for the purchase Money thereof upon the said William Gregson, John Gregson James Gregson, George Case, Edward Wilson & James Aspinal in favor [sic] of the Master of the Bristol Ship who on receipt of the same Bill or Bills of Exchange delivered up & transferred to the said Richard Hanley for the use of his said Owners the aforesaid Prize called the *Zong* or *Zorg* & her Cargo[.]

And your Orators further shew unto your Honors that at the time the said Purchase was made the said Ship *Zong* or *Zorg* having on Board 240 Slaves & Goods sufficient for the purchase of near as many more[.]

---

who owed them private debts. This was done through the plea of *quo minus* by which the plaintiff or plaintiffs alleged that they were debtors to the King and that, since the defendant or defendants owed them a debt, the plaintiffs were thereby the less (*quo minus*) able to pay the King what was due to him. At first this was probably not a fiction but by the eighteenth century it was sufficient simply to make the assertion without specific proof that the plaintiff was an "accountant" or was less able to pay the King what was due to him.

And the said Rich[ar]d Hanley then almost having compleated [sic] his purchase on the Coast & intending soon to set sail for the Island of Jamaica, he appointed Luke Collingwood the Surgeon of the Ship William to be Master or Commander of the Ship *Zong* or *Zorg*[.]

And having put on Board of her Seventeen White People the said Hanley gave directions to the said Luke Collingwood to barter the remaining Part of the Cargo of the same Ship for Slaves or other African produce & then to proceed after the Ship William to Jamaica[.]

And your Orators further shew unto your Honours that when the aforesaid Bills of Exchange were presented for acceptance to the said Owners William Gregson John Gregson James Gregson, George Case, Edward Wilson & James Aspinal six of the Defendants hereto at Liverpool they having been advised thereof & of the said Purchase of the Ship *Zong* or *Zorg* by the said Richard Hanley By Letter confirmed the aforesaid bargain made by the said Richd. Hanley by accepting and paying the same Bills & immediately or soon afterwards the same Defendants caused one or more Policy or Policies of Insurance to be made out in the name of the said William Gregson whereby they insured the said Ship *Zong* or *Zorg* [space left blank][262] Collingwood Master at & from the Coast of Africa & during her Trade & stay there & to her discharge Port or Ports in the British West Indies or conquered Islands upon any kind [119] of Goods or Merchandizes[.]

And also upon the Body Tackle Apparel Ordnance Munition Artillery Boat & other Furniture of the same insured Ship beginning the adventure upon the said Goods & Merchandizes from the loading thereof on board the same Ship & upon the same Ship until she with all her Ordnance Tackle Apparel &c. Goods & Merchandizes whatsoever should be arrived at [space left blank] upon the Ship &c. untill [sic] she had moored at Anchor twenty four hours in good safety & upon the Goods & Merchandizes until the same should be there discharged & safely landed[.]

And it is by the said Policy provided that it should be lawful for the same Ship & in that Voyage to proceed & sail to & touch & stay at any ports or places whatsoever without prejudice to that Insurance

---

[262] Ed. His first name was Luke.

the said Ship &c Goods & Merchandizes for so much as concerned the Assureds by Agreement between the Assureds & Assurers in that Policy were valued at the Sum of £2500, upon the whole of the Ship & on Goods as Interest should appear valuing Slaves at £30, Sterling per Head, Ivory £20. sterling per Hundred weight & Gold at £4. per ounce[.]

And the Adventures & perils which such Insurers were to bear on that Voyage were particularly expressed in the said Policy or Policies in the usual Form.

And your Orators further shew unto your Honors [sic] that they severally subscribed & underwrote one or more of the said Policies of Insurance for the several & respective Sums of Money therein mentioned that is to say your Orator Gilbert in the Sum of £200. your Orator Dawson in the Sum £100. your Orator Bolden in the Sum of £100. & your Orator Thompson in the Sum of £100. your Orator Parker in the Sum of £100. & your Orator Bent in the Sum of £100. All upon Goods, & your Orator Mason in the Sum of £100. Upon the Ship[.]

And your Orators severally confessed themselves paid the Consideration due unto them for the said Assurances at & after the rate of 20 Guineas per Cent. As by the said several Policies of Insurance now in the Custody or Power of the said Defendants some or one of them & whereunto your Orators for greater certainty crave leave to refer when the same shall be produced may & will more fully appear.

And your Orators further shew unto your Honors [sic] that [120] the said Luke Collingwood being appointed Master of the *Zong* or *Zorg* as aforesaid proceeded to barter the remainder of her Cargo of Goods for Slaves on the Coast of Africa & having purchased so many as with the Slaves on Board of her when she was bought by the said Richd. Hanley amounted to 440 Slaves he resolved to leave the Coast of Africa & accordingly on or about the 6th day of September 1781 he set sail from the Island of St Thomas with the said Ship & her cargo for the Island of Jamaica & on the 27th day of November following fell in with the Island but said Luke Collingwood instead of proceeding into some port there either through unskillfulness & Ignorance or with a sinister intent ran the Ship to Leeward of the same Island[.]

And afterwards on the 29th day of same Month of November & on two or three days following under pretence that there was not water in the Ship sufficient for the subsistence of the white People & Slaves untill [sic] the Ship would probably regain the Island of Jamaica, he cruelly ordered 133 Slaves to be thrown alive out of the Ship into the Sea including the 10 Slaves who jumped overboard as herein after mentioned.

And your Orators further shew unto your Honors [sic] that on the 22d day of December 1781 the said Ship *Zong* or *Zorg* arrived in perfect safety & with her Crew & the rest of the Slaves in good Health in the Island of Jamaica[.]

And that the said Defendants have since pretended that the said 133 Slaves which were thrown alive out of the said Ship *Zong* into the Sea & perished including the said 10 were at the rate of £30. per head & according to the stipulation & Agreement in the aforesaid Policies of Insurance of the value of £3990. & that the loss of the said Slaves was a general Average Loss which ought to be borne & paid by the Underwriters on the said Ship & Cargo[.]

And that the same loss amounts to the Sum of £50. per Cent upon the whole Money by them insured on the said Ship & Cargo And the said Defendants have demanded from your Orators payment of the said pretended Average loss in proportion to the several Sums of Money underwrote by [121] Your Orators respectively as aforesaid[.]

And your Orators further shew unto your Honors that[,] apprehending they were not either within the words or meaning of the aforesaid Policies of Insurance liable to pay for the loss of the said Slaves which were by the said unlawful & cruel act of the said Luke Collingwood & without absolute necessity destroyed[,] they refused to pay the said pretended loss & were in hopes that the Defendants would not have repeated their demand.

But now so it is may it please Your Honors that the said Defendants combining & confederating together to & with Colonel Jas. Kelsall of Liverpool aforesaid Mariner with divers other persons at present unknown to your Orators whose Names when discovered your Orators pray they may be at liberty to insert herein with proper and apt Charges against them as Defendants hereto & contriving how to injure you Orators in the Premises they the said Defendants the Owners have not only persisted in making the aforesaid Claim & Demand against your Orators but have lately commenced several Actions in his Majesty's Court of King's Bench against your Orators upon the said Policies underwritten by your Orators respectively as aforesaid to recover payment of the said pretended Loss of £50. per cent[.]

And in order to give some Colour to such proceedings the said Defendants give out & pretend that at the time & times when the said 133 Slaves were thrown overboard the said Ship *Zong* was by stress of wind and Weather & a Lee current driven to Leward of the said Island of Jamaica[.]

And that it was very uncertain at what time she would be able to regain the said Island,

And that there was then very little Water on board the same Ship nor was there any place near where could be supplied with Water & therefore the said Luke Collingwood thinking it more prudent to attempt to preserve the lives of the White People & part of the Slaves than that the whole should be in danger of perishing for want of Water[.]

And in order to lessen the consumption of water on Board ordered the aforesaid 133 Slaves [122] including as aforesaid to be thrown overboard into the Sea[.]

And that if he had not so done the whole Crew & all the Slaves must have perished unavoidably for want of Water & the Ship & Cargo [would] have been totally lost to the Owners thereof[.]

And in Consequence that the Underwriters must have paid to the Owners thereof such total loss Whereas your Orators expressly charge that although the said Ship *Zong* was of Considerable Burthen & capable of carrying 600 Slaves from the Coast of Africa to Jamaica with provisions & water for that number of Slaves[.]

And Although she had on the aforesaid Voyage from Africa to Jamaica only 440 Slaves & 17 White People on Board yet the said Luke Collingwood had on board the said Ship *Zong* when he left the Coast of Africa only an inconsiderable quantity of Water by no means sufficient for the number of People & Slaves on board during so long a Voyage as from the Coast of Africa to Jamaica nor equal to the quantity of water usually taken in like Cases in Ships of the same burthen & with the same number of People on board & bound upon the same Voyage[.]

And that the Puncheons Butts & Casks into which what Water the same Ship had was put were faulty & leaky[.]

And that all or most or great part of the water had drained through the heads or Sides of many of them before they were broached[.]

And your Orators further charge that the said Ship *Zong* was not in immediate want of Water as pretended by the Defendants at the time & times when the said Slaves were thrown overboard[,] that not more than ten days before the said Slaves she might have put into some of the British Windward or Leward Islands in the West Indies or some other place for a supply of Water which she never attempted to do.

And your Orators charge likewise that at the time when the said Slaves were thrown overboard there was not any present want of Water on board the said Ship *Zong*[.]

And that neither the Crew or white People or the Slaves or any of them had before that time been (as they ought) put to short allowance but had had the same daily allowance of Water which they had ever had on any day after [123] the said Ship *Zong* left the said Coast of Africa[.]

And that there were then on board the same Ship several Butts of Water sufficient for the subsistence of all the People in the same Ship during the space of one Week or several days at least. And if the said Luke Collingwood had been afraid the same Vessel would not have reached Jamaica in the space of a Week your Orators charge he might have put all the People to half or less Allowance which is commonly done at Sea when the Crew of a Ship apprehend they shall be in want of provisions In which Case the Water in the *Zong* would have served for the subsistence of all her people for more than a fortnight or some considerable time[.]

And that there was no such want of Water at the time of throwing the said Slaves overboard as created an absolute necessity for so inhuman an Act or will by any means justify the same[.]

And that the said Luke Collingwood might in a short space of time have run into some Island or Place with the same Ship where he could have got a supply of Water & might have got thither whilst his Water had the same been husbanded with the greatest AEconomy & the Crew been put to short allowance would have lasted or he might have met with some Ship at Sea or been supplied in a little time from the Elements with Water for which he ought to have waited instead of committing the aforesaid most inhuman Act, & your Orators charge as Facts which the Defendants the Owners have heard & have reason to believe[.]

And which the Defendant Kelsal knows to be true that the Slaves on Board the *Zong* or *Zorg* or many of them had been sickly on the Voyage & that between the time of her leaving the Coast of Africa & the 29th day of November 1781 Sixty Slaves & upwards & seven white People died[.]

And that a great number of the remaining Slaves on the day last mentioned were Sick of some disorder or disorders & likely to die or not live long[.]

And that the said Luke Collingwood being afraid that by the great Mortality on Board the Ship she would make but a bad Voyage for the Owners he on the Evening of the said 29th day of November called together a few of his Officers & told them that if the Slaves died a natural death it would be the loss of the Owners of the Ship but if they were thrown alive into the Sea it would be the loss of the Underwriters or the said [124] Luke Collingwood expressed himself to the foregoing or the like effect[.]

And in order to palliate his said inhuman proposal the said Luke Collingwood pretended that it would not be so cruel to throw the poor sick Wretches (meaning such Slaves) into the Sea as to suffer them to linger out a few days under the disorder with which they were afflicted or expressed himself to the like effect[.]

And your Orators further charge that the Defendant Kelsal being shocked with the horrid brutality of the said Luke Collingwood's said proposal (as well he might) objected thereto & said there was no present want of Water to justify such a measure[;]

But the said Luke Collingwood prevailed upon the Crew or the rest of them to listen to his said Proposal & the same Evening & two or three or some few following days the said Luke Collingwood picked or caused to be picked out from the Cargo of the same Ship 133 Slaves, all or most of whom were sick or weak & not likely to live & ordered the Crew by turns to throw them into the Sea which most inhuman Order was Cruelly complied with[.]

And your Orators charge that if there had been an absolute & immediate necessity that any Lives should be lost in order to preserve the rest (which your Orators charge was not the case) Lot ought to have been first cast that it might have been known on whom the Lot fell to become sacrificed[.]

And your Orators further charge that all and singular the Facts hereinbefore stated & hereinafter enquired of or a great part thereof would manifestly appear in & By the Log Book of the said Ship *Zong* wherein all the Transactions of the Voyage are entered which is now in the Custody or power of the said Defendants some or one of them & by sundry Journals Books Letters & Papers now or lately in their or some of their Custody or power if the same respectively have or hath not been by their or some of their Order altered obliterated defaced torn burnt or otherwise destroyed & which your Orators have repeatedly by themselves or their Attorney desired the Defendants or some of them to produce[.]

But which the Defendants have always refused to do & have always concealed & still do conceal the same Log Book Journals Books Letters & papers from your Orators sometimes pretending that the said Log Book & the said Journals Books Letters & Papers or some of them were or was lost in the hands of the Agent of the said Ship *Zong* at [125] Jamaica where they now remain & at other times pretending that the said Log Book & the said Journals Books Letters & Papers or some of them were or was in the hands or possession of the said Luke Collingwood at the time of his Death & that he died in the Island of Jamaica & that they were afterwards lost Whereas your Orators charge that the Log Book is a Book belonging to a Ship which is open to all the Crew for them to make & enter therein whatever transactions & Memorandums relative to the Ship or the Voyage they please[.]

And that the same Book is always kept in the Ship & is never carried out of the Ship either by the Captain or any of the Crew unless with some unfair & fraudulent design[.]

And although the Defendants the Owners well know that your Orators untill they can get a sight of the said Log Book Journal Books Letters & Papers will be unable to make any effectual defence at Law to the said Actions commenced against your Orators respectively and the rather because although the Defendant Kelsal kept a Journal untill on or about the 14th day of November 1781 of the proceedings of the same Voyage the said Luke Collingwood with a view of concealing the several Facts which should happen & happened afterwards thereupon then or about that time ordered the same Defendant to desist from any longer keeping the same which he desisted from accordingly[.]

And your Orators charge that sundry Conversations on Board the same Ship passed between the said Luke Collingwood & the Officers & Crew of the same Ship or some of them whereby it will appear as the fact was that the said Slaves were thrown overboard with intent to turn the loss upon the Insurers & to ease the Owners of the risque of the Slaves thrown overboard dying a natural death or with some other fraudulent View in the said Luke Collingwood[.]

And although the said Actions have been only commenced just before the beginning of the present Hilary Term yet the said Defendants the Owners threaten to proceed to Trial in the same several Actions at the Sittings after this present term[.]

All which Actings pretences & concealments [126] of the said Defendants their Confederates are contrary to Equity & good Conscience & tend to the manifest wrong & oppression of your Orators whereby they are the less able to answer his Majesty's demands at the receipt of this Hon[oura]ble Court.[263] In tender Consideration whereof & for as much as your Orators are undefensible [sic] remediless in the prem[is]es without the assistance of a Court of Equity[264] where matters of discovery are properly cognisable & relievable[.][265]

---

[263] Ed. This refers again to the plea of *quo minus* mentioned above.
[264] Ed. The bill is addressed to the equity side of the Court of Exchequer.
[265] Ed. Although it might be necessary for a plaintiff in a common law action to obtain discovery of facts within the knowledge of the defendant or in documents in his or her possession, the common law courts had no power to order such a discovery. Courts of equity, however, asssumed jurisdiction to compel discovery under oath. P V Baker and P St J Langan, *Snell's Equity*, 29th edn, London, 1990, p 28.

To the End therefore that the said Wm. Gregson John Gregson Jas. Gregson Geo. Case Edwd. Wilson & Jas. Aspinal & also the said Colonel Jas. Kelsall & their Confederates when discovered may upon their several & respective Oaths & according to the best & utmost of their several & respective knowledge remembrance information hearsay & belief full true direct & perfect answer make to all & singular the several matters & things hereinbefore mentioned & set forth & that as fully & particularly as if the same were repeated & they thereunto severally & distinctly interrogated[.]

And more especially that the said Defendants Wm. Gregson Jno. Gregson Jas. Gregson Geo. Case Edwd. Wilson & Jas. Aspinal may accordingly as aforesaid answer & set forth whether they did not[266] & at what time fit or cause to be fitted out the said Ship William under the Command of the said Richard Hanley since deceased on the Voyage hereinbefore for that purpose mentioned[.]

And whether the said Richard Hanley or who else did not purchase the said Ship *Zong* with the Cargo there on board of her from such person at such time & in such manner & upon such terms & on such Account as hereinbefore stated or on what other & what number of Slaves & value in other Goods the said Ship *Zong* had on board was she was [sic] so purchased[.]

And whether the said Richard Hanley did not give the Command of the said Ship *Zong* to the said Luke Collingwood & in what station the said Luke Collingwood was before that time[.]

And whether he was well qualified for the command of an African Ship[.]

And whether & about what time they the said Defendants did not cause such Policy or Policies of Insurance as hereinbefore mentioned or any other, & what Policy or Policies to be made out upon the said Ship *Zong* & her Cargo & upon such Terms purport or effect as are herein before mentioned or what other[.]

---

[266] Ed. This part of the bill is phrased in the negative, challenging the defendants to deny the allegations of the plaintiffs and produce evidence against them.

And whether your Orators did not respectively underwrite such Policy or Policies or some of them & for what [127] Sums & when respectively[.]

And whether such Policy or Policies were not made in the names of the said Defendants the Owners or some or one & which of them for the use & benefit of all of them[.]

And that all the Defendants before named & particularly the said Colonel James Kelsal [sic] may answer & set forth according to the best of their respective knowledge remembrance Information hearsay & belief whether the said Ship *Zong* did not at or about the time hereinbefore for that purpose mentioned or what other time set sail from the Coast of Africa & what part of the same Coast for Jamaica and how many white People & also how many Slaves she had then on board & what quantity of water she had then on board & in what & in how many Puncheons Butts Casks or Vessels distinguishing the different number of each species the same Water was contained.

And how many Gallons of water such Puncheons Butts Casks or Vessels respectively contained.

And whether the same were tight in good order & Condition Or whether the same or some & how many at most of each & which sort were not faulty[.]

And whether the Water or great or some & what part thereof did not in the course of the Voyage leak out many or some & how many at most of such Puncheons Butts Casks or other Vessels before the Crew & Slaves on board the *Zong* had occasion to use such Water[.]

And whether or not the quantity of Water on Board the said Ship *Zong* when she left the Coast of Africa was altogether sufficient for & as much as is usually on the like Cases & under similar Circumstances put on board a Vessel of the same size & burthen as the *Zong* & carrying the same number of white & black People as she had on board as she had on board on a Voyage from the same part of the Coast of Africa from Jamaica[.]

And how many of the Slaves on board the said Ship *Zong* died on the said Voyage before the 29th day of November 1781 & of what disorder or disorders & also how many of the white People died before the time last mentioned & likewise how many of the white People are now alive & what are their Names & where do they respectively reside when at their proper & respective houses & where are they now to be met with or heard of respectively & may according [*128*] as aforesaid set forth at what time the said Luke Collingwood or the said Colonel James Kelsall or any other person or who on board the said Ship *Zong* first discovered that the Water on board the same Ship grew low or was nearly exhausted & in what Latitude & Longitude the same Ship then was, & from what Quarters and parts of the Compass the Wind at that time & for two or three Days next afterwards Blew & whether the said Luke Collingwood had not when the want or scarcity of Water was first discovered on Board the *Zorg* or soon & how soon afterwards a fair or some & what opportunity of getting into one of the British Windward or Leeward Islands in the West Indies or into some other & what Island or place in some & what Quarter or part of the World where the Crew might have got a sufficient or some supply of Water for themselves & the Slaves on Board the *Zong*[.]

And whether there was not some & what probability & if the said Defendant shall pretend not a probability whether there was not some & what Expectation or however possibility that the said Collingwood might have got with the same Ship into one of the said Islands or other and what place where he might have been supplied with Water & why & for what reasons the said Luke Collingwood did not attempt to go with the said Ship *Zong* into some Island or Place for a supply of water if the same was wanted and that the said Defendants may accordingly as aforesaid set forth what number of Slaves were on board the same Ship on the Morning of the 29th day of November 1781 & in what state & condition respectively were they strong & healthy or were they & how many of them sick infirm weak or emaciated and under what particular disease or diseases did they respectively labour or were they afflicted[.]

And whether there was then any & what infectious disorder on board the same Ship and whether all the Slaves or how many & which of them on board the Ship had not on the Morning of the aforesaid 29th day of November or when last their usual & full allowance of Water or what other allowance[.]

And when was it first discovered & by whom that the said Ship *Zong* had got to Leeward of the Island of Jamaica and how whether from Ignorance or Design or how [129] otherwise it happened that the same Ship got to Leeward of the same Island & whether on the Evening of the said 29th day of November 1781 or when also the said Luke Collingwood did not call together into the Cabin or some other & what part of the said Ship *Zong* some and which of the Officers or people belonging to the same Ship & who by names & names & tell them or some & or some & which of them that the Ship was got to Leeward of the Island of Jamaica & that they might possible be or should be short of Water before they could regain the same Island in which [case] they must put the Slaves to Short Allowance & that the Slaves would be weak and emaciated when they came to Market & sell for little or nothing & that the Voyage would be ruined or express himself to the foregoing or such like or what other Effect[.]

And whether the said Luke Collingwood did not after the above or some such like or what other discourse propose to the persons then called together or some & which of them that they should be thrown into the Sea or Overboard such part of the Slaves on board the said Ship *Zong* as were sickly weak & of little Value or express himself to the foregoing or the like or what other Effect[.]

And whether the said Luke Collingwood or some other person & who by name then present did not say it (meaning the throwing of such Slaves overboard) would be no loss to the Owners for the Underwriters must pay for the Slaves thrown overboard or to that effect[.]

And whether the aforesaid Conversation or Words or some other to the like purport or effect & what other Conversation did not pass at the time the said Luke Collingwood called together such Officers or People as aforesaid or at any other & what time or times[.]

And that the said Colonel Jas. Kelsal [sic] may deliberate upon & use his utmost endeavours to recollect & then according to the best of his knowledge recollection & belief set forth the whole Conversation & Conversations & the Substance & Tenor thereof respectively which passed on or was or were spoken by the persons present respectively when the said Luke Collingwood called all or some of the Officers & People of [130] the said Ship *Zong* together as aforesaid And whether the said Colonel Jas. Kelsall or who else being shocked by the Inhumanity of the said Luke Collingwood's proposal or for what other reason did not at first object thereto & say then was no occasion for such a measure as throwing any Slaves overboard[.]

And that it would be better to put the Slaves to short Allowance for some time& they might possibly soon or in a few days meet with some Ship or that a shower of rain might supply them with Water enough[,]

Or whether the said Colonel Jas. Kelsall or some other person & who did not remonstrate against the said Luke Collingwood's proposal in some such humane Terms & Language or in Terms and Language to the like or something like the foregoing purport & effect & in what other Terms & Language or to what other purport or effect did he they or any & which of them expostulate with the said Luke Collingwood on that Occasion[.]

And whether immediately or how soon after the said Conversations or what other passed & when particularly 50 or what number of slaves were thrown alive out of the Cabin Window or Windows or from the Deck of the said Ship *Zong* or part through the Cabin Window or Windows & part from the Deck or what other part of the same Ship into the Sea & drowned & whether on the 1st day of December 1781 or when else 42 or how many more Slaves were not thrown alive from the Deck or what other part of the same Ship into the Sea & drowned[.]

And whether soon or how soon afterwards 21 or what other number of Slaves more were not thrown alive from the Deck or what other part of the same Ship into the Sea & drowned & whether all the said Slaves were not thrown overboard by or by the Order of the said Luke Collingwood or who or who else respectively[.]

And whether 10 or what number of Slaves more perceiving the white People were going to throw them overboard did not leap from the same Ship into the Sea & were drowned[.]

And whether all the said Slaves so drowned did not amount to 133 or what other outside number in the whole,

And whether before the said Slaves were so thrown overboard & drowned had the Crew & Slaves of the same Ship been put to any & what short allowance [131] of Water & when first & for what space of time & if not why not[.]

And whether all the said Slaves so thrown in the Sea or the greatest part or some & how many of them at most were not picked out of the whole Cargo as the sickliest weakest or worst part of the Slaves.

And whether a great many & how many of the said Slaves at most that were drowned did not at that time labour under and were afflicted with some contagious or other & what disorder or disorders & would not probably have died a natural death in a few days['] time or some short space of time if they had not been drowned[.]

And whether a great number & how many of the said Slaves so thrown overboard at most were not Women & Children & Infants which would have been of no great Value & of what comparative value individually in proportion to a Prime Man Slave if they had arrived at Market in Jamaica[.]

And whether the said Slaves so thrown overboard or some & how many of them did not understand so much of the English or some other Language understood by the Crew or some of them as to express their such respective Slaves meaning & wants in some degree[.]

And whether the same Slaves or at least such part of them as were Men & able to make resistance or some & how many of them were not & for what reason handcuffed & in Irons when they were so thrown overboard[.]

And whether the same Slaves or many or some & how many of them at most did not pray or earnestly request & with tears in their Eyes or how otherwise or some sign or gesture signs or gestures express or signify a desire that he or she might not be thrown overboard or did not they or some & how many of them in some & what manner & in some and what Language or by some or what Gestures or Signs gesture or Sign respectively express or signify some desire that they he or she might be permitted to live[.]

And whether such Desires & the said Luke Collingwood's Conduct or any & which of them had any & what effect on the said Defendant Mr. Kelsall & the other Officers & Crew or any & which of them & produce any and what Remonstrances Expostulations & Expressions from them respectively & whether one Man Slave who was thrown into the

Sea as aforesaid did not unobserved by any of the Crew catch hold of a Rope belonging [132] to the said Ship *Zong* which hung overboard & by means thereof get into the main or Fore Chains or on some other Chains or part of the outside of the Ship & lay there during the Night he being afraid least if he be discovered the Crew of the *Zong* some or one of them would throw him again into the Sea & drown him[.]

And whether the said Man Slave did not continue & lay close in such place or part untill he was accidentally discovered by some one of the Crew who took him on Board & after making Inquiry & being informed how he had saved himself they did not with a degree of Humanity preserve his life or by what other means was the Life of the said Man Slave preserved[.]

And whether the said Luke Collingwood or any of the Crew of the *Zong* would have adopted such an unparalleled & barbarous Step as throwing 133 Slaves or such number of Slaves as were thrown from the same Ship alive into the Sea if the same Slaves had not been by some disease or diseases weak sickly & of little Value[.]

And whether the said Luke Collingwood did not make a wanton & wicked sacrifice of the Lives of the said Slaves so thrown into the Sea to the Interest of the Owners of the said Ship *Zong* & with the intent & from the motive that the same Owners might put into their pockets thirty Pounds Sterling per Head for every Slave as thrown overboard or with what other intent or from what other motive[.]

And whether the said Slaves so thrown overboard if they had been at a Market for sale in the Island of Jamaica on the same day or day[']s time or times & in the same Condition as to Bodily health & strength & labouring under the same disorders as they were respectively in or laboured under at the several times when they were so thrown in to the Sea & drowned would have been sold at or would have fetched or been worth thirty Pounds Sterling a head to any purchaser or for what other Sum or Sums of Money sterling would they severally or upon an Average one with Another have been sold or been worth[.]

And whether on the said Evening of the 29th day of October 1781 there were on board the said Ship *Zong* several & how [133] many Puncheons Butts Casks or other Vessels full for containing Water & how many Gallons of Water did they contain in all at most[.]

And what Quantity of Water had been usually & upon an average in the Course of the Voyage expended in the regular course of 24 Hours amongst the Crew & Slaves after they first set Sail form the Coast of Africa & when they had on board 440 Slaves 17 white People & before many of them died.

And what quantity of Water had been usually & upon an Average expended in the same Ship in the regular course of the 24 Hours amongst the Crew & Slaves for the space of a Week next preceding the 29th day of November 1781 & how long the water on board the same Ship on the same 29th day of November 1781 would have served for the subsistence of the white People & Slaves then on board of her at the usual rate & allowance if none of it had been wasted or misapplied[.]

And whether it is not very common at Sea when provisions or water become scarce for the People to be put to short Allowance[.]

And if the white People & Slaves on Board of the Ship *Zong* had been put to short Allowance immediately after the discovery was made that the same Vessel was short of Water how many Weeks or days at most might they or any & what number & sort of them probably or possibly & in the course of nature have lived on the water & provisions on Board said Ship if made the most for their Support & why were they mot immediately after such discovery made put to short Allowance[.]

And whether after the Slaves were thrown into the Sea as aforesaid & what time or times & during what time the Crew of the said Ship *Zong* & the surviving Slaves on Board of her or any & which of them were reduced in or had less & how much less than their usual daily Allowance of Water[.]

And if they were so reduced in their Allowance what was the their former daily Allowance & how much & in what proportion was the same produced[.]

And how many Leagues the said Ship *Zong* was distant from the Island of Jamaica at the time when the said Ship Slaves were thrown overboard & how far distant & how many days or hours['] sails was the said Ship [134] from the nearest place & the place which she could have soonest reached & obtained a supply of water from as the Wind then was respectively & why did not the said Luke Collingwood proceed for a Supply of Water to the next place the said Ship could have got to considering the Circumstances of Winds & Weather[,]

And whether soon and how soon & how long & on what particular day or night days or nights after the said Slaves were thrown overboard as aforesaid a great quantity or some & what quantity of Rain did not fall upon the said Ship *Zong*[.]

And whether the Crew & Slaves or some of them did not & at what time & times & when first after throwing the said Slaves overboard catch a large or some quantity & how many Gallons of rain Water at most for the use of the same Ship[.]

And whether on divers days and nights or at divers times and on what particular days & nights between the 29th day of November 1781 and the day on which the said Ship *Zong* arrived at the Island of Jamaica sundry showers or Quantities of Rain did not fall upon the said Ship[.]

And whether the Crew thereof did not catch & save how much in quantity of rain Water sufficient for the sustenance of all the people on Board untill the same Ship arrived at Jamaica[.]

And whether they might not have saved more Rain Water if they had attempted so to do.

And whether upon the Arrival of the said Ship *Zong* at Jamaica there was not on board of her several & how many Puncheons Butts or Casks full of Water or with Water & what quantity of Water in them & whether if the said Luke Collingwood could not have got into any Island or place with the same Ship where he could have obtained a Supply of Water he ought not to have waited & trusted to Providence for obtaining by means of meeting with some Ship at Sea or receiving from the Element a Supply of water instead of making such sacrifice as he did of many lives by throwing the said Slaves into the Sea & drowning them & if not why not.

And whether the same Ship did not arrive at Jamaica on the 22nd day of December 1781,

And whether her passage was [135] longer & how much longer than is usual.

And whether they the said Defendants have not known Vessels as long or longer upon the Passage from the Coast of Africa to Jamaica[.]

And how many Slaves (exclusive of the Slaves so put to Death as aforesaid) had died on board the said Ship *Zong* between the 29th day of November 1781 & the said 22nd day of December following being twenty four days reckoning both these days inclusive & how many Slaves died in the like space of time previous to & next before the said 29th day of November 1781 on board the same Ship[.]

And whether all or how many of the surviving Slaves on board the same Ship did not arrive at Jamaica in good health or how otherwise & how the same happened[.]

And whether it did & doth not & will appear in & by the said Log Book of the Ship *Zong* or some other & what Book or Books Paper or Papers Letter or Letters & in whose Custody or Power what quantity of Water the said Ship *Zong* had on board when she left the Coast of Africa & what quantity of Water was daily expended on board the said Ship & how many Slaves died before the 29th day of November 1781 & in what Condition health & State the remainder were & of what Age & in what health or State & Condition the Slaves severally & respectively were who were thrown overboard & quantity of Water was on board the said Ship *Zong* at that time[.]

And whether there is not in the said Log Book & whether not also in some & what Journal or Journals Book or Books Paper or Papers in the said Defendants or some of their or whose Custody or Power a Memorandum or Memorandums of the resolution of the said Luke Collingwood & his Crew to throw part of the Slaves overboard & of their reasons or some reason for so doing.

And whether there are not also in the same Log Book Journal or Journals Book or Books Paper or Papers or any & which of them a Memorandum or Memorandums of the Showers of rain which fell on the said Ship *Zong* between the said 29th day of November 1781 & the 22nd day of December following & of sundry other articles matters & things relative to the said Ship *Zong* & her cargo necessary or proper for your Orators to know before they can proceed effectually to defend [136] the said Actions commenced against them as aforesaid[.]

And whether a Log Book is not a Book belonging to a Ship which the Captain of her has not business further than another Seaman & than taking care it is kept on safety on Board the Ship[.]

And whether your Orators or some or one & which of them have not by themselves or their Attorney or who else by name applied to the Defendants some or one & which of them & demanded or requested the said Log Book or a sight or Inspection thereof.

And whether said Defendants or such of them as were applied to did not refuse to comply with such demand or request & why they or he so did refuse & whether the said Log Book is not now or when last was in the Custody Possession or Power of the Defendants some or one & which of them & if not in whose Custody Possession or Power is the same or was it when the defendants respectively last saw the same or heard thereof[.]

And whether the same Log Book and some or one & which of the said Journals Books Letters & Papers & Writings which are or were in the Custody or Power of the said Defendants have or some and what part or parts thereof or any & which of them have or has not been by or by the Order or with the Knowledge consent or privity of the said Defendants or the said Luke Collingwood some and one or which of them & at what time & in what manner altered obliterated defaced torn burnt or otherwise destroyed or left or kept in the Island of Jamaica or some other Place or Places and for what reasons[.]

And that the said Defendants may lodge the same Log Book & also the said Journals Books Letters & Papers & all other Letters & papers respecting the aforesaid Slaves or any of them in their or any of their Custody or Power in the Hands of their Cl[er]k in Court in this Cause for the Inspection of your Orators or their Agents with the usual liberties & to be otherwise produced as this Hon[oura]ble shall direct[.]

And that the said Defendants may according as aforesaid set forth whether the said Defendants some or one & which of them have or has not now or lately had some Letters or Letter from some & what persons or person in the said Island of Jamaica or elsewhere from [137] which it would or doth appear that the said Slaves thrown out of the said Ship *Zong* into the Sea were not so thrown for want of Water but with a fraudulent design to make your Orators chargeable with the loss thereof or with some other bad design and that the said Confederate Kelsall may according as aforesaid set forth whether being Mate of the said Ship *Zong* he did not keep a Journal of all the same Ship's proceedings from the time she left the Coast of Africa until the 14th day of November 1781 or down to what other time at latest[.]

And whether the said Luke Collingwood did not at the time last mentioned or when else forbid him the same Defendant to keep a Journal any longer & why & for what reason & with what intent he so forbid him[.]

And whether he the said Defendant did not accordingly & when first desist from keeping a Journal[.]

And that all the said Defendants may set forth whether they do not in their respective Consciences deem the throwing the said Slaves alive into the Sea to have been an unnecessary & inhuman Act & unparalleled in Cruelty in the person or persons who committed the same & if not why not[.]

And whether the said Defendants in their Consciences believe the same was contrived by the said Luke Collingwood for any & what other purposes than defrauding the Insurers & that the same Defendants the Owners might make a good Voyage out of the said Ship *Zong* at the Expense of the Insurers or for one & which of those purposes.

And whether the said Defendants do not in their Consciences condemn the said Luke Collingwood for his aforesaid Conduct & in what respect & for what reasons they so condemn him & if not how do they justify him[.]

And whether if there had been a real necessity for destroying part of the lives on Board the same Ship for the pretended cause aforesaid (the contrary of which your Orators charge to be true) lot ought not to have been cast in some & what manner before the said Slaves were thrown overboard & if not why not & that the said Defendants may make a full discovery of & in all & singular [138] the premises & that in the mean time and untill further Orders of this Hon[oura]ble Court the same Defendants may be restrained from all further proceedings at Law against your Orators or any of them.

May it Please your Honours to grant unto your Orators not only his Majesty's most gracious Writ of Injunction[267] issuing out of & under the Seal of this Honorable [sic] Court to restrain the said William Gregson John Gregson James Gregson George Case Edward Wilson & James Aspinal from proceeding at Law against your Orators touching any of the matters in Question but also his Majesty's most Gracious Writ of Writs of Sub poena to be directed to the said William Gregson John Gregson James Gregson George Case Edward Wilson James Aspinal & Colonel James Kelsall & their Confederates when discovered thereby commanding them & every of them at a certain day & under certain penalty therein to be limited personally to be & appear before you Honours in this Honourable Court then & there to answer the premises & thereupon to Order according to Equity.

---

[267] Ed. The Orators (plaintiffs) seek a common injunction in equity to restrain the defendants from proceeding at law to make a claim against the Insurers. The present bill is undated but it would seem likely that it was drafted after the verdict in the King's Bench (6 March 1783, according to Sharp's account, above, page 293) in order to prevent the defendants enforcing the verdict, but the King's Bench itself then heard the motion for a new trial, as above.

James Kelsall's Answer

The National Archives E 112/1528/173

Fyled Novr. 12th 1783

The Answer of Colonel James Kelsall[268] Mariner one of the Defendants[269] to the Bill of Complaint of Thomas Gilbert John Dawson William Bolden John Thompson John Parker Edward Mason and Ellis Bent Complainants[270]

The said Defendant saving and reserving to himself now and at all Times hereafter all and all Manner of Benefit and Advantage of Exception to the manifold Untruths Incertainties and other Imperfections in the Complainants['] said Bill of Complaint contained for Answer thereunto or into [2] so much thereof as materially concerns this Defendant as he is advised to make Answer unto he answereth and saith

That he admits it to be true that the other Defendants William Gregson John Gregson James Gregson George Case Edward Wilson and James Aspinall in or about the Month of October in the Year [3] of our Lord one thousand seven hundred and eighty fitted out a Ship or Vessel called the *William* under the Command of Richard Hanley since deceased on a Voyage from Liverpool for the Coast of Africa and the British West India Islands and admits that the said Richard Hanley during the Time he was trading for Slaves [4] on the said Coast fell in with a Ship belonging to Bristol which had captured and made Prize of a Dutch Vessel called the *Zong* or *Zorg*[271] with such Cargo on board

---

[268] Ed. Chief Mate of the slave ship *Zong*.

[269] Ed. Kelsall was not in fact a defendant to the action, but a deponent. He swore this deposition as a witness to the events. It seems his solicitor, who drew up this answer, did not use the correct term.

[270] Ed. The original deposition is written on two large parchment sheets so that each line of text is about a yard long. In this transcription the lines have therefore been numbered in the form "[2]" etc., for ease of reference to the original.

[271] Ed. The prize hearing in the High Court of Admiralty says that *"De Zorg"* was captured by the *Sally and Rachell*, a "letter of marque or private ship of war belonging to London commanded by Captain James Hayes". TNA HCA 32/491/9.

as in the Bill mentioned and that the said Richard Hanley agreed to purchase from the Commander of the said Bristol Ship the said Dutch Vessel called the *Zong* or *Zorg* with [5] her whole Cargo then on board her at such Time and in such Manner and upon such Terms and on such Account as in the Bill mentioned[.]

And this Defendant saith he believes that the said Richard Hanley who made such Purchase for the Owners of the said Ship *William* drew a Bill or Bills of Exchange for the Purchase Money [6] of the said Ship and Cargo upon the said other Defendants the Owners of the said Ship *William* in Favor [sic] of the Master of the said Bristol Ship who on Receipt of the same Bill or Bills of Exchange delivered up and transferred the said Ship *Zong* or *Zorg* and her Cargo to the said Richard Hanley for the Use of the said other Defendants[.]

And [7] this Defendant further answering says that at the Time the said Purchase was made the said Ship *Zong* or *Zorg* had on board Two hundred and forty four Slaves but as to the particular or other Value of the rest of the Cargo and Goods on board her this Defendant cannot either from his own Knowledge or otherwise set forth as [8] this Defendant was to Leeward of Anamaboe[272] at a Factory[273] purchasing Slaves when the Cargo of the said Ship *Zong* or *Zorg* was opened[;] further than this Defendant believes that it was of the Value mentioned in the Complainants['] said Bill[.]

And this Defendant admits that the said Richard Hanley having then almost completed his [9] Purchase on the Coast and intending soon to sail for the Island of Jamaica appointed Luke Collingwood now deceased who was previous thereto Surgeon of the said Ship *William* to be Master or Commander of the said Ship *Zong* or *Zorg* and having put on board her seventeen white People gave such Directions as in the said Bill [10] mentioned and that the said Luke Collingwood was well qualified for the Command of an African Ship[.]

And this Defendant further saith that he hath heard and believes that the Owners of the said Ship *William* or the said Defendants William Gregson and James Aspinall for the Benefit of themselves and all the rest of [11] the Owners caused Policies of Insurance to be made out

---

[272] Ed. Anomabu (also known as Anomabo and formerly as Annamaboe), is a town on the coast of modern-day Ghana, 72 miles west of Accra.

[273] Ed. Johnson's Dictionary: "A house or district inhabited by traders in a distant country." Buildings or a fort in which enslaved Africans were held prior to being forced on board slave ships.

upon the said Ship *Zorg*[274] [*sic*] and her Cargo but to what Amount or upon what Terms or to what Purport or Effect this Defendant cannot set forth never having seen any of the Policies of Insurance made thereon so that this Defendant doth not know whether the Complainants [12] or any of them or who also underwrote such Policies or any of them or for what Sum or when they were underwritten or any Thing else relating thereto further than that this Defendant believes the Adventures and Perils which the Assurers were to bear on that Voyage were particularly expressed in the Policy or Policies of such Assurance [13] in the usual Form[.]

And this Defendant saith that the said Luke Collingwood being appointed Master of the *Zong* or *Zorg* as aforesaid proceeded to barter the Remainder of her Cargo of Goods for Slaves on the Coast of Africa and having purchased so many as with the Slaves on board of her when she was bought by the said Richard [14] Hanley amounted to Four hundred and forty two Slaves he set sail in the said Ship *Zong* or *Zorg* on the eighteenth day of August one thousand seven hundred and eighty one from Acra[275] on the Coast of Africa and not from the Island of Saint Thomas for Jamaica with Seventeen white People and the said Four Hundred [15] and forty two Slaves then on board and one hundred and thirty Dutch Butts of Water containing about One Hundred and twenty Gallons each and Twenty Gang Casks or Barrels containing Twenty Five or Thirty Gallons each and that they touched at the Island of Saint Thomas about the twenty fourth or [16] twenty fifth of the same Month and there took in fifteen or sixteen Dutch Butts of Water to replenish those that had been consumed since their Departure from Acra but cannot tell whether the Casks of Water taken in on the Coast were tight or in good Order and Condition or not or if any [or] how many and which sort of [17] them were faulty this Defendant as before mentioned being at a Factory when they were stowed[;]

Saith that on a Survey in the Course of the Voyage two days after they made the Island of Tobago they discovered that about twenty of the aforesaid Butts of Water had nearly leaked out which this Defendant attributes to the bad [18] Management of the Black Coopers who trimmed the Casks as the Cooper belonging to the *Zong* was Sick and unable to work at the Time they were prepared for the Water but on

---

[274] Ed. Careful comparison of the way the writer of the document forms the letter "n" and "r" leads to the conclusion that while the defendant in referring to the ship has earlier used the expression "Zong or Zorg" at this point and later in the document he uses the Dutch name "Zorg" alone, for no apparent reason.

[275] Ed. ie Accra.

such Survey the rest were found tight and in good Order and Condition[.] This Defendant cannot set forth whether any of the said Casks might have leaked [19] before the said Survey as they did not perceive the Leakage before they had finished the second Tier which was soon after their taking their Departure from Tobago as aforesaid[.]

And this Defendant saith that the Quantity of Water on board the said Ship *Zong* when she left the Coast of Africa was altogether sufficient for [20] and more than is usually in like Cases and under similar Circumstances put on board a Vessel of the same Size and Burthen as the *Zong* and carrying the same Number of black and white People as she had on board on a Voyage from the same Part of the Coast of Africa for Jamaica[.]

Saith that Sixty two Slaves died on [21] the same Voyage before the twenty ninth day of November one thousand seven hundred and eighty one but of what Disorder does not know or believe nor can form a Judgment thereof[.]

Says also That six of the white People died before the Time last mentioned of the seventeen white People before mentioned and three more [22] of them were pressed in Jamaica into the King's Service[,] two Dutchmen went from Jamaica to Holland[,] the second Mate was drowned by falling into the Sea from the Black River Jamaica and the Captain died at Kingston in Jamaica to the best [23] of this Defendant[']s Remembrance and Belief this Defendant does not remember the Name of those Six white people that died on the Passage[;] That the Names of those three that were pressed were John Brown Michael Sullivan and George Aston but where they respectively reside when at their proper and respective Houses [24] or where they are now to be met with or heard of cannot tell having never seen or heard of them since they were so pressed[.] Saith that he doth not know the Names of either of the said two Dutchmen or where their fixed Residence is or where they now are having never seen or heard of them since they left the said Ship at [25] Jamaica[;] That the second Mate[']s Name was Joseph Wood but neither knows nor hath heard the Name of one of the three who died in the black River aforesaid but the Names of two of them were Michael Hamon and John Barnes and that the said Captain[']s Name Luke Collingwood[.]

Saith that on or about the [26] twentieth or twenty first of November one thousand seven hundred and eighty one the second and third Mates whose Business it is to take Care of the Water and provisions in the Hold perceived that a large Quantity of the Water had leaked from the lower Tier of Water Casks which caused a General Survey to be made of what [27] was remaining when they found near twenty Butts of Water remaining which was thought a sufficient Quantity to last the Voyage to Jamaica the said *Zong* or *Zorg* being then in twelve or thirteen Degrees North Latitude and about Sixty three or Sixty four Degrees West Longitude to the best of this Defendant[']s Judgment [28] the Wind at that Time and for three Days afterwards blowing at East and East South East which are the usual Trade Winds in that part of the World[.]

Saith that on the fourteenth Day of the said Month of November some Differences arising between the said Luke Collingwood the Captain and this Defendant concerning the [29] said Collingwood having appointed one Stubbs a passenger to take Charge of the said Ship *Zong* or *Zorg*[,] he the said Collingwood suspended this Defendant from his Station of Chief Mate from which he remained suspended 'till the twenty ninth of November aforesaid the Day they perceived themselves to the Leeward of Jamaica [30] when he restored this Defendant to his former Station of Chief Mate and he accordingly then took Charge of the Vessel again in that Capacity[.]

Saith that the said Luke Collingwood did not either through Unskilfulness Ignorance or with any sinister Intent run the said Ship to Leeward of the said Island of Jamaica but being [31] deceived in his Reckoning by the strong Currents which drove the said Vessel with great Rapidity he mistook the Island of Jamaica for Hispaniola and by that Means got to Leeward of Jamaica[,] that perceiving himself out of his Course on the said twenty ninth of November and in a distressful Situation with Respect [32] to the small Stock of water on board her he the said Captain called all hands together to consult what was best to be done when it was the general Opinion that it was impracticable for the said Ship to reach any British Island whatever with the Water which was then remaining on board without being compelled by [33] Necessity to the melancholy Alternative either of reducing the Number of Lives then on board or of attempting to gain the Island of Cuba a Spanish Island which there was a probability of being able to gain though [also] not of gaining any other Island whilst the said Ship[']s Water would last to keep her Slaves and Crew alive [34] but the Captain thought himself not warranted to make that Island as it was an Enemy Port by gaining which he would have lost both Ship and Cargo[.]

This Defendant saith that on the Morning of the twenty ninth of November one thousand seven hundred and eighty one there were Three Hundred and eighty [35] Slaves alive on board the said Ship

Zorg [sic] all of them in Good Health and Condition[,] none of them being sick or weakly infirm or emaciated to this Defendant[']s Knowledge or Belief[;] That there was no infectious or other Disorder on board the said Ship at that Time save that the Crew were much afflicted with the Scurvy[.][276]

[36] Saith that all the Slaves on board the same Ship had on the Morning of the said twenty ninth of November one thousand seven hundred and eighty one their usual and full Allowance of Water and that it was not 'till the Evening of that day a little after Sun set [that it was] discovered by Captain Collingwood [37] that the *Zorg* [sic] had got to Leeward of the Island of Jamaica when they were not able to see Land from the Foretopmast Head[.]

Saith that having made Land the twenty seventh of the said Month of November which the Captain taking for Hispaniola but which was actually Jamaica distant from it South nine [38] Leagues they steered their Course as for Jamaica which was as this Defendant believes the Occasion of the *Zorg* [sic] getting to Leeward of the said Island of Jamaica but this Defendant cannot attribute that Mistake either to Unskilfulness Ignorance or any sinister Intent as many regular bred Seamen Captains in [39] the African Trade from Liverpool have imperceptibly got to Leeward of that Island by Mistake as this Defendant has heard and believes and therefore this Defendant attributes that Event to the said Captain having mistaken Jamaica for Hispaniola by the means aforesaid[.]

This Defendant saith that when Captain [40] Collingwood discovered that Mistake he was distant from Jamaica about Three hundred and thirty Miles but upon that Discovery he immediately altered his Course for Jamaica but in the Evening of the said twenty ninth day of November one thousand seven hundred and eighty one the said Luke Collingwood called together [41] upon the Quarter Deck of the said Ship *Zorg* [sic] all the People or Crew belonging to the same Ship whose Names are before mentioned as far as is in the Defendants Knowledge and Remembrance and acquainted them that the said Ship was to Leeward of the Island of Jamaica and that they should be short of Water [42] before they could regain the same Island and desired to have their Counsel and Advice how to act in that Situation considering the small Stock of Water they had left and upon and with such Counsel and Advice it was then determined by the General Voice of the Crew that part of the Slaves should be destroyed to [43] save the rest and the

---

[276] Ed. The word "scurvy" is inserted between the lines at the beginning of line 35.

Remainder of the Slaves and the Crew put to short Allowance to save them from perishing but this Defendant did not to his Recollection or Belief hear the said Captain Collingwood or any Person on board the said Ship at that Consultation say that by short Allowance the Slaves would be [44] weak or emaciated when they came to Market and sell for little or nothing or that the Voyage would be ruined or express himself or themselves to any such or such like Effect[.]

And this Defendant saith that the said Luke Collingwood did not at or after the above Discourse or Consultation propose to the Crew there [45] assembled or any of them to this Defendant[']s Knowledge or Belief that that they should throw in to the Sea or overboard such Part of the Slaves on board the said Ship *Zorg* [sic] as was weak sickly and of little Value or express himself to that or such like Effect though he believes he heard some one of the Crew say (though [46] he cannot recollect whom in particular) that the throwing overboard such Slaves would be no Loss to the Owners of the said Ship if she was insured or utter Expressions to such or the like Effect after the Slaves were thrown overboard though nothing of that Sort was mentioned at the Consultation to the best of this [47] Defendant[']s Remembrance and Belief and this Defendant saith to the best of his Recollection and Belief no particular Conversation passed at the Time the Crew were called together as aforesaid or at any other Time afterwards save such as last mentioned and save each Person's giving his Assent or Dissent to the [48] Proposal made by the said Luke Collingwood of throwing Part of the Slaves overboard and save that this Defendant himself who was shocked with the Idea of taking away so many Lives objected thereto and accompanied the Captain into the Cabin and there told him that there did not seem to this Defendant [49] an Occasion to put the Measure concluded on into Execution hastily and that it would be better to put the Slaves and Crew to short Allowance for a day or two and that they might possibly in the mean Time meet with some Ship or that Providence might afford them some Showers of Rain which might supply them [50] with water enough or to such or such like Effect and cannot with any Certainty further set forth in what terms or Language or to what Purport or Effect this Defendant or any other of the said Ship[']s Crew expostulated with the said Luke Collingwood on that Occasion but says that on such Objection or Remonstrance [51] of this Defendant the Captain said he thought they should not trust to so uncertain an Event in the Distress they then were as they should involve themselves in deeper Difficulties by keeping the whole of the Slaves on board considering their very reduced Stock of Water and that the

Opinion of the whole Crew was with him [52] the said Captain and therefore the first proposal of the said Captain was concluded to be put in Execution and about Eight o'Clock in the Night of the said twenty ninth of November one thousand seven hundred and eighty one (it having been previously so determined by the Crew which was but a short Time though [53] not immediately after the Consultation and Conversation that had so passed) the said Luke Collingwood ordered fifty or sixty of the said Slaves to be taken out of the Women's and Boys['] Rooms indiscriminately for that Purpose and fifty four of them were thrown alive singly through the Cabin Windows of the said [54] Ship into the Sea and drowned all of whom were in good Health and Condition considering the Length of the Voyage[.]

Saith that on the first of December following forty two stout healthy Men Slaves were thrown alive from the Quarter Deck of the said Ship into the Sea and drowned and that at several [55] Times between the first and twenty second of the said Month of December but on what Times or Days in particular this Defendant cannot recollect thirty six more marketable Slaves (though not so good as the former by reason of having been put and kept to short Allowance from the said twenty ninth of [56] November but however very good Slaves considering the Hardships they had endured) were thrown into the Sea from the Quarter Deck of the said Ship and drowned in Consequence of the Determination of the Crew by or by the Order of the said Luke Collingwood[.]

However the said Luke Collingwood's Order that [57] the said Slaves should be thrown overboard as aforesaid was in order to preserve the Crew and the Remainder of the Slaves from perishing and this Defendant saith that Ten other Slaves who were upon Deck fearing they might suffer the unhappy Fate of those destroyed spied Opportunities at different Times [58] when unobserved of leaping overboard and leapt from the said Ship into the Sea and were drowned so that the Outside Number of Slaves so drowned amounted to One Hundred and forty two in the whole and this Defendant saith that the Crew and Slaves of the same Ship had not been put to any short [59] Allowance before the first Number of Slaves were thrown overboard on the said twenty ninth of November as aforesaid but that those which were thrown overboard afterwards as well as the Crew had from that Time to wit from the said twenty ninth of November one thousand seven hundred and eighty one untill [sic] [60] the respective Times they were thrown overboard been put to short Allowance of Water[.]

This Defendant saith that the usual full Allowance of Water upon the Voyage was three half Pints Per man per Day but when put to short

Allowance on the said twenty ninth of November one thousand seven hundred and eighty one the [61] three half pints were reduced to half a Pint Per Day Per man which same short Allowance was continued as well to the Crew as the Slaves and they all had so much less (after the Rate of that reduced Allowance) than their usual daily Allowance of Water until they were in Sight of Jamaica Harbour when they were [62] supplied with Water by some Shower of Rain which fell and they then increased their Allowance[.]

This Defendant saith that the Slaves first thrown overboard were all taken out of the Women's and Boy's Rooms indiscriminately (and not picked out of the whole Cargo as the sickest and weakest or worst Part of the Slaves) and [63] that the others were taken out of the other Rooms in the same Manner without Respect to sick or healthy none of them being sick or unhealthy to this Defendant[']s Knowledge or Belief but all of them marketable Slaves[.]

This Defendant admits that it is very common at Sea when Provisions or Water become scare for the [64] people to be put to short Allowance [;] But this Defendant cannot form a Judgment how many Weeks or Days at most after the Discovery of the Ship *Zorg's* [sic] Scarcity of Water on the said twenty ninth of November one thousand seven hundred and eighty one (at which Time the white People and Slaves on board her were all put to [65] short Allowance of Water) they or any and what Number and Sort of them probably or possibly and in Course of Nature would or might have lived on the Water and Provisions on board the same Ship if made the most of for their Support and their being so put to short Allowance was immediately after the said [66] Discovery of the Scarcity of Water[.]

This Defendant saith that none of the Slaves drowned to this Defendant[']s Knowledge or Belief at the Time they were so drowned laboured under or were afflicted with any contagious or other Disorder and therefore can form no Judgment whether any of them might have died a natural [67] Death in a few Days or in a short Time if they had not been drowned but believes if so many as aforesaid had not been drowned many of them would have been seized with Madness for want of Water and died in the [same] State as the thirty six Slaves did which are hereinafter mentioned and this Defendant further [68] saith that the first fifty four Slaves so thrown overboard as aforesaid were Women and Boys but none of them Infants save one (not reckoned in the Number of good and valuable Slaves) but the said fifty four Slaves in general would each of them have been equal in Value individually to a Prime Man Slave if they [69] had arrived at a Market in Jamaica and that the rest were all Prime Men Slaves[;] And this Defendant further answering says that the Slaves which were first thrown overboard had [']till that Time had their full Allowance of Water and therefore did not express their Want of any Thing nor can this Defendant [70] set forth whether any or if any how many of them did understand so much of the English or some other Language understood by the Crew or any of them so as to express their or any of their respecting[277] Meanings and Wants in any or in what Degree but saith that those thrown overboard on the said first of [71] December in their own Languages understood by the Crew or some of them expressed their want of Water[;] Saith that all the Men Slaves as being able to make Resistance were handcuffed and in Irons from their first coming on board (as is usual) to prevent an Insurrection and that they were thrown [72] overboard so handcuffed and in Irons[;]

Saith that those Slaves thrown overboard on the said twenty ninth of November were brought up singly in the Night and thrown overboard and therefore were Ignorant of what they were going to suffer or be done with and that amongst those who were thrown [73] overboard on the said first of December there was one Man who spoke English amongst them and told this Defendant that the Slaves were murmuring on Account of the Fate of those who had been drowned and understanding that it was on Account of the Want of sufficient Water that they [74] begged they might be suffered to live and they would not ask for either Meat or Water but could live without either [']till they arrived at their destined Port when they desired they might have their Victual boiled in fresh Water[.]

This Defendant doth not recollect that save as aforesaid the said [Second parchment] [75] Slaves or any of them prayed or earnestly requested with Tears in their Eyes or otherwise by any Sign or Gesture Signs or Gestures expressed or signified a desire that they he or she might not be thrown overboard or in any Manner or in any and what Language Sign or Gesture [76] Signs or Gestures respectively express or signify any Desire that he she or they might be permitted to live[;] But saith that the Captain considering it less shocking to destroy the Slaves by drowning than to suffer them to expire in the Sight of himself and the Crew and of each other which [77] had been actually the Case of Thirty six Slaves who died in a State of absolute Madness for want of Water and he having the Opinion of this Defendant and the rest of the Crew corresponding with his own took that Method as the shortest

---

[277] Ed. Word appears to be "respecting", but "respective" might fit the context better.

and least painful Mode of destroying them[.]

This [78] Defendant saith that the Desires of the Slaves to be permitted to live so communicated to this Defendant by such one of the Slaves as before mentioned and the said Luke Collingwood[']s Conduct had such Effect on this Defendant as before mentioned but doth not recollect that such Desires if [79] communicated to any others of the Crew or the said Luke Collingwood[']s Conduct had any or if any what Effect on the other Officers and Crew of the said Ship or any of them or produced any or if any what Remonstrances Expostulations or Expressions from them or any of them respectively[.]

This [80] Defendant saith that one Man Slave who was thrown overboard into the Sea aforesaid and (unobserved by any of the Crew) catch [sic] hold of a Rope belonging to the said Ship *Zorg* [sic] which hung overboard and by means thereof got into the Larboard[278] Main or Forechains[279] part of the outside of the said [81] Ship and lay there during the Night being afraid that if he should be discovered the Crew of the *Zorg* some or one of them would throw him again into the Sea and drown him and in the next Morning he was there discovered by some of the Crew who after making Enquiry and being [82] informed how he had saved himself took him aboard and preserved his Life by keeping him amongst the remaining Cargo of Slaves[.]

This Defendant saith that the dreadful Necessity of the Situation which the Crew and Slaves were in for want of Water compelled the said Luke Collingwood and [83] the Crew of the said Ship to adopt the Step (barbarous as it may appear) of throwing the aforesaid Number of Slaves overboard though none of them were afflicted with any Disease or were weak sickly or of little Value to this Defendant[']s Knowledge or Belief and verily believes that the said Luke Collingwood's [84] only Motive for causing the said Slaves to be thrown overboard was their want of a sufficient Quantity of Water to serve them during the Voyage and to preserve his own Life and the rest of the Crew as well as the remaining Cargo of Slaves in the said Ship[;]

And this Defendant further answering [85] says if the Owners of the said Ship recover Thirty Pounds Per Head for the said Slaves destroyed they will nevertheless sustain a Loss of six Pounds Per Head

---

[278] Ed. OED: The side of a ship which is to the left hand of a person looking from the stern towards the bows. Ed. An older word for the port side.

[279] Ed. Strong iron plates bolted to the side of the ship with holes in them adjacent to the main or foremast to secure the lower shrouds of the main or foremast. Shrouds were a set of ropes stretched from a ship's side to a masthead to offset lateral strain on the mast.

upon those destroyed as those Slaves which arrived at Market fetched upon an Average thirty six Pounds Sterling per Head and those [86] thrown overboard if their Supply of Water had been sufficient to last them the Voyage and bring them to market would have been equal in Value[.]

Saith that on the Evening of the said twenty ninth of November one thousand seven hundred and eighty one there was on board the said [87] Ship *Zorg* [sic] Five and an half Dutch Butts of Water three of which were good and two and an half Sour and scarce fit for Use each of which Butts contained the Quantity they are above specified to contain that the Consumption of Water during the Voyage was variable and uncertain sometimes amounting [88] to two Butts a day in hot Weather and one and an half in temperate Weather amongst the Crew and Slaves which was continued as this Defendant believes till the Day they discovered their Deficiency of Water which is before particularly mentioned but this Defendant cannot ascertain the [89] particular Quantity of Water consumed on board after his Suspension from his Office of Chief Mate till the Time of his Reinstatement as aforesaid therefore cannot say what Quantity of Water had upon an Average been expended in the same Ship in the regular Course of twenty four Hours [90] amongst the Crew and Slaves for the Space of a Week next preceding the twenty ninth Day of November one thousand seven hundred and eighty one as he was not restored to his former Station until that Day[280] but believes that the above Quantity might be continued 'till that Day as they found no want of Water 'till that Time[.]

Saith that no Water [91] was wilfully wasted or misapplied and that it is always usual at Sea when Provisions or Water become scarce for the Crew to be put to short Allowance and that as well the white People as the Slaves of the said Ship *Zorg* immediately after the want of Water was discovered were put to [92] short Allowance at half a Pint Per Man Per Day and that their full Allowance had been three half Pints Per Man Per Day as aforesaid and that such short Allowance was continued 'till they arrived at Jamaica save after the Shower of Rain which fell as before mentioned when they [93] were within Sight of Jamaica Harbour after which they increased their Allowance[.]

Saith that the said Ship *Zorg* [sic] was distant about Three Hundred and Thirty Miles to the Westward of the Island of Jamaica to the best of his Judgment at the time the first Slaves were thrown overboard but

---

[280] Ed. The words "as he was not restored to his former Station until that Day" are inserted here between lines 89 and 90.

[94] he cannot form a judgment as to the Distance the said Vessel then was from the Island of Cuba which was agreed by all the Crew to be the nearest place (as the Wind then was) that the said Ship could have soonest reached and obtained a Supply of Water from and cannot tell how many Days [95] Sail she was from that place as the said Vessel was very foul and leaky and the few white People she had on board were weak and sickly and unable to work the said Vessel which was a very slow and uncertain Sailer.

This Defendant saith the said Captain declined proceeding for a Supply of Water [96] to the said island of Cuba as being an Enemy Port the Entering into which would have been the Loss of his Ship and Cargo[.]

This Defendant saith that in beating back to Jamaica after their Water was nearly exhausted they had a Fall of Rain but how soon how long or on what particular Day [97] or Night Days or Nights after the Slaves were thrown overboard or after the first of December such Fall of Rain happened this Defendant cannot set forth not having any Entry made thereof from whence to ascertain the Time and Quantity better than that he believes it was sometime between the [98] sixth and ninth of that Month and that from that Rain the Crew of the said Vessel caught about Sixty Gallons at most for the Use of the said Ship and that after making the said Island of Jamaica there was another Fall of Rain but on what particular Day or Night Days or Nights this [99] Defendant cannot remember or set forth of which last Rain they caught two Butts of Water at most which sustained the Crew and the remaining Slaves 'till they arrived in Black River in Jamaica and which was all they could catch and that it only rained the said two different Times from the said [100] twenty ninth day of November 'till the said twenty second Day of December the Day on which the said Ship arrived at Jamaica[.]

Saith that on their Arrival in the Harbour there was not on board of her above half a Barrel of the said last mentioned Butts as after coming in Sight of Harbour they allowed [101] their Slaves a larger Quantity than what they had before done as they then could run into Harbour under their Lee for a Supply[.]

This Defendant further saith that if the said Luke Collingwood could have got into any British Island or place of Safety in any Quarter or Part of the World where he could [102] have obtained a sufficient or any Supply of Water for the Crew and Slaves on board the *Zorg* [sic] he certainly would have done so but when the want or Scarcity of the said Ship[']s Water was first discovered or at any Time between that Time and the said Ship's Arrival at Jamaica the said Luke Collingwood had [103] not any Opportunity of so doing and the Crew being against his waiting or trusting to Providence for obtaining a Supply either from some Ship which they might meet at Sea or from the Element he took the Lives from the said Slaves by drowning them as aforesaid.

This Defendant verily believes that [104] on the first Discovery of the want of the said Ship *Zorg's* [sic] Water as aforesaid there was neither any Probability Expectation or Possibility that the said Luke Collingwood might have got with her into any of the Islands in the Bill mentioned or any other Island or Place of Safety where he might have been [105] supplied with Water which was the Reason why he did not attempt it[.]

Saith he believes the said Ship *Zorg* [sic] arrived at Jamaica on or about the twenty second Day of December one thousand seven hundred and eighty one after a Passage of upwards of four Months which Passage is usually performed [106] in seven or eight Weeks[.] Saith that he never knew any vessel be so long in a Passage from the Coast of Africa to Jamaica before the Voyage before mentioned and that to the best of this Defendant's Recollection and Belief Thirty six Slaves died on board the said Ship *Zorg* [sic] between the twenty ninth of [107] November one thousand seven hundred and eighty one and the twenty second of December following inclusive (exclusive of those that were put to Death as aforesaid) but cannot remember how many died in the like Space of Time or in the Course of the Voyage previous to the said twenty ninth of November [108] one thousand seven hundred and eighty one not being suffered to keep the Log Book after his Suspension as aforesaid[.]

Saith that all the surviving Slaves on board the said Ship *Zorg* [sic] arrived at Jamaica in good Health considering the Hardships they had experienced during their Voyage[.]

Saith that it did and [109] would appear by the Log Book of the said Ship *Zorg* [sic] (which this Defendant delivered up to the Captain the said Luke Collingwood at Jamaica but has never seen it since nor does he know in whose Custody or Power the same is) but not by any other Book or Books Paper or Papers Letter or Letters (to the [110] Knowledge or Belief of this Defendant) unless some Entry thereof can be found in the said Ship[']s Journal what Quantity of Water the said Ship *Zorg* [sic] had on board when she left the Coast of Africa and what Quantity of Water was daily expended on board the said Ship and how many Slaves died before [111] the said twenty ninth day of November one thousand seven hundred and eighty one and in what Condition

Health and State the Remainder were (but it is not usual to set down the Ages of Slaves) who were thrown overboard and what Quantity of Water was on board the said Ship *Zorg* [sic] at that Time [112]

Saith that to the best of this Defendant[']s Recollection a Memorandum of the Resolution of the Crew to throw Part of the said Slaves overboard was entered in the said Log Book with the Reasons which founded the said Resolution but in no other Book or Books Paper or Papers (unless in the said [113] Ship's Journal) to this Defendant's Knowledge or Belief But saith that there are also in the same Log Book Memorandums of the Showers of Rain which fell on the said Ship *Zorg* [sic] between the twenty ninth Day of November one thousand seven hundred and eighty one and the said twenty [114] second Day of December following and of sundry other Articles and Things relative to the said Ship *Zorg* [sic] and her Voyage all of which have been in Substance related to this Defendant according to the best of his Recollection and Belief[.]

But whether all or any of these Articles Matters or Things are necessary or [115] proper for the Complainants to know before they can proceed effectually to defend the Action commenced against them this Defendant cannot take upon himself to judge of or determine[.] This Defendant saith that a Log Book is a Book belonging to a Ship which is kept by the Chief Mate and [116] which no Person has a Right to inspect without Leave of the Captain or Chief Mate unless he understands how to keep a Journal and believes the Captain of a Ship has no Business with the Log Book further than another Seaman who understands keeping a Journal[281] save taking Care that the Log Book be kept in Safety on board the Ship[.] [117]

This Defendant saith that he does not know of his own Knowledge whether the Complainants or any or which of them have or hath by themselves or himself or his or their Attorney or any Body and whom also by a Name applied to the said Defendants or any or which of them and demanded or [118] requested the said Log Book or a Sight or Inspection thereof but hath heard and believes they have or some or one of them hath been applied to for that Purpose[.]

Saith he doth not know though he believes that the Defendants or Defendant who were or was applied to declined (not having it in [119] their Power) to comply with such Demand or Request but no otherwise refused to comply with such Request than by alledging they or he had not such Log Book in their or his Custody or Power for this

---

[281] Ed. The words "who understands keeping a Journal" are inserted above the line.

Defendant conceives it would be their Interest to produce it if it was in their Power or Custody[.] [120]

This Defendant saith as he believes that the said Log Book is not now in the Custody Possession or Power of the Defendants or any of them nor does this Defendant know or has heard or can form a Belief in whose Custody Possession or Power the same now is but says that the same was [121] in the Possession of the said Luke Collingwood when this Defendant last saw it and this Defendant knows nothing further respecting it[;]

And this Defendant saith that the same Log Book which was in the Custody or Power of this Defendant until his Delivery of it to the said Luke Collingwood as [122] aforesaid or any of the Journal Books Letters Papers or Writings which are or ever were in the Custody or Power of this Defendant when this Defendant so delivered the said Log Book to the said Luke Collingwood or at any other Time had not been in any respect altered obliterated defaced torn burnt or otherwise [123] destroyed by the Order or with the Knowledge Consent or Privity of this Defendant or the said Luke Collingwood or any of the said other Defendants or kept or deposited in any other Place or Places save the said Island of Jamaica where this Defendant hath heard that it was left by the said Luke [124] Collingwood or by him lost or misplaced before he died[.]

This Defendant saith that neither he nor any other of the said Defendants to this Defendant[']s Knowledge or Belief had any Letter or Letters from any Person or Persons in the said Island of Jamaica or elsewhere from which it would or doth [125] appear that the said Slaves thrown out of the said Ship *Zorg* [sic] into the Sea were not so thrown for Want of Water but with a fraudulent Design to make the Complainants chargeable with the Loss thereof or with any other bad or sinister Design[.]

This Defendant saith that he kept a Journal [126] of the Ship[']s Proceedings as Mate of the said Ship from her Sailing from Acra until his Suspension on the said fourteenth of November one thousand seven hundred and eighty one which he has now delivered into the hands of his Clerk in Court for the Inspection of the Complainants if they [127] shall be disposed to inspect the same and saith that on the fourteenth day of November one thousand seven hundred and eighty one the said Luke Collingwood for the Reasons which this Defendant has before given and for no other that this Defendant knows of forbid [sic] this Defendant to [128] keep a Journal as is usual when Officers are disgraced in the Manner that the said Collingwood disgraced this

Defendant and that this Defendant accordingly desisted from keeping a Journal from that Time to the day he was so restored as aforesaid and this Defendant saith [129] that he does now in his Conscience believe and deem that the throwing overboard the said Slaves alive into the Sea was an Act of absolute Necessity in the Person or Persons who committed the same to preserve their own Lives and the Lives of the Remainder of the Slaves as [130] also the Ship and Cargo from perishing for want of Water or being captured by making and entering into an Enemy Port for a Supply of Water and so becoming an Enemy[']s Prize and not an inhuman Act or unparalleled Cruelty[;]

And this Defendant saith that he also believes in his [131] Conscience that the drowning [of] such Slaves was not a Scheme contrived by the said Luke Collingwood for the Purpose of defrauding the Insurers and that the other Defendants the Owners might make a good Voyage out of the said Ship *Zorg* [sic] at the Expense of the Insurers or for any of those [132] Purposes but that it was as well to preserve his own Life and those of the Crew and remaining Slaves and the said Ship as for the Interest of all concerned therein and therefore doth not condemn the said Luke Collingwood in his Conscience but considers his Conduct justifiable and pityable [sic] as he could [133] not but be shocked as the Executioner of so fatal a Necessity[;] And this Defendant saith that casting Lots amongst the Slaves would have created great Murmurings Suspicions and Delay as some of the Slaves understood English and therefore the Measure pursued was in this Defendant[']s [134] Opinion the safest shortest and soonest put in Execution and preferable to any other which would have created Delay and that Lots ought not to have been cast before the Slaves were thrown overboard[;]

And Lastly this Defendant denies all unlawful Combination or Confederacy charged [135] against him in the said Bill and without that that any other matter or Thing in the Complainants['] said Bill contained material or necessary for this Defendant to make Answer unto and not herein or hereby well and sufficiently answered unto confessed or avoided traversed or denied is true [136] All which Matters and Things this Defendant is ready to aver maintain and prove as this Honourable Court shall award and humbly prays to be hence dismissed with his reasonable Costs and Charges in this behalf as he conceives without just Cause had and sustained.

Colonel James Kelsall [signature]

[137] This Answer was taken and the above named Colonel James Kelsall was duly sworn to the Truth [138] thereof upon the Holy Evange-

lists at the Office of Robert Carr Solicitor for the said Defendant [*139*] situate in the Parish of Liverpool in this County of Lancaster on the twenty sixth day of July in the twenty [*140*] third Year of the Reign of his present Majesty King George the third and in the Year of our Lord [*141*] one thousand seven hundred and eighty three by Virtue of the Commission hereunto annexed before us

[signatures]
Peter Ellames
Robt. Carr

Gregson's Answer

The National Archives E 112/1528/173

Fyled March 8th 1784

The Answer[282] of William Gregson Esquire John Gregson James Gregson George Case Edward Wilson and James Aspinall Six of the Defendants to the Bill of Complaint of Thomas Gilbert John Dawson William Boldon John Thompson John Parker and Edward Mason Complainants[.]

The said Defendants saving to themselves all Advantages and benefit of Exception that can be taken to the many untruths incertainties [sic] and other Imperfections in the Complainants['] said Bill of Complaint contained for answer unto so much thereof as those [2] Defendants are advised is any way material or effectual for them or any of them to make answer unto, They[,] these Defendants[,] answering say as followeth[,]

And first these Defendants admit That at or about the time in the said Bill for that Purpose mentioned [3] They fitted out a Ship called the William under the Command of Richard Hanley since deceased on a Voyage from Liverpool for the Coast of Africa and the British West India Islands and that whilst the said Richard Hanley was trading for Slaves on [4] the said Coast of Africa he fell in with a Ship[283] belonging to Bristol which had made Prize of a Dutch Vessel call the Zong otherwise the Zorg with a Cargo on Board consisting of Slaves Goods and Merchandize calculated for the African Markett [sic] [5] which Ship the said Richard Hanley purchased from the Commander of the said Bristol Ship with her Slaves Goods and Merchandize on board her for a Sum agreed upon between them and drew one or more Bill or Bills of Exchange for the Purchase [6] Money upon these Defendants or some

---

[282] Ed. The original deposition is written on large parchment sheets so that each line of text is about a yard long. In this transcription the lines have therefore been numbered in the form "[2]" etc., for ease of reference to the original.

[283] Ed. The prize hearing in the High Court of Admiralty says that *"De Zorg"* was captured by the *Sally and Rachell*, a "letter of marque or private ship of war belonging to London commanded by Captain James Hayes". TNA HCA 32/491.

of them as Owners of the said Ship William in Favour of the Master of the said Bristol Ship who on delivery to him of such Bill or Bills delivered up the said Ship Zong or Zorg and her Cargo to the said [7] Richard Hanley for the use of his Owners at which time as they have heard and believe there were on Board the said Ship Zong or Zorg Two hundred and forty four[284] slaves and Goods sufficient for the Purchase of near as many more and the said Richard Hanley [8] having then almost compleated [sic] his Purchase on the Coast and intending soon to sail for the Island of Jamaica appointed Luke Collingwood Surgeon of the Ship William to be Master or Commander of the said Ship Zong and which [the] said Luke [9] Collingwood was well qualified for such Command and the said Richard Hanley having put seventeen White People on board her gave the said Luke Collingwood directions to barter the Goods and remaining Part of her Cargo for Slaves and other African [10] Produce and then to proceed after the Ship William to Jamaica[.]

These Defendants admit that when the said Bills of Exchange were presented for Acceptance to those Defendants Owners of the Ship William at Liverpool they having been advised [11] thereof and of the Purchase of the said Ship Zong by the said Richard Hanley by Letter, confirmed the said Richard Hanley's bargain and purchase by accepting and paying such Bills and these Defendants some or one of them immediately or soon[285] afterwards [12] caused several Policies of Assurance to be made out in the Name of the Defendant William Gregson and one[286] in the Name of the Defendant James Aspinall whereby they insured the Ship Zong Luke Collingwood Master in such or the like terms and [13] manner and with such Provision as in the Bill mentioned and with such respective values set upon the said Ship slaves and other Goods and Merchandize and such Adventures and Perils to be born[e] by the Assurers as in such Policy and Policys expressed in [14] the usual form and that the Complainants severally underwrote one or more of the said Policy or Policys [sic] of Insurance for such several and respective Sums of Money upon Goods and upon [the] Ship as in the said Bill mentioned and by such Policy and Policies the [15] Complainants confessed the premium for such Insurance paid as in by such policy and policies in the Custody of these Defendants some or one of them or their Broker may appear[.]

---

[284] Ed. The word "four" is inserted above the line.
[285] Ed. The words "or soon" are inserted above the line.
[286] Ed. The word "one" is inserted above the line.

These Defendants say that as to their own personal Knowledge being [16] entirely ignorant of the Transaction of the said Ship Zong's late Voyage from Acra to Jamaica and [having heard the Answer of the other Defendant Colonel James Kelsall read over to them they][287] believe the same to be in all aspects true and therefore creave [sic] leave to refer thereto for and as the Answer of these Defendants to the Allegations Matters and [17] Things in the Complainants said Bill suggested alledged [sic] and set forth they saying that they these Defendants cannot make any further or other Answer thereto save than by such Reference to the said Kelsall's answer and by such further Answer of [18] these Defendants as hereinbefore and after set forth.

These Defendants say as they believe that the Number of Slaves which were so drowned and perished as mentioned in the same Answer of the said Colonel James Kelsall were at the Rate of thirty Pounds a [19] Head and upwards and according to the Stipulation and Agreement in the said policies of Insurance of the Value of three thousand nine hundred and sixty Pounds and that the loss of the Slaves was a General average loss which ought to be born[e] [20] and paid by the Underwriters on the said Ship and Cargoe and these Defendants have accordingly demanded from the Complainants such Average loss in proportion to the several Sums of Money by them underwritten on the said Ship and Cargoe [21] amounting as these Defendants compute to the Sum of Twenty Eight Pounds two shillings per Cent on the Whole Money so by them insured which the Complainants refused to pay either for the reason in the said Bill suggested or some other wherefore these [22] Defendants have some time ago commenced several Actions in his Majesty[']s Court of King's Bench against the Complainants upon the Policies by them respectively underwritten to recover Payment of the said Loss of Twenty Eight Pounds two Shillings [23] per Cent[,]

And these Defendants further say that soon after the said Ship Zong's Arrival at Liverpool from the Voyage in the said Bill mentioned the Journal Book of and relating to the said Voyage which came in her was delivered up to these Defendants some [24] or one of them[,]

And that these Defendants have left the said Journal Book in the Hands of their Clerk in Court in this Cause and these Defendants crave leave

---

[287] Ed. The words in brackets are inserted above the line.

to refer to the same there to manifest and ascertain such of the Facts in the Bill mentioned and [25] enquired after as are therein set down[,]

And these Defendants further answer and each for himself say they or any of them never saw the said Ship[']s Logbook or had the same in their or any of their Custody or Power nor can form any belief touching the same [26] other than such as is mentioned in the said Answer of the said Defendant Kelsall[,]

And all these Defendants each answering for himself further say that neither they or any of them have or hath or lately had in their or any of their Custody or Power any Books [27] Letters or Papers besides the said Journall [sic] Book so left in the hands of their Clerk in Court wherein all or any of the transactions of the said Voyage are entered and that neither such Journall Book or any Books Letters or Papers relating to all or any the [28] Transactions of the said Voyage hath or have been by them or any of them or their or any of their orders altered obliterated defaced torn burnt or any otherwise destroyed[;]

But these Defendants further say that soon after the Purchase of the said Ship Zong they received [29] from Richard Hanley their Captain of the Ship William a Letter from Cape Coast road[288] dated March sixteenth One thousand seven hundred and Eighty and advising of such Purchase and recommending to these Defendants to make Insurance and three Letters [30] from the said Luke Collingwood after his appointment to the command of the said Ship Zong the first of them dated April third One thousand seven hundred and Eighty one Anamatoe [sic] Roads Ship de Zorg the second of them Anamatoe Ship Zorg [sic], June twenty fourth [31] One thousand seven hundred and Eighty one and the third Kingston, Jamaica, February thirteenth One thousand seven hundred and Eighty two[;] And one Letter from Coppells and Aquillar the Agents or Factors of these Defendants dated Kingston Jamaica twelfth [32] January One thousand seven hundred and Eighty two after the said Ship Zong's arrival there and two other paper Writings one of them being an Account of the Cargoe [sic] on board the Ship Richard alias the Zorg when purchased on the Coast and the other of them the Account [33] of Sales of the Cargoe of the said Ship Zorg or Zong and which are all Letters and Papers relating to the said Ship and

---

[288] Ed. OED "road: 3.a. A sheltered piece of water near the shore where vessels may lie at anchor in safety; a roadstead."

her Voyage and transactions therein in the Custody or Power of these Defendants or any of them to their or any of their Knowledge Remembrance and [34] belief all which they have left in the Custody of their Clerk in Court for the Inspection of the Complainants and with all the Libertys usual on such Occasions[.]

These Defendants admit the Complainants by Mr Ellames their Sollicitor [sic] in this Cause have repeatedly applied to [35] these Defendants or some of them to produce to them or some of them the said Ship Zong's Log Book but cannot recollect that he so applied for a Production of the said Ship's Journal-book or any other books Letters Papers or Writings belonging to the said Ship or [36] which Applications these Defendants or such of them as was or were so applyed [sic] to assured the said Mr Ellames that the same Log-book never came to their Possession nor did they know where it was.

These Defendants admit that the Log book is a book belonging to a Ship [37] which is open to all the Crew for them to make and enter therein whatever transactions and memorandums relative to the Ship or Voyage they please but any thing respecting in whose Custody after a Voyage ended the Log-Book of a Ship ought to be cannot say or set forth[,] [38]

And these Defendants each speaking for himself deny they know or believe the Complainants will be unable untill they can get a sight of the said Log-book Journal Book and Papers or any of them to make an effectual defence at Law to the said Actions [39] commenced against them or any of them respectively either because the Defendant Kelsall kept a Journall until or about the fourteenth day of November One thousand seven hundred and Eighty one of the proceedings of the same Voyage or because he omitted continuing [40] the same from that time either for the Reason in the said Bill suggested or some other[;]

And these Defendants so far as their respective Knowledge, Information and belief extend[,] deny that the said Luke Collingwood with a View of Concealing any Facts which should [41] happen or happened afterwards thereupon there or about that time ordered the said Defendant Kelsall to desist from keeping the said Log Book[289] tho' they admit as from his Information they believe that he desisted accordingly from keeping the same until he was by [42] the said Luke Collingwood

---

[289] Ed. Kelsall in his answer said Luke Collingwood ordered him to stop keeping his own journal. The log book was the responsibility of the captain.

restored to his Office of Chief Mate at such time as in his answer to the said Bill is mentioned,

And these Defendants in like manner also deny that sundry or any Conversations on board the same Ship passed between the said [43] Luke Collingwood and the Officers and Crew of the same Ship or any of them whereby it will appear or that the Fact was that the said Slaves were thrown overboard with Intent to turn the Loss upon the Insurers and to ease the Owners of the Risque [sic] of the Slaves [44] thrown overboard dying a natural Death or with any other fraudulent view in the said Luke Collingwood as by the said Bill is uncharitably and unjustly suggested.

For these Defendants cannot in Christian Charity for the said Luke Collingwood but hope that his [45] sole and only view and Motive for throwing such Slaves overboard was to preserve the rest of them as well as his Officers and Crew from perishing for Want of Water as he could not in time get into any of the british [sic] or other friendly Islands where he might have [46] obtained a supply of Water[.]

These Defendants admit that tho' their Actions against the Complainants were only commenced just before the beginning of last Hilary Term yet they did intend to proceed to Trial therein at the Sitting after the same term[.] [47]

And these Defendants deny all unlawful Combination or Confederacy charged against them in the said Bill without that that [sic] there is any other[290] Matter or Thing in the Complainants said Bill contained material or necessary for these Defendants to make answer unto and not [48] herein or hereby well and sufficiently answered unto confessed or avoided traversed or denied is true[.]

All which Matters and things these Defendants are ready to aver maintain and prove in this honourable Court shall award[291] and humbly pray to be hence dismissed with their reasonable [49] Costs and Charges in this behalf as they conceive without just Cause had and sustained[.]

---

[290] Ed. The words "any other" are inserted above line 47.
[291] Ed. The words "shall award" do not seem to make sense within the sentence. Perhaps some words were omitted.

[50] This answer was taken and the above named Defendants William Gregson, John [51] Gregson James Gregson George Case Edward Wilson and James Aspinall were duly sworn to the [52] Truth thereof upon the Holy Evangelists at the Office of the said William Gregson situate in Castle [53] Street in the Parish of Liverpool in the County of Lancaster at eleven o'Clock in the forenoon [54] of the twenty third day of January in the twenty fourth Year of the Reign of his Majesty King [55] George the third and in the Year of our Lord One thousand seven hundred and Eighty four by Virtue of the [56] Commission hereto annexed before us -

[signatures]
Peter Ellames
H. Brown

Extract from Martin Dockray MS

Squire Law Library, University of Cambridge

Captives and Captors

The *Zong* sailed from Africa for the West Indies on 18 August 1781 with 442 slaves on board, according to the evidence given by her Mate to the Court of Exchequer in London. In March 1781 a total of 244 people had been bought from the Alert privateer. Some of those slaves are likely to have died before the Atlantic voyage began, so that if the Mate was telling the truth at least another 200 Africans carried off by the *Zong* must have been purchased between March and August on the Gold Coast. It is possible that the *Zong* also carried some ivory and gold. Back in Liverpool, her owners certainly thought it worthwhile to insure these items as well as the slaves.

The *Zong's* logbook is not known to have survived, although a journal of the voyage did eventually reach Liverpool. But the vessel's progress from west to east along the coast of what is now the state of Ghana can be traced from the records of the insurance litigation and corroborated by other sources, notably the papers of the Company of Merchants trading to Africa. The Company's servants on the coast noted and regularly reported to London on shipping arrivals and departures. The *Zong* is mentioned from time to time in the Company's routine correspondence as well as in the day books and accounts kept by each fort, several times in the records of payments to free canoemen - typically made in gallons of brandy - for moving people or goods between the ship and shore.

In the first part of the year, from March to June 1781, the *Zong* was at Cape Coast Castle and at the nearby British fort at Annamaboe. The archives of the Africa Company in London contain a copy of a letter written to the Castle in April by her captain, Luke Collingwood. [T70/1547]

In May, Collingwood was present at an auction in the Castle when the personal property of Governor Roberts, who died a month or so earlier, was sold as Dead Men's Effects. The standard practice of the Company when one of its officers died on the Coast was to arrange a public auction of the man's possessions. Long experience had shown that to avoid endless disputes with relatives of the deceased, detailed accounts of sales had to be made and forwarded to London. At the Roberts' auction, Collingwood treated himself to two items including a pair of silver plate candlesticks, price two pounds ten shillings. [T70/1483]

In June 1781 Collingwood appears again in the Company's records, with another unusual transaction. In need of extra supplies after the outbreak of war, the Company asked for help from the captains of the English slave ships at Cape Coast. Collingwood lent gunpowder to the Company: 7 and a half barrels, valued at six pounds a barrel. [T70/772, T70/ 1047, T70/1125; T70/1046; T70/1453]

A few days later, on 18 June, the *Zong* finally left Cape Coast roads, sailing for safety in company with two London slavers, the *Adventure* and [the] *Lord George Germain*.[292]

The three ships moved ten miles or so to the east of Cape Coast Castle to Annomaboe, then rated as the second English trading centre on this part of the coast in terms of importance. The *Zong* was seen there on 21 June by the only Royal Navy ship in the area, HMS *Champion*. Collingwood also wrote to his owners from this port on 24 June. On 19 or 20 July she moved further east to Tantumquerry [T70/1153; T70/1168; T70/1546] landing supplies for the Company along with a passenger, Charles Graves, Governor of the neighbouring fort of Winnebah. It is likely that the *Zong* remained at Tantumquerry for a few days before continuing eastwards to Accra. She finally left the Gold Coast on 17 or 18 August. [T70/1547 and litigation]

No details have been traced that would help to identify any of the enslaved Africans taken on board at these places, although women and children certainly formed part of the *Zong's* human cargo. Liverpool ships often kept business records of the items given in exchange for each slave or group of slaves, allocating a number to each individual in the ship's papers. The *Zong* seems to have followed this practice. In the Court of Exchequer her owners acknowledged that they had received an account of the cargo on board the ship when it was purchased, together with an account of the sales of the cargo on board. These items have not been found and the only information about the *Zong's* prisoners now available comes from a newspaper advertisement placed by the firm of Coppetts & Aguilar in Jamaica in

---

[292] Ed. Lord George Germain was a British soldier and politician who was Secretary of State for America in Lord North's cabinet during the American War of Independence. Piers Mackesy, 'Germain, George Sackville, first Viscount Sackville (1716–1785)', ODNB, 2004; online edn, May 2009 [http://www.oxforddnb.com/view/article/10566], accessed 17 July 2016.

January 1782. The survivors of the voyage were offered for sale by the brokers on board the ship on 9 January 1782 and described as "200 choice young Coromantee, Fantee and Ashantee Negroes".

This statement does not help much in identifying the origins of any of the individuals. It is possible that the words "Fantee" and "Ashantee" referred to the ethnic origins of individuals carried off by the crew of the *Zong*. The Fanti people occupied the coastal belt around Cape Coast, south of the Ashanti region in the south-central area of modern Ghana. But care and accuracy in brokers descriptions cannot be relied on and the advertisement may have referred to the places that individuals had passed through rather than to their ethnicity. Coromantee in particular was a description frequently applied in the British West Indies to slaves shipped from Kormantin, 20 miles or so east [?] of Cape Coast Castle.

What about the killers? It is not possible to name the whole crew of the *Zong* at the time of the deaths with absolute certainty. A little information came to light in the course of the proceedings in the court of King's Bench. The only witness called at trial was a man named Robert Stubbs. Stubbs went on board the *Zong* as a passenger.

He gave evidence that the ship sailed from Africa with a crew of 17, and that 7 of the men had died before the first African was thrown overboard. Stubbs confirmed that Luke Collingwood was the captain and identified one other member of the crew, James Kelsall, as the first mate. These facts were recorded by a short-hand writer commissioned by the anti-slavery campaigner Granville Sharp to take a note at one of the hearings; the facts were later included in published accounts of the case.

Further facts about the crew emerge from the unpublished record of the proceedings in the Court of Exchequer. The Mate of the *Zong*, James Kelsall, was made a defendant to this claim along with the *Zong's* owners. His response to a demand for information from the insurers was contained in a formal document called an Answer, prepared with the help of his solicitor and sworn at Liverpool on 26 July 1783; it was filed with the court in London on 12 November of that year. Kelsall agreed that the ship sailed from Africa with a crew of 17 and gave the names of 8 of the men; he put the deaths among the crew at 6 before the first African was killed. Kelsall's statements about the crew did not give much information to the insurers. According to Kelsall, six members of the crew died before the killings began, a seventh man, Joseph Wood, drowned before reaching Jamaica, while the captain and three more men died shortly after the ship arrived at the island. His evidence was that all the remaining members of the crew quickly moved on after reaching Jamaica. Two Dutchmen returned to Holland while three more men - John Brown, Michael Sullivan and George Aston - were pressed in Jamaica into the British Navy. If Kelsall was telling the truth, the insurers were not likely to be able to find any more witnesses among the five surviving members of the crew. But was he telling the truth? Kensall's Answer was regular in form. It was more or less consistent with the evidence given in King's Bench and apparently credible. All the names he mentioned appear in the *Zong's* muster roll. There are, nevertheless, a number of points of detail on which Kelsall's evidence did not match the information contained in the roll.

In 1782 a muster roll had to be completed by the captain or the owner of a (British) ship returning to an English port. Rolls were required in order to show the length of time each man had served on board. This information formed the basis of the duty to account for Seamen's Sixpences, the sum of money payable to the Royal Naval Hospital at Greenwich for each week a man worked on a merchant ship. Compliance with the duty to [pay and file a muster roll] was enforced by statutory penalties and the use of informers. The muster roll for the 1781-2 voyage of the *Zong* has survived in the Public Record Office in London, half-hidden among the other Liverpool rolls for 1782, for the name of the ship was changed when she arrived at Jamaica, first to the *Richard of Jamaica* and then to the *Richard*. She was probably named after Richard Hanley who purchased her at Cape Coast Castle. Sailing under the name *Richard*, the *Zong* arrived at Liverpool from Jamaica in July 1782 and using this name, John Gregson signed the muster roll detailing the names of men who worked on the ship at any time between March 1781 and July 1782. The roll contains 48 names. The last 18 men named on the roll had nothing to do with the homicidal events of 1781. They joined the ship in Jamaica in 1782 and served only on the run to Liverpool. But the other 30 names are men who are shown as joining the ship before she left Africa. Nineteen men are shown as entering the ship in March after she was bought by Captain Hanley of the *William*. All the names given by Kelsall can be found in this group. Twelve of the new crew came from the *William*, including the captain, Luke Collingwood and James Kelsall himself. Three were members of the captured Dutch crew of the *Zong*: Pieter Germonpree, the Derdewaak, of Neusen or Nensen, Christiaan Hoor, Oppermeester, from Rotterdam and Johannes Andreas Horr, Derdemeester, also from Rotterdam. It is possible that these three men may not have been on board voluntarily. A privateer taking a prize like the *Zong* into port for adjudication was required by the Standing Instructions for Commanders to bring in three or four of the most senior members of the crew of the captured ship for examination by the Court. Nevertheless, the appearance of the names of these men on the muster roll suggests that they had signed articles and agreed to serve for pay on the voyage to Jamaica.

Four of the nineteen men who joined the *Zong* in March 1781 cannot be found in the muster rolls of the *William* or in the Dutch crew list of the *Zong*. One individual, Richard Dick, may have been an independent trader on the Coast; a man of this name is mentioned in African Company records. But nothing is known of the way in which the remaining three men - Nicholas Welsh, James Sill and John Brown - came to join the ship. Very likely they came out of one of the English ships that called at Cape Coast Castle in early 1781. But not all muster rolls have survived so that it is not possible to be sure. The first part of the *Zong's* muster roll, dealing with men who joined the ship in March 1781, is consistent with the evidence given by Kelsall and is probably substantially accurate. But the roll also adds facts not given by the mate. It lists 11 new men as joining the ship in June. There is no hint in the muster roll of the way in which these 11 men came to join the ship. Kelsall made no reference to this group or to any of these men. Nevertheless, the entries in the roll are probably accurate. Most of these men can in fact be traced as arriving in Africa in a Liverpool privateer. The *Brilliant*, master Robert Bently, sailed from Liverpool in January 1781. On the 20 April 1781, she was noted in the day book at the Africa Company's fort at Appolonia, [T70/1001] no more than a hundred and twenty miles or so to the west of Cape Coast Castle. Her muster roll shows 9 of the men as discharged on 27 April, making it possible that they joined the *Zong* some where on the Coast in May or June. Kelsall's failure to mention these men is odd but not especially suspicious. No one asked him where the *Zong's* crew came from and and he was not, according to the common practice in the Court of Exchequer, required to answer questions that had not been asked.

In addition to the 11 men shown as entering the ship in African waters, the *Zong's* roll also shows 11 men as leaving the vessel before the transatlantic voyage began, something else not mentioned by Kelsall in his sworn statement. One man was said to have drowned. As to the rest, a key entry in the *Zong's* roll states that Francis Cornforth left the ship when he "Ent'd the *Champion*. Ent'd 22nd May 1781." Nine other men named lower down the roll are then said simply to have "Ent'd 22nd May 1781", suggesting that they too joined *Champion*.

This entry undoubtedly refers to His Majesty's Ship *Champion*, Captain West, a 24-gun frigate sent out from England to protect the African Company's annual store ship and then to inspect the forts and settlements and estimate Dutch strength on the Coast. She arrived at Cape Coast roads on 24 May. *Champion's* muster-table [ADM 36/9746] shows that four men from the *Zong*, including Francis Cornforth, did join the warship on the day she arrived. They were listed in her books as supernumeraries, carried for victuals only. All four sailed with *Champion* when she left Cape Coast for Sao Tome and the West Indies. But there is no reference in the *Champion's* logs to the six other men mentioned in the *Zong's* muster roll as "Ent'd 22nd May 1781". If these six men did not enter the *Champion*, what became of them? Did they remain on board *Zong*? Kelsall in his evidence mentioned the names of three of these six men - John Barnes, George Arto or Aston and Michael Sullivan - and said they sailed with the him. It is of course possible that Kelsall lied to the Court of Exchequer. But there may be an innocent explanation for discrepancies between Kelsall's evidence and the *Zong's* muster roll. There are a number of clear errors in the roll: one man is show as sailing to Jamaica with her who certainly joined *Champion*; another is shown as deserting the ship at a time when she was at sea. The likely explanation for the differences between the *Zong's* muster roll and Kelsall's evidence is that the clerk in Liverpool who prepared the muster roll knew that a number of men had left the ship in Africa, but could only guess at their names and the reasons for their departure. Where did they go? It is possible that the missing men entered one of the other English ships in the area. In late May 1781, HMS *Champion* led an attack on the Dutch fort at Commenda and was supported by most of the English slave ships known to have been in the area: *Camden*, Captain King, *Adventure*, Captain Muir, and *Lord George Germaine* [sic] , Captain Thorburn. The attack failed after a day or two, repulsed by a garrison that had been strengthened by 40 Dutch seamen, who were in the area only because they had been captured and then released by English privateers. *Zong* did not take part in this attack but it is possible that some members of her crew did join in and, in the event, did not return to their ship.

There is, however, a simpler way to explain what happened to the six missing seamen. The rate of mortality among the crews of slave ships in 1781 was high; higher than in any other branch of shipping. A few years after the *Zong* left Africa, statistics were published showing that on average one seaman in five died on each slaving voyage. Modern historians have confirmed this high level of mortality on British ships in the period. A long stay on the Coast was virtually certain to increase the risk of death, so that it is perfectly possible that the missing men simply died before the *Zong* sailed for the West Indies. Nevertheless, it is at present impossible to be sure about the names of all the members and total size of the crew of the *Zong* at the start of the Atlantic voyage. Despite this uncertain, the identity of some of the white members of the crew of the *Zong* is beyond dispute. The captain of the ship was Luke Collingwood, previously surgeon of the *William*. Collingwood had made his career in the slave trade. When at home in Liverpool he lived at Highfield Street, [Gore's *Liverpool Directory*, 1777, 1781] with his wife Sarah and a family that included his sons Robert and Luke, aged 9 and 5 in 1780. Collingwood's early years are a mystery. A boy of the same name was apprenticed to Mr Edward Bell, Barber-Surgeon of Newcastle-upon-Tyne, for 7 years in 1722. [P J & R V Wallis, *Eighteenth Century Medics*, 1988][293] This boy became, perhaps, the Luke Collingwood shown in the Medical Register 1783 as a surgeon in nearby Bishop Auckland. But this is unlikely to be the man who commanded the *Zong*, although the similarity in name and profession suggests that they may have been related. This man was old enough to be the father of the captain of the *Zong*.

In his will - made in 1764 - Luke Collingwood named Liverpool as his home and described himself as a surgeon bound on a voyage to sea. He was already married to Sarah and was at least 21 years old by that date, possibly older. Liverpool muster rolls reveal some details of his subsequent career. In 1773–4 he worked on the slave ship *Jane*. Under Captain Hanley he made slaving voyages on board *Gregson*, 1775 and *Ellis*, 1776-77. He subsequently cruised on the privateer *Vulture*, 1779–80, his last voyage before entering *William* in October 1780.

[Collingwood's son Robert followed his father into the family trades, first into medicine and then to the sea. Robert Collingwood was apprenticed for 4 years to Thomas Avison apothecary-surgeon of Liverpool in 1788, with his mother, the widow Collingwood, paying a high permium of £38. Robert died unmarried in 1793. His mother remarried the same year, picking another sailor, Joseph Williamson.]

Collingwod and his crew were not the only Europeans on board the *Zong* when the ship left Africa in August 1781. At least one and perhaps two passengers sailed on the ship. The records of the African Company contain a letter of July 1781 from Cape Coast Castle to Lon-

---

[293] Ed. P J and R V Wallis, *Eighteenth Century Medics*, Project for Historical Biobibliography, 1988.

don, announcing that XYZ,[294] a former employee of the Company and Robert Stubbs, Governor of Annamaboe [Anomabu] until his recall to London, had taken passage on the ship. Stubbs association with the *Zong* has long been known. He was the only person called to give evidence at the trial of *Gregson* v *Gilbert* who could speak about the events that occured on board. He was offered to the Courtl as an honest and impartial witness. That was not correct.

In 1781 when the *Zong* left Africa, Stubbs was 52 years old, perhaps a little older. At the hearing in the King's Bench in Westminster Hall, Lord Mansfield said that Stubbs had described himself as "bred to the Sea, that he was upwards of Forty years in the Service [and] that he was afterwards appointed to the Government of Annamabo". Counsel for the owners of the *Zong* summarised Stubbs' evidence in similar terms, repeating the phrase "bred to the sea" and adding that Captain Stubbs had been "Master of a Man of War & frequently gone in the particular voyage this ship went upon". Since Stubbs' professional opinion of the way the *Zong* had been handled was in issue in the case, his qualifications and experience are unlikely to have been understated. Surviving offical and business records confirm most of these claims, although not quite all. When Stubbs went to sea, the master of a man-of-war was the most senior non-commissioned officer on board and was a specialist navigator. No record of service by Stubbs as a master in the British Navy has been traced. But there is no doubt at all that he had a long career as a mariner, merchant and slave trader. His experience on merchants ships would have qualified him for appointment as master of a smaller vessel, so that it is possible that he did serve for a short time in the Navy. The words bred to the sea were a claim to the special virtue thought in the eighteenth century to attach to someone who had mastered a trade after following it from an early age and who could be expected to know it from top to bottom. It was not unusual for boys as young as eight years old to go to sea, but most began later, between the age of eleven and fifteen. Before that, Stubbs must have had some formal schooling; he could read, write and understand trading accounts. It is possible that he served an apprenticeship, but this was not a practice followed by all those who became master mariners. Many captains of merchant ships in Stubbs' time had not done so, picking up their training while working on board, occasionally supplementing practical experience with

---

[294] Ed. Professor Dockray may have inserted the letters "XYZ" as a marker to be filled in later, or the name may be omitted in the original.

instruction on shore in mathematics or navigation. Stubbs was born in 1728 or 1729. His claim to more than forty years experience suggests that he began his career around 1740 at the age of 11 or 12.

The earliest public record of him on a merchant ship dates November 1753, when in his own words, he entered himself as Chief Mate on board the slave ship *Black Joke*, a snow of 120 tons. The record of this employment has survived because the voyage resulted in an arbitration at Garraways Coffee House and then an acrimonious court case between the captain and the ship's owners in which Stubbs was required to give evidence. The voyage began in London in November 1753 and took much longer than the planned 9-15 months, with the ship calling at places as far apart as Sierra Leone, Cape Mount, Cape Coast Castle, Anamaboe, Tantum Querry, the River Cameroon, River Caboon and Nazareth. [PRO E 207/153/1: E 133/18/ 48 and 49] The defendants to the action *Barton v Cooper* in the Court of Exchequer were John Cooper, Sherman Godfrey, Henry Savage, Charles Fowlis, John Potts, Joseph Bird, John Greaves, John Pickett, Richard Gammon, George Challenor, Ebenezer Blackwell, James Farmer, Edward Page, James Johnson, Isaac Worth and Samuel Hough. Stubbs deposition in the case was eventually suppressed on the grounds that proper notice of his examination had not been given to Barton. Stubbs himself left the ship on the Gold Coast in April 1755.

Black Joke eventually returned to London with some of its original cargo still unsold in November 1755. Stubbs sea-going career continued in the spring of 1756 when he rejoined *Black Joke* as master, and sailed from London with instructions to carry slaves from Gambia to Barbados.

The next year, records from the Seven Years' War show him in command of a small vessel - the *Supply* - owned by John Biggin, a Billingsgate coal merchant and a transport contractor to the British government. Stubbs' ship was one of a number of vessels chartered to the Commissioners of Victualling. His particular task was to carry beef to Stade on the river Elbe for delivery to allied troops. By February 1758 Stubbs was back in London, [PRO ADM 7/90; E 133/18/49] this time as captain on board the ship *Anthony* - the property of the London-based merchant Anthony Bacon - planning a voyage to Virginia. Stubbs returned to Senegambia in the snow *Senegal* in 1760. This voyage was disrupted when the snow was first captured and then ransomed by a French privateer. Stubbs was back in Senegambia in 1761, in *Friendship*, 100 tons. On both occasions he was employed by Biggin and Bacon, who held the victualling contract for the garisons in the area. The Friendship's cargo was recorded as including flour, bread, pease and a massive quantity of 3,000 gallons of vinegar. [T413/116–117] At the time these voyages were made, the French forts and settlements on the great Senegal river had fallen under British control. At a low point in the Seven Years War, members of the African Company managed to persuade the British government to mount a speculative expedition to the region. A tiny naval squadron, assisted by 4 or 5 private ships fitted out by the trade, arrived in April 1758 at the bar at the mouth of the river. The bar, a major obstacle to navigation, was the only real defence for the the key French post of Fort St Louis. When the attackers managed to haul vessels across the obstruction under fire, Fort St Louis promptly capitulated and Britain became for a few years the dominant European power on the river.

Stubbs was certainly at the renamed Fort Lewis again in March 1764, when, as Biggin & Bacon's chief agent in the country he made a journey up river to Podor. The trip up river was regarded as both arduous and a danger to health by English seamen. A supplementary crew of Africans, hired at Fort St Lewis, was commonly regarded as necessary in order to make voyage. The sights to be seen by a traveller on this journey were recorded in lyrical terms by M Adanson in *Voyage to Senegal* (1749)[295] who noted "most beautiful tamarisks, red gum-trees, and several sorts of thorny acacias ... The rich soil of this country is a great encouragement to gardening." Elephants, birds, crocodiles, sea-horses (hippopotami) and "an infinite multitude of other very extraordinary animals" were enthusisatically viewed. Stubbs probably paid more attention to navigation than to the fauna, although the gum trees might have taken his interest. Gum arabic was one of the important products of the region and a vital and expensive commodity for London's silk industry. Before the attack on Fort Lewis the gum had to be acquired from the French indirectly, via Dutch intermediaries. Capture of an important source of the commodity was one of the main objects of the 1758 expedition.

Stubbs' trip to Podor resulted in a bad-tempered dispute with the commander of Fort Lewis. Accused of attempting to monopolize trade at Podor by excluding other English merchants, Stubbs counter-attacked and complained to his prinpcipals that he was being obstructed. The rights and wrongs of this affair, distorted by the slow and formal

[295] Ed. Michel Adanson, *A Voyage to Senegal, the Isle of Goree, and the River Gambia... Translated from the French [i.e. from the "Histoire naturelle du Sénégal"]. With notes by an English gentleman, who resided some time in that country.* [With a map.] London, J Nourse & W Johnston [sic], 1759.

correspondence with London, cannot now be easily untangled. Nevertheless, the Commander's distaste for Stubbs is unmistakeable: "...a person whose universal character is so very indifferent." Although he described himself as a mariner to the end of his life, Stubbs appears to have left the sea after the trip to Podor and to have established himself as a merchant in London. He became a freeman of the African Company in 1765 and appears as a ship owner in the records of the slave trade for the first time in that year, when he dispatched the *Union* to Bonny. This venture, in partnership with another London merchant, carried 165 slaves to Jamaica. The following year, Stubbs dispatched the same vessel to Bonny, this time carrying 200 slaves to Antigua. Records confirm his ownership of just one more slave ship, the *Mary* (or *Mary & Samuel*) which sailed for Senegal in 1770 and carried 100 slaves to Maryland.

This is virtually all that is known for certain about Stubbs' slave trading activities before 1780 when he arrived on the Gold Coast as Governor of Annomabo. He may nevertheless have been involved in other ventures. The records of ownership of London slave ships in the second half of the eighteeth century are far from complete and, in any event, English slave traders in Senegal - the centre of Stubbs' trading interests - are known to have made use of French vessels, so that it is quite possible that Stubbs was involved in other slaving voyages; he is shown in London directories trading from premises near the River Thames during the whole of the period between 1767 and 1780.

Stubbs' first recorded business address was Belvidere Yard on Narrow Wall, Lambeth, a site on the south bank of the River, downstream of Westminster Bridge. Narrow Wall was at one time the name given to the marsh wall that separated drier ground from the marginal land on the bank of the River. In Stubbs' day it referred to a road that followed the line of the medieval wall. Belvidere House was a substantial old building. In the 1720s it had been used for a time as a pleasure garden: "Charles Bascom is now settled in the house called Belvidere, upon the river, over against York Buildings. He sells all sorts of wines and accomodates guests with eatables of every kind in season, especially the choicest riverfish." [Ducarel, Lambeth][296] But by the time Stubbs came to occupy Belvidere Yard, the neighbourhood had changed and the old marshland between Narrow Wall and the River was mostly

---

[296] Ed. See Andrew Coltee Ducarel (1713–1785), *Historical Particulars of Lambeth Parish and Lambeth Palace in addition to the histories by Dr. Ducarel in the Bibliotheca Topographica Britannica*, By S Denne, London, 1790. (Miscellaneous Antiquities. No. 5. 1791, etc.) 1780, etc.

occupied by wharves, timber and stone yards. Inland, contemporary maps show a ribbon of buildings along Narrow Wall and to the south, the site of the notorious Cuper's Gardens pleasure grounds which had closed a year or two earlier.

The approach to Waterloo Bridge covers the site today. Near at hand were some well-known manufacturing enterprises, including the famous Coade Stone factory and the celebrated Vinegar Manufactory owned by Mr Mark Beaufoy, a notable supporter of the campaign to abolish slavery.[297]

In eighteenth century London, as in other major English ports, slave traders and abolitionists were near neighbours. This was an area that Stubbs must have known well in 1765. His long-time employer John Biggin had traded from Belvidere Yard in earlier years. [Kent's *Directory*, 1761; *Complete Compting House Companion*, 1763] Stubbs almost certainly rented these premises from Biggin and may well have taken over the Senegal victualling contract in which Biggin had been interested. Stubbs traded from and may have lived at Belvidere Yard for the remainder of the decade. Four of his children - Thomas, 1765, George, 1768, Frances, 1769 and Henry, 1770 - were baptised in the parish church, St Mary at Lambeth, at the other end of Narrow Wall, under the walls of Lambeth Palace. He seems to have remained in the parish until 1771, when he left Belvidere Yard and moved to Wapping, probably as a result of temporary insolvency. [B 4/21] But he must have settled with creditors quickly.

In the spring of 1772 he embarked on a new career when he obtained a licence to act as a broker in the City of London, most probably acting as a middleman in matching ships, cargoes and customers, as well as trading on his own behalf from substantial premises in Mill Street, St Saviour's Dock, a site downstream from London Bridge on the Bermondsey side of the River. St Saviour's Dock is today a fashionable residential area. In 1772 it was mixed neighbourhood with tradesmen, sea captain and craftsmen occupying small houses abutting the wharves and warehouses. Coal, stone and grain merchants dominated the water frontage, with surrounding streets filled with the nauseous stench of fellmongers, leather dressers and tan yards. Stubbs remained in Mill Street until the end of the decade, although towards the end of this period he also traded from addresses north of the River, at 24

[297] Ed. Mark Beaufoy (1718–1782). He was the father of Mark Beaufoy (1764–1827), astronomer and physicist: Anita McConnell, 'Beaufoy, Mark (1764–1827)', ODNB, 2004; online edn, January 2008 [http://www.oxforddnb.com/view/article/1866], accessed 30 April 2016.

Bishopsgate and at the Senegal Coffee House, Cornhill, in the City of London. Not much is known about the Senegal, but its name, the interests of merchants who used it in the 1770s and its location close to the famous Jamaica Coffee House, suggest that it was one of the centres in London for West African and slave traders. Stubbs' connection with these places came to an end in 1779 when he gave up his broking and trading businesses and accepted a post with the African Company on the Gold Coast.

The lease of his Bermondsey premises was assigned, the broking licence surrendered and Stubbs sailed for the Coast in December 1779, accompanied by his son George, then just twelve years old. The reason Stubbs' sought this move are obscure. Possibly his businesses in London had been affected by the American war, although the new salary of £300 a year, with the prospect of making more by personal trading and through his contacts in London may have been sufficient inducement. But whatever the reason, he now became one of the most important of the Company's servants in Africa, holding the posts of Governor of Annamaboe and Vice-President of the Council at Cape Coast. On board the Company's annual storeship for the voyage to Cape Coast Castle, he joined a group of men sent out by the Company to take over the key posts on the Coast and to investigate complaints made against the previous incumbents. [T70/1544] Stubbs managed to retain his own posts for less than a year. Complaints about his conduct began to be sent back to London almost from the moment the storeship arrived at Cape Coast Castle in March 1780. Refusing to undertake any public business, he was active only in his own interest, concentrated all trade in his own hands and excluding both independent traders and the other officers of the Company from any dealings with the captains of the ships that called at the Fort. He quarrelled with everyone; the President and Council, his deputies at Annamaboe and the residents of his town, who put Fetish on the Fort Gate, blocked the entrances and sent messengers to Cape Coast Castle asking for Stubbs to be removed. In the end, irritated by his greed and insolence and fearful of his malice, Stubbs was suspended from office early in 1781 by the President and the Council of Cape Coast.

On 26 January, in the 18th century version of a dawn raid, a Council member and the officer commanding the garrison at Cape Coast Castle arrived at the Fort at Annamaboe at 5.30 am. Suspecting that they might be met with violence, they entered the Fort with a peaceful request for breakfast and then suddenly drew pistols. With the support of 15 canoemen armed with knives, they seized Stubbs who, on his own evidence, was then dragged naked from the Fort and deposited on the beach below the high water mark where they "very indecently exposed me, holding my hands and feet for some time amongst a vast number of Black people both Men and Women, and pulled and bruised me violently; they then ordered me into the Fort again, dragging me on the ground as before by my hands and feet..." [BT6/14] Released later that day, Stubbs fled to safety on board the *William*, then anchored in the roads. Even by the sordid standards of the African Company, Stubbs' ritual degradation was unusual. But looked at in the context of Stubbs' vicious career, it was simply a more [dramatic] incident in an old pattern. Stubbs was a person of no particular importance before he stepped aboard the *Zong* in 1781. The reason that so much information about his earlier career can be found in public records, is that so many of the chapters in his life ended in controversy or disaster. In Stubbs' hands, even the simplest things could be sent awry. The routine carriage of a small cargo of beef to Stade in 1757 led to a dispute about two missing casks which disappeared while in Stubbs' care. Years after his own death, the lease of his Bermondsey premises was challenged by his landlord's successors, who clearly suspected that to secure a low rent, Stubbs had made an under-the-counter payment, to their prejudice. Even the voyage out from London to Cape Coast Castle ended in rancour. Stubbs accused another of the Company's servants of destroying the ship's stores and later, of having been a pimp in a bawdy house, of endeavouring to raise a mutiny and of going with Governor Roberts "on the Highway robbing together." Writing later to London about the vexations of the voyage, Captain Lewellin reported to London "My opinion of Mr Stubbs is, that he is a Wicked and Treacherous Character". [T70/1695] None of this information, of course, was given to the Court of King's Bench when the action of Gregson v Gilbert was tried.

[Robert Stubbs died in 1787, His will - dated 13 October in the year - was made at Dartmouth Hill, near Blackheath and was witnessed by two neighbours, Robert Tillot (probably his landlord) and Thomas Walker. [Lewisham Local Archives: Land Tax Records 1787, 1788] Stubbs left one shilling to each of his five children "I do not leave them more because I have expended large sums of money in their maintenance and education". The residue of his estate was left to wife Mary and younger sons George and Henry. Unkown to his father, George had died a few months earlier in Africa. The boy, then 13, had been left behind at Cape Coast Castle when Stubbs sailed away on the *Zong*: after holding a number of appointments with the African Company, at his death aged 19, George commanded the trading fort of Commenda.]

Minor Cases

De Grey Opinion

NYHS Granville Sharp Collection.

[1]

Opinion of Mr Attorney General De Grey[298] (now Lord Chief Justice of the Common Pleas)

Mr Storer might have an Interest by Contract in the Service of this Female Slave. But no property in her person by the Law of this Country. And therefore no authority to direct Swetman to carry her away.

The Husband had a right by Marriage according to the Laws of this Country to that Relation, and Mr Storer having no property in her Person could have none by the Marriage.

(Copy)

---

[298] Ed. The opinion is undated, but William de Grey became attorney general in August 1766 and was appointed lord chief justice of the Common Pleas at the end of 1770; Gordon Goodwin, 'Grey, William de, first Baron Walsingham (1719–1781)', rev M J Mercer, ODNB, 2004 [http://www.oxforddnb.com/view/article/11571], accessed 17 April 2015.

Cay v Crichton

NYHS Sharp MS.

[1]

Case

Prerogative Court, May 11th. 1773

Cay and Crichton

A. B. Deceased, in 1769, among other effects, left behind him a Negro Servant. Crichton the Executor, was called upon by Cay to give in an Inventory of the Deceased[']s Goods and Chattels, which he accordingly did, but omitted the Negro. This Omission was made the ground of exception to the Inventory, as being therefore not perfect. Upon Argument, it was said by the Counsel on behalf of Crichton, that, by a very late Case in the King's Bench of Knowles (or more properly Stewart)[299] and Somerset, Negroes were declared to be free in England, and consequently, they could not be the subject of Property, or be considered as any part of a personal Estate.

It was answered, that the Cause above mentioned was determined only in 1772; that A. B. died in 1769, at [2] which time Negroes were, in some respects considered as Property, and therefore that he ought to have been included in the Account.

The Judge (Dr. Hay)[300] said, that this court had no right to try any Question relating to Freedom or Slavery; but as Negroes had been declared free by the Court which had the proper Jurisdiction, that determination referred to them, as well at the preceding time, as at the present; and therefore directed, that Article, in which the Negroe was mentioned to be stuck out of the Exceptive Allegation.

---

[299] Ed. The words in brackets are inserted above the line.

[300] Ed. Sir George Hay (25 January 1715–6 October 1778); Matthew Kilburn, 'Hay, Sir George (1715–1778)', ODNB, 2004 [http://www.oxforddnb.com/view/article/12719], accessed 16 April 2015.

Hylas v Newton[301]

York Minster Library COLL 1896/1
Granville Sharp Letter Books

[11]

A Short Report of[302]
A Trial before Lord Chief Justice Wilmot in the Court of Common Pleas on Saturday 3d December 1768

Thomas John Hylas... Plaintiff
John Newton Esqr... Defendant

The Affair was stated for the Determination of the Court as follows. "Plaintiff and his Wife Mary were Negro Slaves Born in Barbadoes[.] the Plaintiff was the property of Miss Judith Aleyne,[303] the Wife was the property of Mrs Newton[,] Wife of the Defendant[.] They so being Slaves, were brought over by their several Masters and Mistresses in the Year 1754[.] they were married by consent of Miss Aleyne and Mr Newton in the Year 1758. In the Year — the Plaintiff left [the] Family with the consent of Mrs Newton[304] and in the Year 1766 they sent away the Plaintiff[']s Wife Mary without his consent; upon the whole if the Court should be of Opinion that she did not continue the Negro Servant of the Defendant, they will find a Verdict for the Plaintiff and one Shilling Damages"[.]

---

[301] Ed. See also Gerzina, *Black England*, pp 76–78; Katherine Paugh, in her article "The Curious Case of Mary Hylas: Wives, Slaves and the Limits of British Abolitionism" (2014) 35:4 *Slavery & Abolition: A Journal of Slave and Post-Slave Studies* 629–651, rather oddly equates, without argument, marriage, or at least marriage in the eighteenth century, with slavery and argues that the judge was guilty of hypocrisy in denying the claim of the master to remove Mary from England against her will by reason of her marriage.

[302] Ed. The words "A Short Report of" are inserted above the line. A note in the top left margin states that "The Whole Trial at length by the short Hand Writer is in another volume". This has not so far been traced.

[303] Ed. Usually spelled "Alleyne".

[304] G#. Memdm. He was soon afterwards commanded to return again but he refused to comply and Mr. Newton found that he had no power to compell him in this Country and when Mr. Newton brought an Action against Mr. Hone whose servant Hylas then was, he was desired by Sir Fletcher Norton to drop it.

The Jury brought in their Verdict for the Plaintiff with one shilling [12] Damages, as directed by the Court.

Thus the Plaintiff[']s right to his own Liberty as well as that of his Wife is established by this Determination; and also that Damages are due in such a case; but it requires a further Explanation why the Damages were set so low.

By the advice of the Plaintiffs Council [sic] the action was brought merely for damages whereas it ought to have been laid for the Recovery of his Wife from Slavery in Barbadoes as well as Damages.

The Defendants Council were so sensible of this Error, that they did not fail to turn it to the advantage of their Client.

Sir Fletcher Norton[305] first Council for the Defendant even in his opening of the Trial observed the omission, and insinuated that the Plaintiff did not want to have his Wife again, as he had asked for nothing but Damages, and consequently that the taking her away was no great loss to him "Therefore (says he) we will meet you half way: if you will give up your Action for damages, we will restore the Woman to the Plaintiff."

This was a manifest acknowledgement of Sir F. N. that the Plaintiff had a right to considerable Damages and consequently to his Wife [13] and that the restoring the Woman, on the Condition above mentioned, was the only means the Defendant had to avail himself of the Error on the Plaintiff[']s Council in bringing the Action merely for damages.

(Copy)

---

[305] Ed. Philip Laundy, 'Norton, Fletcher, first Baron Grantley (1716–1789)', ODNB, 2004; online edn, May 2006 [http://www.oxforddnb.com/view/article/20342], accessed 3 May 2015.

Sharp's Remarks on Hylas v Newton

York Minster Library COLL1896/1

[14]

Some Remarks on the Case of John Hylas and his Wife Mary.

The freedom of John Hylas is indisputable, even though it should be admitted that the Villenage Doctrines are still Law and that the West India Slavery is justly entitled to succeed it and to be established upon that obsolete foundation.

Hylas lived more than a Year and a day in a free State without being claimed; by which circumstance alone he is certainly enfranchised; tho' there are several other circumstances besides, which seperately [sic], would have been amply sufficient for that purpose. The effect of these circumstances is proved and confirmed by the subsequent proceedings of the Master who lately pleaded by his Council [sic] to Hylas's Action in a Court of Record, without demanding him as his property. Hylas therefore, being free, his Wife must necessarily be allowed to be free also; "for that his Wife and he be one person (*Vir et Uxor sunt quasi Unica persona quia caro una Sanguinis unus.* Bracton Lib. 5 p. 416) in the Law" Lit. Lib 2 p. 112) [15]

Sir John Fortesue in the 42 Chapter of the Book (*de laudibus legum*) quotes our Lord[']s Words in the Gospel to this purpose "*Jam non sunt duo, sed una caro.*"[306] Upon which he thus reasons, "*et cum masculinum concipiat fæmininum, ad masculinum quod dignius est, referri debet tota caro sic facta una.&c.*"[307]

So that it is most certainly true, that the Woman follows the condition of her Husband, and if he be free, so must She likewise.

It must therefore appear that Mr Newton has forcibly carried away and Transported, contrary to Laws of God and Man, a Free Woman

---

[306] Ed. "They are no more twain but one flesh." Quoted by Fortescue, *De Laudibus Legum Angliæ*. The translation into English published A.D. MDCCLXXV (1775) and the original Latin text, with notes by A Amos, Cambridge, printed by J Smith, printer to the University; Cambridge, 1825, ch 42. Cincinnati, 1874, Legal Classics Library reprint, 1984, p 161.

[307] Ed. "And forasmuch as the male comprehends the female, the whole flesh, so made one, ought rather to regard and to be referred to the male, as the more worthy." Ibid.

the Wife of a Free Man, at a time when She was Resident in this Kingdom, and consequently, a subject. He is therefore certainly liable to all Penalties of the Habeas Corpus [Act][308] against such flagrant offences, and if the Courts of Law do not adjudge those penalties against him, I know not how they can be excused from the charge of doing a manifest injustice to Hylas, who is as much entitled to £500 Damages at the least besides treble Costs, by this Act of Parliament, as the first Lawyer of the Kingdom would be, if he should lose his Wife in the same manner. Howsoever the proposition may be received. I flatter myself that, It cannot be easily or, at least, justly be rejected, if what I have wrote elsewhere upon the Habeas Corpus Act, thoroughly weighed and considered. [16]

On the other hand perhaps it may be said, that Mr Newton is entitled at least to the Value of his former Slave, and may sue the husband for the same; according to the Doctrine of Sir John Fortescue, in a similar Case, when a Freeman married a Neif, (Naif) or Native - *"recuperabit versus liberum ilium* (says he) *omne damnum quodipse sustinuit ratione deperdite Servitii, et amissæ Ancillæ."*[309]

But even if it should be admitted that this is Law at present as Sir John Fortescue says *"Summa et forma Legis Anglia in casu jam enarrato* fo. 103"[310] (though I hope I have clearly shewn elsewhere that all such Doctrines are obsolete) Yet Mr Newton should consider that the utmost Damages, which can reasonably be allowed him for the Loss of his Female Slave will not exceed £30, if he is allowed so much, for I heard of a Young Woman, who was offered for sale at £20 which is very inconsiderable when compared with the Damages due from himself to Hylas, according to the Habeas Corpus Act.

But it may also be said, perhaps, that Hylas cannot prosecute upon the Act because it is near 3 Years ago, since the offence of Transporting his Wife was committed, whereas the prosecution according to the Act must be within 2 Years.

Nevertheless it must be remembered that the Offence against the Act [17] continues as long as the Wife is retained in Slavery, and that the husband, therefore, may with propriety bring his Action according

---

[308] Ed. Habeas Corpus Act 1679, 31 Car II c 2, s 12.

[309] Ed. *"recuperabit versus Liberum ilium omne Damnum quod ipse sustinuit Ratione deperditi Servitii, et amissæ Ancillæ."* "Yet he shall recover against the free-man all his damages which he hath sustained by reason of the loss of his bond-woman" Fortescue, Ibid, p 163.

[310] Ed. *"Summa et Forma Legis Angliæ, in Casu jam enarrato."* Ibid, p 253. "the sum substance and manner of proceeding according to the laws of England, in the case now declared." Fortescue, ibid p 163.

to the said Act, even seven Years hence, or as long after that time as his Wife should remain under that unlawful confinement beyond the Seas; provided that it was not in his power, for want of Money or Friends, to demand her sooner, or for any other reasonable cause, as that he durst not for fear of the Master; lest he himself should likewise be trepanned[311] and Transported.

But the present opinion and inclination of our Courts is, it seems, with respect to the Habeas Corpus Act, and the West India Slavery is supposed to be very different from what I have here laid down.

Yet I have never been able to trace out a sufficient reason for this, neither have I ever met with any person that could.

This supposed Opinion, therefore, is rather to be esteemed a general prejudice that a proper Authority, and so ought not to avail in the least, unless Reason (I mean legal Reason warranted by Authority of Law) prevails also.

It was on Account of this supposed Opinion (I presume) that Hylas's Council thought themselves obliged to bring the Action for Damages alone, who it seems, ought to have been principally, for the recovery of the Wife. [18] So that this same supposed opinion has occasioned a manifest Injury to Hylas, which in the end must appear very unworthy of the Courts.

The poor Man indeed was asked in Court, whether he would have his wife or Damages? He replyed he desired to have his Wife.

But why this cruel alternative? If he had a right to his Wife (which cannot be denied) he most certainly had a right to Damages also, in consideration of the Violent and unpardonable outrage committed against himself in the person of his Wife, for which no pecuniary allowance whatsoever can really make him amends, at least I should think so, was the case my own.

It was nevertheless, insinuated in court, that Hylas had not much regard for his Wife; that he rather wished for Damages, than to recover the person (though the event proved otherwise) and therefore that the Damages should be proportioned to the loss which might appear to be sustained.

But this is a new Doctrine as repugnant to the Law of God as to the common Law of this Kingdom, for according to both [of] these, a Man and his Wife are considered as One, that is, One flesh, which I have already shewn.

---

[311] Ed. In the sense of to catch in a trap; to entrap, ensnare, beguile. OED.

Now they are either One flesh, or they are not so, for no third Person whatsoever has any right to define a Medium, either with respect to their [19] conjugal Relationship, or their mutual affection. The Law must ever suppose that both these are intire; especially when sufficient Proofs of a lawfull Marriage are not wanting, and the Parties themselves do not sue for a Separation.

It is therefore very plain and clear that Heylas as a husband has a right to his Wife by the Laws of God and Man and as a subject of England has a right likewise to very considerable Damages as well by the Habeas Corpus Act as by the common Law and common Justice.

Nevertheless before the Cause was opened, near even during the time that the Clerk was tendering the Oath to the Jury Sir Fletcher Norton came into Court and acquainted the judge, that now the great important Question concerning the right of retaining Slaves in England was likely to come before his Lordship, signifying at the same time that it is a point of great difficulty, and that a judicial determination much to be wished for, or to that purpose &c.

Sir Fletcher likewise observed afterwards, that there is now in Town upwards of 20,000 Negroes - I could have told him that there would soon be 20,000 more, the important and difficult point, as he calls it, was to [20] be determined on his side of the Question, whereas if it was clearly proved on the other hand that Negroes become free on their landing in England, it is very certain that their West Indian Masters who are so tenacious of this kind of property would for the most part be prevented thereby from bringing them.

Now it may safely be allowed that the cause which Sir Fletcher espoused (Vizt. the right or rather wrong, which the West Indian claims as his prerogative forcibly to Transport a Person out of the Kingdom) is "a point of real difficulty". It is so difficult, indeed, that it cannot possibly be admitted, until some Valuable Statutes are Annulled by proper Authority; and until the common Law and custom of this Realm is totally changed; which time, I hope we shall never see.

The Slaveholder[']s Council must first of all convince the whole Legislature, King, Lords, and Commons, that some singular benefits will arise to the Community if they will condescend to give a Sanction to such flagrant Breaches of the Peace as that particular transaction, which was then before the Court.

But it will be still more difficult for the Slaveholder[']s Council to find just Arguments for this purpose; though one of them burst into a [21] loud contemptuous laughter at the very mention of damages for such an outrage.

How far this kind of Eloquence (in which that Gentleman seemed so happily to excell) might influence or prejudice the Judgment of his hearers I know not; but sure I am, that such a method has no more connection with sound and just Reasoning, than it has with good manners.

But to return to the Important Question. One of the Slaverholder[']s Council wished that it might now be determined.

He could not mean, I think, that he wished it to be determined in favour of the oppressed, because that is sufficiently determined already, as well by the common Law and custom of England (which is always favourable to Liberty) and the Freedom of a Man from Imprisonment, as by the 12th Section of the Habeas Corpus Act which expressly determines the point "that no subject of this Kingdom of England Dominion of Wales or Town of Berwick upon Tweed shall be sent Prisoner into Scotland &c. or into Ports, Garrisons Islands or places beyond the Seas and that every such Imprisonment is hereby enacted and adjudged to be illegal &c." [22]

So that really there is not any difficulty at all in the Question notwithstanding that I have heard some very grave and learned Lawyers affirm the contrary to my great astonishment and mortification.

But none[,] neither [of] those Gentlemen I speak of, have as yet made it appear that there is anything so commendable or worthy of imitation in the West India Slavery, that it deserves to be admitted also into this Kingdom.

The Information of the Gentlemen of Barbadoes on the late Tryal may perhaps point out to them the prodigious convenience of such Laws to Men who have lost all sense of Humanity; But they will not be able to demonstrate that the least advantage will arise thereby to any other sort of people whatsoever.

And therefore I hope they will no longer persist in defending so bad a cause, least they should bring upon themselves also the charge of Inhumanity according to the maxim of the great Chancellor Fortescue *"Impius et Crudelis Judicandus est qui Libertati non favet"*.[312]

(Copy)

---

[312] Ed. "He is to be adjudged impious and cruel who does not favour liberty." Co Lit 124 citing Fortescue c 42; Fortescue, ibid, p 162. Fortescue has: *"Quo impius et crudelis judicandus est, qui libertati non favet"*. Fortescue, *De Laudibus...* trans Gregor and Amos, Cincinnati, 1874, Legal Classics Library reprint, 1984, p 276.

Legislation

Habeas Corpus Act 1679

11. And for preventing illegal Imprisonments in Prisons beyond the Seas; Be it further enacted by the Authority aforesaid, That no Subject of this Realm that now is, or hereafter shall be an Inhabitant or Resiant of this Kingdom of England, Dominion of Wales, or Town of Berwick upon Tweed, shall or may be sent Prisoner into Scotland, Ireland, Jersey, Guernsey, Tangier, or into Parts, Garrisons, Islands or Places beyond the Seas, which are or at any time hereafter shall be within or without the Dominions of his Majesty, his Heirs or Successors; and that every such Imprisonment is hereby enacted and adjudged to be illegal; and that if any of the said Subjects now is or hereafter shall be so imprisoned, every such Person and Persons so imprisoned, shall and may for every such Imprisonment maintain by virtue of this Act an Action or Actions of False Imprisonment, in any of his Majesty's Courts of Record, against the Person or Persons by whom he or she shall be so committed, detained, imprisoned, sent Prisoner or transported, contrary to the true Meaning of this Act, and against all or any Person or Persons that shall frame, contrive, write, seal or countersign any Warrant or Writing for such Commitment, Detainer, Imprisonment or Transportation, or shall be advising, aiding or assisting in the same, or any of them; and the Plaintiff in every such Action shall have Judgment to recover his treble Costs, besides Damages, which Damages so to be given, shall not be less than five hundred Pounds; in which Action no Delay, Stay or Stop of Proceeding by Rule, Order or Command, nor no Injunction, Protection or Privilege whatsoever, nor any more than one Imparlance shall be allowed, excepting such Rule of the Court wherein the Action shall depend, made in open Court, as shall be thought in Justice necessary, for special Cause to be expressed in the said Rule; and the Person or Persons who shall knowingly frame, contrive, write, seal or countersign any Warrant for such Commitment, Detainer or Transportation, or shall so commit, detain, imprison or transport any Person or Persons contrary to this Act, or be any ways advising, aiding or assisting therein being lawfully convicted thereof, shall be disabled from thenceforth to bear any Office of Trust or Profit within the said Realm of England, Dominion of Wales,

or Town of Berwick upon Tweed, or any of the Islands, Territories or Dominions thereunto belonging; and shall incur and sustain the Pains, Penalties and Forfeitures limited, ordained and provided in and by the Statute of Provision and Proemunire made in the sixteenth Year of King Richard the Second; and be incapable of any Pardon from the King, his Heirs or Successors, of the said Forfeitures, Losses or Disabilities, or any of them.

12. Provided always, That nothing in this Act shall extend to give Benefit to any Person who shall by Contract in Writing agree with any Merchant or Owner of any Plantation, or other Person whatsoever, to be transported to any Parts beyond the Seas, and receive Earnest upon such Agreement, although that afterwards such Person shall renounce such Contract.

Act of Scottish Parliament, 1701 c 6

(Criminal Procedure Act 1701,
Short title given by the
Statute Law Revision (Scotland) Act 1964 (c 80), Sch. 2)

1701 c 6... And His Majestie with advice and consent forsaid farder Statutes and Ordains that upon application of any prisoner for Custody in order to tryal whither for capital or bailable Crimes to any of the Lords of Justiciary or other Judge or Judicatory competent for judgeing the crime or offence for which he is imprisoned and the said prisoner his produceing the said double of the warrand of his imprisonment under the Keepers hand the said Judge or Judicatory competent... are hereby Ordained within twenty four hours after the said application and petition is presented to him or them to give out letters or precepts direct to messengers for intimating to his Majesties Advocat or Procurator fiscall and party appearing by the warrand to be concerned if any be within the Kingdom to fix a dyet for the tryal within sixty dayes after the intimation Certifieing his Majesties Advocat or Procurator fiscall and the said party concerned that if they failyie the prisoner shall be discharged and set at liberty without delay For doing whereof the said Judge or Judicatory competent are hereby expressly warranted and strictly required and ordained to do the same... unless the delay be upon the prisoners petition or desire And the dyet of the tryal being prefixed the Magistrats of the place or Keeper of the prison shall then be oblidged to deliver the prisoner to a sufficient guard to be provided by the Judge his Majesties Advocat or Procurator fiscal that the prisoner may be sisted before the Judge competent And his Majesties Advocat or Procurator fiscal shall insist in the lybell and the Judge put the same to a tryal and the same shall be determined by a final sentence within fourty dayes if before the Lords of Justiciary and thirty dayes if before any other Judge And if his Majesties Advocat or Procurator fiscal do not insist in the tryal at the day appointed and prosecute the same to the conclusion as aforsaid His Majestie with advice forsaid Statutes and Ordains that the dyet shall then be simpliciter deserted and the prisoner immediately liberat from his imprisonment for that crime or offence And if no process be raised and execute within the time allowed or in case of not insisting at the dyet and bringing the process to a conclusion within the forsaid space it shall be lawful to the prisoner to apply to the Justice General Justice Clerk or any of the Lords of Justiciary or Judge competent respective And upon his application and instructing that the limited time by law for insisting or concludeing the process is elapsed and Instruments taken thereupon the said Justice General Justice Clerk Lords of Justiciary and Judge competent shall be oblidged within twenty four hours to issue out Letters or precepts direct to Messengers for chargeing the Magistrats or keepers of the prison where the prisoner is detained for setting him at liberty... And the prisoner being liberat in manner forsaid it shall not be lawfull to put or detain him in prison for the same Crime... Provideing allwayes that in case of imprisonment for treason the prisoner shall not have access to apply for prefixing of a dyet for process for fourty dayes after his imprisonment which are hereby allowed for prepareing of the process After elapseing of which time the... Lords of Justiciary or any one of them are hereby required upon the application of the prisoner to issue furth precepts as in other cases And in case of not insisting or prosecuteing the process as aforesaid the prisoner shall be liberat upon sufficient baill to Compear at any time when called within twelve moneths for his good and peaceable behaviour in the mean time the said baill not exceeding the double of the baill in other crimes... And farder Discharges all closs imprisonments beyond the space of Eight dayes from the commitment... and his Majestie with advice and consent foresaid Enacts and Declares that action and process for wrongous imprisonment shall prescribe if not pursued within three years after the last day of the wrongous imprisonment And process being once raised the same shall prescribe if not insisted in yearly thereafter...

Slave Trade Act, 1788

(Sir William Dolben's Act[313])

28 Geo 3, c 54

An Act to regulate, for a limited Time [one year], the shipping and carrying Slaves in British Vessels from the Coast of Africa.

12. No Insurance to be made against any Loss, except the Perils of the Sea, &c.

And be it further enacted by the Authority aforesaid, That from and after the first Day of August one thousand seven hundred and eighty-eight, it shall not be lawful for any Owner or Owners of any such Ship or Vessel to insure any Cargo of Slaves, or any Part thereof, on board the same, against any Loss or Damage, save and except the Perils of the Sea, Piracy, Insurrection, or Capture by the King's Enemies, Barratry of the Master and Crew, and Destruction by Fire; and that all and every Policy of Insurance, hereafter made contrary to this Act, shall be, and the same is hereby declared to be null and void, to all Intents and Purposes whatsoever.

[Continued by:
Slave Trade Act, 1789, 29 Geo 3, c 54, s 9;
Slave Trade Act, 1790, 30 Geo 3, c 33, s 8;
Slave Trade Act, 1791, 31 Geo 3, c 54, s 8;
Slave Trade Act, 1792, 32 Geo 3, c 52, s 1, earlier Acts recited]

---

[313] Ed. Shyllon, *Black Slaves*, pp 205–207; Sir William Dolben, third baronet (1727–1814), politician and slavery abolitionist, Nigel Aston, 'Dolben, Sir William, third baronet (1727–1814)', ODNB, 2004 [http://www.oxforddnb.com/view/article/7780], accessed 29 December 2015.

Slave Trade Act, 1793

33 Geo 3, c 73

An Act to continue, for a limited Time, and to amend several Acts of Parliament for regulating the Shipping and carrying Slaves in British Vessels from the Coast of Africa.

10. And whereas, by the said Act of the thirty-third Year of his present Majesty's Reign, and the several preceding Acts, it is enacted, that, from and after the first Day of August one thousand seven hundred and ninety-three, it should not be lawful for any Owner or Owners of any Ship or Vessel to insure any Cargo of Slaves, or any Part thereof on board the same, against any Loss or Damage, save and except the Perils of the Sea, Piracy, Insurrection, or Capture by the King's Enemies, Barratry of the Master and Crew, and Destruction by Fire; and that all and every Policy of Insurance thereafter made contrary to the said Act should be, and the same are thereby declared to be null and void to all Intents and Purposes whatsoever: And whereas the Owners of Ships and others concerned in the Trade to Africa, understanding that it was merely intended by the above-mentioned Provision of the said Act, to prescribe and specify the particular Kinds of Loss and Damage for which alone all Indemnity should thereafter be recoverable in respect to Cargoes of Slaves, and not to interfere with or vary the particular Forms of the Policies of Insurance, whereby such Insurances had been theretofore effected, have continued to make Insurances on the Perils and Dangers allowed to be insured by the said Act, in the same general Terms as are contained in the common Policies theretofore used in other Insurances on Ships and Goods: And whereas Doubts have arisen respecting the Validity of such Insurances so made on Cargoes of Slaves, on account of the Policies whereby the same are effected, not being expressly restrained to the particular Peril and Dangers which are by the said Provision of the said Act alone saved and excepted as the Subjects of lawful Insurance: For Remedy whereof, and for the more effectual Security of such Persons, be it therefore enacted, and it is hereby enacted by the Authority aforesaid, That nothing in the said Act, or any former Act contained, shall extend, or be construed to extend, to make void any Insurance already made, or which hereafter shall be made, upon Ships, Slaves, Goods, and Merchandize, in

the same general Terms with the Policies now commonly made use of in all other Insurances on Ships and Goods; (that is to say,) on account of their expressing to be made, against the Risks and Perils of the Seas, Men of War, Fire, Enemies, Pirates, Rovers, Thieves, Jettisons, Letters of Mart and Countermart, Surprisals, Takings at Sea, Arrests, Restraints, and Detainments of Kings, Princes, and People of what Nation, Condition, or Quality soever, Barratry of the Master and Mariners, and of all other Perils, Losses, and Misfortunes that have or shall come to the Detriment or Damage thereof:

Provided nevertheless, That under such Policies of Assurance so made, or to be made, no Loss or Damage shall be hereafter recoverable on account of the Mortality of Slaves by natural Death or ill Treatment, *or against Loss by throwing overboard of Slaves, on any account whatsoever*,[314] or against Loss or Damage by Restraints and Detainments by Kings, Princes, People, or Inhabitants of Africa, where it shall be made appear that such Loss or Damage has been occasioned through any Aggression for the Purpose of procuring Slaves, and committed by the Master of any such Ship, or by any Person or Persons commanding any Boat or Boats, or Party or Parties of Men belonging to any such Ship, or by any Person or Persons acting by the Direction of any such Master or Commander respectively.

Slave Trade Act, 1794, 34 Geo 3 c 80, s 10;
Slave Trade Act, 1795, 35 Geo 3 c 90, s 1;
Slave Trade Act, 1797, 37 Geo 3 c 104, s 1;

Slave Trade Act, 1798

38 Geo 3 c 88

An Act for regulating, until the first Day of August one thousand seven hundred and ninety-nine, the shipping and carrying of Slaves in British Vessels from the Coast of Africa.

25. Clause in former Acts respecting the Certificates of Qualification required to be given by Masters, recited.

---

[314] Ed. Emphasis supplied. The phrase is repeated in the Slave Trade Act, 1794, s 10.

[In other respects the Act is the same as 37 Geo 3. c 104 (Slave Trade Act, 1797).]

And whereas by an Act, passed in the thirty-second Year of the Reign of his present Majesty, and which was afterwards continued by several subsequent Acts, passed in the thirty-third, thirty-fourth, and thirty-fifth Years of his said present Majesty's Reign, it was enacted, That from and after the first Day of August one thousand seven hundred and ninety-two, it shall not be lawful for any Person to become a Master, or take or have the Command or Charge of any such Ship or Vessel, at the Time he shall clear out from any Port of Great Britain, for purchasing and carrying Slaves from the Coast of Africa, unless such Master or Person taking or having the Charge or Command of any such Ship or Vessel, shall have made Oath, and delivered in to the Collector or other Chief Officer of the Customs, at the Port where such Ship or Vessel shall clear out, a Certificate, attested by the respective Owner or Owners, that he has already served in such Capacity during one Voyage, or shall have served as Chief Mate or Surgeon during the Whole of two Voyages, or either as Chief or other Mate during three Voyages, in purchasing and carrying Slaves from the Coast of Africa, under Pain that such Master or other Person taking or having the Charge or Command of any such Ship or Vessel, and also the Owner or Owners who shall hire or employ such Person, shall for every such Offence respectively forfeit and pay the Sum of five hundred Pounds:

And whereas Doubts have arisen respecting the Construction of the above-mentioned Clause, whether the Certificate thereby required to be delivered in to the Collector or other Chief Officer of the Customs, should be attested by the respective Owner or Owners of any Ship or Vessel wherein the Person or Persons then about to take the Command of the Ship or Vessel required to be cleared out, had formerly sailed in some or one of the Capacities by the said Act specified and required, or by the respective Owner or Owners of the Ship or Vessel in which such Person or Persons was or were then about to sail as the Master or Commander thereof, as believing the Facts stated in the Affidavit of such Person or Persons then about to have or take the Charge or Command of any such Ship or Vessel to be true:

And whereas in consequence of such Doubts, the Collectors, or other Chief Officer of the Customs at the Ports of London and Liverpool, doubting the Meaning and Construction of the said Acts, have required and taken Certificates attested in both the Ways before mentioned, and cleared out Ships or Vessels under each Form of Certificate, in consequence of which great Inconveniences have arisen, and Doubts have been made touching the Legality of the Policies of Insurance made upon such Ships or Vessels;

be it therefore further enacted by, the Authority aforesaid, That nothing in the said former Acts of Parliament hereinbefore mentioned, or in any of them contained, shall extend, or be construed to extend, to impeach, invalidate, or make void, any Policy or Policies of Insurance which shall have been made before the passing of this Act, by reason or in consequence of any Certificate or Certificates which have been required and given in order to the clearing out any Ship or Vessel, employed in the Slave Trade, to the Coast of Africa, by the Owner or Owners of the Ship or Vessel then about to clear out and to sail, or by the Owner or Owners of some other Ship or Vessel in whose Employ the Person then about to sail had been formerly employed and sailed, to as always the Matter contained in the said Affidavits so made or to be made as aforesaid, shall be true in Substance and Matter of Fact, or to inflict any Penalty or Penalties upon the Owner or Owners of such Ship or Vessel.

Slave Trade Act, 1799

39 Geo 3 c 80

An Act for better regulating the Manner of carrying Slaves, in British Vessels, from the Coast of Africa.

24. Former Acts recited.

And whereas by an Act, made in the thirty-third Year of his present Majesty's Reign, and several preceding Acts, it is enacted, That, from and after the first Day of August one thousand seven hundred and ninety-three, it should not be lawful for any Owner or Owners of any Ship or Vessel to insure any Cargo of Slaves, or any Part thereof, on board the same, against any Loss or Damage, save and except the Perils of the Sea, Piracy, Insurrection, or Capture by the King's Enemies,

Barratry of the Master and Crew, and Destruction by Fire, and that all and every Policy of Insurance thereafter made contrary to the said Act should be, and the same are thereby declared to be null and void, to all Intents and Purposes whatsoever: And whereas the Owners of Ships, and others concerned in the Trade to Africa, understanding that it was merely intended by the above mentioned Provision of the said Act, to prescribe and specify the particular Kinds of Loss and Damage for which alone an Indemnity should thereafter be recoverable in respect to Cargoes of Slaves, and not to interfere with, or vary the particular Forms of the Policies of Insurance whereby such Insurances had been theretofore effected, have continued to make Insurances on the Perils and Dangers allowed to be insured by the said Act, in the same general Terms as are contained in the common Policies theretofore used in other Insurances on Ships and Goods:

And whereas Doubts have arisen respecting the Validity of such Insurances so made on Cargoes of Slaves, on Account of the Policies whereby the same are effected not being expressly restrained to the particular Perils and Dangers which are by the said Provision of the said Act alone saved and excepted as the Subjects of lawful Insurance:

For Remedy whereof, and for the more effectual Security of such Persons, be it therefore enacted, That nothing in the said Act, or any former Act contained, shall extend, or be construed to extend, to make void any Insurance already made, or which hereafter shall be made, upon Ships, Slaves, Goods, and Merchandize, in the same general Terms with the Policies now commonly made use of in all other Insurances on Ships and Goods; (that is to say,) on Account of their expressing to be made "against the Risks and Perils of the Seas, Men of War, Fire, Enemies, Pirates, Rovers, Thieves, Jettisons, Letters of Mart and Countermart, Surprisals, Takings at Sea, Arrests, Restraints, and Detainments of Kings, Princes, and People, of what Nation, Condition, or Quality soever, Barratry of the Master and Mariners, and of all other Perils, Losses, and Misfortunes, that have or shall come to the Detriment or Damage thereof."

Letters

Letter from Blackstone to Sharp

NYHS Granville Sharp Collection

20 February 1769

[1]

Memorandum

(This letter was received in consequence of Mr Blackstone's perusal of the Book[315] against Slavery in M.S. before it was Printed, and some alterations and additions were made to the Book in Answer to this Letter from Pages 136 to 146 and particularly in Page 138.)

Sir,
I have the favour of yours, and am much obliged to you for the Entertainment and Instruction I received from your Papers; and also for the kind Attention you have shewn to me, with regard to any Citations from my Commentaries.

My Books are now *Publici Juris*, and every Gentleman has a Right to make what Citations her pleases from them; nor can I reasonably be displeased at his doing so. I only desired not to have a Passage cited from my first Edition as decisive in favour of your Doctrine (Book 1. Ch. 1) which I thought I had been sufficiently explained and guarded by what followed in Chap. 14. but when I found it had been misunderstood both by yourself and others, I found it necessary to explain it more fully in my subsequent Editions. You are welcome to make what use you judge necessary of these corrected [2] Editions; and also of another Passage in Vol. II Page 402 where the same Doctrine is occasionally hinted at. For you will observe, that I have never peremptorily said, that "The master hath acquired any right to the perpetual Service

---

[315] Ed. Granville Sharp, *A Representation of the Injustice and Dangerous Tendency of Tolerating Slavery; or of admitting the least Claim of Private Property in the Persons of Men, in England*, London, 1769.

of John Thomas, or that the Heathen Negroe did owe such Service to his American master". I only say that "if he did, that obligation is not dissolved by his coming to England and turning Christian." It did not become me to pronounce decisively, on a matter *Adhuc subjudice*;[316] whatever the Inclination of my own Opinion may be.

You want no assistance with regard to the nature of Villenage; a thing totally distinct from that of Negro Slaving; except that it may be collected from the Law of Villenage, how little a matter will serve (in the humanity of the English Law) for Evidence of Manumission. The only Argument that can be drawn from it against you is, that as Villenage was Allowed by the common Law, it cannot be argued that a state of Servitude is absolutely unknown to and inconsistent therewith. You will see my Ideas of Villenage in Book II. Page 90, &c. [3]
I return your two Books herewith and remain
Sir
Your most Obedient
Humble Servant
Wm. Blackstone

Lincolns Inn Fields
20th Febr. 1769

Memorandum

Mr Blackstone[']s suggestions in favour of the Master[']s Claim are fully answered in pages 136 to 146 in the Printed Book.

(Copy)

---

[316] Ed. While still under judicial consideration.

Letter from Dr Fothergill to Sharp

NYHS Granville Sharp Collection

Letter from Dr Fothergill[317] to Granville Sharp

Dr. Fothergill presents his respects to G. Sharpe [sic] and returns the M.S. which his Brother was so obliging as to put into the Drs. Hands. He has perused it with attention, and with much satisfaction. For the honour of his Species, he wishes most sincerely that such pungent applications to the hearts of Man grown callous were unnecessary.

Could not another Argument be drawn in favour of the humanity of Negroes from this circumstance? That tho' in the Islands a White who kills a Black may compound for the crime, yet in England I believe no such precident [sic] exists. A Master who stabbed his Black Servant, or any other Black would probably swing for it.

Dr. F. requests G. Sharp's acceptance of a Book, which at least has the merit of being Printed by Baskerville. The sentiments it contains, are humane and will so far be agreeable.

15th Inst.

(Copy)

---

[317] Ed. John Fothergill (1712–1780) was a distinguished physician, at St Thomas's Hospital, London, a naturalist and was active in the anti-slavery movement. Margaret DeLacy, 'Fothergill, John (1712–1780)', ODNB, 2004; online edn, October 2007 [http://www.oxforddnb.com/view/article/9979], accessed 31 October 2015. He came from a Quaker family and among his Quaker friends was the merchant and botanist Peter Collinson. Collinson traded with America, and was the English patron of the American botanical collector John Bartram. Collinson was also a correspondent of the Swedish naturalist Carl von Linné (Carl Linnaeus), whose work he helped introduce to England. In 1762 he bought an estate at Upton in Essex where he grew thousands of species of plants. The estate later became West Ham Park. It was through Collinson that Fothergill and Benjamin Franklin became acquainted. Collinson was the London agent for Franklin's Philadelphia Library. In 1745 Collinson wrote to Franklin about electrical experiments and sent him experimental equipment. The next year Franklin wrote to Collinson of his experiments. Collinson and Fothergill then arranged for the publisher of the *Gentleman's Magazine* to publish his account as a pamphlet with an unsigned preface by Fothergill. In 1743 Fothergill became the correspondent from the English Friends' yearly meeting to the Philadelphia yearly meeting. He soon became a respected political adviser to the Quaker members of the Pennsylvania assembly. In 1757 the assembly sent Franklin to London. On his arrival he fell ill and became Fothergill's patient. They became fast friends and collaborators.

Blackstone's Commentaries

William Blackstone, *The Commentaries on the Laws of England*, First edition published by the Clarendon Press at Oxford, 1765–1769. Second edition, vols 1, 2, 1766–67; *The Oxford Edition of Blackstone*, Wilfrid Prest, gen ed, 4 vols, vol 1 with an Introduction and notes and textual apparatus by David Lemmings.

Words deleted in the second or later editions of the Commentaries are indicated by strike through. Words inserted in the second or later editions are indicated by underlining.

Book 1

p 123
And this spirit of liberty is so deeply implanted in our constitution, and rooted even in our very soil, that a slave or a negro, the moment he lands in England, falls under the protection of the laws, and so far becomes a freeman; though the master's right to his service may [probably] possibly still continue.[318]

p 412
And now it is laid down, that a slave or negro, the instant he lands in England, becomes a freeman; that is, the law will protect him in the enjoyment of his person, his liberty,[319] and his property.

Yet, with regard to any right which the master may have acquired, by contract or the like,[320] to the perpetual service of John or Thomas, this will remain exactly in the same state as before: for this is no more than the same state of subjection for life, which every apprentice submits to for the space of seven years, or sometimes for a longer term.

---

[318] Ed. The 2nd edition, 1766, p 127 added the words underlined including the word "probably". In the 4th edition, 1770, the word "probably" was replaced with "possibly". *The Oxford Edition*, pp 86, 273, varia, 331 (3); Shyllon, *Black Slaves*, pp 59–61; Wilfrid Prest, *William Blackstone: Law and Letters in the Eighteenth Century*, Oxford, 2008, pp 250–251.

[319] Ed. 2nd edition, 1766, p 424.

[320] Ed. 2nd edition, 1766, p 424.

p 413
The law of England acts upon general and extensive principles: it gives liberty, rightly understood, that is, protection, to a jew, a turk, or a heathen, as well as to those who profess the true religion of Christ; and it will not dissolve a civil ~~contract~~ obligation, ~~either express or implied,~~[321] between master and servant, on account of the alteration of faith in either of the contracting parties: but the slave is entitled to the same ~~liberty~~ protection[322] in England before, as after, baptism; and, whatever service the heathen negro owed to his ~~English~~ American[323] master, the same is he bound to render when brought to England and made[324] a christian.

Book 2

p 402
And this doctrine seems to have been extended to negro-servants, who are purchased, when captives, of the nations with whom they are at war, and continue therefore in some degree the property of their masters who buy them: though, accurately speaking, that property (if it indeed continues)[325] consists rather in the perpetual service, than in the body or person, of the captive.

---

[321] Ed. 2nd edition, 1766, p 425.
[322] Ed. 2nd edition, 1766, p 425.
[323] Ed. 2nd edition, 1766, p 425.
[324] Ed. 2nd edition, 1766, p 425.
[325] Ed. 5th edition, 1773, p 402.

Bibliography

Books

Adanson, Michel, *A Voyage to Senegal, the Isle of Goree, and the River Gambia... Translated from the French [i.e. from the "Histoire naturelle du Sénégal"]. With notes by an English gentleman, who resided some time in that country.* [With a map.] London, J Nourse & W Johnston [sic], 1759.

Alford, Terry, *Prince Among Slaves*. New York; London, Harcourt Brace Jovanovich, c 1977.

Baker, John, *The Diary of John Baker, barrister of the Middle Temple, solicitor-general of the Leeward Islands being extracts therefrom, transcribed and edited with an introduction and notes by Philip C. Yorke... a record of life, family history and society, 1751–1778, in England (mostly in Sussex and London) and the Leeward Islands, and of two travels abroad.* London, Hutchinson, 1931.

Baker, John H, (John Hamilton) *An Introduction to English Legal History*. 4th edn, London, Butterworths, 2002.

Baker, J H (Sir John Hamilton), *English Legal Manuscripts: vol. II. Catalogues of the Manuscript Year Books, Readings, and Law Reports in Lincoln's Inn, the Bodleian Library and Gray's Inn.* Zug, Switzerland and London, c.1975–1978.

Behn, Aphra, *Oroonoko: or, the Royal Slave. A true history.* London, Will Canning, 1688.

Bingham, Tom (Thomas Henry), *The Rule of Law*. London, 2010.

Bird, James Barry, *Laws respecting Masters and Servants; articled clerks, apprentices, journeymen and manufacturers. Comprising as well the laws respecting...* London, [1795].

Blackstone, William, *The Commentaries on the Laws of England*, originally published by the Clarendon Press at Oxford, 1765–1769. 4 vols; *The Oxford Edition of Blackstone*, gen ed Wilfrid Prest, 2016.

Blunt, Reginald, *Paradise row; or, A broken piece of old Chelsea, being the curious and diverting annals of a famous village street newly destroyed, together with particulars of sundry noble and notable persons who in former times dwelt there...*, London, Macmillan, 1906.

Brown, Archibald, *A New Law Dictionary and Institute of the Whole Law*. London, 1874.

Bundock, Michael, *The Fortunes of Francis Barber: The True Story of the Jamaican Slave Who Became Samuel Johnson's Heir*. Yale UP, New Haven, London, 2015.

Carretta, Vincent, *Equiano, the African: biography of a self-made man*. Athens, University of Georgia Press, c 2005.

Carretta, Vincent, *Phillis Wheatley: Biography of a Genius in Bondage*, Georgia, 2011.

Chater, Kathleen, *Untold Histories: Black People in England and Wales during the period of the British Slave Trade c. 1660–1807*. Manchester, 2009.

Cugoano, Ottobah, *Thoughts and Sentiments on the Evil and Wicked Traffic of the Slavery and Commerce of the Human Species, etc.*. London, 1787.

Cugoano, Ottobah, *Thoughts and sentiments on the evil of slavery; or, The nature of servitude as admitted by the law of God, compared to the modern slavery of the Africans in the West-Indies*. by a native. London, printed for, and sold by, the author, etc., 1791; reprint Harmondsworth, Penguin, 1999. [The British Library has a copy of the 1791 edition with the author's name printed at the end as "Quobna Ottobouh Cugoano".]

Dabydeen, David, John Gilmore, and Cecily Jones, eds *The Oxford Companion to Black British History* Oxford, 2007.

Douglass, Frederick, *Narrative of the Life of Frederick Douglass*. Boston, Anti-Slavery Office, 1845.

Dresser, Madge and Andrew Hann (eds), *Slavery and the British Country House*. English Heritage, 2013.

Dunn, Richard and Rebekah Higgitt, *Ships, Clocks & Stars: The Quest for Longitude*. London, Royal Museums Greenwich, 2014.

Earle, Thomas F, Kate J P Lowe, eds. *Black Africans in Renaissance Europe*. Cambridge, 2005.

Equiano, Olaudah, *The Interesting Narrative of the Life of Olaudah Equiano, or Gustavus Vassa, the African*. Second edition. London, Printed and sold for the Author, by T Wilkins, etc, [1789].

Gerzina, Gretchen, *Black England: Life before Emancipation*. London, John Murray, 1995.

Goodwin, George, *Benjamin Franklin in London: the British Life of America's Founding Father*. London, 2016.

Gordon-Reed, Annette, *Thomas Jefferson and Sally Hemings: An American Controversy*. Charlottsville: University of Virginia Press, 2000.

Gronniosaw, Ukawsaw, *A Narrative of the Most remarkable Particulars in the Life of James Albert Ukawsaw Gronniosaw, an African Prince, As related by himself*. Bath, 1772.

Guild, June Purcell, *Black laws of Virginia: a summary of the legislative acts of Virginia concerning Negroes from earliest times to the present*. Virginia, Richmond, Va, Whittet & Shepperson, 1936.

Hague, William, *William Pitt the Younger*. London, Harper Collins, 2004.

Halliday, Paul D, *Habeas Corpus: from England to Empire*. Cambridge, Mass; London, Belknap, 2010.

Hargrave, Francis, *An argument in the case of James Sommersett a negro, lately determined by the Court of King's Bench: wherein it is attempted to demonstrate the present unlawfulness of domestic slavery in England. To which is prefixed a state of the case. By Mr. Hargrave, one of the counsel for the negro*. London, printed for the author: and sold by W Otridge, opposite the New Church, in the Strand, MDCCLXXII. [1772].

Hening, William Waller, *Statutes at Large; Being a Collection of all the Laws of Virginia*. 13 vols Richmond, Va, 1809–23.

Hoare, Prince, *Memoirs of Granville Sharp, Esq, Composed from his own Manuscripts and Other Authentic Documents in the Possession of his Family and of the African Institution*. London, 2 vols, 1820, 2nd edn 1828.

Hoyles, Martin, *Cugoano Against Slavery*. Hertford, Herts, 2015.

Inglefield, John Nicholson, *Capt. Inglefield's Narrative, concerning the loss of His Majesty's Ship the Centaur, etc*. London, Printed for J. Murray... and A Donaldson, 1783.

Jacob, Giles, *The Law Dictionary*. 1811.

Jacob, Giles, *The Law Dictionary: Explaing The Rise, Progress, and Present State of English Law*, corrcted and greatly enlarged by T. E. Tomlins, 6 vols Lawbook Exchange reprint, Union, NJ, 2000.

Kea, Ray A, *A Cultural and Social History of Ghana from the Seventeenth to the Nineteenth Century*. Lewiston, NY, 2012.

Kiralfy, A K R, *Potter's Historical Introduction to English Law*. London, 1958.

Lascelles, E C P, *Granville Sharp and the Freedom of Slaves in England*. Oxford, OUP, 1928.

Made, Simon van Groenewegen van der, *Tractatus de legibus abregatis et inusitatis in Hollandia*. Lugduni Batavorum, 1649.

Marshall, P J ed, *The Oxford History of the British Empire*. vol II "The Eighteenth Century". Oxford, OUP, 1998.

Maxwell, John Francis, *Slavery and the Catholic Church: The history of Catholic teaching concerning the moral legitimacy of the institution of slavery*, Chichester, the Anti-Slavery Society for the Protection of Human Rights, 1975.

Montesquieu, Charles de Secondat, baron de, *De l'esprit des loix... Nouvelle edition, avec les dernieres corrections & illustrations de l'auteur*. Edinbourg, G Hamilton & J Balfour, 1750.

Newton, John, *Thoughts upon the African slave trade. By John Newton, Rector of St. Mary Woolnoth*. London, printed for J Buckland, in Pater-Noster-Row; and J Johnson, in St Paul's Church-Yard, M.DCC.LXXXVIII. [1788].

Oldham, James, *Mansfield Manuscripts & the Growth of English Law in the Eighteenth Century*, Chapel Hill, NC, 2004.

Olusoga, David, *Black and British: A Forgotten History*, London, Pan Macmillan, 2016.

Onyeka [Nubia], *Blackamoores: Africans in Tudor England, their Presence, Status and Origins*. Narrative Eye, 2013.

Polson, Archer, *Law and Lawyers: or, Sketches and Illustrations of Legal History and Biography*. London, 1840.

Potter, Harry, *Law, Liberty and the Constitution: A Brief History of the Common Law*. Woodbridge, Boydell, 2015.

Prest, Wilfrid, *William Blackstone: Law and Letters in the Eighteenth Century*, Oxford, 2008.

Prest, W R, *The Letters of Sir William Blackstone, 1744–1780*. London, Selden Society, 2006.

Reeves, John, *History of the English Law, from the Time of the Saxons, to the End of the Reign of Philip and Mary*. 4 vols, Dublin, 2nd edn, 1787.

Rodger, N A M, *The Command of the Ocean: a Naval History of Britain, 1649–1815*, London, Allen Lane, 2004.

Rogers, Nini, *Ireland, Slavery and Anti-Slavery: 1612–1865*. Basingstoke, Palgrave Macmillan, 2009.

Sancho, Ignatius, *Letters of the Late Ignatius Sancho, an African*, ed Frances Crewe. sold by subscription.

Sancho, Ignatius, *Letters of the Late Ignatius Sancho, an African*, ed V Carretta, 1998.

Savary des Brûlons, Jacques, *The Universal Dictionary of trade and commerce*, translated from the French by Malachy Postlethwayt. London: printed for John and Paul Knapton, in Ludgate-Street, 1751–55.

Schama, Simon, et al, *Rough Crossings: Britain, The Slaves and The American Revolution*. London, BBC, 2005.

Schwarz, Philip J, *Twice condemned: slaves and the criminal laws of Virginia, 1705–1865*. 1940- [Baton Rouge], Louisiana State University Press, c 1988.

Sessarakoo, William Ansah, *The Royal African: or, Memoirs of the young Prince of Annamaboe, etc.* London, W Reeve, etc, c 1750.

Sharp, Granville, *A Representation of the Injustice and Dangerous Tendency of Tolerating Slavery, or of Admitting the least Claim of Private Property in the Persons of Men in England*. London, Printed for B White, 1769.

Sharp, Granville, *The Sailors Advocate*, 1727–8; republished as *The Sailors Advocate: first printed in 1727–8: to which is now prefixed, some strictures, drawn from the statutes and records, relating to the pretended right of taking away men by force, under the name of pressing seamen*. London, Printed for B White... and E and C Dilly, 1777.

Shyllon, Folarin Olawale, *Black Slaves in Britain*. London, OUP for the Institute of Race Relations, 1974.

Shyllon, Folarin Olawale, *Black People in Britain 1555–1833*. London, New York, Ibadan, OUP for the Institute of Race Relations, 1977.

Sobel, Dava, *Longitude: The True Story of a Lone Genius Who Solved the Greatest Scientific Problem of His Time*. London, Fourth Estate, 1998.

Stephen, Sir James Fitzjames, *A History of the Criminal Law of England*. 3 vols, London, Macmillan, 1883.

Temple, Sir William, *An Introduction to the History of England*, London, 1708.

Thomas, Hugh, *The Slave Trade: The Story of the Atlantic Slave Trade, 1440-1870*. London, 1997.

Turner, J W C, *Kenny's Outlines of Criminal Law*, 18th edn. Cambridge, 1962.

Vinogradoff, Sir Paul, *Villeinage in England: Essays in English Mediaeval History*. Oxford, Clarendon, 1892, reprint 1968.

Virginia. *Acts of Assembly, passed in the colony of Virginia, from 1662, to 1715*. Volume I. London, MDCCXXVII. [1727] [Eighteenth Century Collections Online].

Waldstreicher, David, *Runaway America: Benjamin Franklin, Slavery, and the American Revolution*. New York, Hill and Wang, c 2004.

Walvin, James, *Black and White: The Negro and English Society, 1555–1945*. London, Allen Lane, 1973.

Walvin, James, *The Zong: A Massacre, The Law and The End of Slavery*. New Haven and London, Yale UP, 2011.

Wentworth, John, *A Complete System of Pleading: comprehending the most approved precedents and forms of practice; Chiefly Consisting of Such as have Never Before been Printed...* in 10 vols, London, printed for G G and J Robinson, Paternoster-Row, [1797]–99.

Wallis, P J and R V, *Eighteenth Century Medics*. Project for Historical Biobibliography, 1988.

Articles and Chapters in Books

Armstrong, Tim, "Catastrophe and Trauma: a Response to Anita Rupprecht" (2007) *The Journal of Legal History* 347–356.

Cairns, John W, "After Somerset: The Scottish Experience" (2012) 33:3 *The Journal of Legal History* 291–312.

Costello, Kevin, "Habeas Corpus and Impressment, 1700–1756" (2008) 29:2 *Journal of Legal History* 215–251.

Davis, David Brion, "The Problem of Slavery in the Age of Revolution, 1770–1823", Cornell University Press, 1975, Ithaca, NY, 1975), chap 10; Oxford University Press edn, with a new preface, 1999.

Drescher, Seymour, "Manumissions in a Society without Slave Law: Eighteenth Century England" (1989) 10 *Slavery and Abolition* 85–101.

Fisher, Ruth Anna, "Granville Sharp and Lord Mansfield" (1943) 28:4 *The Journal of Negro History* 381–389.

Glasson, Travis "'Baptism doth not bestow Freedom': Missionary Anglicanism, Slavery, and the Yorke-Talbot Opinion, 1701–30" (2010) 67:2 *The William and Mary Quarterly* 279–318.

Hay, Douglas, "England, 1562–1875: The Law and Its Uses", in Douglas Hay and Paul Craven, eds, *Masters, Servants, and Magistrates in Britain and the Empire, 1562–1955*, Chapel Hill an London, 2004.

Jones, Neil, "The Zong: Legal, Social and Historical Dimensions" (2007) 28:3 *The Journal of Legal History* 283.

Kennedy, Duncan, *The Structure of Blackstone's Commentaries* (1978–1979) 28 *Buffalo Law Review* 205.

Lewis, Andrew, "Martin Dockray and the Zong: a Tribute in the Form of a Chronology" (2007) 28:3 *The Journal of Legal History* 357–370.

Lobban, Michael, "Slavery, Insurance and the Law" (2007) 28:3 *The Journal of Legal History* 319–328.

Mtubani, C D Victor, "African Slaves and English Law" (1983) 3:2 *Botswana Journal of African Studies* 71–75.

Mtubani, Victor C D, "The Black Voice in Eighteenth-Century Britain: African Writers against Slavery and the Slave Trade" *Phylon* (1960–), Vol. 45, No. 2 (2nd Qtr., 1984), 85–97.

Oldham, James, "New Light on Mansfield and Slavery" (1988) 27 *Journal of British Studies*, No. 1, 45–68.

Oldham, James, "Insurance Litigation Involving the Zong and Other British Slave Ships, 1780–1807" (2007) 28:3 *The Journal of Legal History* 299–318.

Paugh, Katherine, "The Curious Case of Mary Hylas: Wives, Slaves and the Limits of British Abolitionism" (2014) 35:4 *Slavery & Abolition: A Journal of Slave and Post-Slave Studies* 629–651.

Paley, Ruth, "After *Somerset*: Mansfield, Slavery and the Law in England, 1772–1830." in *Law, Crime and English Society, 1660-1830*, ed Norma Landau Cambridge: Cambridge University Press, 2002, 165–184.

Richardson, David, "The British Empire and the Atlantic Slave Trade 1660–1807" in P J Marshall ed, *The Oxford History of the British Empire* vol II "The Eighteenth Century", Oxford, OUP, 1998.

Rizzo, Betty, "The Elopement of Francis Barber" *English Language Notes* (September 1885), 35–38.

Rupprecht, Anita, "'A Very Uncommon Case': Representations of the Zong and the British Campaign to Abolish the Slave Trade" (2007) 28:3 *The Journal of Legal History* 329–346.

van Cleve, George, "'Somerset's Case' and Its Antecedents in Imperial Perspective" (2006) 24:3 *Law and History Review* 601–645.

Washburn, Emory, "Somerset's Case, and the Extinction of Villeinage and Slavery in England" *Massachusetts Historical Society, Proceedings for 1863–1864*, pp 307–26.

Watner, Carl, "*In Favorem Libertatis*: The Life and Work of Granville Sharp", (1980) 4:2 *The Journal of Libertarian Studies* 215–232.

Webster, Jane "The Zong in the Context of the Eighteenth Century Slave Trade" (2007) 28:3 *The Journal of Legal History* 285–298.

Wiecek, William M, "Somerset: Lord Mansfield and the Legitimacy of Slavery in the Anglo-American World" (1974) 42 *University of Chicago Law Review* 86–146.

INDEX OF PEOPLE, PLACES & THINGS

Abdul-Rahman Ibrahim Ibn Sori, Prince
    held as slave in USA, 67, 173 n
Adams, President John Quincy, 67, 173 n
African Company, 365, 366, 373, 374
    archives, 361
Airlie, Earl of, 60
Ajumako village, Ghana, 10
Alta Vela island, 84
Amazing Grace, hymn, 49
Ann and Mary, vessel, 156
Anomabu, 59, 67, 71, 368
Anomabu, Ghana, 244, 336, 362, 373
    fort, 361
    Robert Stubbs, 294
    Stubbs, former Governor, 256
Antigua, 31, 49, 64
Aristotle, 205
Ashburton, Lord, *see* Dunning, John

Bacon, Anthony, London merchant, 369
Baker, John
    Middle Temple member, 26
    slave owner, 26
    Solicitor General, Leeward islands, 11, 26
Baldwins Gardens, London, 48
Ballindean, Perthshire, 60
Banks, Mrs, 47, 113–115, 119, 123, 124 n
    lived at 22 Paradise Row, Chelsea, 113 n
    mother of Sir Joseph Banks, 113 n
    sent habeas corpus, 115
Banks, Sir Joseph, naturalist, 47, 113 n
Barbados, 11, 180, 245, 248
Barber, Cedric, 20
Barber, Francis, 17–20
    beneficiary under will of Dr Johnson, 18
    Bishop's Stortford Grammar School, 18
    black servant of Dr Johnson, 17
    born on Bathurst plantation, Jamaica, 17
    Dr Johnson, and, 38
    married Elizabeth Ball, 19
Bartram, John
    American plant collector, 397
Bashan, 174
Bathurst, Dr Richard
    brought Francis Barber to London, 18
Beach, Thomas, Coroner of London, 43, 92
Beaufoy, Mark
    abolitionist, 372
    father of astronomer and physicist, 372
    vinegar manufacturer, 372
Beckford, William
    slave owner, 268
Beckford, William Thomas
    inherited slave fortune, 268
Beef, Jack
    servant of John Baker, 11
    went to a ball, 11
Beethoven, Ludwig van, 13
Behn, Aphra, 173 n
Belle, Dido Elizabeth
    baptism, 20
    grandniece of Mansfield, 20
Belvidere Yard, 371
Benezet, Anthony, 46
    abolitionist, 97
    of Philadelphia, 97
Berkeley, Bishop, 26
Bermuda scheme, 26
Biggin, John, London merchant, 372
Bingham, Thomas, Lord Bingham, 65
Black Boys Hill, Bristol, 16
Black people
    number in England, 382
    occupations, 8
Blackstone, William
    Commentaries, 38
    professor of English law at Oxford, 38
Blanchard, William Isaac
    69 Fetter Lane, of, 135
    shorthand writer, 2, 135
Bligh, Captain, 82

Boston, Massachusetts, 48
Boswell's *Life of Johnson*, 60
Boswell, James
    Knight case, 60
Bounty, HMS, 82
Bridgetower, George Augustus
    performed with Beethoven, 13
    violinist, 13
BSBE
    abbreviation, 7
    number in England, 210
Burke, Edmund
    black servant, 29
    Cugoano wrote to, 11
    Somerset comment, 29

Cade, Elizabeth
    godmother of James Somerset, 48
    rebukes Mansfield, 236
    refuses to "buy" Somerset, 235
Campbell, Baron, LC, *see* Campbell, John
Campbell, John, Baron Campbell, 29
    Somerset comment, 29
Canute, King, 66
Cape Coast Castle, 59, 361–363, 373, 374
Carolina, 108, 112, 133
Castillo, William
    freed by Admiralty, 41
Cavendish-Bentinck, William
    Duke of Portland, 308
    prime minister, 308
    Sharp's letter to, 307, 308
Cayman (Camanes), Grand, 249, 258 n
Charles II, King
    the "black boy", 16
Cheap, ward of, London, 157
Chelsea, 112, 146
    ale house, 103
    parish of St Luke, 102
Chelsea College, 125
Chelsea Physic Garden, 113
Cheltenham, 61
Circassians, 174
Clarkson, Thomas, abolitionist, 3
Clay, Secretary of State Henry, 67 n, 173 n
Cockell, Serjeant
    on starving slaves, 80
Codrington Library, Oxford, 27

Codrington, Christopher
    bequest to C of E, 27
    slave owner, 27
Coffee house
    Garraways, 369
    Jamaica, 373
    Senegal, 373
    Sharp notes before trial, 3, 139
Coffee, Captain, 110
Colchester, 11
Collars, slave, 15–16
Collingwood, Luke, 298
    address, 367
    captain of the *Zong*, 336
    death, 75, 295
    doctor, 246, 266
    fraudulent plan, 318
    master of *Zong*, 292
    ordered slaves thrown overboard, 299, 316
    prevailed on crew, 318
    reinstated chief mate, 339
    sick and not able to command, 246
    sinister intention, 314
    surgeon, 272
    surgeon on ship William, 313, 336
    suspended chief mate Kelsall, 75, 339
Collinson, Peter, 397
Colour, or race, 103, 125, 126, 131, 146, 177
    black population in England, 175
Company of Merchants trading to Africa, 361
Cook, Captain James, 82
Cosway, Richard, 10
Cromwell, Oliver, 58
Cuba, 11, 85, 339
Cugoano, Ottobah
    abolitionist, author, 10–11
    born in Ajumako village, Ghana, 10
    wrote to prominent people, 11
Culloden, Battle of, 60
Curran, John Philpot, 29
Custom House, 113

Davy, William, Serjeant, 4, 5, 49, 50, 66, 67, 69, 153, 156, 158
    Somerset, for, 4, 158

Dead reckoning, 258 n
Demane, Harry
    saved from slavery by Sharp, 10
Diallo, Ayuba Suleiman, aka Job ben Solomon
    translated Sloane's Arabic MSS, 13
Dido Elizabeth Belle, *see* Belle, Dido Elizabeth
Dockray, Prof Martin, xi, 6, 83, 361
Dolben, Sir William
    act regulating slave trade, 79
    act restricting insurance, 388
    Cugoano wrote to, 11
Dominican Republic, 85, 86
Douglass, Frederick, 38, 68
Dr Johnson's house, Gough Square, 20
Drummond, James
    black boy with collar, 15
    Jacobite, 15
    titular Duke of Perth, 15
Dunning, John, Lord Ashburton, 4, 5, 102, 137, 138
    appeared for slaveowner in Somerset, 129
    criticised by Sharp, 129
    Jonathan Strong case, consulted, 44
    Lord Ashburton, becomes, 95
    solicitor general, 63, 64, 95
    Somerset, against, 3
    Thomas Lewis, for, 3

Equiano, Olaudah
    author, abolitionist, 9
    told Sharp of the *Zong*, 5
Esterházy, Prince, 13
Estwick, Samuel, 221
    version of Mansfield judgment, 221
Eyre CJ
    Sir James Eyre, 62
Eyre CJCP, 61
Eyre, Sir James, 44
    advised Sharp that Strong case was hopeless, 62
    barrister, as, 62
    CB, 95 n, 95
    CJCP, 95 n
    Recorder of London, 95

Fanti people, 363

Fenchurch Street, London, 42, 92
Fonthill Abbey
    built with slave fortune, 268
    William Thomas Beckford, 268
Fort St Louis, 370
Fothergill, Dr John
    adviser to American Quakers, 397
    anti-slavery activist, 397
    associate of Sharp, 397
    Franklin's experiments, helped to publish, 397
    friend of Benjamin Franklin, 397
    naturalist, 397
Franklin, Benjamin
    knew Fothergill, 397
    London house, 17
    Peter, personal servant, 17
Franklin, William
    "King", personal servant, 17
Frazier, wine merchant in Havannah, 132

Gainsborough, Thomas, 10
Gang casks, 246
Garraways Coffee House, 369
George III, King, 11
Georgia, 13
Germain, Lord George, 362
Gibraltar, 81
Gloucester, 61
Gloucestershire Archives, 1, 2, 39 n
Glynn, John, Serjeant, 153
Gold Coast, 103
Graves, Admiral Sir Thomas, 260
Gravesend, 115, 122
    mayor of, 123
Green, William
    Afro-Briton, abolitionist, 10
Greenwich Observatory, 82
Gregson, William, 353
Grenada, 84
Grey, William de
    1st Baron Walsingham, 32 n
    AG, opinion, 31
    attorney general, 375
    CJCP, 375
    opinion, 375
Gronniosaw, Ukawsaw, 11
    published first account in English of slavery by former slave, 11

published first book by a black person in England, 11
Grose J, 80
Guantanamo Bay, 58
Guinea, 115

Hackney Coach, 92
Hadrian's Wall, 7
Haiti, 86
   successful revolt, 18
Haiti, Republic of, 85
Hamlet, John
   slave on St Christopher, 62
Hanley, Richard, 364
   deceased, 295, 335
   master of the William, 295, 335, 353
   purchased ship *Zong*, 336
Hardwicke, Lord LC, *see* Yorke, Philip
Hargrave, Francis, 4, 5, 58, 199, 200, 205
Harrison, John
   clock-maker, 81
   H4 and H5 chronometers, 82
Havana, 46
Havannah, 109
Hay, Sir George
   judge of prerogative court, 29, 376
   view of *Somerset*, 29
Henley, Robert, Earl of Northington LC
   Henley LC, 32
   Baron Henley, created, 32
   Earl of Northington, created, 32
   Henley LK, 26
   LC, becomes, 26
Hill, George
   collector of manuscripts, 51
   serjeant-at-law, 51
Hispaniola, 71, 72, 83, 84, 244, 272, 289
   Alta Vela island, 84, 85
Holburne, Admiral, 42
Hospital, St George's, 125
   Hyde Park, 116
   Lanesborough House, 116 n
   Tooting, 116 n
Howe, Captain, 34
Howe, Charlotte
   a black woman, 34
   a pauper, 34
   baptised, 34
   bought in America, 34
Hutchinson, Thomas
   governor of Massachusetts, 57

Immigration, fear of, 175
Independence, American War of, 362 n
Inglefield, Captain, 260, 265, 270, 282
   HMS *Centaur*, 260

Jacobite Rebellion, 1745–46, 59
Jamaica, 80, 112, 122, 133, 146, 156, 158, 244
   mistaken for Hispaniola, 244, 245, 251
   Morant Point, 84
Jamaica Coffee House, 373
Jefferson, Thomas
   Sally Hemings, controversy, 68
   slave owner, as, 68
Johnson, Samuel
   advertisement for Barber, 19
   Francis Barber, took as servant, 18
   Knight case, 60
   loudest yelps for liberty, 18
   negro children committee, 17
   supported slave insurrections, 18

Kames, Lord, 60
Kelsall, or Kelsal, Col James, 71, 75, 273, 292
   affidavit, in KB, 273
   answer in Exchequer, 73, 76–77, 83, 335–351
   chief mate of *Zong*, 73, 278, 279
   deposition in Exchequer, 299, 335
   London, went to, 250
   subpoena, but not found, 71, 251
   suspended from duty, 75
Kendall, Larcum, clock-maker, 82
Kennedy, Duncan, 38
Kenwood House, 20, 57
Kerr, James, 44
   Jamaica slave owner, 43, 92
Kidderminster, 11
Kingston upon Thames, 14
Kingston, Jamaica, 85
Kite, Sir Robert, Lord Mayor, 43, 92
Knight, Joseph, 59
   born on Guinea Coast, 59
   demanded wages, 60

servant to Jacobite, 59
sold in Jamaica, 59
taken to Scotland, 60
Knowles, Captain, 232
Knowles, Captain John, 199, 209, 211, 215
commander of vessel *Ann and Mary*, 156

L'Ouverture, Tousaint, 18
Laird, David, ship captain, 92
Lambeth, 371
League, nautical, 264
Lee, John
defends throwing slaves into sea, 271
solicitor general, 254, 293
Yorkshire accent, 293
Letter of marque, *see* Marque, letter of
Leward, or leeward, 257
Lewis, Thomas, 14, 46, 95, 97, 102
admitted being servant, 133
attempt to impress, 105, 135
born on Gold Coast, 103
defendant claimed he was his property, 105
earlier attempt to kidnap, 103
English, left home to learn, 107
evidence, 46
gives evidence, 47, 106
habeas corpus, 105
kidnapped in Chelsea, 104
lived in Chelsea, 103
New York, worked in, 110
Sharp comment, 237
shipwrecked, 104
Liberia, 2
Lilburne, John, 23, 58
Lincoln's Inn Fields, 15
Lincoln's Inn Hall, 25, 26, 208
Lincoln's Inn, London, 51
Dampier MSS, 51
Hill MSS, 51
Lindsay, Captain Sir John
nephew of Mansfield, 20
Linnaeus, Carl (Carl von Linné), 397
Lisle, David
beat Jonathan Strong, 42, 92
slave owner, 42, 91, 94
Littleton, Sir Thomas, 70

Lloyd Baker, Thomas, 2
Longitude
at sea, greatest scientific problem, 81
Board of, 81
chronometers, 82
Galileo, 81
John Harrison, 81
Larcum Kendall, 82
moons of Jupiter, 81
problem, 81, 251 n
solution, 81
Zong error, 83–86, 258, 272

Mackey, Brian, 8
Maine, Sir Henry, 15
Mansfield, Lord LC, *see* Murray, William
Mansfield, Sir James, 5
Marcus Aurelius, Emperor, 7 n
Marlow, John, 48
Marque, letter of, 46, 335 n
Martinique, 11
Massachusetts Historical Society, 48
Milford, Lord, 14
Mincing Lane, London, 42, 91
Mont Orgueil, Jersey, 58
Montagu, John, 2nd Duke of Montagu, 12
Montesquieu, 176, 205
Moors, 7
Morocco, Sultan of, 67, 173 n
Murray, William, Earl of Mansfield CJKB
advised widow to "buy" Somerset, 235
Kenwood House, 57
leaves slavery issue to jury, 237
navigation error not peril of sea, 79
rebuked by Elizabeth Cade, 236
shocking case, 245
slaves same as horses, 255
will, 21

National Maritime Museum, Greenwich, 2
New England, 111, 133
New York, 46, 110, 112, 117, 132, 133
New York Historical Society, 2
Newspaper, 127
advertisement for runaway, 120
Newton, Rev John

Antigua, on, 49
  slave captain, 49
Newton, Rev. John
  plantation conditions, describes, 49
Norman Conquest, 66
North, Lord, 97, 309
  prime minister, 308
  Sharp's letter to, 308
Northington, Earl of, LC, *see* Henley, Robert
Norton, Sir Fletcher, 377, 378, 382
Norwich, 11

Oglethorpe, James
  founder of Georgia, 13
  purchased freedom of Ayuba Suleiman Diallo, 13
Old Bailey, 16, 33, 174, 271, 303
Oroonoko, novel
  Aphra Behn, 67 n, 173 n
  Serjeant Davy on, 173

Paley, Dr Ruth, 83
Pensacola, 46, 112, 117, 133
Pepys, Samuel, 13
Perth, Sheriff of, 60
Philadelphia, 46, 74, 110
  yearly Quaker meeting, 397
Philips, Sir John, 14
Phillips, Lady, 14
Picton, Cesar
  coal merchant in Kingston upon Thames, 14
  Picton House, Kingston upon Thames, 14
  Senegal, brought from, 14
Pines, Isle of, 249
Pitcairn Island, 82 n
Pitt, William
  Castillo case, 41
  control of slave trade, 79
  prime minister, 72
  treasurer of Court of Exchequer, 72
Pope Callixtus III, 28
Pope John Paul II, 27, 28
Pope Leo, 28
Pope Nicholas V, 27
Pope Sixtus, 28

Portland, Duke of, *see* Cavendish-Bentinck, William Henry Cavendish
  prime minister, 73
Postlethwayt, Malachy, 176 n
Poultry Compter (jail), 91 n
Poultry Counter (jail), 91
Pratt, Sir Charles, AG, 26
Psalms, 294

Quakers, American, 397
Quashey
  from Fante day-name Kwasi, 17
  Jamaican name, 17

Rodger, Dr Nicholas
  naval historian, 83
  sceptical of *Zong* account, 83
Royal Hospital Chelsea, 221 n
Rush, Benjamin, abolitionist, 46

Sailors, 151
St Augustine, 109, 132
St Bartholomew's Hospital, 42, 91
St Christopher, 62
Saint Domingue, 85 n, 85, 86
St Lucia, 245, 248
St Marylebone (St Mary le Bon), parish of, 157
St Paul, 134
St Saviour's Dock, 372
St Thomas's Hospital, London, 397
St Vincent, 29, 61, 63
  manumission, 63
Saintes, Battle of the, 260
Sainto Domingo, 85 n, 86, 258
Sally and Rachell
  privateer, 335 n
Salusbury, Sir Thomas, 33
Sancho, Ignatius, 12
  author, abolitionist, 9
  first black Briton to vote, 9
Santa Cruz, 103, 108, 117, 132
São Tomé (St Thomas), 82, 262, 298, 337
Satie, John, 45
Savary, Jacques
  dictionary of trade and commerce, 176
  translated by Postlethwayt, 176
Sawver, Captain, of the Fanny, 115
Sawyer, Captain Philip, 47

Scarman, Leslie, Lord Scarman, 65
Scilly Isles, 81
Scott, William, Lord Stowell
  executor of Dr Johnson's will, 65
Seaward, Captain Philip, 121
  of the West Indiaman, 115
Senegal Coffee House, 373
Septimius Severus, Emperor, 7 n
Servants
  black, in England, 7–22
Sessarakoo, William Ansah, 67
Seven Years' War, 369, 370
Sharp, Granville, 155
  abolitionist, 1–2
  cost of transcripts, 295
  criticism of King's Bench, 293
  criticism of lawyers, 129 n
  criticism of Mansfield, 148, 150
  criticism of solicitor general, 293
  Cugoano wrote to, 11
  Dunning, infuriates, 95
  God's punishment
    hurricanes as, 308
    loss of American colonies, as, 308
  guilt of country, 293
  impressment, 150
  instructed Blackstone in Kerr case, 44
  Sierra Leone, founder of, 2
  slavery abolition, 308
  sued by James Kerr, 44
  sued with brother James by slave owner, 93
  warning to prime minister, 308
Sharp, James, 92
Sharp, William
  surgeon, 91
  treated Jonathan Strong, 91
Sherlock, Thomas, 185
Ship
  Adventure, slave ship, 362, 366
  Anne and Mary, 158, 232
  Anthony, 369
  Black Joke, slave ship, 369
  Brilliant, privateer, 365
  Camden, slave ship, 366
  Danish, 108, 116, 132
  Fanny, a snow, 115
  Friendship, 369
  HMS *Champion*, 362, 365, 366
  HMS *Neptune*, 42
  HMS *Thames*, 34
  Jane, slave ship, 367
  Lord George Germain, slave ship, 362, 366
  Mary, or *Mary and Samuel*, 371
  Sally and Rachell
    letter of marque, 353 n
    privateer, 335
  Senegal, snow, 369
  Supply, 369
  Thames, 43, 92
  Union, slave ship, 371
  Vulture, privateer, 367
  William, slave ship, 312, 335, 336, 353, 364, 367, 374
Ships
  brig, 108, 109
  snow, 115
  West Indiaman, 115
Shovell, Admiral Sir Cloudesley, 81
Sierra Leone, 2, 37
Slave ships
  sour water, 247, 263
  water allowance, 263
Slaves
  Jamaica, number in, 210
  value, 210, 293
  Zong
    10 jumped overboard, 264, 283, 284
    64 died of disease, 244, 270 n, 284, 298
    7 whites died on voyage, 298
    number on, 244, 246, 298
    number thrown overboard, 262–264, 284, 292, 294, 297, 298, 308
    one regained ship, 294
Sloane, Sir Hans
  Arabic MSS, 13
  founder of British Museum, 12
Smith, Robert
  English merchant, 108
  merchant at Santa Cruz, 111, 117, 127, 132
Smollett, Tobias
  approached by Johnson re Francis Barber, 19

naval surgeon, 19
novelist, 19
Society for the Propagation of the Gospel in Foreign Parts, 27
Solicitor General, 293
Somerset, James
   address in London, 48
   baptised "James Summersett", 48 n
   Dunning appears for slave owner, 3
   taken from Boston, not Virginia, 48
   witnesses obtained habeas corpus, 48
Sons of Africa, 9
Spanish privateer, 47, 108, 109, 132
Stowell, Lord, see Scott, William
Strong, Jonathan, 62, 63
   beaten by master, 42
   black servant, 42, 46
   freed by Lord Mayor, 43
   Sharp secured his release, 44
Stubbs, George, 374
Stubbs, Robert
   birth, 369
   bred to the sea, 244, 368
   character, 371, 373, 374
   copy of evidence, 256
   death, 374
   evidence, 245, 246, 248, 252, 256, 262–264, 266–269, 271, 272, 363
   evidence at trial, 71
   governor of Anomabu, 244, 294, 368, 373
   in charge of Zong, 339
   in London, 369
   no record of service in Royal Navy, 368
   only witness, 244, 256, 268, 275
   passenger on Zong, 253, 278, 339, 363
   violently assaulted, 373
   will, 374
Sugar, 176
Summersett, James, see Somerset, James

Tacky's Rebellion, Jamaica, 18
Talbot, Charles

Solicitor General, 25, 208, 221
Talbot, Lord, see Talbot, Charles
Tantumquerry, 362
Thames Ditton, 14
Thames, river, 371
Tobacco, 176
Tobago, 248, 251, 253, 256, 337
   French, taken by the, 244, 245
Trade Wind, 249
Tuberon, Cape, 258

Vails, 36
Virginia, 156, 171, 204
Voyage
   average time, 272
   time take by Zong, 273

Wales, Prince of, 11
Walkin, Thomas, 48
Wallace, James, barrister, 138
Walpole, Horace, 14
   comment on Cesar Picton, 14
Walpole, Robert, 14
Walsingham, Baron, see Grey, William de
Waterloo Bridge, 372
Watermen, 103
Watson, William, Dr, 125
Wells, Nathaniel, 8
West India Company, 204, 209
Westminster Bridge, 371
Wharf
   Bull, 113
   Mrs Banks's, 113
Wheatley, Phillis, 29 n
Wilberforce, William, 79
Wilkes, John, 19
William, slave ship, 295, 313
   Richard Hanley, master, 312, 321
Williams, Anna
   character, 19
   Dr Johnson's housekeeper, 19
Williams, Francis
   called to the bar, 12
   Jamaican, 12
   read law at Cambridge, 12
Windward Islands, 84
Winnebah, 362

York Minster Library, 2
Yorke, Charles, 26

Yorke, Philip, Earl of Hardwicke LC
    as Lord Hardwicke LC, 232
    Attorney General, 25
    criticises Holt CJ, 31
    Lord Hardwicke LC, becomes, 30
    Mansfield mentions opinion, 221, 232
    slavery, view of, 30

Zong
    10 slaves jumped overboard, 264
    62 slaves died on voyage, 338
    64 slaves died of disease, 269 n
    7 whites died on voyage, 269 n
    bought by owners of ship *William*, 312
    captain died at Kingston, Jamaica, 338
    Dutch, 312
    Dutch crew, 364
    Hispaniola not sighted, 72
    insurers, 293
    Joseph Wood, second mate, 338
    journal
        chief mate kept, 350
        in Liverpool, 361
    leakage of fresh water, 338
    Liverpool, 292
    location when leakage of water found, 339
    log book, 348
        delivered to captain in Jamaica, 348, 350
        not found, 72, 247, 250, 319, 348
        should stay with ship, 349
    longitude error, 251 n, 339
    muster roll, 364
    name, 292
    name change, 364
    number of slaves when set sail, 337
    number of whites, 246, 337
    owners, 295
    prize of Bristol ship, 312, 353
    prize vessel, 335
    rain collected, 78, 247, 248, 262, 263, 269 n, 276, 283, 284, 289, 300
    scurvy afflicted crew, 340
    second mate drowned, 338
    second mate Joseph Wood, 338
    Sharp learned of massacre from Equiano, 5
    slave ship, 335
    slaves thrown in sea, 262–264, 284, 292
    Stubbs in charge of ship, 72
    Stubbs' address, 76
    three crew died at Black River, 338
    three crew impressed, 338
    water supply, 247, 259, 262, 263, 265, 269, 273, 280
    water supply when set sail, 337

INDEX OF SUBJECTS

Accident, common, 257
Admiralty
    criminal jurisdiction, 292
    slavery, and, 42
Admiralty, High Court, 64
Admiralty, High Court of, 33, 335 n
African flora and fauna, 370
Ambassador, 174
Apprentice, 196
    master cannot force out of kingdom, 62, 219
    voluntary act, 194
Apprenticeship, 214
    as to BSBEs, 62
    implied
        as to BSBEs, 44, 63, 95
        Blackstone and, 64, 96
Ashurst J, 183, 184
Aston J, 138, 147, 184

Bail, 165
Baptism, 135, 169, 173, 196
    effect, 134, 168, 169, 185, 224, 226
    frees slaves, 179
Barbados
    laws, 308
Barter, 314
Bill of exchange, 336
Bill of lading
    for alleged slave, 122
Bill of sale, 115, 127
    for black person in England, 92, 94
Black loyalists, 37
Black Poor, Committee for the Relief of the, 36
Blackstone, William
    Commentaries, 95
    implied apprenticeship as to BSBEs, 95
    implied apprenticeship theory, 44
Bracton, 379
BSBE
    abbreviation, 7
    arguments as to status, 30
    baptism, 28

Blackstone, 40
    conflicting legal views, 28
    consensus emerging, 32
    differences from colonial slaves, 37
    implied apprenticeship suggested, 44
    manumission, 37
    sheriffs, 33
    sheriffs, role of, 33
    status not based on contract, 15, 22
    villeinage, 50, 54
    wages, 35
Burroughs, Master, 184

Cannibalism and the common law, 74
Capital punishment, 167
Certiorari, 146
Christianity, 160, 164, 169, 173, 185
Coke, Sir Edward, CJKB
    confession on record, 162
    villeinage, on, 162
Colour, or race
    common law and, 66
    equal right to life, 259
    whether relevant, 103, 117, 131
Common Pleas, Court of
    'grave' serjeants in, 167
Confession upon record, 167
    action in court, 162
    villein, of being, 162
Contract
    cannot make self a slave by, 162, 184
    express, 195
    in England to buy slave in America legal, 187
    in England to buy slaves abroad legal, 183, 187
    in England to sell slave in England illegal, 183
Coroner of London, 43, 92

Dead Men's Effects, 361
Dead reckoning, 82

log method, 82
Death, appeal of, 163
Declaration, 94, 96, 289
Detinue, 34
Doctors' Commons, 64 n
Doe, John, fictitious litigant, 94
Domesday Book, 165
    recited in statute, 165
Donatio mortis causa, 32
Douglass, Frederick
    slave owners' children, 69
Dower, 180
Duelling, 45
Dunning, John, Lord Ashburton
    solicitor general, 44
Dyer's Reports, 217

England
    air too pure for slavery, 22, 29 n, 170, 192, 201, 212, 218
    free, on setting foot in, 172, 182
Exchequer, Court of, 293
    authentic copy, 293
    bill on equity side, 293, 311
    common injunction, 333
    discovery, 320
    discovery available of equity side, 72
    equity side, 72
    injunction to stop proceedings at law, 72
    quo minus, 312 n
    quo minus clause, 320
Exodus 21.2, 185

Forster J, 134, 183, 185
Fortescue, 379
France
    admiralty court case, 203
    edict of 1685, 203
    edict of 1706, 208, 209
    edict of 1716, 203
Freedom
    presumption of, 107, 147
    the grand object of the laws, 204

Gaius, 68
Grey, William de
    CJCP, 31
    refuses master the right to remove slave, 31

Grotius, Hugo, 201

Habeas corpus, see also Writ, 4, 105, 115, 123, 150, 151, 380–382
    "Cromwell's Guantanamo Bay", 58
    1679 Act, 57
    1816 Act, 58
    Henley LC, 32
    Holt CJ, 32
    Lord Bingham, 65
    Lord Scarman, 65
    masters, in favour of, 33, 117
    no subject to be sent out of England, 383
    not appropriate remedy for property, 34
    return to writ, 156, 224, 227
    Somerset legacy, 65
Hardwicke, Lord LC, see Yorke, Philip
Henley, Robert, Earl of Northington LC
    as LC, in favour of freedom, 32
Holt, Sir John CJKB, 182, 197
    Butts v Penny not good law, 180 n, 181
    slave free once in England, 24
    slavery legal in Virginia, 182
    slaves free in England, 182, 197
    trover does not lie for a black person, 180 n, 181
    trover not for negro, 24
Homicide
    innocent persons, 78, 300–302
Hudson, General, 125
Hutchinson, Thomas
    American slave owners, on, 57
    comment to Mansfield, 57
    governor of Massachusetts, 57

Impressment, 105, 117, 150–152
Independence, American War of, 37
Indictment, 146
Infidel Prince, subjects of, 168
Infidels, 160, 161, 169, 174, 192
Information
    assault, 183
    taking away a black person, 183
Injunction, common, 333
Insurance
    natural death, 80
    perils of the sea, 72, 79 n, 79, 80

Sir William Dolben's Act, 388
Insurance policy, 244
    slaves as goods, 269, 303
    slaves same as horses, 245

Judges
    12 common law, opinion, 133, 225
Judgment
    motion in arrest of, 245, 254
Jury
    grand, of Middlesex, 146
    special verdict, 180
    trial by, 166

Kenyon, Lloyd, Lord Kenyon CJKB
    critic of Mansfield, 63
    humanity, principles of, 80
    on insurance of slaves, 80
    per incuriam, 62
    refuses habeas corpus, 62
Kenyon, Lord, see Kenyon, Lloyd
King
    can prescribe form of making law in Virginia, 174
    no power to make law in England without parliament, 174
King's Bench, Court of, 293
    discovery of documents not available, 72
    motion for new trial, 293
    shorthand notes, 293
    verdict, 293

Landfall, 84
Lawrence J
    on the *Zong* case, 80
Lawyers
    criticised by Sharp, 129
Letter of marque, see Marque, letter of
Littleton, Sir Thomas, JCP, 162
    confession on record, 161
    villeinage, on, 160
Longitude
    Act, 81
    prize for solution, 81
Lord Mayor
    frees Jonathan Strong, 43, 92
    warrant, 120
Lord Mayor of London, 43

Magistrate, 105, 115

Magna Carta
    free men, 168, 171
    jury trial, 171
Mainprize, 165
Mansfield, Lord LC, see Murray, William
Manumission, 178
    law of St Vincent, 63
    no law in England, 37
Marque, letter of, 335 n
Massachusetts
    legality of slavery, 48
Master and servant, 14, 15, 129
    whether person can hire himself for life, 184
Mayhem, appeal of, 163
Minor, contract by, 61
Mirror of Justices, The, 160
Mistake, 244, 245, 250, 257
    cause of delay, 289
Moors, 66, 172
Murder, 255, 267, 269, 271, 292, 297, 298, 308
    admiralty jurisdiction, 308
    necessity no defence, 73
    proof of, 288, 290
Murdrum
    collective punishment, 66
    discrimination in favour of Normans, 66
Murray, William, Earl of Mansfield CJKB
    being black not evidence person is slave, 117
    common law judges, point of law for, 133
    evidence of Lewis material, 132, 147
    fiat justitia, ruat cœlum, 219
    granted habeas corpus to masters, 117
    habeas corpus, use of, 150
    leaves property issue to jury, 116
    masters and slaves, on, 135
    no right to send person abroad without consent, 225
    presumes a person free, 107, 146
    slavery in England never determined, 117, 139
    Somerset case, recommended parties settle, 218
    Somerset ruling, on, 56

special verdict, 132, 133
summing-up to jury, 132, 146
witness giving evidence of own freedom, doubts, 137, 147, 148

Ne exeat regno
   not on demand for money, 31
   writ, 31
Necessity
   absolute, 245–247, 256, 261, 283, 286
   Lord Hobart on, 261
   no defence to murder, 74
   on *Zong*, 244–246
Northington, Earl of, LC, *see* Henley, Robert

Perils of the sea, 250
Plantations, 175
   America, 156, 186
     owners slaves liable for debts, 186
   slave trade, 172
Planters, West Indian, 224
Powell J, 182
Prerogative Court, 376
Press Gang, 128, 135
Press warrant, 151
Privateer (letter of marque), 46
Proclamation of Lord Mayor of London
   black apprentices, against, 44
Protestant religion, 164
Pufendorf, 201

Quantum meruit, 35
Quo minus clause, in Exchequer bill, 72, 312 n

Race, 191, 194
   common law took no account of, 181, 182
   proclamation against black apprentices, 44
Rape, appeal of, 163
Recognizance
   estreat, 137, 138, 147
   respited, 138, 148
   Somerset, in, 235
Recorder of London, 95
Reversion, 180

Roe, Richard, fictitious litigant, 94
Royal Navy
   all on board free, 20, 42
   black servants impressed, 33
   Castillo case, 41
   Francis Barber joined, 19
   murder of black boy, 33
   slavery, not recognised, 41
Rushworth's *Historical Collections*, 22, 170
Russian slave, 23, 202, 212
Rutherforth, Dr Thomas, 201

St Germain, *Doctor and Student*, 3
Saracens, 161, 169, 192
Saxons, 160
Scotland, law of, 59, 204
Scott, William, Lord Stowell
   conflict of laws, 64
   doctorate in civil law, 64 n
   personally opposed to slavery, 65
   Somerset case, on, 64
   Somerset comment, 29
Seamark, 84
Servant
   implied
     no such doctrine, 195
   indenture
     by BSBE, 62
     by slave might be manumission, 61
     with BSBE, 61
Servants, 134, 196
   contract, 195
   for a term, 194
   for life, 194
   wages, not always paid, 36
Service, perpetual, 40, 41
Sheppard's *Abridgement*, 207
Sheriff
   City of London, of, 43
   Perth, of, 60
Sheriffs
   Bristol, Burke's letter, 29
Slave
   bill of sale for slave in England invalid, 44
   cannot contract to make self, 162, 184
   capture in war cancels claim to, 132, 133, 138

in Virginia, sold in London, 182, 183, 187
only statute to use word, 166
Russia, from, 170
Slave trade, 308
  Dolben's Act, 79 n
  inconvenience to underwriters if liable for mortality of slaves, 255
  regulation, 79
  Sharp on, 293
Slave Trade, Society for the Abolition of the, 1
Slavery
  nature of, 200
  whether in England, 116, 117, 120, 159, 225
Slaves
  baptism, effect of, 224, 226
  captives in war, 130, 182
  chattels, as, 156
  entail of, in will, 268
  infidels, as, 179
  one third commonly died of distemper on ship, 285
  real property in Barbados, 180
  real property in Virginia, 172
  St Paul on, 134
  transferable by deed in Virginia, 182
Star Chamber, Court of, 23, 202
Stowell, Lord, *see* Scott, William

Talbot, Charles
  as CJ, 232
  property right in black people, 134
  Solicitor General, 228
Talbot, Lord, *see* Talbot, Charles
Trespass
  abbot, for a monk, 180
  for loss of service, 180 n, 208
  Granville Sharp sued for, 93
  per quod servitium amisit, 24, 180 n, 208
Trial by jury, 166
Trial, New
  order for, 245
Trover, 34, 179, 181, 221, 228
  does not lie for black person, 180
Turks, 66, 172

Underwriters
  liable if slaves killed in engagement, 255
  not liable for mortality of slaves, 255
  not liable if slaves died a 'natural death', 255
Utility, principles of, 268

Vagabond, 166
  imprisonment without trial by jury, 165
Verdict, 23, 24, 31, 47
  special, 23
  Zong case, date of, 293
Villeinage, 159–170
  manumission, 70, 162, 164
  origin, 159
  service, 160
  Sir William Temple, on, 160
  slavery, and, 159
Villeins
  confession on record, by, 161, 162, 167
  in gross, 160, 161, 202, 213, 225, 228, 233
    not subject of property, 161
    severed from manor, 160
  last case in England, 169
  not all who held by villein service were, 160
  not subject of property, 161
  prescription, by, 161, 162
  regardant, 160, 169 n, 202
  regardant, abolished, 225, 226, 233
  Restoration, whether existed at, 163
  revolt of 1377, 165
Virginia
  law
    punishment of slaves, 178
  laws, 156, 171, 172, 178, 193
    1682 Act, 172
    1705 Act, 172
    assembly makes, 174
    did not affect GB, 172, 174, 193
    punishments of slaves, 178
  power of Crown in, 174
  slaves real property, 182
  slaves transferable by deed, 182
  statute, 67

Wilmot CJ, 186
Writ
    habeas corpus, 4, 33, 47
        black people, for, 32
        Holt CJ, 32
    indebitatus assumpsit, 24
    Ne exeat regno, 31
    trespass for loss of services, 24
    trespass per quod servitium amisit, 24
Wyclif, John, 164

Year Books, 214, 217 n
Yorke, Philip, Earl of Hardwicke LC
    as Lord Hardwicke LC, 134, 228
    cites own opinion, 224
    Mansfield mentions opinion, 228
Yorke-Talbot opinion, 22, 25–28, 30, 31, 40, 44, 62, 221, 226, 228, 230
    circulated by slave owners, 22
    Granville Sharp, cited, 93
    Lofft report, 232
    Lord Mansfield on, 208
    Mansfield discounts, 28
    pledge to West Indian slave owners, 224, 226
    shaky foundation, 30
    social effects, 16
    villein in gross, 69

Zong
    Africans thrown overboard in chains, 71
    first case of its kind, 255
    insurance policy, 249
    Lawrence J on, 80
    motion for new trial, 71
    necessity doubted by underwriters, 73
    necessity no defence to murder, 73
    owners abandoned insurance claim, 73
    perils of the sea, navigation error not, 72
    verdict, date, 293
    volume in NMM, 2